Real Black

Real Black: Adventures in Racial Sincerity

John L. Jackson Jr.

The University of Chicago Press :: Chicago and London

John L. Jackson Jr. is assistant professor of cultural anthropology at Duke University and the author of *Harlemworld: Doing Race and Class in Contemporary Black America,* also published by the University of Chicago Press.

The University of Chicago Press, Chicago 60637
The University of Chicago Press, Ltd., London
© 2005 by The University of Chicago
All rights reserved. Published 2005
Printed in the United States of America

14 13 12 11 10 09 08 07 06 05   1 2 3 4 5

ISBN: 0-226-39001-2 (cloth)
ISBN: 0-226-39002-0 (paper)

Frontispiece: "Anthroman," drawn by Stanford Carpenter.

A version of chapter 3 appeared as "The Soles of Black Folk: These Reeboks Were Made for Runnin' (from the White Man)," in *Race Consciousness: African-American Studies for the New Century,* edited by Judith Jackson Fossett and Jeffrey A. Tucker (New York: New York University Press, 1997). A version of chapter 4 appeared as "Ethnophysicality, or an Ethnography of Some Body," in *Soul: Black Power, Politics, and Pleasure,* edited by Monique Guillory and Richard C. Green (New York: New York University Press, 1998). A version of chapter 6 appeared as "An Ethnographic Filmflam: Giving Gifts, Doing Research, and Videotaping the Native Subject/Object," *American Anthropologist* 106, no. 1 (2004): 32–43; © 2004 by the American Anthropological Association.

Library of Congress Cataloging-in-Publication Data

Jackson, John L., Jr.
  Real black : adventures in racial sincerity / John L. Jackson, Jr.
    p.   cm.
  Includes bibliographical references and index.
  ISBN 0-226-39001-2 (cloth : alk. paper) — ISBN 0-226-39002-0 (pbk. : alk. paper)
  1. African Americans—Race identity—New York (State)—New York.
  2. African Americans—New York (State)—New York—Social conditions.
  3. Black Hebrews—New York (State)—New York. 4. Harlem (New York, N.Y.)—Social life and customs. 5. Brooklyn (New York, N.Y.)—Social life and customs. 6. New York (N.Y.)—Race relations. 7. New York (N.Y.)— Social life and customs. I. Title.
    F128.68.H3J335   2005
    974.7′1—dc22

                                                    2005007799

♾ The paper used in this publication meets the minimum requirements of the American National Standard for Information Sciences—Permanence of Paper for Printed Library Materials, ANSI Z39.48-1992.

For Lena

Contents

1

Real Fictions

We have entered a realm of all-performance-all-the-time. This is not to say that "the real" has disappeared, but it is to acknowledge that it is impossible to recognize "the real" without a concept of performance in view.   **Peggy Phelan**

Sincerity is key. If you can fake that, you've got it made.   **George Burns**

Welcome to the desert of the real.   **Morpheus/Slavoj Žižek**

: : :

Working with Watermelons

"Look here, let me tell you something," Bill says, wiping down the counter in front of him with a frayed and dirty white towel. In another uncanny example of those sometimes short-circuited differences between people and their things, the towel matches his own gray-bearded scraggliness. It is a resemblance that I jokingly point out to him just about every chance I get. Bill even laughs occasionally, grudgingly, almost agreeing with my not-so-innocent comparison. But he also blames *me* for his tattered, raglike state—me and people just like me. "And I'm serious about this," he continues, "serious as cancer about this here. So you listen to me. Listen good to what I'm saying. You think you have all those degrees and letters behind your name; people make you think you're a big shot.

I don't care about any of that, none of it. It don't mean nothing to me. Nothing! Absolutely nothing!"

"What makes you say that?"

"W-w-w-what m-m-makes you s-s-say that?" he mocks inexplicably, as though I had just stuttered, which I had not. So I simply furrow my brows, smile with nervous politeness, and continue watching his handiwork. My eyes cannot help but follow Bill's machete blade—sharp, silver strokes back and forth against lush, wet redness. He is cutting whole watermelon into halves, those halves into quarters, each quarter into smaller cubes, and those same cubes into even tinier bite-size chunks— all to be packaged for sale in 20 oz., Saran-wrapped plastic containers. When the cutting is done, he will march the chopped watermelon pieces upstairs to the sidewalk and arrange them atop a metal foldout table that one of his daughters, Margaret, should already have draped in kente cloth. Bill is running late and has missed the morning rush of commuters and pedestrians, but he is working on several different kinds of projects this day, which means that he slows his chopping down even more just to lecture me:

"You are like all these other black people running around here who refuse, absolutely refuse, to follow their own destiny. Refuse to do it. You'd rather follow someone else around. They can't teach you what I can teach you. They can't teach you your destiny. They can't teach you that. They can't teach you how to stand up like a man and control your own resources. Control your destiny. Raise your family. These black women here, the worst thing they have are African American men like you. That's why they go after everybody else—West Indians, West Africans, Panamanians—anybody but you. Because they're raising you instead of you raising them, instead of you taking care of them and showing them how to take care of themselves. You know who I respect? You know who? Palestinian women. They raise warriors. Warriors! They raise warriors, while we send people to Duke University. It's a damned shame."

As Bill cuts, sweats, and scolds, he braces himself against the rusting metal countertop inside the leaky kitchen basement of a small Pentecostal storefront church. The church is letting him temporarily use its building, along with a portion of the sidewalk out front, as a base for his family's vending operation. He will sell watermelons and health books here for the next few months—either as long as they let him, or until he finally does what he has been threatening to do since the very first day I met him: "give up on these ungrateful black people once and for all" and "let go of the ghost."

This morning, however, Bill simply continues to work, cutting up watermelons in his brand new location, a spot that seems to be doing minor wonders for his vending business's productivity. The church, conveniently located right on 125th Street, Harlem's key commercial drag, is only a couple of blocks from the supermarket where he buys his melons, on a good morning, for $5.99 apiece. It is also across the street from Harlem's only commuter rail stop, just forty more yards from the bustling IRT subway line, and a mere five traffic lights down from the one-room, second-story loft where he stores his thousands upon thousands of book titles, collected over some fifty years of bookselling—once as a storeowner, now as a street vendor. Bill's books clutter just about every square inch of his wood-paneled loft space, precarious hard-covered towers that peak at the paint-chipped ceiling above and leave only the thinnest, snaking footpath from the front door to the back window. With Harlem's housing stock rising rapidly these days, and everyone trying to cash in on the changes, Bill's landlord has already officially started the eviction process. If he can get Bill evicted and "flip the apartment," he can charge more than triple the current amount in rent. Deciphering the proverbial "writing on the wall," Bill has already begun to search out alternative storage spaces, even as he simultaneously contemplates walking away from the books and the loft and the watermelon altogether, part of his threatened attempt to "let go of the ghost." Today, however, Bill is not talking about any of that. He just keeps cutting up those melons as he simultaneously reproaches me for my misguided life choices.

The first morning I catch Bill's daily watermelon-chopping routine in its newly Pentecostalized location, he makes sure to introduce me to the pastor's mother, an elderly matriarch who spends about as much time milling around the basement most mornings as Bill does—sweeping floors, dusting cabinets, scavenger-hunting for something or other that a church member might need, silently leaving Bill alone to do his watermelon work. That day, the first chance he gets, Bill stops her briefly to let her know that I am writing a book and will be following him around as part of my research. "If you want to write a book about Harlem," he says to both of us, "you gotta start with a place like this one. This is a real black church. Working for the community. Open every day. Every day. And lovely people. How many other churches around here would let me do what I'm trying to do here? Let me set up like this here? Full access to everything, whatever I want. I just try to keep the place clean. Make sure that when I leave, it's just the way I found it. Respect their building."

By the time I make my first visit, Bill has not been working out of the church for more than a couple of weeks; so everything is still relatively new to him, even ad hoc. He is only beginning to figure out his daily system, some kind of efficient method for negotiating this new space. There is a broken, cluttered, room-temperature freezer in the back where he stores his uncut melons and related business supplies: an assortment of knives, two large cutting boards, plastic containers, spoons and wrapping paper, aluminum bins, napkins, brown paper bags, and Clorox bleach. A storage room upstairs, right next to the main sanctuary, houses his three metal foldout tables, a rickety shopping cart, two collapsible canvas stools, and several crates of health-related paperbacks. The church's kitchen, just below that, has a running faucet, a sputtering gas stove, and one large, metal garbage can that he uses to discard rinds and seeds. "This place is just perfect," he almost croons. "It's like it was built especially for me. Just right. I couldn't have designed it any better than this. We don't need anything more than this. This is just the way we need it."

When Bill finally gets a chance to introduce me to the pastor herself, an angular and serious-faced woman who designs, manufactures, and sells her own clothing on the side, he is effusive about the church's hospitality. Since he appreciates her letting him use the space and does not want to wear out his welcome, Bill makes sure to tell her exactly what he has already told her mother: that I will be hanging around with him in the basement some mornings and "learning something about Harlem, if that's okay." "Sure," she says nonchalantly, wishing me luck before heading out the church lobby and up the block in search of fabric for a new design idea. Bill and I will not be too far behind her. He is preparing to take me on my first vending trip to Jamaica, Queens, where he says black people treat him much better than they do in Harlem. "People in Harlem don't read," he sneers matter-of-factly, rewiping the countertop and tossing his doppelgänger of a towel into a dingy heap in the corner.

Bill hands me a melon sliver to taste and inserts the last few chunks into three remaining plastic containers. He is in a relatively good mood today, which is probably why he feels comfortable enough to divulge some of his cherished trade secrets: strategies for choosing the tastiest Pathmark watermelons, special techniques for slicing them (accumulated over five decades of vending), and foolproof tricks for packing the containers so that they appear most appealing to pedestrians. Bill is quite meticulous about all this, mildly famous in certain local circles for his fastidiousness—even though his same white towel will be a makeshift scabbard for his stored machete's rusty blade; despite tiny pools of watermelon juice running along the floorboard by his worn, wing-tipped shoes; and regardless of how much his liberal application of Clorox (on what seems to be every reachable flat surface in the entire kitchen) chokes the last of the oxygen from the basement air. Bill is clearly very good at what he does, and these techniques keep his family fed.

He quickly fills his last few containers with watermelon pieces, puts everything else back in his storage space, and promises to return later that afternoon for a more thorough cleaning. For now, he is more focused on getting to the subway station and setting up in Queens. All the while, of course, he continues reprimanding me for my many ignorances. I smile awkwardly as I listen, not always knowing what else to do with my eth-nographic face, and Bill even finds my smile disheartening.[1]

"I don't know why you're smiling," he censures. "This is serious stuff. You don't even know how messed up and sick they have you. You can't even see it. And you're worse than some of these broken-down peo-ple out here on the street. Because at least they can see it. They know something's not right. They can't tell you exactly what's wrong, but they know something's not right. You? You think you're living the American Dream. Brainwashed! You don't even know what knowledge is. I can show you knowledge. Stick with me. I'll show you what they can't teach you at your Duke University. You ever took a class on numerology? On astrology?"

Before I even get a chance to answer with the no he expects, Bill launches into a discussion of his wife's many psychic powers. He does take some credit for training Gina (making her drop out of college, quit her secretarial job, and practice her "calling"), but he also readily ad-mits that she is actually the one with all the "natural gifts."[2] After more than a decade's worth of astrological experience, she now does individ-ual psychic readings for about $10 an hour—or sometimes even less, depending on how much her clients can afford. "We try to work with people," Bill says, "but she'd be making ten times as much if she had an office in mid-town. Twenty times that much. But these people need the knowledge. They need it, so we bring it to them."

Bill and Gina regularly organize psychic fairs (at least a few every year) to sell astrology books and to teach others about the basic me-chanics of psychic energy. Many of the titles in Bill's book-filled loft are new-age treatises on numerology, palmistry, and the astrological sci-ences. "Gina," he says, "has read just about all of them." Even though she was always naturally gifted, he boasts of helping her to improve on those gifts, to master her craft, to follow her destiny. His books supple-mented her intrinsic abilities, which means that if Gina is not watching watermelons or helping Bill sell books at another vending table further west, she is leaning over a kitchen table in someone's Harlem or Brooklyn apartment conducting a personal reading. Gina and Bill take astrology very seriously. It is their "life and love." In fact, one of the first things they ask any new acquaintance is nothing more than an antiquated pickup line for other people: "What's your sign?" It serves as a kind of pickup line for them too, but in a decidedly different sense. I divulged my astrological sign to Bill within seconds of our first handshake. In fact, he was still squeezing my hand, not intending to let go until I had answered his question. I told him that I was a Cancer, and he just shook his head sympathetically. "Boy," Bill responded, "you're going to have one tough year. Whew!"

Bill may not have Gina's "natural" gifts, but he does know some of the basics. For example, he can tell you how Malcolm X's death was unequivocally fated by the stars, why Africans ever got enslaved in the first place, and what President George W. Bush really cares about in the Middle East—all with recourse to astrological signs and numerological equations. This doesn't make him a "crackpot," he maintains, because it isn't all that different from the stuff he learned almost half a century ago as an undergraduate at MIT and Boston University—or from what he learns nowadays in the lectures he still frequently crashes at Columbia University. "The *right* knowledge can be power," Bill says, "not any old knowledge, the *right* knowledge. That's what I'm trying to give people." And he accepts the increased social responsibility that seems to come with such knowledge. Still, Bill and Gina have a more playful side, too.

"We used to have all kinds of fairs and carnivals for the kids," he says, as we carry his watermelon containers up the church steps and out to the sidewalk. "Not just astrology events. We did all kinds of things. We had rides for the kids, and clowns and things. Games. We'd set the whole thing up. From beginning to end. Rides and clowns. Collect money and organize the thing, manage everything. We did it all."

"And what happened?"

"Whatever happens when you take the time to invest in *us*? What usually happens? You get burned. They turn on you. Black people aren't like white people. They have no loyalty. They have no sense of destiny. They have no desire to be self-sufficient and self-employed. They want to keep sucking on their momma's teat. They want to cry about, 'The white man did this, the white man did that.' Garbage! Nonsense! The white man didn't do a thing to you. I love white people. And I have respect for white people."

"Why is that?"

"Because they understand the importance, the undeniable importance, of destiny. Destiny! Everything I learned, I learned from white people. They're brilliant."

"Black people aren't brilliant?"

"Look around Harlem, and you tell me. You think white people would let Harlem look like this if they lived here? You think they'd have their young girls walking around the street in these tight jeans like they're prostitutes? They think about the big picture. They think about their own destiny. They want to be their own boss. They want to conquer and control. All we want to do is suck wind up under the white man, just like you, at somebody's Duke University. It's pathetic. You should be ashamed of yourself."

"White people work at Duke, too, you know. Plenty of white folks are right there, 'sucking wind' with me."

"But the institution is theirs," he says, raising his voice slightly, gesticulating with a clenched fist as he arranges the watermelons on the kente'd tabletop. "It's their daddy's institution. So they are accepting their destiny, which is what they should be doing. What's your excuse? All you want to do is suck wind up under the white man and get your little paycheck and take it home to your wife, who probably controls you. Do you let your wife walk around the street in pants?"

"What?"

"You heard me. Do you let your wife wear pants?" Bill temporarily stops laying out the watermelon containers to wait for my answer.

"She wears pants, yeah. Why?"

"You have your wife walking around there at Duke University, while you're sucking wind up under the white man for his little job, and you think you know something. It's sad. It's really sad. It breaks my heart to see you ignore your own destiny for someone else's."

"What kind of destiny have you grabbed?" I shoot back. "Cutting watermelons is supposed to be better than teaching? Don't we need more black teachers?"

"No."

"No?"

"No! Absolutely not. Absolutely not. Not if they're teaching them what you're teaching them. What can you teach children? How to work for the white man? How to suck wind up under the white man? How to work *better* for the white man? More efficiently? Change to the other teat?"

"And you think this is better?" I gesture toward the watermelons on the vending table where his youngest daughter is sitting. Margaret appears to be ignoring our conversation, listening to her Walkman and polishing off a cardboard-boxed fast-food breakfast.

"This is self-sufficiency," he responds. "You want to know my problem? My problem is that I want to help black people. I want to help people like you. If I didn't want to do that, I'd be out there making the money, greasing my palms. I have all the knowledge, the right knowledge. All the books, that's why I sell them, even though nobody in Harlem wants to read them. Everything you need to know is in those books. You ever read *The Choice*, by Samuel Yette?"

"I don't think so. Why?"

"Teaching at Duke University, and you haven't even read anything. See if they have that down there in Duke's library. *The Choice*, Samuel Yette, Y, E, T, T, E. Read it, and then tell me what you're teaching. It's a hard book to find, but I have a copy, one copy, or else I'd have given you one. I want you to read that book. I told you, white people taught me everything I know, but I'm so stupid. I want to try to teach some of it to black people. I must be crazy."

"And so why do you keep trying to help black people if they don't want to be helped, or if they don't seem to listen?"

"I'm foolish. My poor mother raised me to care about these wretched people, and so I'm stuck. Gina and I have tried to do all these things for black people. Fairs, flea-markets, bookstores. You think they'd support us? Of course not. That's not how black people are programmed. They can't be warriors. They don't want to be warriors, because they're scared. They'll pay for a reading, but they won't take the time to study it themselves, to seize their own destiny. They'll take it as quick fix but not to live their life by. And they definitely don't want to learn anything from another black person. I have this one girl, real young, twenty-five; we might see her in Queens today. I'm trying to get her to join my family and help with the business. You see me; I'm too old. I can't do this all by myself. But if I could just get some younger people to believe in this, to see my vision and seize their destiny, then I'll be doing something. You're an anthropologist. You should know what I'm talking about. Polygamy! That's what we need as a people. But you can't get most of these brainwashed black women out here to listen to that. They don't want warriors. They want winos."

"But this girl says she wants to join your family and raise warriors?" I ask, incredulous.

"That's what she says, but you know, sometimes people just talk, especially black people. All talk, no action. No sense of destiny. You know what my problem is though? You know what the problem is with Gina and I? I'll tell you. We're too sincere. We're too sincere, and it's killing us. It's killing her. She could use some help from a younger woman. Someone she can train. Someone she can talk to. She can't talk to me. She does, God bless her, but I cry for my wife. I wish she'd never found me. I took her out of school, made her come and sell books with me on the street. It's sick, but she believed. And she'll tell you she's the happiest woman in the world. I've been doing this for fifty years. If I would just suck wind, and let my wife suck wind, get an office job, our daughter would be so much happier. She wouldn't be embarrassed around her friends that her daddy sells watermelons on the street. I could take the easy route, for their sakes. But instead, this is what I do. This is what I do instead." Bill shakes his head despairingly from side to side as he fills a sagging plastic shopping cart with books for our day-trip to Jamaica, Queens.

Sincerity, Authenticity, and Something-Elseness

When Bill and I had this particular conversation, one of many we shared just like it, I did not yet know that I was trying to write a book about the relationship between sincerity and race—analytically disentangling sincerity from authenticity's sticky webs (even while simultaneously spinning other knotty nodes of their continued convergence). I still had not quite figured out that I wanted to offer a distinct notion of sincerity (distinct, that is, from academic and popular definitions of "authenticity"), to ask questions about how vernacular slogans like "keeping it real" help to explain some of contemporary society's preoccupations with its own limits and contours. Going back over this specific discussion with Bill many months later, I was puzzled and fascinated by his abovementioned invocation of sincerity ("We're too sincere, and it's killing us"), a belief he uses both to explain his own personal failures and to implicate other black people in them, including me. What is this deadly sincerity, and how might it add further specificity to current academic discussions about racial authenticity, a popular trope for critical race theorists and other scholars of identity? *Real Black: Adventures in Racial Sincerity* is an effort to ask that two-pronged question recursively, bending the genre of ethnography to flesh out some of the most important conceptual elements we use, individually and collectively, to craft our conflicting responses to the enigmatic workings of race.

At the same time, this book is also a rumination on the ethnographic project itself, a response to challenges arising from the alleged crises in representation and analysis of the late 1980s, crises that still haunt the discipline to this day.[3] I want to use the concept of racial sincerity to flag the many complicated, if usually implicit, fault lines of a social science discipline that I learned to take seriously in the mid-1990s, a social science still battling with itself about the relative importance of natures vs. cultures, structures vs. agencies, collectivities vs. individuals, sciences vs. humanities, domination vs. resistance, objectivity vs. subjectivity, form vs. content, and fact-finding vs. fictionalization.[4] Racial sincerity's articulation with (and distinction from) racial authenticity does not fall too far from this same series of ever-spiraling binaries—even though sincerity/authenticity, while shadowing them all, cannot be straightforwardly graphed too specifically atop any one of these seemingly oppositional pairs. This book attempts to parse some of what is potentially most valuable about the differences and similarities that connect and disconnect racial authenticities from racial sincerities, to wring social significance from what might seem, for some, mere semantics. Every rhetorical gesture, then, is a purposeful and self-conscious theorizing of race through writing—and writing through race—that showcases a few of the ways in which these two interrelated terms (*sincerity* and *authenticity*) can be mined for subtly distinctive political and epistemological implications.

In researching *Real Black,* I have tried to choose my ethnographic subjects carefully, cautiously, while also playing with the methodological fantasy that it is they who have chosen me. Bill is a special case, infamous around certain stretches of Harlem for his provocative opinions about everything from male-female relationships ("a woman's job is to obey her husband, no matter what, end of discussion") and sartorial sins ("black women started destroying the black community once they started wearing pants") to formal education ("the only schooling black people need today is astrology") and white-collar work ("sucking wind up under the white man"). Bill clearly enjoys confounding people's commonsense assumptions about the world, including a relatively young anthropologist conducting research on his home turf. And he does have a following in Harlem. The same people who disagree with his sexist opinions (often publicly and vehemently) still treat him with a modicum of kindness and respect. Residents appreciate and recognize his self-proclaimed sincerity, even as they accept the fact that he might sometimes just be saying things to get a rise out of them, a miniature version of the very paradox that anchors this book's larger argument. Saving a fuller discussion of Bill's controversial views for another time, I am most interested here in the criticism he levels at himself and his wife for being "too sincere." I want to think about how he uses a conception of sincerity to make sense of his own life-chances and the potentially doomed futures of a larger black community that has lost sight of its "destiny."

Bill is one of my *key informants* and interlocutors, and I have learned quite a bit from him during our many exchanges, though maybe not always what he would have wanted to teach. At the same time, Bill is also a recognizable character in a larger story about contemporary social life. Whether or not he is reduced to his status as a street vendor and potential evictee, Bill can stand as a placeholder for everyone whose lives are shaped by macro-level processes buzzworded with terms like *gentrification, deindustrialization, transnationalization, globalization,* and *Empire.*[5] I want to tell a bit of this wider story, only with a slight difference. I want to tell a tale about how people think and feel their identities into palpable everyday existence, especially as such identities operate within a social context that includes so many causal forces beyond their immediate control.

Real Black is also an "argument of images," an ethnographic portrait painted with the quixotic brushstrokes of anti-essentialism, brushstrokes that indicate how race is overimagined as real (and really slippery) in American society.[6] This same portrait hovers closely over wider contemporary debates about "identity politics" and alternative possible futures of the nation-state. In one such iteration of things, the United States of America is said to be founded on an individualism that distinguishes it from non-Western cultures and civilizations, which supposedly privilege kin-based, religious, and communal ties over individual autonomy and "the natural rights of man."[7] In American politics, it often translates into right-leaning politicians carrying the torch for an individualist ethos that they pit against the group mentalities of their opponents across the aisle—with clear inferences for relative degrees of patriotism. This sometimes gets glossed as a discussion about what it means to be a *real* American (someone who privileges an unfettered global marketplace and respects individualism) as compared to a communist, reverse-racist, Islamic apologist who worships at the shrine of multiculturalism and takes group categories far more seriously than the individuals boxed in by them.[8] Of course, it is the group-based category of "American" that is often used to ground such political claims, troubling any absolute characterization of them as simply individualist.[9]

In contemporary American electoral and cultural politics, where individuals get defined against special-interest groups, sincerity is the attribute most often called upon to make sense of public debates and controversies: from dismissals of Jesse Jackson's racial politicking on Wall Street as little more than an attempt to scare up investment capital for his African American business cronies, to doubts about Dick Cheney's public endorsements of an "Iraqi freedom" that concomitantly serves his vested interest in Halliburton profits. Such assessments criticize the guilty party, at least partially, for a certain lack of sincerity, which is qualitatively different from an assumed deficiency in social or political authenticity (even if the latter accusation is actually the ultimate goal).[10] One of the time-tested mechanisms for deeming authority inauthentic is to first prove it insincere. Florida's butterfly ballots, Bush's claims about Iraqi weapons of mass destruction, and Reverend Jackson's relatively recent financial and familial scandals are all used to question sincerity first—and then, as a logical extension, authenticity. Were those butterfly ballots and police investigations part of a larger coordinated and concerted effort to disenfranchise elderly blacks who were most likely to vote against the governor's brother? Did Bush really believe Iraq had nuclear capabilities, or did he just need a powerful justification for preemptive strikes? How can Jackson be religious advisor for a Lewinsky-scandalized President when he has such a sordid and unfaithful matrimonial history himself? In all of these cases, political authenticity gets attacked sideways—through challenges to sincerity. However, that fact hardly reduces the two terms to simple equivalency. Even when they are working in tandem, which is not always the case, the two notions have distinctive properties. Using linguistics as a suggestive metaphor, their relationship can be described as syntactical, not semantic; indexical, not iconic.[11] There is a connection between them, but they are not isomorphic. Sincerity and authenticity have very different ways of imagining the real, different ways of "keeping it real," and so *racial* sincerity, which should not be confused with *racial* authenticity, exemplifies an epistemologically distinct rendering of race, identity, solidarity, and reality. *Real Black: Adventures in Racial Sincerity* attempts to highlight some of what is most important, practically and theoretically, about that distinction.

Faking Sincerity

Authenticity functions as a valuable term in contemporary academic discussions about race and racism. It explains what is most constraining and potentially self-destructive about identity politics. Philosopher Kwame Anthony Appiah uses the suggestive model of "scripting" to describe social authenticity's pitfalls. "Collective identities," he writes, "provide what we might call scripts: narratives that people use in shaping their life plans and in telling their life stories."[12] The problem is that these tales can be both "too tightly scripted" and corrosively mobilized to make social differences appear absolute and natural.[13] We have scripts for American patriotism that disqualify anyone who, say, wears a *burka*. We write scripts for masculinity that mean not having sex with other men, scripts for blackness that mandate walking with a pimp strut, for femininity, à la Bill's pronouncements, that would ban real women from wearing pants, and on and on—from the seemingly mundane to the extraordinary. These scripts provide guidelines for proper and improper behavior, for legitimate and illegitimate group membership, for social inclusion or ostracism. We use these scripts as easy shorthand for serious causal analysis, and scholars who invoke "racial authenticity" usually do so to talk about how such scripts delimit individuals' social options—describing how racial identity can be made to function a lot like social incarceration, a quotidian breeding ground, claims Paul Gilroy, for even more brutal forms of fascism.[14]

People from opposing political and theoretical backgrounds bemoan the shortsightedness of racial authenticity tests and their attempts to predetermine social possibility.[15] Here, race is seen as the restrictive script we use to authenticate some versions of blackness, whiteness, brownness, yellowness, and redness while simultaneously prohibiting others. It creates potentially myopic political responses to various forms of alienation and determinism, responses that (1) replace bourgeois individualism with reified histories of collective resistance, (2) alchemize capitalism's iron cages into communalist utopias, and (3) mistake after-the-fact, ad hoc psychological descriptions for biocultural proscription.[16] Authenticity names and frames these kinds of exercises and their critiques, but what happens when we think of race in terms of sincerity and not just authenticity? When we theorize race as Bill does: something predicated as much on being sincere as authentic? Could it be analytically useful to extricate sincerity from authenticity? And is there anything left out of academic discussions about racial authenticity, left over, that might make it intellectually profitable to consider sincerity authenticity's excess? Its inassimilable remainder?

Invocations of authenticity do not exhaust the necessary deliberations we all should have about what makes race tick. A turn toward what I am calling *racial sincerity* might add some nuance to contemporary considerations of social solidarity and identity politicking. Moreover, it could help us to compose a diverse series of questions about how (and why) race is lived so intimately and affectively, questions that vary slightly from those that indispensable aspects of social constructionism and anti-essentialism already emphasize.[17]

This book is an extended ethnographic attempt to mark that difference between *sincerity* and *authenticity,* and one productive place to start such a delineation is with Lionel Trilling's book based on his 1970 lectures at Harvard University, lectures about what he called the "cognate ideals" of authenticity and sincerity.[18] For Trilling, sincerity and authenticity are both modern, if not modernist, sensibilities linking individual practices to broader intersubjective contexts. He outlines a history and genealogy of sincerity in Europe ("the birth and ascendancy of the concept but also its eventual decline, the sharp diminution of the authority it once exercised") and connects that analysis to his ideas about everyday performances and presentations of self.[19] "Society requires of us that we present ourselves as being sincere," he writes, "and the most efficacious way of satisfying this demand is to see to it that we really are sincere, that we actually are what we want our community to know we are. In short, we play the role of being ourselves, we sincerely act the part of the sincere person, with the result that a judgment may be passed upon our sincerity that it is not authentic."[20]

Sincerity demands its performance, Trilling argues, and with that demand, authenticity usurps sincerity's social power and pride of place. We cannot trust sincerity, he asserts, because in the modern age people aspire to (and perform) categories that they do not, in fact, actually occupy. They can, for instance, put on social airs, even if they do not have the aristocratic pedigree to back it up. Comedian George Burns is often quoted for aptly stressing sincerity's relevance for Hollywood acting: "Sincerity is key," he says. "If you can fake that, you've got it made." Burns is famous for this pithy rendition of acting's debt to sincerity, a debt that equates actors with professional sincerity-fakers.[21] According to Trilling, we are all social actors in this very theatrical sense, and it is a potentially faked and feigned sincerity that demands authenticity testing as further validation of our professed genuineness.[22]

Commonsense usages of the terms *sincerity* and *authenticity* reflect some of Trilling's arguments about the relevant differences between these two terms. Authenticity conjures up images of people, as animate subjects, verifying inanimate objects. Authenticity presupposes this kind of relationship between an independent, thinking subject and a dependent, unthinking thing.[23] The defining association is one of objectification, "thingification": a specialist applying his or her expertise to a seventeenth-century silver candlestick, or a newly discovered Picasso, or any item dusted off from a dead grandfather's attic and brought before the appraisers of PBS's *Antiques Roadshow.* Authenticity presupposes a relation between subjects (who authenticate) and objects (dumb, mute, and inorganic) that are interpreted and analyzed from the outside, because they cannot simply speak for themselves.[24]

Sincerity, however, sets up a different relationship entirely. A mere object could never be sincere, even if it is authentic. Sincerity is a trait of the object's maker, or maybe even its authenticator, but never the object itself, at least not as we commonly use the term. Instead, sincerity presumes a liaison *between subjects*—not some external adjudicator and a lifeless scroll. Questions of sincerity imply social interlocutors who presume one another's humanity, interiority, and subjectivity. It is a subject-subject interaction, not the subject-object model that authenticity presumes—and to which critiques of authenticity implicitly reduce every racial exchange.[25] In this sense, analyses that deal exclusively with discussions of "racial scripts" dehumanize, much like the processes they ostensibly critique. They turn us all into mere objects of our own social discourses, less the actors who read and interpret scripts than the inert pages themselves.

A brief etymology of the two words is also instructive. *Sincerity,* Trilling tells us, comes from the Latin term *sincerus* (originally applied to things, not people), meaning without wax, unadulterated, not doctored. Authenticity, however, derives from the Greek *authenteo:* to dominate or have authority over, even *to kill* (implying quite a bit more intersubjectivity than its present *Antiques Roadshow* incarnation—and also a nice analogy for what authenticity testing does to people's sense of individual agency). Sincerity was once about things, and authenticity about relations between people. In the present, their connotations have been reversed. To talk exclusively in terms of racial authenticity is to risk ossifying race into a simple subject-object equation, reducing people to little more than objects of racial discourse, characters in racial scripts, dismissing race as only and exclusively the primary cause of social domination and death.[26] At the same time, this position kills some of what is most interesting about the hows and whys of racial living. Authenticity is only part of race's story, and racial sincerity implies something more, what Ralph Ellison might have called the "something else" of race, "something subjective, willful, and complexly and compellingly human."[27] Racial sincerity is an attempt to apply this "something-elseness" to race, to explain the reasons it can feel so obvious, natural, real, and even liberating to walk around with purportedly racial selves crammed up inside of us and serving as invisible links to other people.

Homo Transparentus

Cambridge, Massachusetts. It both is and is not a long way from Bill, Gina, and their watermelon vending in Harlem, New York. I am eating lunch at Harvard University with a table full of thirty-something physicists, philosophers, and social scientists. One of them has a thought-exercise for the group, something to occupy our time for the next forty-five minutes or so while we finish our meals. The idea actually emerges as a function of another colleague's generous summary of my first book and its arguments about what might be dubbed *racial kinesics,* the anthropological study of how we use bodily movements to make sense of racial categories and to describe/ascribe intraracial and interracial differences.[28] After the synopsis, everyone else at the circular table nods respectfully, peppers me with a few perfunctory questions, and then quiets down to allow one of the philosophers to pose his question: "What kind of beings would we be," he queries, between forkfuls of lettuce and olives, "if everything we said were completely transparent to other people? If we could never misrepresent our true feelings? If there was no way to dissimulate or lie? No way to be misunderstood or misapprehended? What if everything we ever meant were clear? Language, in that sense, perfect? No excess, no ambiguity, no misinterpretation. What kind of world would that be? What kind of species would we be?"

Almost immediately, the group attaches a psychoanalytic rider to this hypothetical world: We must also, then, be a species whose members are totally and completely self-transparent. We would always have to know what we, ourselves, actually mean when we say things. There could be no unconscious repression. No sublimation that escaped our understanding and recognition. No Freudian slips from our unlying lips.

"So, of course, this is a world where the psychologists are all out of work," the eavesdropping psychologist at the adjoining table playfully interjects. "Talk about the subconscious. How can we ever think about interdisciplinarity when academics really have such serious psychological issues to work out? Such fears of their own unconscious?" With this additional nod to self-transparency duly noted, alongside the psychologist's caveat about the serious repressions intrinsic to our very exercise, we argue back and forth with one another for the next hour about what such ultratransparency might mean for our definitions of humanity.

I have used this little lunchtime thought experiment in several of my undergraduate courses over the last couple of years, usually trying to get students thinking about the limits of language, about how social categories get assembled as interpretive devices and decoding techniques for helping us see *into* otherwise opaque human beings, for reading between the lines of what people might tell us about themselves in search of even more latent truths and certainties. Classifications by race, class, gender, sexuality, ethnicity, and nationality are all such shortcuts, templates we use in lieu of absolute interpersonal transparency. We employ them to get at the truth of the world, to get at *the real world*, which is why it is so much more comforting to think about these categories as natural occurrences and not man-made conventions.[29] If race were a mere by-product of some collective "racial contract," just something we made up, the social transparency it seems to provide would be only a ruse, a dissembling fiction, just so much more opacity.[30] However, if we can convince ourselves that we just found these social categories in nature, stumbled upon them even, and simply proved them true in subsequent research studies, then we can marshal them as cues and clues for understanding who and what we really are underneath it all.[31] Racial sincerity and authenticity are both ways of thinking through how we find these shortcuts for knowing ourselves and others—for locating *the real* in (and in the intentions of) everyone around us. The difference is that authenticity theorizes this as an unbalanced relationship between the powerful seer and the impotently seen, the latter being a mere object of the seer's racial gaze and discourse, a rendition of identity that Frantz Fanon famously illustrates with the exclamations of a child, "Look, a Negro . . . Mama, see the Negro! I'm frightened!"[32]

As much as they add tools to the theoretical arsenal of anti-essentialism (and purportedly "anti-anti-essentialisms"), critiques of racial authenticity may also be anchored in the very same kind of objectifying and thingifying that they attempt to debunk, relegating people to the status of racial objects much as authenticity tests themselves do.[33] People are always simply somatic extensions of social scripts, embodiments of predetermined dialogue, little more than flesh-and-blood racial objects. Sincerity, however, is an attempt to talk about racial *subjects* and subjectivities. Race is not singularly and exclusively about authenticating others—or, more specifically, it is about authenticating others who concomitantly escape solitary confinement within the pre-scripted categories that others impose. Without absolute social transparency, we use social categories like race to help us grope around in the darkest caverns of our own personal uncertainties. But authenticity tests and racial scripts do not exhaust race's social import; they just begin a never-ending conversation about how the opacity of social identities and individual intentions gets clarified—and only ever temporarily so.

Authenticity attempts to domesticate sincerity, rein it in, control its excesses. It demands hard, fast, and absolute sure-footedness, whereas racial sincerity wallows in unfalsifiablity, ephemerality, partiality, and social vulnerability. Sincerity highlights the ever-fleeting "liveness" of everyday racial performances that cannot be completely captured by authenticating mediations of any kind.[34] Where authenticity lauds content, sincerity privileges intent—an interiorized intent that decentralizes the racial seer (and the racial script), allowing for the possibility of performative ad-libbing and inevitable acceptance of trust amid uncertainty as the only solution to interpersonal ambiguity. With sincerity as a model, one still does not see into the other, one still does not know if one can trust the other's performances (a partiality and steely eyed skepticism it shares with authenticity discourse); however, one recognizes that people are not simply racial objects (to be verified from without) but racial subjects with an interiority that is never completely and unquestionably clear. Racial subjects demand a mutual granting of autonomy and interiorized validity that outstrips authenticity's imperfect operationalizations.

Sincerity and authenticity, like certain opposing strands within the discipline of anthropology itself (as well as between and among all social science fields), are at war with one another, battling for hegemony and explanatory efficacy vis-à-vis everyday displays of racial self-making. For every effort at racial authentication, there is only the most ambiguous confidence—trailed by lingering epistemological doubts.[35] The scripts we read from are never enough. Or rather, they are always too much—overly long and convoluted. They strain our actorly capacities for memorization. There are far too many pages, lines, cues, characters, and stage directions to shore up a racial performance once and for all. And since we can only see people's insides through these externalized variables (like how they deliver their lines and execute prescribed social blocking), we are also always suspicious of our own social epistemologies. We know that we cannot simply trust these performed doings and sayings, even if they are all we have. As an oft-cited Azande saying advises, explaining the camouflaged qualities of witchcraft, "One cannot see into a man as into an open basket."[36] We cannot take racial performances at face value. Performers can lie, misrepresent, cheat, backstab—even as they fool us all the while with perfect inflections and intonations. Sincerity is another way to talk about these racial concerns and uncertainties, to stare negativity in its face, but it is not nearly a smoking gun.[37] Sincerity, after all, is everything, but once you can fake it. . . . In fact, to make things all the more complicated, sometimes what we think about as fake may not be fake at all—at least not in terms of sincerity's fuller logic.

Leo Felton's Spiritual White Supremacy

Authenticity tests and notions of social fakery do not help us to make sense, for example, of someone like Leo Felton, the main character in a New England news story that was picked up by the national media while I was still living in Cambridge, Massachusetts. Leo Felton is a neo-Nazi skinhead who was arrested in Boston for trying to pass off counterfeit bills at a local convenience store. After a little more investigating, the police found that Felton and his girlfriend, Erica Chase, were using this money-scam to help finance something even more sinister: a terrorist plot to blow-up Jewish monuments throughout the city. Felton was summarily arrested and then—even more fascinatingly—outed. The police determined that this light-skinned, would-be Italian skinhead was born to a black father and white mother at the end of the free-loving 1960s. This Aryan racist was black! Felton's story was compelling to media outlets because he was a retooled version of Hollywood's classically tragic mulatto. In a postmodern "Imitation of Life," Felton's mixed-raced ancestry made it so hard for him to fit in with other black children that he chose, instead, to pass for white. But not only did Felton pass for white, he passed for a white, neo-Nazi skinhead who attacked black people because of their race (often landing himself in jail as a consequence) and plotted to blow up Jewish landmarks with the money he acquired trying to pass off fake bills at a Boston-area Dunkin' Donuts.[38] The doubled counterfeiting (passing off fake money while passing off a faked whiteness) was lost on no one. How could Felton know his interracial family history and its implications for his own social identity, especially in the context of America's one-drop rule of hypodescent, and still choose to pass as a skinhead, still identify with white supremacy so unabashedly and violently?

Felton's answer was simple. He wasn't living a lie, only a deeper, more significant racial truth. All his life, he felt white on the inside, an avowed allegiance to whiteness that outpaced his own apparent racial contaminations. He was materially black, but spiritually and soulfully white, only keeping the specifics of his family biography hidden from skinhead friends because their thinking was overly indebted to "nineteenth-century materialism."[39] According to Felton, we are all racial materialists who wrongly believe race to be solely contingent upon blood and biology.[40] In prison, reading anything he could get his hands on that was sympathetic to the Nazi cause, Felton came upon a book, *Imperium,* written in the middle of the last century under the pseudonym Ulick Varange. The author was a lawyer from Chicago who served

in World War II and then on postwar tribunals in Europe before quit-
ting to write the two volumes of this book, his opus, wherein he predicts
the future unification of Europe against its many propagandistic enemies
and "Cultural Distorters." Varange is described in the book's 1962 pref-
ace as a "sincere patriot," only his patriotism is based on the celebration
of group differences, not Americanist individualism. He wants to talk
about group-based identities, especially race, and about the organizing
principles behind them. "Race is not the way one talks, looks, gestures,
walks," Varange writes, "it is not a matter of stock, color, anatomy,
skeletal structure, or anything else objective. Men of Race are scattered
throughout all populations everywhere, through all races, peoples, nations. . . . Race in the subjective sense is thus seen to be a matter of
instinct." [41] For Varange, race is about what you feel in your gut, what
you sense in your soul. It is not simplistically reducible to skin color or
to any metaphorical invocations of "blood" as proxy for racial difference.[42] You intuit race. It is something one commits to as a function of
what one feels, even if phenotypic expressions are given primacy in most
analytical formulas. Skin color, facial features, and hair texture do not
completely predetermine it. Race's origins may be connected to genes,
but that genetic past does not delimit its present manifestations. According to Varange, race is sui generis, using all of nature's materials but combining them (soul, body, mind, and spirit) into a whole that is irreducibly different from any of its constitutive parts. After reading Varange's
manifesto, Felton could begin to understand how the whiteness he felt
inside expurgated any inauthenticities adhering to him as a function of
his parents' race-mixing. His investment in whiteness and white supremacy was, for him, a sincere counterpoint to externally imposed, materialist, and authentic notions of whiteness that were mechanically predicated on "blond hair and blue eyes." [43]

Felton's story is useful because it can be mined for some of the many
subtle slippages between racial authenticity and racial sincerity. In terms
of racial authenticity, he is passing for something he is not, hiding his
family secret from other skinheads because he knows how they will read
it, how they will read him: as fake, phony, impure, nonwhite, illegitimate, half-bred, black. Even so, Felton can feel something inside of himself that is not captured by these bodily or ancestral authenticity tests,
something that he invokes to trump anything that genetically or epider-
mally predetermines exactly how "race matters." [44] According to Felton,
race does not matter, that is, is not reducible to testable materiality. The
interiority of race is not about blood, genes, or purely white ancestry.

This interiority is predicated on a spiritual connection to race that grounds identity in intention, faith, belief, inclination, and commitment. One of the wonderfully troubling ironies in all of this, of course, is that Felton can maintain this spiritualist reading of his own racial sincerity at the same time that his record of physical violence against other people is steeped in the very racial materialism he otherwise disavows. On the street, Felton attacks "Blacks" and "Jews" who do not seem to be granted the same spiritual voluntarism he allows himself, "Blacks" and "Jews" whose racial limits are wholly determined by their assumed ancestry and biology.

The rest of *Real Black* is an extended meditation on this relationship between imagined racial authenticities (born of materialist factors like blood and genes, or of performative ones like social activities) and differently imagined racial sincerities that complicate such straightforwardly materialist and literal readings of racial identity. In fact, the entire notion of passing—which Felton's narrative could be considered little more than a fantastical and extreme version of—must be reconsidered once sincerity becomes another analytic for thinking race. Passing is founded on a certain privileging of authentification.[45] The categories are fixed, and successful passers simply use one part of the social script to perform an identity that they (and others, given enough pertinent biographical information) would imagine themselves not to truly embody. However, Felton's story hints at some of the ways in which authenticity and sincerity are at each other's throats—an embattled state of affairs that should not be dismissed simply because authenticity can often use notions of sincerity in the service of its own objectivist aims, or because sincerity can sometimes seem like just another way of successfully passing other people's authenticity tests. Sincerity can be co-opted by authenticity, and vice versa, but they are not the same thing. When actors/tour guides re-enact colonial Williamsburg for visiting families, authenticity is always at issue (are the clothes, stoves, houses, and accents authentic), but sincerity, in some very obvious ways, is certainly not at stake.[46] What tourists would demand, for instance, that their costumed tour-guides really believe themselves emissaries from the past? For colonial Williamsburg to feel "real" has nothing to do with whether the performers imagine themselves to be more than mere performers. Someone who takes his or her role to heart might provide good fodder for newspaper puff-pieces but would probably get fired rather quickly if her adherence to such realness became too steadfast (i.e., if she refused, say, to break the temporal fourth wall even during emergencies that threatened the lives of guests). Such subtle but important differences between sincerities and authenticities help to explain much of the bickering, battling, and gnashing of teeth that present-day race entails.

Authenticity, we know. Academics write about it, criticize it, deconstruct it. But I want to talk about its cognate ideal, sincerity, particularly racial sincerity—a racial sincerity that Leo Felton took from *Imperium* to justify his own counterintuitive and antimaterialist claims to whiteness, a racial sincerity that can only ever be unequivocally trusted or safely tested in some impossibly transparent, human never-neverland, and a racial sincerity that Bill has used to explain his own racialized life choices and their potentially deadly consequences: "We're too sincere, and it's killing us." Does sincerity kill? Or is the murderer, as its Greek root implies, authenticity instead? Or better yet, what if they each kill *the real,* but in very different ways, using drastically different techniques?

Ethnographobias and Ethnographrenia

Racial sincerity is this book's explicit through-line, but the concept has several thematic running buddies, conceptual bedfellows—terms and ideas that assist in parsing racial sincerity's theoretical purchase. For instance, I am interested in a certain kind of *ethnographic sincerity,* something that one can map onto both the research and write-up phases of anthropology's intellectual project. To conduct fieldwork is to engage in a certain kind of research-based sincerity that is related to, but analytically distinct from, questions of ethnographic authenticity.[47] Like academic discussions about race, anthropological debates of the late 1980s and early 1990s organized themselves almost exclusively around an authenticity paradigm: teaching future anthropologists to decode rhetorical strategies that created a certain kind of ethnographic and scientific authority.[48] However, anthropologists have also used sincerity as an implicit component of authenticity's toolkit, a sincerity expressed in everything from disinterested, scientific objectivity to applied social activism. Ethnographies are supposed to make the intentions of anthropologists clear and transparent, so when anthropological icon Bronislaw Malinowski's diaries contradicted the Trobriand-friendly sympathies of his more official books, or when Napoleon Chagnon was accused of deceiving and diseasing the Yanomamo in South America, or when Margaret Mead was attacked for misrepresenting Samoan culture to justify her critique of American social norms (or even when Guatemalan activist Rigoberta Menchu's autobiography was dismantled as a purposefully political fiction), these were all criticisms of authority and authenticity filtered through the sliding glass door of ethnographic in/sincerity.[49]

This notion of ethnographic in/sincerity is especially interesting if we assume all ethnographies to be what Lee Clarke would call "fantasy documents," attempts to emplot and narrativize responses to natural and/or man-made disasters that are stories told less for effectivity than affectivity, stories more about symbolic value than saving lives.[50] The orderliness of inter-institutionally coordinated routes and procedures mandated after a nuclear bomb's detonation in a suburban neighborhood (the stipulated school bus paths, instructions for parents to meet children at designated holding areas as opposed to panicking in flocks by local schools, imagined scenarios of hyper-synchronicity and unrealistically confineable blast zones) is, Clarke contends, a methodological fiction. It literally papers over the fact that we are all dangling on the brink of unimaginable chaos and catastrophe beyond our capacity for collective response.

Obviously, in most anthropological writing, the stakes are not nearly so high. The phenomenon being represented is not doomsday or Armageddon, but a quotidian place and time and people that the anthropologist has actually experienced and studied firsthand. Where's the fantasy in that? In the anthropologist's head, surely, but also in the imagined objectivity of the written monograph, its hoped-for transparency, its assumed authenticity as a function of long-term empirical fieldwork. In this instance, the outside anthropologist is the authenticator, and the natives are the objects. Or maybe the book is the object that the readers, with agency, authenticate through their accolades. In either sense, ethnographies are attempts to portray an everyday reality that easily outdoes and overpowers any effort to capture it, to write it down—even with the use of realist narratives that convincingly create the impression of cultural transparency by rendering social differences measurably real. What is not always assumed is a certain coevalness of cross-cultural subjecthood.[51] Like authentication, anthropology often turns contemporary subjects into objects of modernity's past.[52] The objects can be authentic or inauthentic (and the anthropologist maintains the same dual potential), but it is the avowed sincerity of the anthropologist that often serves as the most important entry point for subsequent discussions about authority, authenticity, and ethnographic accuracy in the field.[53]

Real Black: Adventures in Racial Sincerity is an attempt to theorize this anthropological sincerity, the ways in which we might displace subject-object equations within the ethnographic project to make room for intersubjectivities that presume the agency and interiority of one's interlocutors (even as we always already remember that such interiority is not tantamount to true, unfettered, and completely transparent self-knowledge).[54] This kind of intersubjectivity, however, can be frightening, and I want to use the term *ethnographobia* to mark neologically the kinds of fears that accompany anthropological writing, fears about ethnographic partiality and the impossibility of ever capturing that elusive *real* in print. Anthropologists are heavily invested in uncovering "the real thing," but they are also deathly skeptical of it, of language's capacity to render it.[55] Ethnographobia summons every author's fears about "writing culture," marks meta-ethnographic critiques of ethnography as a genre full of disingenuous conventions, and stresses the many unshakable fears anthropologists have about writing's intrinsic incompleteness, including the fear that we may never be up to the task of representing the political *fluidarity* and cultural complexity of the villages, cities, suburbs, and global networks within which we do our research.[56]

Ethnographobia, however, is not just about a writer's apprehensions. It is also meant to emphasize some of the fears endemic to fieldwork, reasonable fears about conducting something as murky, qualitative, and jumbled as fieldwork, a rite of passage that is not so much taught (in too few methodology courses) as endured (especially for the graduate student facing a first dissertation), almost like some kind of disciplinary hazing process. The fear starts with the research design, but one has mentors and advisors to help with that. It is what happens once one plops down into the field itself that is most daunting. For me, it meant getting over a life-long struggle with shyness by using simple tricks, research-based mind-games, my own techniques for cutting the ethnographic watermelon (to borrow from Bill's project) so that it appears most appealing to my informants. For example, I would sometimes pretend to be other, more famous anthropologists when I was out conducting my ethnographic fieldwork. The first time I tried it was with a man in his thirties in a local Harlem dive who had just finished offering up an amazing spiel on a two-minute news story blaring from NY1 (an all-news channel) on the television monitor overhead. I was sitting in a corner thumbing through the *Amsterdam News* when this stranger's response to that NY1 piece (about the eighteenth-century African burial ground inadvertently excavated in 1991 during an otherwise routine building construction project in downtown Manhattan) made me want to introduce myself and get his story. After several surreptitious minutes of watching him from the corners of my eyes, I finally asked myself, WWZNHD? That is, what would Zora Neale Hurston do? She would march right up to this man and get his story, strike up a conversation and get on with it, already. What if I pretended to be Hurston, I thought? And then, right then, for the first time, I did: I became Zora Neale, channeling her fearless eccentricities to jumpstart my legs all the way over to the stranger's barstool.

While I was still a graduate student, Hurston always seemed my most effective ethnographic prompt. Imagining myself in her shoes, as a bold, no-nonsense, Southern black woman, seemed somehow exploitative, but it also really worked—so well, in fact, that I tried other ethnographic icons: Franz Boas, John Gwaltney, Margaret Mead. I was no longer just John Jackson, bashful and reticent, easily unnerved and intimidated. I was, instead, Ulf Hannerz, hanging out on a Washington, D.C., street corner that I was able to psychologically drag all the way up to New York City whenever I needed to. This was one way for me to get over the ethnographic phobia I had, a phobia about approaching unknown strangers—and for reasons that I often felt uncomfortable even trying to explain. Without these minor performative fictions, I did not stand an ethnographic chance.[57]

I started this anthropological ancestor-channeling more than ten years ago, when I first began doing ethnographic fieldwork in Brooklyn and Harlem, New York. Eventually, this specific timidity-inoculation was not enough. I could no longer suspend my disbeliefs. Boas could not really get access to some of these folks, and Hurston would probably not even suffer others. I needed something more, someone more, a stronger ethnographic fix. That is when I began to think of myself less as the utilitarian reincarnation of some long-dead cultural anthropologist, and more as a kind of ethnographic superhero: Anthroman©®™ was born!

Imbued with super-scientific powers beyond the "I can walk through walls and leap tall buildings" kind, I imagined Anthroman as a cross between Harry Potter and Huckleberry Finn, less Superman than Blankman, that klutzy Coke-bottle-eyeglasses-wearing hero slapstickishly portrayed by comedian Damon Wayans, a grandmother's old housecoat for a cape, an orthopedic shoe for a deadly boomerang.[58] Anthroman was a way for me to envision stepping outside of myself, to be fearless about social research by visualizing myself protected from harm by my own superhuman powers of observation and analysis. It somehow felt safer than just being some inconsequential graduate student asking black nationalists, or drug dealers, or architects, or grandmothers, or street vendors, or anyone else intrusive questions about their everyday lives and loves.

In this sense, Anthroman is responsible for conducting much of the research over the ten years that this book (re)presents. Even when not explicitly invoked, Anthroman is always lurking somewhere on the page, between the lines, a trickster figure with a squiggly, Gothic letter "A" stenciled into the chest region of an oversized white t-shirt. And he/I wielded that purloined letter to insightful effect—even if I sometimes felt like little more than Hester Prynne's illegitimate mulatto half-sister's brother-in-law's babydaddy. I imagined myself with an Anthrosense, one that tingled and vibrated whenever valuable anthropological data wafted through the air. I demanded that no culture-making escape my purview. Anthroman spotted ethnographic significances where mere mortals saw only bricks and mortar, high-rises and graffitied storefronts, angry-black-male-family-deserters, and the welfare queens who emasculated them. I used Anthroman as a psychological and methodological conceit that helped me to watch myself protectively from above, allaying some of my anxieties in (and of) the field.

Here, again, sincerity is part of what I want to underscore: ethnographic rapport is predicated on the anthropologist's performances of self being considered genuine and transparent by subjects in the field. For many of the people I wrote about in *Harlemworld,* this sincerity meant that my investment in them should not have been reducible to the glossy cover of a nonfiction hardback. When I liberally disseminated free copies to several of the people captured, almost taxidermically, against its pages, they admired the well-designed cover, appreciated my autographed thank you notes, and thumbed through the chapters hastily for shreds of their own stories. But they were also quite clear about demanding that the book's completion and publication not mean the end of our relationship. If our interactions had been exclusively about completing a book manuscript, some of these Harlemites, especially the ones I came to know most intimately, would have felt a little cheated.

The world-renowned observational filmmaker Fred Wiseman promises no such personal relationships to the subjects in his films. Sharing a panel with him at a University of Michigan conference on ethnography several years ago, I listened as he made it clear to all in attendance that once his filming is complete, his relationships with the subjects in those films are also terminated. He is there to make films, not friends. When the production is done, he moves on to postproduction and, eventually, the next documentary. Although some anthropologists might follow a similar model, and actually find it more honest and ethical, I did not always delimit my ethnographic relationships so narrowly. Moreover, I cannot believe that I would have acquired the kinds of access to people that I sometimes did (however much or little) had I not made it clear to many of my "informants" from the start that I was investing in their stories not just as a researcher, but also as a human being interested in getting to know them more personally—maybe even as a friend.[59]

Another irony, of course, is that I often began these same relations with Anthroman or Zora Neale as my proxy. Anthroman sized up social situations and approached potential interlocutors with a performance of self that seemed most situationally appropriate, most likely to put them at ease. The presentation of self I invoked to approach that thirty-something NY1 heckler in a Harlem bar was drastically different from the tactic I used to allay the suspicions and apprehensions of an elderly Haitian-American woman living alone and facing eviction; or of a Black Hebrew Israelite who thinks all blacks are Jews and all whites, red devils; or with Bill during our very first (and all-day-long) interaction, when he initially asked me to quit my job and sell books with him on street corners. What does this say for the sincerity of an anthropologist who self-consciously manipulates self-presentation toward these ethnographic ends? The anthropologist/informant relationship is predicated, especially for the so-called native ethnographer, on the mutual search for sincerity: that anthropologists are not misrepresenting themselves for the sake of rapport, and that informants are not simply giving anthropologists what they think they want to hear. These are further fears of the ethnographic encounter that the term ethnographobia seeks to summon: a fear that the anthropologist cannot distinguish a real from an unreal (a real self, a real other), cannot trust what passes for real: from self to other, from other to self. This can almost become a kind of ethnographic schizophrenia, ethnographobia as ethnographrenia, a distrust of any "real" that we think we experience. And how do we write this realness when we know it to be little more than a social construction? When we realize that it is real and fake at the same exact time? Writing such an ethnophrenia demands more than "blurred genres."[60] It means recognizing such a state as the very organizing principle for the fieldwork process itself, for what it feels like trying to figure out "the real" from bits and pieces of everyday detritus piled on top of one another and then flattened out in book-length ethnographic accounts.

Part conspiracy theory, part rant, part novelistic storytelling, and part autoethnography, *Real Black* is written to capture some of this ethnophrenia, representing the many voices in/of ethnographic texts that turn the romantic impulse for multivocality into the scarier disorder of multiple personalities: now Hurston, now Boas, now Anthroman; now Bill, now Gina, now Leo; now Trilling, now Fanon, now my graduate school professors—and on and on.[61] This ethnophrenia characterizes (1) the unwieldy nature of field research at its core, (2) the writerly ethos to capture something about the truth of content through the necessary mediation of form, and (3) an epistemological uncertainty about the very reality of one's most cherished *reals*. How does one write about realness, and commitments to it, without recourse to prominent academic arguments about naturalization and essentialism? What are the differences between and among contested *reals,* and how do we resolve their heuristic disputes? Where does sincerity take us that authenticity cannot go? These are all versions of quintessentially anthropological questions, but anthropologists do not nearly corner the market on such preoccupations, not in the least.

Reality TV and Keeping It Real

It is a bit ironic that the vernacular phrase "keeping it real" finds its closest colloquial synonym in the call to "represent." Most academics learn, either from the study of semiotics or the writings of Michel Foucault, to think of "the real" and "the represented" as two distinct, and even mutually exclusive, things.[62] One might fool us by standing in for the other, but they are still metaphysically discrete. There is something, however, about this everyday correspondence of reality with its representation (to be "real" is to "represent" for a place where one is from and for others who live there with you) that further unpacks the sociocultural importance of what I'm calling racial sincerity. Each chapter in this book serves as an ethnographic performance of the bond between sincerity and reality, between representations and their supposed *reals*.

As a racial construct, blackness "represents" (indeed, overrepresents) the real. It is a decidedly real fiction. In hip-hop culture, in various forms of black spirituality, and in contemporary debates about identity and belonging in a gentrifying Harlem, invocations of "the real" help to explain how people make sense of the world by combining models based on authenticity with those based on sincerity, cobbling together these two separate routes to the realness of everyday life—and most often using one half of that dyad to challenge and confound the other. *Real Black: Adventures in Racial Sincerity* tries to analyze this duality by showing that race is more than just what relegates people to selfsame versions of impoverished objecthood, to little more than racial *things* that are externally narrated and scripted out of any form of agency or subjectivity.

My attempt to construct this argument through ethnographic examples culled from Harlem and Crown Heights, Brooklyn, should not, however, imply that such imbrications of sincerity and authenticity are specific to the black community—that African American obsessions with the real are a function of racial exceptionalism. This is society's obsession, and our mainstream media outlets are the prime indicators of that fact. We satirize the real with humorous "mockumentaries," purposefully confuse it with films like *The Blair Witch Project*, prioritize it during network newscasts, and highlight its familial schisms on shows like *Jerry Springer*. Reality TV offerings like *Big Brother, The Bachelor, The Bachelorette, Survivor, The Apprentice, Wife Swap, Fear Factor, The Swan, Celebrity Poker, The Simple Life,* and *Temptation Island* help to chart a journey back from the days of authenticity to our renewed contemporary and collective interest in sincerity. If Trilling marked the modernist demise of sincerity at the hands of a murderously authentic ethos, we may presently be witnessing sincerity's big payback. I try to make this argument with recourse to a certain kind of performative ethnography, but even if we go on with our discussion of contemporary television production for a while longer, we can see the fault lines quite clearly there as well.[63]

Authenticity is far less operative for Reality TV. The usual metaphors do not quite work in that genre. There are no screenplays, few lines for actors to memorize and recite. No retakes from different camera angles. The current proliferation of Reality TV programming (usually chalked up to the bottom-line of lowered production costs) can also be seen as a certain replacement of actorly authenticity with purportedly non-acted sincerities. Faked sincerity, no matter how stellar and Oscar-caliber the performance, is no longer enough, George Burns's credo notwithstanding. More than a Coca-Cola ad campaign, we all want "the real thing": real tears, real anger, real oddity, real sex. The fact that these non-actors could be faking their own depictions of sincerity is something to be ferreted out, something to be exposed. The success of these shows is an outgrowth of their ability to display a seemingly transparent sincerity, not sincerity's masterly simulation.

It is this unquenchable thirst for "the really real" that empowers sincerity, displaces authenticity, and drives the paparazzi's flashbulb frenzies. Celebrity is predicated on it, this backstage access, this simulacra of transparency. We know the staged and filmed performances are simulations, even when well done, so we long for the realities that underpin them: of shoplifting waifs, of child-molesting rock stars, of Johnny Cochran–defended sports icons. These breaking news stories assure us that there is a real behind our televisual and cinematic recreations of it, a real that similarly grounds our fanciful imaginings of race, imaginings that began outpacing simple biology long ago.[64]

Real Black: Adventures in Racial Sincerity attempts to explain how such hungers for the real get fed and fought over in contemporary society. Each chapter takes on this preoccupation with the real, recursively exhibiting the kinds of sincerities that give race meaning and significance in people's everyday lives. Authenticity is not the only operative window into vernacular notions of realness, and the chapters that follow offer a series of interrelated lenses for viewing the real through the sincere— less a linear, narrative march toward definitive conclusion than a circular re-rehearsing of several connected phenomenological queries (a mirror of the same spiraling manner in which race is experienced). Chapter 2 asks, who are "real Harlemites," and how are they determined—with recourse to how much mathematics and how much more mysticism? Using gentrification and globalization to define Harlem's larger political and economic milieu, this chapter takes Bill and Gina's numerology, along with often-disparaged notions of the "ghetto fabulous," and begins marking some of the distance separating sincere and authentic realities. Henri Lefebvre's distinction between qualitative and quantitative space-making becomes a foil for navigating some of that conceptual terrain. "Real Harlemites" is also a methodological critique, a thumbing of the nose at a different kind of numerical deification: the way we bow before statistical idols, negotiating the coldness of life by donning "a mathematical frock coat."[65] The point here is simply to argue that part of sincerity's power extends directly from the realization that it is utterly irreducible to statistical representation.

And what are we to make of spiritual sincerity? That is, how can a New York City public high school make sense of its gospel choir's "real bodies," especially once those bodies are seemingly taken over by Holy Ghosts? Chapter 3 invokes semiotics and spirit possession to talk about the darknesses and unfalsifiabilities that constitute sincerity—as well as our institutional attempts to rein those attributes in. It is this darkened, interiorized, and unfalsifiable aspect of sincerity, I would argue, that makes it most disturbing, powerful, and unwieldy.

According to a group of Black Hebrew Israelites in Crown Heights and Harlem, what constitutes "real Jews" is also seriously unwieldy— and even up for grabs. Chapters 4 and 5 examine how the practice of Black Jewry, at least among a certain sliver of the worldwide Black Jewish community, has changed substantially over time and space—from one that trumpets authenticity's hegemony to another that champions the primacy of interiorized Judaic sincerities. The Worldwide Truthful Understanding (WTU) Black Hebrews provide an almost stunning instance of sincerity's reclamation of the real. In the first of these two chapters, "Real Jews," I look at the group's cosmology in 1994, the way they reckoned belonging, and their conspiratorial views of the world. This chapter thematizes conspiracy-theorizing as an alternative spying of realness, as a model for the writing of urban ethnography, and as a vision of the world that works at cross-purposes with ancestral and authentic equations for identity. In chapter 5, "Real Publics," I examine how this same group's self-definitions have changed by 2004—and ask what that alteration might mean for the sincerity/authenticity divide. Moreover, I place black religiosity into a larger discussion about the gendering of black public spheres—using this context to showcase some of the everyday tensions between sincerity and authenticity.

Do bodily differences adequately constitute anthropology's "real natives," and what does that mean for the "real, white, male anthropologists" they ostensibly are not, especially in our media-saturated social world, where visual images provide ubiquitous and detailed examples of group differences? Chapter 6 looks at the relationship between visual anthropology and native anthropology, two related efforts at defining human reality and particularity. Just as the film camera is asked to offer a transparent and minimally mediated window into the world around it, the primeval native is believed to provide an equally clear lens for spying what is most real and natural about humankind.[66] "Real Natives" examines the category of native anthropology by looking at my own attempts to use digital video equipment while conducting research in New York City.

In an age of purported Original Gangsters (and their transatlantic cultural cousins, Original Rudeboys), who are hip-hop's "real emcees," and why are they so obsessed with some purported equivalence between *keeping things real* and *representin'*?[67] Chapter 7 examines hip-hop's preoccupations with realness, which are clearly as much about racial sincerity as authenticity—and predicated as much on the sacred and the spiritual as on graphic violence and sexism. The chapter asks about the kinds of gender work that sincerity helps emcees to confound and/or reproduce through attempts at singing and rhyming on record.

Just as I would like my own fictionalizing methods (i.e., channeling anthropologists, pretending to be superscientific heroes, and writing novelistic dialogues at the start of apparent ethnographies) to assist me in rethinking the limits of anthropological possibility and reality, the idea of changing real names can help us to think through some of the real fictions of racial nominalism. What does naming and renaming mean for issues of racial sincerity? Is sincerity merely authenticity by another name? If not, why not? I use chapter 8 to look at how names and name changes (along with name-dropping) structure ethnography as a research method and overdetermine the everyday lives of groups and individuals depicted in particular ethnographic accounts.

I end *Real Black* with a chapter entitled "Real Loves," more epilogue than full-fledged conclusion, where Bill and Gina have the last word. They explain what the notion of "real love," as they use it, should mean for African Americans today. Summarizing my arguments about why racial sincerity is different from conventional assumptions about racial community and authenticity, I use Bill's bittersweet notion of sincerity— a racial sincerity, a deadly sincerity—as critical counterpoint to academic platitudes about race's essentialist underpinnings.

Real Black looks at "the real" in contemporary black life, at what it means for African Americans to "keep it real," "stay real," and "be real" to one another and to the world at large. I am less interested in deconstructing these naturalized racial "reals" than in showing their productive force—and not always and exclusively toward dehumanizing ends. The "real" need not be a desert, or at least not just that (the pronouncements of Morpheus and Žižek notwithstanding). Vernacular notions of realness are about ideas of sincerity and authenticity that are not easy to reconcile, ideas that I have been trying to wade through as an urban anthropologist working in New York City. I want to use this book to show how sincerity critiques authenticity's explanatory categories, even while authenticity imagines the sincere to be fully operationalizable and externally ratiocinated.

Each chapter should also be read somewhat skeptically, as a specific attempt at writerly sincerity. I am thinking here of the kind of black vernacular writing that authors like Greg Tate, Nelson George, dream hampton, Mark Anthony Neal, Joan Morgan, and Jelani Cobb exemplify with seductive aplomb, an offspring of everything from Paul Laurence Dunbar's dialect poetry and Zora Neale Hurston's "free indirect discourse" to Black Arts Movement chants by the likes of Nikki Giovanni.[68] One critique of this writerly impulse, of this literary Ebonics, is to dismiss it as little more than a rhetorical attempt at racial authenticity: a mobilization of vernacular English to show off one's cultural expertise, one's ghetto pass. And some of that is probably undeniable. However, it is also about divining a certain kind of racial self, an attempt at rendering a writerly "I" that stylistically marks its racial difference through syntactic and semantic variation.[69]

Real Black endeavors to show how and why many of the African Americans I have met in New York City under the auspices of social scientific research cannot imagine themselves alive without a black person (or persona) inside them—a black person of their own sometimes idiosyncratic, always contingent, choosing; a black person carving out tiny bits of agency and humanity within larger material and macrostructural constraints. At the same time, this book is a confessional tale about my own continued, post-constructionist investments in race (recognizing, of course, that I should most certainly know better). Moreover, it is an attempt to unpack, à la Clifford Geertz, vernacular laws that distinguish racial winks from racial twitches, since these specific details of racial realism and essentialism are vitally important.[70]

This is "Annayya's Anthropology," where minoritarian voyeurism becomes inadvertent self-exposure and shock.[71] Anthropology has left its uninventoried traces on me, at least the real *me* I believe myself to be.[72] Imagining myself studying black people, and studying anthropology's representations of black difference, I find that anthropology has already bounded my stories in its disciplinary webs—Orientalist webs that my self-identified nativist identity does not safely allow me to escape (or to cease from weaving). And so I have been trying to write this book, on and off, for close to ten years now, and I finally decided to "give up the ghost already," as Bill might say, and let it go.

Just as Anthroman has been my own admittedly puerile invention for pretending myself into participant observation, for vouchsafing my anthropological authority, and for allaying my ethnographobias about writing, reading, and doing anthropology, so is *Real Black* an effort to proclaim something about race (and the pretending of race) that authenticity theories leave out: a racial "something else" to be engaged and studied more than merely transcended. Not simplistically sentimental or essentialist, the notion of racial sincerity might help us to point our collective index fingers in the general direction of such Ellisonian something-elseness, along with the values it attaches to ideas about race, reality, and their interconnections. This something-elseness illustrates the ambivalent, conflictual attributes of our racial selves—racial selves that many of us could almost not imagine living without.[73] At the same instant, Bill's reference to the deadly, even suicidal, aspects of such sincerity belies any attempt to offer it up as an easy, final solution to the difficult problems of racial reasoning in the twenty-first century.

2 Real Harlemites

124 was spiteful.   **Toni Morrison**

Raw, the one, like five divided by four . . . reciprocated and multiplied by more.
                                                                        Jay-Z

In the background is the Jefferson and Lincoln Memorial. Each one of these
monuments is nineteen feet high. Abraham Lincoln, the sixteenth president.
Thomas Jefferson, the third president, and sixteen and three make nineteen
again. What is so deep about this number nineteen? Why are we standing on
the capital steps today? That number nineteen, when you have a nine you have
a womb that is pregnant. And when you have a one standing by the nine, it
means that there's something secret that has to be unfolded.   **Louis Farrakhan**

: : :

Figuring Harlem

There is a bookmark floating around Harlem, New York,
that does a great job of demonstrating the complicated
mathematics of Manhattan, a mathematics that divides its
time between sincere and authentic versions of geographical realism. I first spotted it during the summer of 2003.
Disseminated by a local real estate company, it serves as
their calling card, prominently displayed in the entranceway to their tiny, cluttered storefront office. This is an office space in one of those subsections of Northern Man-

hattan that assert their symbolic distance from the rest of Harlem by using ever-quainter, lofty, and deracialized place-names like Morningside Heights, Hamilton Heights, SoHA, NoHA, SpaHA, and, in this particular instance, Manhattanville.[1]

The bookmark is simple and ingenious, really. On the front, the company's name, phone number, and Web address frame a full-color reproduction of Manhattan's portion of the New York City Transit Authority's iconic and ubiquitous subway map, with only a hint of the Bronx and a sliver of Queens peeking in from the corners. On the flip side, another listing of the company's URL crowns their "Arithmetic of the Avenues" chart, introduced as follows: "Here's a simple way to locate the cross street for an address on an avenue. Just take the number of the avenue building, cancel the last digit and add or subtract the number below. That's the nearest cross street." Underneath those instructions, *1444 Amsterdam Avenue,* a Harlem address, is provided as illustration: remove the final 4 from 1444 to get 144, divide 144 by 2 to get 72, and then add 59 for a grand total of 131, which means that 1444 Amsterdam is closest to the intersection of Amsterdam and 131st Street. Every single Manhattan avenue is then listed below, along with a truncated version of each avenue's respective equation: Columbus and West End Avenues require that you add 60, not 59; for St. Nicholas and Lenox Avenues, you add 110; you need only add 3 for Avenues A, B, C, or D; with Riverside Drive you divide by 10 (instead of 2) and add 72 for your answer. Then there are avenues like Fifth and Broadway that require a variety of additive amounts based on different groupings of street numbers, some even calling for subtraction instead of addition to determine final locations.

This is clearly a very useful device for many prospective homebuyers, especially outsiders who want to locate properties as efficiently as possible so that they can beat their competitors to the bargaining table. However, in all my previous years of researching and residing in Manhattan, I had never before noticed such a master key to the city, even though several popular magazines and local phonebooks regularly publish the same wallet-sized "Street Finder" (minus the real estate company's contact information) for their own citywide readerships. As a minor consolation, I realize that I am not alone in my imperceptiveness. This distillation of Manhattan addresses was unknown to almost all of the Harlem residents I ever asked about it. People could usually recall more general rules of thumb (Fifth Avenue halves Manhattan into East and West; even-numbered streets run eastward, and odd addresses are on the northern sides of those streets—also facts noted on the bookmark),

Keep this handy to locate the nearest cross street to any address in Manhattan.

Arithmetic of the Avenues

Here's a simple way to locate the cross street for an address on an avenue. Just take the number of the avenue building, cancel the last digit and add or subtract the number below. That's the nearest cross street.

Ex.   **1444 Amsterdam Av**
        (144⟨X⟩) / 2 = 72 + 59 (from chart below)
        = 131st street.

Av A, B, C, D ...... add 3
1 Av & 2 Av .... add 3
3 Av .... add 10
4 Av .... add 8
5 Av .... Up to 200 add 13
.... Up to 400 add 16
.... Up to 600 add 18
.... Up to 775 add 20
.... 775 to 1286 drop last
    figure and deduct 18
.... Up to 1500 add 45
.... Up to 2000 add 24
Av of the Americas [6 Av]
.... deduct 12
7 Av .... add 12
    Above 110th St add 20
8 Av .... add 9
9 Av .... add 13
10 Av .... add 14
11 Av .... add 15

Amsterdam Av .... add 59
Broadway ....
.... 754 to 858 deduct 29
.... 858 to 958 deduct 25
. Above 100th St deduct 30
CPW . divide house number
        by 10 and add 60
Columbus Av ..... add 60
Lenox Av add110
Lexington Av ..... add 22
Madison Av ......add 27
Manhattan Av .... add 100
Park Av .... add 35
Park Av South ..... add 8
Pleasant Av ..... add 101
St Nicholas Av ... add 110
RSD divide house number by
10 and add 72 up to 165th St
West End Av ...... add 60

East   Cross Street   West

Fifth Avenue divides the city East from West. 12 East 79th Street is east of Fifth. 12 West 79th street is west of Fifth.

The progression of house numbers is logical — 100 per avenue block. Please note: Madison and Lexington are not true avenues, and so have only 50 numbers per block.

Manhattanwide
1-49 .... 5th & Madison Av
50-99 .. Madison & Park Av
100-149 .... Park & Lex Av
149-199 ..... Lex & 3rd Av
200-299 .... 3rd & 2nd Av
300-399 ..... 2nd &1st Av
400-499 .... 1st & York Av
    (Av A below 14th St)
500-599 ..... Av A & Av B

Even streets generally run east, odd ones west. Odd numbered buildings are on the north side of cross streets. Even ones are on the south side.

Below 59th St
1-99 .... 5th & 6th Av
100-199 ..... 6th & 7th Av
200-299 .... 9th & 10th Av
300-399 .....7th & 8th Av
400-499 .....8th & 9th Av
500-599 .. 10 th & 11th Av

Above 59th St
1-99 ....Central Park West
        & Columbus Av
100-199 .....Columbus Av
        & Amsterdam Av
200-299 ......Amsterdam
        & West End Av
300-399 ..... West End Av
        & Riverside Dr

but few of the Harlemites I queried had ever used (or even seen) such an intricately mapped out series of equations for locating Manhattan destinations. Of course, they do not bumble around the city missing appointments because they cannot quickly figure cross streets. This does, however, highlight an otherwise commonsense recognition that the lived experience of a neighborhood does not cultivate such strict mathematical formulas for rendering geographical certainty: Lexington Avenue, add 22; Madison Avenue, 27; Park Avenue, 35 (not to be confused with Park Avenue South, where you only need to add 8).

This particular way of parsing place resonates with what Henri Lefebvre famously described as a relationship between "quantified" and "qualified" spaces, which I want to remap as a discussion of authentic vs. sincere social spheres.[2] Lefebvre's two options frame a related series of dialectical contradistinctions between abstract and concrete space, productive and unproductive space, public and private space, capitalist *utilizers* vs. community *users* of space.[3] His neo-Marxian argument distinguishes quantified "spaces of consumption" from the more emancipatory and qualified "consumption of space." Quantified spaces are predicated on exploitative surplus values that presage already corrupted exchange values. Qualified spaces privilege the egalitarian impulses of an unapologetically nonproductive use-value that counters "bourgeoisified" expropriations of the same social landscape. Lefebvre tries to theorize along the fault lines of an ecological "class warfare," pitting "quantifiable, profitable, communicable and 'realistic'" considerations of space on the one hand against more subjective, proletarian, lived, imaginary, and ideal spaces on the other.[4]

In this chapter, I want to rewire Lefebvre's distinction between "real" and "ideal" spaces, connecting it to a consideration of hot-button urban issues in contemporary black America. I am thinking, most specifically, about the potential threat that gentrification poses for a place like Harlem, New York, a place statistically portrayed as some five square miles inhabited by three hundred thousand predominantly poor and working-class African Americans and Latinos.[5] Understanding some of the conceptual routes back and forth between the *real* and the *ideal* (in this case, real and ideal Harlem, real and ideal Harlemites) might be a useful way of contrasting a mere "history of neighborhoods to a history of the techniques for the production of locality" in a self-consciously global twenty-first century.[6] Since the chapter examines the linkages between gentrification and race in America's urban core, this is also, quite clearly, a story about globalization, even though certain provincial assumptions might imagine that globalism would be better spied in other parts of the world—in the seemingly more exotic instantiations of racial difference found in places other than those black ghettos that often abut the very academic campuses where scholarly research on globalization and race is conceptualized and debated.[7] I am interested in the realisms and idealisms of everyday forms of African Americanness, everyday forms sometimes obscured from ethnographic view as a function of their taken-for-granted proximity and visibility.

There are many different ways to chart paths linking real spaces to ideal ones, reconnecting the sincere to the authentic in contemporary black America, but they probably take an entirely different math from the "machine-oriented" variety circulated by that Harlem realtor's bookmark.[8] What I am imagining, however, might still be called a "mathematical anthropology," even without any substantive discussion of the "distance metrics" and Guttman scalings that ostensibly mesh quite nicely with the bookmark's measured graphing of urban geometry.[9] Its Manhattan-by-numbers recipe is reminiscent of a similar kind of globalization-by-numbers ethos that often entails little more than counting up the bodies and currencies and jobs and industries that cross nation-state boundaries, envisioning ourselves able to locate the specifics of global processes in these traveling individual, political, financial and corporate entities.[10] Instead, I am thinking here of a more mystical and slippery mathematics—a mathematics of illusion, allusion, ephemerality, and contingency, a burlesque mimicking of realness that might comprehend globalization more through sympathetic magic than improved empiricism.[11] This is Bill and Gina's mathematics, as much anthropological numerology as "firm" and factlike numerical transparency.[12] And one way to hint at such a seemingly oxymoronic notion (of embodied and "ambiguous numbers") is to invoke late-nineteenth-century scholar Charles Sanders Peirce's mathematician father, Benjamin Peirce, someone who reveled in his intellectual incomprehensibility to such a degree that he once proudly proclaimed an anthropologist, Louis Agassiz, the only person in all of Harvard University capable of consistently understanding him.[13]

Benjamin Peirce was clearly a well-respected mathematical mind of the mid-nineteenth century, but he was also notoriously impenetrable—and not just because the concepts he talked about were difficult to understand. His math was laced with just the kind of mysticism I am looking for; there was elusiveness in his metaphors. As an example of such myth-making mathematics, former Harvard University President Charles W. Eliot relayed the somewhat apocryphal story of "an intelligent Cambridge matron" who remembered one specifically cryptic line

from a Peircean public lecture delivered in 1862, a line that has been offered up time and again as an example of Peirce's intellectual eccentricities: "Incline the mind to an angle of 45 degrees, and periodicity becomes non-periodicity, and the ideal becomes the real." [14]

Here we have one mathematician's cryptic directive for travel between ideality and reality. There is a geometry at play here, but its lines
reek of allegory. They stink with the stench of synecdoche. I want to invoke a similarly figurative and funky mathematics to talk about present-
day Harlem's ideal and real instantiations—imagining Daddy Peirce
standing on his soapbox at 125th Street, leaning against a lectern on the
corner of Lenox Avenue, a bushy head cocked slightly to one side (at a
45 degree angle, no doubt), eyebrows scrunched, eyes squinting, in an
attempt to see the everyday differently, to spot chaos where others believe they see clear and universal patterns, the sharply obvious contours
of a matter-of-factly real world. What happens when we look at the commonsense, stereotypical, and overstudied Harlem with Peirce's canted
and curious posture? What do we notice about the place that we have
not quite seen before? Is there anything we recognize anew? And can we
even trust what we think we notice? Examining how local Harlemites describe their neighborhood and determine local belonging, I use Lefebvre
and a notion of metaphorical mathematics to frame my ethnographic
engagement. Chronicling the social forces that conspired to perpetuate
a racialized and classed urban housing market, historian Gilbert Osofsky penned what is still the most famous historical representation of
Harlem, a story he subtitled "The Making of a Ghetto." [15] I want to talk,
instead, about the making of a "ghetto fabulous," where ghetto fabulousness is defined as the belief that one can use qualitative means to
outstrip assumed quantitative boundaries of place and social position.
This same ghetto fabulousness helps to articulate a related story about
race, identity, and sincerity in contemporary Harlem, a story that does
not culminate exclusively in demographic, statistical, and quantifiable
accounts of seemingly authentic, historical ghetto-making.

Lefebvrean Sincerities

To invoke a Harlem of the present is to talk, first and foremost, about
pressing and controversial issues of gentrification—local, national, and
transnational processes of urban change and conflict that have many
suburbanites salivating, a lot of grassroots activists agitating, and more
than a few low-income tenants quaking in their boots. A discussion of
gentrification demands recognition of Harlem's storied history, along

with the neighborhood's self-reflexive capacity to invoke that past as a way of justifying particularly imagined futures. Founded in the seventeenth century as a rural outpost and built up in the late nineteenth century for a burgeoning white middle class, Harlem is now globally recognized as the small-scale geographical quintessence of black racial difference. A racially segregated housing market combined with the Great Migration and the miscalculations of white realtors to spawn an early-twentieth-century overcrowding of the community with black migrants from the southeastern United States and various islands in the Caribbean—as well as continental Africans, who arrived later.[16] However, that alone does not explain Harlem's international notoriety. The area is most famous today because of the cultural and literary "Renaissance" it spawned in the 1920s and 1930s, a time that grounds current neighborhood nostalgia about figures like Langston Hughes, Rudolph Fisher, and my own much-channeled Zora Neale Hurston—about how they once so proudly walked this neighborhood's sacred streets. Here, again, we find an analogy to Lefebvre's distinction between quantified and qualified places. There are more black residents in other American locales (like Chicago or even the borough of Brooklyn right across the East River), but Harlem's symbolic purchase is imagined to outstrip strict demographic calculations. There are black bodies in Harlem today, but that fact alone does not exhaust the explanations for Harlem's symbolic value. Residents maintain that numbers alone could never fully capture what makes Harlem *Harlem*.

Varying assumptions of belonging in this racialized neighborhood (assumptions translated through Lefebvre's quantified/qualified dialectic, assumptions that help explain Harlem's worldwide reputation) underpin fundamental disputes about class, race, and community in urban America. For example, one might say that there are two distinctly quantified notions of space (two mathematics of membership, if you will) at work in current discussions about gentrification in Harlem. One emphasizes the market as final arbiter of residential validity, while the other highlights the purported dislocation of low-income residents as a deal-breaking by-product of renewed middle-class and corporate interest in once-forgotten urban cores. The first claim is a mathematics of the marketplace (privileging housing prices and residential demand); the second is a mathematics of mobility (highlighting urban pioneers and concomitant displacements). The contrasts between these interconnected claims help to disentangle two distinctive brands of privatization: one based on neoliberal assumptions that the market can do no wrong (a version of Lefebvrean quantification); the other an extension of more qualified space-making, what theorist Pierre Mayol describes as the "insides" of local neighborhoods, those "third spaces" of playfully "poetic geographies" that create local intimacies within the most global of teeming cities.[17]

Lefebvre's critique of quantified social spaces privileges a class-based analysis that is more than operative in Harlem, but I want to advocate a point of view that looks at the quantified/qualified fault lines of *race,* an equally important analytical lens for spying space, place, struggle, and social change. Some provincial assumptions about contemporary Afro-America notwithstanding, to think about gentrification in Harlem means analyzing the global, a notion of local living inextricably linked to international tracks of racial mobility and processes of racial segregation—a kind of *georaciality* where the international ebb and flow of people through local places demands certain affective investments from them, including racial frameworks for determining community and reckoning belonging.[18] With America's current "war on terror" and its implications for theories of supposedly "new" imperialisms, it is important to remember that any articulation of empire's "changing sameness" must also help to explain just what the global looks like in places like Harlem, New York.[19] Similarly, theories of globalizing "flows" and transnational "scapes" must account for the entrenched and institutionalized non-*flow*ingness and ine-*scap*ability of race in contemporary American society—and all around the world.[20] One can talk about globalization's racial underpinnings without intimating a racial essence that naturalizes the connections between brown-hued bodies in different parts of the world, an anti-essentialist fear that helps explain some of the reasons why race often gets written out of discussions about a fragmented global order. The culturally specific incarnations of racial reasoning found in different countries around the world belie a powerfully coherent organizing principle for planetary inequality, an organizing principle mappable along the selfsame epidermal ladder from light to dark bodies.[21] Today's Harlem, a gentrifying Harlem, is also shot through with such color-coded significances, a color-coding that tints the lenses local residents use to see international influences on their small Manhattan community, a small community undergoing some very big changes.

Gentrification Studies

The study of gentrification has become a veritable cottage industry within the social sciences.[22] Coined in 1960s England, the term is usually used to mark middle-class reclamation of formerly forsaken urban regions.[23] In the United States, most renditions of gentrification start with a discussion of deindustrialization and suburbanization in the middle of the twentieth century.[24] Improvements in transportation technology, expansions in highway construction, and precipitous rises in service-sector employment helped to encourage a middle-class exodus from packed urban centers.[25] Corporate divestment accompanied this urban evacuation, as middle-class suburban families spent their disposable incomes—which lower-class urbanites left behind did not possess—at the cash registers of increasingly transnational big businesses.

By the mid-1970s, as a function of this other "great migration," most academic and popular stories about urban Americana understood it as little more than a class-specific locus of poverty and deprivation.[26] In New York City, which was flirting with bankruptcy on Mayor Abraham Beame's watch and about to hand over the financial reins to a post-Rockefeller governor's state-sponsored institutions, Harlem Day was getting its inaugural kickoff at about this time (a gamble on the rejuvenating powers of cultural tourism), just when the city foreclosed on over a thousand mismanaged or abandoned buildings in the neighborhood. When the larger national discussion of urban decay was linked to considerations of race and ethnicity, the out-migration of middle-class African Americans was also used as a trump card for claims about urban cultural pathology and social marginalization.[27] Once members of the black middle class began following their white counterparts out of already racially segregated urban areas, the stage was set for arguments about the intergenerational transmission of familial dysfunction within poor black and Latino communities as a consequence of their social and cultural isolation. This social isolation was asked to explain perpetual black poverty by both the political left and right.[28] Inner-city communities were conceded to the poor, while "equalizing institutions" like schools and other important governmental interventions were weakened by the disappearance of urban tax dollars.[29]

In that context, cities were said to require more, not less, federal and corporate support, and intended improvements entailed cajoling corporate America and middle-class families back into urban centers. Local institutions with religious ties, such as the Harlem Congregations for Community Improvement and the Abyssinian Baptist Church, were vocal participants in this rallying cry, leveraging such new investments to redefine themselves as stewards of infrastructural community development. As their new buildings went up and affluent tenants moved in, these religious connections helped to justify the discourse of social resurrection in Harlem, of a community that was being "born again."[30] With this renewed middle-class in-migration comes an increase, the story goes, in resources for local services, especially public schools, an attractive consumer base for corporate reinvestment, and a redevelopment circle that builds on itself to enrich depressed urban locales. This notion of gentrification as urban salvation is, of course, only half the story. Many detractors (and in Harlem, they are organizing and mobilizing every day) argue that renewed middle-class interest in urban areas means nothing more than low-income tenant dislocation and displacement. The prices of apartments and houses, which were once below market rates, have risen to meet that market—and with this rise, poorer residents are said to be priced out of the homes and neighborhoods they once occupied.

Much of the literature on gentrification interrogates this dislocation hypothesis, often with differing definitions of displacement and less-than-perfect measures for comparing its rates in gentrifying and nongentrifying neighborhoods.[31] Most recently, studies in Boston and New York City have argued that low-income displacement might be mitigated by the existence of already vacant apartment buildings (developers refurbished those before going after occupied homes)—and by poor tenants' dogged determination to stay put and take advantage of their slowly improving local environs. These studies attempt to problematize simple arguments about gentrification as low-income dislocation, and they offer up a more complicated picture of its ills and gains. In Harlem, where residency has always historically included a certain embrace of racial community, these debates about residential dislocation intensify cultural conflicts that fuel various kinds of identity politicking.

As late as the 1980s, Harlem was still considered somewhat gentrification-proof, specifically because of its symbolic connection to African Americans and its stereotypical media representation as violent and dangerous.[32] However, even before Harlem Congressman Charles Rangel helped to usher in a new era with the 1996 Empowerment Zone legislation, Harlem's outer edges, along stretches like 110th Street, touching the northern end of Olmstead's Central Park, were already sites of renewed, middle-class residential interest and reoccupation. With the Empowerment Zone, hundreds of millions of dollars worth of government loans and subsidies have made it all the more enticing for stores like Disney, Pathmark, Old Navy, Radio Shack, The Gap, Starbucks, and Magic Johnson Theaters to take a chance on the Harlem consumer, and many residents welcome this renewal of retail variety. The argument offered is simple: Harlem should have what any and every other community boasts (fancy cafes, convenient movie theaters, huge shopping centers), and corporate America should provide it. Anything short of that is deemed a slap in the face. One woman being videotaped for a documentary I am coproducing on gentrification specifically likened a pre–Empowerment Zone Harlem to Beirut, besieged by both everyday violence and the subtler deprivations of state neglect. "Why should I live in a Beirut type of environment?" she queried rhetorically during a local storeowners' meeting convened in a neighborhood barbershop to discuss gentrification's impact on a string of mom-and-pop shops along one northern Harlem block. "Why should I have to do it when the rest of New York is the cultural capital of the world?"

Housing Hoodoo

In an eatery around the corner from the realty office that gave out that bookmark, I am speaking with Dana, a competing realtor, about all the relatively new and much-publicized interest in Harlem housing. She has just been in the realty business for a couple of years, but even in such a short time, she has noticed substantial shifts in local demand. Dana starts to tell me this story by summarizing a movie—or, at least, a movie pitch. It is one of her many screenplay ideas, this one based on the life of a fictitious Harlem realtor who gets killed by a crazed client obsessed with a specific, nineteenth-century brownstone on an especially quaint Harlem street. Dana is one of four realtors I will meet over a five-day period who are all writing, revising, or selling original screenplays! Los Angeles is no longer the only place that cultivates such cinematic aspirations.

The plot for Dana's script pivots on a century-old curse that turns one Harlem house's Queen-Anne quaintness (its hand-crafted oriel windows and remote, recessed porches) into an intoxicating and deadly obsession. The story's violence is not about gunplay; she makes that clear. ("We have too much shoot-'em-up already.") Instead, the film ends with the realtor, the story's main character, slowly choked to death by an otherworldly (or othertimely) apparition in the small, overgrown yard of the house. The realtor is left limp and breathless under a large, full moon. The ghost, an early-twentieth-century, white resident of the house, possesses the prospective buyer, turning him into a crack addict and then forcing him to perform the suffocating deed. Dana, the realtor-screenwriter, is still working kinks out of her script's third act. It came to her in a dream, she says, "clear as day" in her mind, but she wants to start typing it out with her screenwriting software before too long. "I'll e-mail it to you when it's done," she says. "I promise."

This horror story is not the only script that Dana is working on, either. She has several, at various stages of near-completion, and thinks of herself more as a frustrated writer/video director than a full-fledged real estate agent. A resident of Greenwich, Connecticut, just beyond the five boroughs, she only sells homes in Harlem a couple of days out of the week. The rest of her time is spent doing unrelated, part-time office work in downtown Manhattan—that is, when she's not plugging away at her scripts and story ideas. Most of these stories, she assures me, have little to do with Harlem real estate, but she does see things that merit fiction-alization every time she visits her office in Upper Manhattan—with every single house showing, with every final sale.

That very week, a different screenwriting real estate agent had wit-nessed an exchange that epitomized Harlem's fast-paced, gentrification-driven changes. She describes this one house off Mount Morris Park as completely gutted and sandwiched between two equally dilapidated rowhouses (one of them home to a "deranged squatter"). As if that were not enough, she says, the house also has a caved-in roof that had some-how plunged all the way down to the ground floor. When you open the front door and walk inside, she laughs, you can look up and see the sky. A few years ago, even completely refurbished (and not yet sporting its windowless sunroof), the owners could hardly have gotten more than a hundred thousand dollars for that house, she guesses, and even that would have been wishful thinking. Now, they are asking for $700,000. Not only that, they have already turned down a $675,000 offer. "The roof's in the basement," she reiterates. "Did I tell you that? I did say that, right? That's the kind of Harlem housing [market we have] right now. People are losing their minds. They see green, and they know it."

Sitting across from her in a Manhattanville eatery, Anthroman jots down the numbers feverishly; I want to make sure that I get things ex-actly right: 675,000; 700,000. I have a cassette recorder in my bag, but she is leery about being taped, so I scribble sloppily instead. As I do, she reminds me that this very restaurant, the one I've taken her to for lunch this Saturday afternoon, is also a beneficiary of gentrification's changes, the newest and most upscale business on the city block it shares with one Senegalese diner, several bodegas, and a Chinese take-out restaurant at the far northern corner. It is the latest addition to a bustling streetscape full of Latino toddlers and preteens on bicycles, African American se-niors toting shopping carts from the housing project across the street, and white Columbia University students quietly coming and going from their upstairs apartments.

She emphasizes the fact that every other patron inside this restaurant is white, except for the two of us. I assure her that I had already noticed and jotted that fact down: seventeen patrons, nineteen including us. She then launches into her theory of "the neighborhood squeeze," a version of social mobility in Harlem that is related (but not reducible) to gentrification. African Americans are in the middle of a double push, she says. Gentrification prices them out from the top; they cannot afford the rents for renovated apartments, which is why you have more and more Harlem restaurants patronized by white customers. At the same time, "the rug is being pulled out from beneath them," as poorer Latinos and Africans, "people from overseas," are willing to pay more money for cheaper, unrenovated housing units. "They get squooshed in the middle," she offers, and they will eventually have to leave. "It's sad," she admits, "but I don't think it's anybody's fault. That's just how things go. You have to educate yourself if you want to stay here. They have to learn how to take advantage of the changes, if they can. If not, you won't be here for long."

Helping Homebuyers

Using a small digital video camera, I am recording the last-minute preparations for Harlem's Sixth Annual Community Homebuyers Fair. Everyone at the Greater Harlem Real Estate Board, a seventy-five-year-old, nonprofit organization, "the oldest African American housing trade association in the United States," is comparing notes for the next day's eight-hour event. They are expecting some fifteen thousand attendees, which would make it "the largest community-based Homebuyer's event in the nation." [33] With fiscal sponsorship from every major bank in New York City, the Homebuyer's Fair is billed as an opportunity to do exactly what the Harlem realtor-screenwriter I lunched with advised: promote homeownership among poorer Harlem families. The fair provides attendees with one-stop access to everything they might need for the process: "realtists, realtors, developers, building contractors, suppliers, mortgage lenders, financial planners, insurance specialists, architects, nonprofit housing specialists, and government agents . . . free credit reports, pre-purchase affordability tests, as well as pre-qualifications and pre-approvals for mortgages." [34] There will be workshops, seminars, and appearances by local and national celebrities—along with free ice cream for all those who arrive before supplies run out, not an unimportant perk on a hot July in the city.

Earlier that month, the head of Harlem's Real Estate Board took part in a Harlem Homeowner's event in the Adam Clayton Powell State Office Building, the architectural backdrop for their Harlem Homebuyers Fair (and on exactly the same floor where Bill and Gina organized their last psychic fair). The real estate company with the "Arithmetic of the Avenues" bookmark had sponsored a small gathering for current home-owners (the other side of that housing market transaction) intended to give them a sense of all the assistance potentially at their disposal when-ever (and if ever) they decided to sell their Harlem properties.

You did not need to be actively selling anything to attend. Orga-nizers just wanted homeowners to meet real estate agents who could answer any questions they might have about home-selling procedures. Again, I wielded my video camera, interviewing everyone I could find (estimators, lawyers, realtors, contractors—each with his or her own pamphlet-laden booth), asking them about what they stood to gain from such an event. Each of them spouted basically the same party-line about making sure that Harlem homeowners know (1) the home-selling basics and (2) that their particular business is available for consultation. The turnout was not as large as the real estate company had hoped, but it was still an upbeat afternoon, with attendees exchanging business cards and personal stories about their Harlem experiences. "It is just about making contacts," one realtor offered, "a way to get your name out there and see where other people are at."

The executive director of the Harlem Real Estate Board was there to promote his upcoming Homebuyers Fair, along with a longer series of workshops throughout the year that were billed as "powerful, cost-effective homebuyer training services that inform, educate, empower, in-spire, and motivate." They promised to "transform local residents into local Homeowners." [35] He agreed to let us videotape their preparation for the Homebuyers Fair, which is why I had my camera in their faces as they went over last-minute details before the big event. There were still porta-potties to pick-up, workers to enlist, a few hundred flyers to distribute, and a huge outdoor tent to construct. The main organizers mapped out their every step and stayed up all night (a group of some five part-time workers and a few more familial volunteers) to make sure that everything was taken care of. The next morning, on the day of the event, several thousand people (just about all of them black and/or Latino) snaked around the block as they waited to register for admittance. Once they made it to the other side of the police barricades and into the tented affair, they would find applications for unfinished townhouses and apartment buildings (oversized blueprints and drawings of those future sites propped up securely on contiguous folding tables), booths full of legal aid attorneys and real estate developers, newly published "home-buyer reference guides," and kiosk after kiosk of soliciting realtors.

One of the first tables, closest to the entrance, included a pile of booklets on "Tenants' Rights," booklets produced by the State Attorney General's office. (Thinking of Bill's pending loft eviction, I picked up an extra copy.) The "tenant," of course, is the most explicitly invoked explanation for a homebuyer's fair in the first place. Turning renters into homeowners is the very raison d'être of the Harlem Real Estate Board, which has consulted with more than 800 families through the years and helped some 160 of them into new homes. After seven hours in the blazing sun, the ice cream long gone, and even Congressman Rangel's rousing speech a distant memory, I see several journalists interviewing attendees about their assessments of the event. In a few days, local weeklies will officially proclaim the Real Estate Board's fair an unequivocal success, but for now, the tents are not even down before organizers start thinking aloud about the future; they might just get twenty thousand people to come out next time around.

Tenant Activists

There are clearly many more renting tenants than the Harlem Real Estate Board can ever fully house—and that lopsided math is exactly what Netta Bradshaw, a local Harlem tenant-activist, wants everyone to remember. She is part of a citywide network of urban activists from places like Harlem, Chinatown, the Lower East Side, and Flatbush, Brooklyn, who are intent on keeping poorer tenants housed in their apartment buildings—even and especially in response to gentrification-specific pressures to oust them.[36] Many of Bradshaw's clients could be found roaming around the tables at the Homebuyers Fair, trying to imagine a life without landlords and threats of eviction. In the name of these same tenants, local activists designate certain neighborhoods "Gentrification-free Zones," areas from within which they refuse to allow a single local tenant to be removed without public demonstrations and legal appeals.

"Everybody can't own a home in Harlem," Bradshaw says, racing through an obstacle course of pedestrians along Harlem's main thoroughfare. Already late, she is on her way to yet another meeting. This one is about challenging mandatory work requirements for public housing tenants. Still, she takes the time to offer me her views on gentrification and homeownership. It is important to debunk myths from all comers, she proclaims, to get the truth out there. "That's just unrealistic [thinking everyone can own a home]. We have to make sure that anyone can live with dignity and self-respect in this community. They don't deserve to be harassed by landlords or ignored by politicians because they don't have campaign contributions. That's what we're fighting against."

For Harlem tenant-activists, residential dislocation is a given, and it can happen in any number of ways. For example, over the last few years, Columbia University has repeatedly met with local Community Boards in Northern Manhattan to let them know about the institution's request for a zoning change to construct several new buildings in Manhattanville, just minutes away from their main anchorage point in the contiguous neighborhood of Morningside Heights. Such rezoning usually increases the proportion of students to nonstudents in any given area. To activist groups like the Coalition to Preserve Community, one of the more organized local responses to proposed university encroachments, this creates a not-so-subtle slope toward displacement. Students are considered "soft tenants," usually only intending to stay in a community for a relatively short period of time: the number of years it takes them to matriculate and earn their degrees. With less truly long-term investment in the local neighborhood, soft tenants are much more willing (and, since most are middle-class college students, financially able) to pay market rates for apartments conveniently located close to their campuses. These same tenants also leave quickly, maybe signing a lease for a year and then looking to find a new place for the subsequent fall term, which translates into their units being regularly "renovated" (which need not mean actually doing very much) and their rents raised higher and faster than would be possible without a tenant's departure. In a New York housing market where rent control is really a thing of the past, and rent regulation has ever-widening loopholes, these soft tenants are just one more explanation for the declining political leverage of poorer local residents.

According to Bradshaw, market-based incentives for removing tenants have seduced many an unscrupulous landlord into filing frivolous lawsuits in the hope of ousting long-term tenants. And whom do they go after? Not so much African American residents, activists argue, as Panamanians, Dominicans, Haitians—and especially elderly female tenants whose native language is not English. This is one obvious inflection of gentrification's global relevance to local stories of residential displacement, an understanding of gentrification that spies a patterned manipulation of what might be called diasporic differences in the service of profiteering, since there are certainly some African Americans among the ranks of these overly litigious landlords. For Bradshaw, this is not just a race issue. "Owners and tenants have different incentives," she says. "And a lot of people will try to make money at the expense of other people if they have half the chance. And we don't want to give them that chance. Black, white, or whatever."

Bifurcating Black Middle Classes

There are, according to Bradshaw and others, at least two black middle classes in contemporary Harlem: the old guard that never left and a newer group that has recently arrived. For many of the Harlem activists, these two black middle classes represent diametrically opposed interests—not least because the older guard views the younger set as a threat to their local authority. When newspapers and magazines represent the black powerbrokers of Harlem, they also use this dual model of older, liberal, civil rights patriarchs in one corner and newer, conservative, corporate-friendly upstarts in the other. As overstated as the distinction might be, there are many ways that activists like Bradshaw attempt to use such frameworks to reeducate tenants about class politics, complicating binary racial formulas for a schema that pits the older middle-class residents against newer ones, with poorer local tenants using that rift as a leverage-point for getting their demands heard and their needs addressed.

This bifurcation of Harlem's black middle class also delineates another major fault line between (1) those who explain their relationship to the community in purely materialist, market-based terms and (2) those who justify their presence as a function of race-based social community and commitment.[37] For some, this old-guard/new-guard divide graphs easily onto what I am labeling a market/membership distinction. For others, market and membership drives dissect old and new black middle-classes alike. According to Bill, for instance, it is important to note that most of Harlem's newest arrivals are not even African Americans. "Just because somebody's got dark skin," he offers, when Bradshaw and I stop to peruse his book table (so that she can provide advice on his pending loft eviction), "that doesn't mean they deserve to be here. People fought for this community, and we got folks from all over the place coming in to capitalize on it, except for us, and not the *us* that just got off the boat from Africa or somewhere setting up a business to sell us nonsense. We gotta get rid of that foolishness. Black people gotta be smarter than that. These other people come here and buy cars and homes, and live the lifestyle we say we want. They take our women; they take our money; they take our destiny." Bill's nativist screed has a history that can be traced to earlier xenophobic renditions of Harlem's African American particularity vis-à-vis West Indians.[38] His analysis of the diasporic circulation of women, money, and destinies is also a fanciful misreading of the actual gendered dynamics of on-the-ground local

activism, where women are not simply items of exchange among diasporic men, but are disproportionately overrepresented among the neighborhood's most powerful grassroots political activists. The collaborative
research of anthropologists Leith Mullings and Alaka Wali indicates
that this lopsided overrepresentation of women in urban activist circles
may even worsen already serious health disparities.[39] These same African American women, who are among the most vocal and active residents on both sides of this issue (pro-gentrification homeowners and
anti-gentrification tenant activists), may exemplify a kind of "Sojourner
Syndrome" that adds serious health-related concerns to the already taxing lives of African American women, the very women dismissed out of
hand by Bill's masculinist rhetoric.

Veronica Boynton is head of a local Homeowners association in
Central Harlem. She moved into the neighborhood more than twenty
years ago and was able to buy a brownstone in the community during Harlem's below-market, pre-gentrification era. In the early 1980s,
she purchased her home for about $34,000. It is now worth closer to
$500,000—and the value may still be rising. Boynton takes me on a
tour of "the ruins," a local name for the string of nine infamous, turn-
of-the-century rowhouses that were seized by the government under
eminent domain in the 1960s and slated for a drug rehabilitation center.
Amid fierce NIMBY (Not in My Backyard) resistance, the plans were
scrapped and the buildings left mostly to decay—only the corner edifice
consistently utilized, most recently as an all-women's jail. The Community Preservation Corporation (a nonprofit agency started in 1974 to improve the city's deteriorated housing stock) finally turned the strip into
a series of market-rate condominiums slated to sell for at least $200,000
each. To many tenant activists, this is just another example of "unbalanced" urban growth, the kind that privileges middle-class interests over
the needs of poorer Harlemites. For residents like Boynton, however, it
is simply another feather in Harlem's newly plumed cap—and a nice
ending to a long, embattled saga. Any other interpretation, she says, is
just ridiculous.

"If you want to stay in Harlem," she proclaims confidently, "just pay
your rent. That's it. Sure, we don't want landlords taking advantage of
poor people, but we have courts to take care of that. It may not work
perfectly, but it works. The only people not safe are those who don't
want to pay their rent and need to be thrown out of here, and that's just
a portion of the people who live here. Besides," she adds, "you look at
some of these [tenant] activists; I never see black people in their offices.
I used to work next to one, and I would watch the people who went in

and out of there. They were all white people, so what kind of community are they talking about helping?" For Boynton, the "white threat" comes not from gentrification, but from the gentrification activists themselves, defined as fronts for outside white interests. At the same time, she trusts the courts to weed out criminal landlords who are less of an issue, in her opinion, than obstinate tenants refusing to pay rent. And here we see part of gentrification's contentious fault line: Boynton puts her faith in the very institutions that Bradshaw most readily distrusts.

Boynton and I are sitting at Settepani, a two-year-old gourmet bakery on Lenox Avenue, one of a cluster of smaller local businesses that are competing with corporate America for storefront space and Empowerment Zone money. Settepani is a trendy new business co-owned and operated by an Ethiopian woman who greets me with a friendly smile of familiar recognition after only my second visit. Its well-prepared offerings are small and Soho-priced. Settepani's menu is based on light tuna salads and an assortment of coffees. The staff is diasporic and multi-hued. It is the kind of establishment that members of both the new and old black middle classes look upon with pride. It is where Maya Angelou, a recent Harlem homeowner, takes many of her neighborhood meetings, where I once spotted Kareem Abdul Jabar strolling outside, where residents convene midday for coffee and conversation—certain residents, that is.

Settepani marks itself (and its surrounding sidewalk space) as a decidedly middle-class location. Across the street and within a stone's throw of Settepani's stylish awning, abandoned buildings and chicken shacks with no air conditioning serve as the stony backdrops against which local Harlemites chat and pass their time, sitting atop milk crates and folding chairs, sometimes playing dominos, sometimes listening to music, sometimes just ogling passersby. Directly in front of Settepani, however, the outdoor space is much more carefully configured. A row of lightweight dining tables and chairs line the storefront's exterior wall, chained and padlocked to one another and to the store's metallic storm gates. These outside seats and tables are as much about performances of middle-classness as they are viable spaces for dining on Settepani cuisine. This is a rendition of public space with recognizably middle-class implications—and it signals, from afar, just who belongs and who does not. It serves as a deliberate rejoinder to the chicken shacks and the graffitied front stoops of nearby establishments, a direct refusal of (and rebuttal to) their presentational alternatives. It is also what, for some, potentially flags the space as feminized and homosexual. One twenty-five-year-old Harlemite always describes the place to me as "faggoty," with clear implications for residential disqualification. This homophobic characterization is his main reason for not wanting to eat there. For him, middle-class status is articulated through homosexuality—two equally soft versions of public life—in contradistinction to the more stereotypically hardened performances of lower-class black masculinity.

These class-specific (and homosexualized) markings of space are some of the more obvious sites for social antagonisms and clear-cut displacements in a gentrifying community. Whether or not poorer Harlemites are being displaced from their homes, there are very obvious examples of the ways in which middle-class uses of space (and a concomitant Disneyfication that evacuates all conspicuous class differences from the public sphere) accomplish a certain social displacement from public view, imposing an obviously class-inflected loss of access to certain public locales.[40] It is a displacement that, coupled with "quality of life" policing, fuels the fires of antagonism that rage along the cement sidewalk spaces of many urban cities.[41]

This reconfiguration of public space has serious implications for Harlem's poorest residents, especially when many of them have already been relegated to a kind of exclusive publicness. The welfare state starts the process by evacuating privacy from the home, turning what was once intimate seclusion into a matter of public record, especially as social workers document the presence or absence of men in welfare recipients' homes. In this context, access to privacy becomes a solely bourgeois privilege, and when this publicness is all one is allowed, privatization of public space may be the most obvious riposte. Flip-flopped feet on concrete sidewalks, bright pink rollers in unkempt and auburn-streaked hair, the slouchiest of stoop-sitting—they all assert a very powerful counter-privatization.

These class-inflected uses of sidewalk space are especially important when we think about how public places gain personal, political, and private significances.[42] Residents' paths to and from, say, laundromats and corner bodegas, Chinese or Senegalese restaurants, their children's public schools, and so on, become vain attempts at tiny patches of peripatetic privacy within an overdetermined landscape of market-based privatization and accompanying state-sponsored public expansion. Pierre Mayol also calls these kinds of personal pathways forms of "privatization," a wonderful counterpoint to neoliberal notions of the private as ineluctably and exclusively linked to property ownership.[43] These intimate and idiosyncratic paths through public space are not equivalent to individual ownership in any simple sense. If anything, this is an ownership of space that money cannot actually buy.

Redefined privatization is another way to invoke Lefebvre's notion of qualified spaces untamed by market forces. It is a disavowal of mathematical resolutions and reducibilities. This is not solely about how spaces symbolize (as black or white, rich or poor); it is also a rehearsal of social belonging tethered to people's everyday practices and senses of self. To look out onto one's public sphere and see what was another abandoned storefront (open space for all, especially the least successful) alchemized into a gourmet bakery for a growing middle class, is a different order of displacement entirely, a kind of psychological and semiotic displacement from the sites of one's own, formerly less-fettered, everyday pedestrianism. At the same time, when a purported privateness behind locked apartment doors becomes subject to the probing publicity of the state apparatus, private sidewalk spaces emerge as important battlefields. Gentrification becomes a way to show how the public gets privatized (in capitalistic ways) by the middle-class interests of places like Settepani, Native (another new restaurant across the street), Hue-Man Books, and other recent business additions.

Such a realization (that gentrification is as importantly about reprivatizing public spaces as it is about evicting building tenants) might mean imagining the activist and corporatist renditions of space (their mathematics of mobility and marketability, respectively) as two sides of the same coin, analogous in many ways to the "Avenue of Arithmetic" equations that offer a bird's eye view of contemporary urban living. Forced to make sense from below not above, local actors can be seen vying for authority in a slightly different discussion about who is and is not a real Harlemite, about who does and does not truly belong. A look at the remainders (what's left out of most popular mathematics of Manhattan) might allow us to see conflicting forms of urbanity in contemporary black America—instances of racial privatization that draw middle-class African Americans to Harlem even as their very presence reinforces the forms of corporate privatization that necessitate extreme performances of public privacy as subversive response to a shrinking private realm that has become little more than public playground for the authenticities monopolized by middle-class consumerism.

Edificial Ekphrases

Lefebvre's discussion of the hegemony of quantifiable and mathematical conceptions of space is a clear attempt to theorize contemporary globalization, even if he traces this impulse back to seventeenth-century philosophy, and regardless of the fact that we presently read him from beyond his own seemingly antiquated 1970s context. Critical geographer David Harvey's tripartite schema ("historical-geographical-materialist") is an equally processual rendering of space and its importance to globalization.[44] In both instances, space (as analytical construct and everyday experience) is not just an innocent context for power's machinations; it is a malleable tool in the processes of subjectivation, routinization, institutionalization and resistance that inform/deform social action.

Gentrification, then, is a lens for glimpsing the same globalization that theorists like Frederic Jameson and Arjun Appadurai have been known to unpack by way of differently pentamerous formulas. For Jameson, this means examining technological, political, cultural, economic, and social components of the phenomenon.[45] For Appadurai, it results in his oft-cited flowscapes model: ethnoscapes, financescapes, ideoscapes, technoscapes, and mediascapes, a critical response to both linear social evolutionism and Wallersteinian macrostructural analyses.[46] I want to argue for another important *scape*. We might call it a kind of *racioscape*, one that marks the color/culture compressions that pull far-flung corners of the African diaspora into greater and greater everyday contact on the streets of neighborhoods like Harlem—where Creole-speaking Haitian tenants are disproportionately targeted for eviction, where Ethiopian storeowners successfully win Empowerment Zone funding to open up Italian eateries, where Latinos and West Africans are believed to put a "squeeze" on Afro-American residential life-chances, and where class differences between and among African Americans are often diasporically internationalized (as us vs. *us*) and even homosexualized to determine the limits of authentic community. The notion of racioscapes speaks to the inescapably non-*flow*like constancy of racial inequality as an effective analytical template for understanding globality, diasporic relations, and transnational interconnections in the past, present, and foreseeable future. Any discussion of globalization that does not make race one of its central analytical components threatens to offer an impoverished notion of globality that reproduces inequalities through its theoretical silences.[47]

When race is both a public and private commodity, understanding commercialization is key. Double-locking doors can be read as an emphatic declaration of privacy, especially with Empowerment Zone money downsizing more and more of the public sphere. Indeed, Harlem's public landscape has changed drastically in the last few years, but the process of change is still ongoing. That is, there is an unevenness to Harlem's public revamping, and one window into this incompleteness is provided by the Times-Square-sized advertisements splotched over the still-abandoned and dilapidated buildings that sit surreally tooth to jowl against all of Harlem's brand new local establishments with their shiny neon storefronts. These jumbo ads are not just erected along the unused sides of buildings, the empty and windowless spaces tailor-made for such billboarding. More usually, such ads are placed right over windows themselves—windows that are sometimes boarded up, sometimes bricked over, and sometimes still-glassy implications of the lives that once animated their most intimate and private insides.[48] These abandoned apartments bespeak the selfish and irresponsible custodianship of Harlem during the mid-twentieth century, when a middle-class exodus led owners to abandon their low-income housing stock. Advertisements atop abandonment also mark the slowness of Harlem's current transformations, a reinvigorated interest that cannot quite completely cover up/over a history of neglect—one sordid public space underneath another. But not only are the apartments themselves abandoned, a remnant of the tenants who once lived inside; the advertisements themselves are abandoned as well—left to dangle for a futurity not yet realized, tethered to a material present of brick, glass, and cement that exposes the injustices of a past rife with restricted covenants, overcrowded apartments, and absentee landlording.

Showing images of images draped over abandoned histories is a shorthand lesson in racial visuality as told through architectural desertion and reappropriation.[49] These ads don't just sell athletic wear (which some 99 percent of them ostensibly do). They also advertise the very absurdities of capitalist revaluation—the powerful will-to-profit of its economic mandates. Hanging huge ads over empty residential space only draws attention to the forgotten and forsaken—even as it tries to resignify waste as wanton material excess. But the dingy facades of these early-twentieth-century structures challenge such a redefinition. The buildings themselves instantiate a kind of edificial captioning that literally concretizes critical commentaries about the images swathed above them.

One would almost not even see the bricked-up buildings without their incomplete obstruction by these jumbo billboards. And then there are those semitransparent ads, the ones that only partially hide faintly discernible open windows beneath them, animating those same pseudo-private insides—insides where, before heading outside, people are slinking their feet into flip-flops and throwing colorful scarves over their uneven hair rollers. The pedestrian wanderer below gasps at the obviously Faustian pact that tenants must have signed, condemning themselves to varying degrees of darkness behind the sun-stopping mesh, plastic and

cardboard advertisements. What manner of literality is this? What is really being hawked in Harlem's public sphere?

The "Ghetto Fabulous"

Clearly, Harlem is a diasporic and global place. Race, racial ideology, racial essentialism, and racial diasporas are challenged, deconstructed, and reconfigured on its cement sidewalks daily, with recourse to morphing racioscapes that recognize global pressures and processes from the tiniest points of local specificity. Even though parsed differently in various parts of the world, race is still an importantly international unit of social analysis, not because it has some kind of biological, genetic, and precultural reality, but because race-inflected differences are fundamental organizing principles for global capital, regardless of nation-specific classificatory schemas. In this scenario, race is that seemingly quantifiable rubric whose irrepressible remainders haunt our every attempt to mathematicalize it into scientific validity. Its biological anchors can be disproved, but its effects are nonfalsifiable. Even to think in terms of falsification is to fall victim to a ploy, to authenticity's traps. And therein lies race's social power—its ability to evade the most careful and rigorous of social scientific analyses. The ethnographic goal, then, is not to look for something redemptive about race (an intellectual wild-goose chase if ever there was one), but rather to find the pockets of qualitative possibility that mystify the mathematical equations people use for figur-

ing self and other in contemporary societies overdetermined by race—an overdetermination that begs for some recognition of the symbolic remainders that exceed naively rationalist and realist responses. To think about an ethnography of the racioscape is to imagine an engagement with what is usually left over from (and left out of) academic theories of racial essentialism and social constructedness. It is ethnography of the fake, the simulated, the counterfeit, if only insofar as such a predilection helps us peek through reality's opened back doors.

The vernacular notion of "ghetto fabulousness" is a tiny example of just such an ethnographic impulse, a spying of the real's backside. To be ghetto fabulous is to embrace a sense of self utterly irreducible to one's assumed location at the residential and spatial bottom of national or international pecking orders. Ghetto fabulousness takes the quantified assumptions of localized marginality and transforms them into a qualitatively different kind of lived experience, a way of traversing the sociospatial margin that privileges personal and intimate privatizations over the market-based instrumentality of social scientists, government agencies, and economic modeling. This is not simply a depressing enslavement to designer clothing—foolish ghetto residents living beyond their means in authentic Versace, Prada, or even Burberry fashion. Ghetto fabulousness, when at its most fabulous, epitomizes a consumerism and commercialism that revels in knock-offs and wears them, sincerely,

against the grain of societal expectations. Think, again, of those designer flip-flop slippers on the street corner, slippers that turn public
space into another kind of privateness, countering jumbo ads that transform the privacy of tenement apartments into mere extensions of commercial publicity. Here, too, ghetto fabulousness is predicated on the
workings of the global market, a global market where imitation Gucci,
DKNY, and Sean Jean products flood the sidewalk. Ghetto fabulousness would not survive without this low-end global commodification of
trademark infringement, without such brash disregard for international
trade laws. Ghetto fabulousness uses this underside of the global to challenge its own confinement, to declare the social margins quite central
to the people who live there, even as they struggle for more access to
a global mainstream.[50] But those two fronts (mainstream and fringe)
should not be confused. Ghetto fabulosity is only misread when glossed
in the most vulgarly Bourdieuian terms: as a lack of middle-class symbolic capital that makes itself known by the loud impropriety of, say,
bright red spandex jumpsuits worn with black faux-fur tops.[51] Just as
exorbitant price tags can be flouted, mainstream sartorial codes are similarly dismissed—not out of pure ignorance, but as an assertion of self-
validity.[52] These tactics are not immune to cooptation, but they are also
not solely delimited by that potentiality. Even as "ghetto fabulous" websites invite readers (1) to "vote" on a Ghett-O-Meter about whether individuals photographed are really "ghetto fabulous" as opposed to just
"ghetto" or (2) to follow the saga of fictitious Harlem drug dealers as a
serialized prequel to an independent film shot on location in real Harlem housing projects, the notion of ghetto fabulousness is fighting its
own reduction to the plane of sheer authenticity.[53] But ghetto fabulous
can only be defined—and unwieldily—by its resistance to purported
definitions, by its dismissal of external validation. It will not be voted
on—or quietly acquiesce to the results.

Ghetto fabulousness offers an entirely different calculus for social
valuation. It changes mere numbers-crunching and vote-tabulating into
something more like Bill and Gina's numerology, morphing an externally verifiable racial authenticity into a kind of racial sincerity that is
more difficult to falsify, a sincerity that comes through the faux and
fudged, a sincerity that celebrates its own conspicuous alternatives to
middle-of-the-road racial realities. This is some of what it might mean
to write blackness as blue/s, to embrace the very *thingness* of sociality,
and to master not a racial science but an "art of being black."[54] Far
from utopian transcendence, ghetto fabulousness is an utter immanence,
a dwelling close to the materiality of an everyday existence that frus-

trates our very best efforts at mathematical and rhetorical realism, especially when such math is used dismissively to determine who does and does not *count*.[55] Demanding a newfangled geometry of race, ghetto fabulousness relishes remainders. And it may just necessitate a turning of the head 45 degrees so as to see the real ideally and the ideal, quite possibly, only ever partially, as real.

3

Real Bodies

Thou art a scholar; speak to it, Horatio.

Marcellus, in William Shakespeare's *Hamlet*

God giveth it a body as it hath pleased him, and to every seed his own body. All flesh is not the same flesh: but there is one kind of flesh of men, another flesh of beasts, another of fishes, and another of birds. There are also celestial bodies, and bodies terrestrial: but the glory of the celestial is one, and the glory of the terrestrial is another. There is one glory of the sun, and another glory of the moon, and another glory of the stars: for one star differeth from another star in glory. So also is the resurrection of the dead. It is sown in corruption; it is raised in incorruption: It is sown in dishonour; it is raised in glory: it is sown in weakness; it is raised in power: It is sown a natural body; it is raised a spiritual body. There is a natural body, and there is a spiritual body.

1 Corinthians 15:38–44

God is the baddest ass in the firmament.

Gordon Etheridge, in John Gwaltney's *Drylongso*

∴ ∴ ∴

Big-Butted Bodies

"That boy can flat-out sing," Shanita proclaims, carefully draping a hot, just-ironed pair of BOSS jeans over a wire hanger. Stretched out across this seventeen-year-old's pecan-sandy-colored comforter, I take note of her gentle meticulousness, as effectively thorough and cautious as the pants themselves are hastily produced and shoddy, counterfeits purchased from a dreadlocked street vendor nervously stationed atop a subway's air vent in downtown Brooklyn. Literally bootlegged: Shanita only decided to buy them because they fit so nicely over her favorite pair of knee-high leather footwear. The pocket-sized notepad on my lap is filled with half-legible jottings on facts just like this, mostly details about Shanita, her mom, her friends, and their everyday lives that I will never find a way to translate into the stuff of ethnography.

Shanita's living room is the same size as my mother's, but the layout is different. My mother's apartment is on the southern side of this very building, its windows frowning over cemented sidewalk space at a little corner of Kings Highway in Brooklyn, a corner not more than fifteen minutes from the Canarsie tenement buildings of my wide-eyed, bloody-kneed childhood. Shanita's place, along the building's northern end, has a view of a walled-off back lot of metal-meshed garbage cans, chipped and discarded bricks, shards of broken soda bottles, and sometimes worse, much worse, like the time "this motherfucker was like wailing and crying and shit, and wasn't nobody doing nothing except saying shit like 'Be quiet down there 'cause some folk got jobs to go to in the morning.' And come to find out the next day that this guy is lying dead back there." But that was a good while ago, and Shanita assures me that "ain't much happen back there since then."

The slightest afternoon breeze brings a rhythmic clack, clack, clacking from a bedroom window in the back of the apartment that is not quite snug in its fiberglass grooves. Feeling sick and physically weak from the flu, Shanita's mother, Lucy, has decided to take off from work, trying her best to rest amid the bedroom's staccato soundtrack. Anthroman, in the living room of their one-bedroom apartment, lounging on Shanita's bed, one of two twin-sized mattresses sandwiching the shag-carpeted living room's color television, half-watches as Lucille Ball performs her syndicated shtick on a thirteen-inch color television in the far corner. However, I can hardly concentrate. Something about Shanita's description of her schoolmate Tyrone (the "boy" she claims "can flat-out sing") has my special Anthrosense tingling, which means, of course, that there is valuable qualitative data to be grasped. I brim with ethnographic expectation.

"Flat-out sing?" I skeptically quip back. "He's awwiight!! I mean, if it's that boy I saw at your school's last gospel concert, the one with the foot-high fade, looking like Lord-knows-what, he ain't all that."

"I don't know how you muster up the nerve to talk about someone else's singing," Shanita reprimands, "especially when you can't even Sing Sing prison." [1]

"Don't make prison jokes like every black man has to relate," I warn. "I'm just saying, he's good, but you biguppin' him like he's the 'brother from another planet.'" [2]

Shanita folds another pair of jeans in half lengthwise, a water-filled iron hissing with her every touch. "Anyway, Luther Vandrone," she continues, "that wasn't him. David was at the concert before. That is the person you seen. Tyrone wasn't even there last time. But he's gonna be the one everyone can't wait to see this time around though, with his big-butt self. You know what? A friend of mine from school was playing around and shit saying that she did a survey and found that every black person knows at least one person from the neighborhood where they grew up who had a big butt. And that usually the person was named Tyrone. And I was like, 'Oh shit, there was a boy who lived in 9308, and he sure did have a huge butt—like a woman's.' We would all clown on him when he did stupid shit, too. Those were the good old days." Shanita's nostalgia is self-consciously feigned and facetious.

"Damn, you all may be on to something," I say, thinking back to my earliest years in a housing project complex that was home to at least one big-butted Tyrone. Maybe two.

"And there was always at least one big-headed person, too," she resumes, laughing. "I don't know if they all have the same name, but we always called them watermelon heads. We got one in the choir now, but he is quiet. He can sing too, but it's Tyrone we wanna see on Thursday night."

"Why?" I ask.

"'Cause we gonna see some drama."

"Drama like what?" I lean in toward her.

"Well, the principal said that no one can 'catch the Holy Spirit' or anything like that on stage, and that as soon as anyone did, he would stop the concert, and the person would get suspended. And even when we just practicing, Tyrone be looking like he about to break down and faint or something."

"From the Holy Spirit?" I ask her to clarify.

"I don't know, but Tyrone, when he starts getting into a song, especially *Firmament*, which we will be singing on Thursday night by the way, he be really getting into it."

"Getting into it like how?"

"Like body shaking and stuff. He be like crying and . . ."

"And the school told you all that they would not allow that?" I interrupt.

"Mmhmm."

"And what did you all say?"

"Nothing. What we gonna say? We just all wanna see what happens with Tyrone Thursday night at the concert. You coming, right?"

How could Anthroman miss it? It promised to be a concert that would pit authenticity against religious sincerities, that would reread the distance separating administrative rules from the unruliness of interiorized spiritualities. The discussion of singing souls and Holy Spirits that I'll try to unpack in this chapter can serve as a useful model for the differing logical polarities of contemporary racial reasoning, analogizing the distinction between authentic verifications and sincere vulnerabilities. The connection between institutional mandates (in this case, assumptions about appropriate decorum for public performances) and the interiorized, intentional bodies they assume—and upon which they seek to act—foregrounds a debate about "the body as a site of knowing."[3] These particular teenage bodies are partially co-constructed and constrained at one and the same time by the principal's clear-cut mandate.[4]

Extending the last chapter's numerological anthropology of public privacies to this one's discussion of semiotic spiritualities, I want to argue that the possessed body, Tyrone's big-butted and Holy-Ghosted body, marks an impasse between sincere and authentic versions of reality, pinpointing the everyday issues at stake in philosophical debates about race's metaphysical and epistemological purchase.[5] Anthroman's scholarly job, then, much like that of Shakespeare's Horatio, is to speak to the ghosts and specters and spirits and phantoms that exceed and confound some of our attempts to police ourselves through authenticity, to fix the realities of social identity.[6] Toward that end, it is important to unpack at least two interrelated suppositions underpinning the high school administration's categorical ban on the Holy Ghost. First, the principal's office might dismiss such spirit possession as mere performance, distinguishing genuine religiosities from mockery or playacting: Are these high schoolers really being possessed, or are they just performing possession, willful agents pretending to relinquish their agency and subjective interiority to some celestial spirit—and maybe just to get away with hijinks that might not otherwise be tolerated? This aspect of the principal's suspension threat reduces these adolescents' spirit possession to the kinds of pranks and horseplay that commonly land students in detention. The principal's decree also neatly divides internal states from their appropriate external contexts, emphasizing the difference between

socially acceptable and unacceptable places to genuinely "catch the
Holy Spirit." Why should the general public be subjected to witnessing
such spirit possession? And during a high school's annual spring concert
no less? The spiritual subject is granted (and demanded to perform) intentional control over its inanimate body matter. And shouldn't all religious bodies be held to such a standard, one seemingly flouted with
every emergence of the Holy Ghost in this New York City public school?
How should an anthropologist interested in the specificities of racial
reasoning understand these socio-spiritual bodies and their relationship
to institutional prohibitions? What might they rehearse about the connection between sincere and authentic renditions of the real?

Theologian Vincent L. Wimbush provides a suggestive model for
reading sacred texts (which these singing bodies ephemerally become)
through, in, and as "darkness." "A reading of darkness," he argues, "as
psychosocial reorientation, as self-possession and critical point of departure, as a higher critical gaze, can reorient and redefine the agenda
of interpretation." [7] For Wimbush, "reading darkness" is a hermeneutic
and an everyday practice, "a way of being in and seeing the world . . . in
emergency mode, as through the individual and collective experience of
trauma." [8] This darkened reading as a response to trauma is exactly how
Kathleen Stewart characterizes realness more generally, especially in the
context of a contemporary world over-theorized with conspiracies, a
"REAL [that] emerges as trauma . . . a pathological public sphere focused
on trauma, trauma, trauma. The mantra of trauma." [9] For Wimbush and
Stewart, trauma is a reading of social life that imagines the taken-for-
grantedness of seeing as liability. Reading darkly means, among other
things, a kind of knowing not predicated straightforwardly on sight. It
is to feel, grope, invent, even pretend for the real—and most especially
because the stakes are so high. Michael Taussig cites Walter Benjamin
to describe the quotidian as always already "nervous," in a perpetual
"state of emergency," another ethnographic iteration of the volatile
everydayness of trauma, an everydayness, an everyday darkness, that
privileges tactility over visuality. [10] Wimbush, Stewart, and Taussig are
also interested in how we read and write these everyday emergencies,
how we mobilize them toward analytical ends—and without simply
flicking on some objectivist light-switch.

The body as "nervous system" is quite powerfully performed by the
jutting, gesticulating, dancing, shouting, shaking, twitching, and con-
vulsing singer taken over by the Holy Ghost. To see Tyrone and these
other choir bodies in the *dark,* to read them "darkly," is to ask questions
of them that help us to continue thinking through the heuristic distance

between racial authenticities and sincerities, a distance that shows how realness gets divined by way of two separate methodologies and interpretive strategies: external verification through the myth of transparency vs. an acquiescence to the interior and opaque authority of a social "other." The principal's attempt to police these possessed adolescent bodies is a textured analogy for some of the ways in which authenticity would like to rewire sincerity's excesses and invisibilities to its own goals. Sincerity presupposes an otherly inside that can never be fully verifiable, never unambiguously spied. Authenticity's world, however, is topsy-turvy, reading the surfaces of the social for fully externalized proof of internal machinations, intentions, and meanings. In this chapter, I examine darknesses of/on the body through two analytically distinctive notions of soul: one predicated on salvations and second comings; the other, on racial essences and irrationalities.[11] These two versions of soul (an ostensibly universalizing ethos vs. a form of expressive racial particularity glossed with recourse to things like soul music, soul food, soul brothers and sisters, etc.) mark time between sincere and authentic ways of reckoning realness, race, and reason. I also want to use this chapter to think more explicitly about the limits of autoethnography, about how a performative suturing of self into ethnographic subject matter operates as another kind of possession ritual. Writing the threats, fears, and obsessions of spirit possession performatively, I think, demands that we offer the "I" as always already oversaturated with its own potentially exorcizable ghosts and goblins—familial, citational, and psychological ones all at once. "Real Bodies" puts such cloudy reflexivities into critical conversation with one high school gospel choir's *soul*ful performance of the slippery distinctions between seeing and feeling corporeal insides.

Dead Bodies

When disentangling bodies, spirits, souls, and ghosts, it makes sense to begin by waxing eschatological, musing over the unknowable relationship between, say, fleeting souls and their eventually rotting corpses. Talk of the soul easily traffics in discussion of death. And where do all these many floating souls of decaying, dead flesh go when their time has come? Most of the residents I have worked with in Harlem and Brooklyn would undoubtedly offer hell and heaven as the best possible answers, depending on the moral histories of the decomposing bodies in question. But what about those living, breathing bodies still struggling too much to fret over the fate that may await them? Where do they go? A smaller majority of the same New Yorkers go to church services, so that the translation from body to spirit means eternal life for the soul involved. With that in mind, I decided to attend a few different houses of worship in preparation for the high school's gospel concert, an attempt to complete some ethnographic work on contemporary black religiosity by connecting that conversation to some of my own childhood experiences with the terror of religious possession.

As a preteen sporting clip-on ties to Sabbath School sessions on Saturday mornings, I remember our Seventh-Day Adventist church's conservative congregation being adamant about a very specific articulation of individuals' bodies in its sanctuary. Seventh-Day Adventism in Brooklyn in the 1980s (particularly within my predominantly West Indian congregation) represented the kind of asceticism that denied ecstatic displays of spirituality.[12] The music and dancing of the outside world was deemed corrupting, while the overly taut strictures against movie-watching, club-hopping, jewelry-wearing, and pork-eating were meant to save practitioners from the excesses of this outside world. The distinction between sacred and profane, religious and worldly, was mapped quite explicitly onto the singing and dancing Christian body, and this was not solely a Seventh-Day Adventist preoccupation. It was a distinction that animated doctrinal debates in otherwise very different religious denominations.[13] In our congregation's rendition of the impasse between sacred and secular, generational differences animated the fault lines between acceptable and unacceptable worship practices. Many of the older members never wanted younger, newly baptized converts to rechoreograph church motion—be that motion in the pews, behind the pulpit, or up in the choir loft. "God is one, infinite and perfect," Pastor Joseph's argument went and still goes. "He don't change, so why change church doctrine, making church more worldly, with all the heavy drum music and hand clapping?" Like other traditionally staid denominations, the SDA church has liberalized many of its ceremonial practices since the mid-1980s.[14] Even so, contemporary congregations often remain rather Pauline in their thoughts on exactly what church services should performatively entail.

"If God didn't want women to talk in his church when the Bible was written," a septuagenarian deacon in a predominantly Caribbean Protestant church reasons, "then that mean he don't want them talking in it now as preachers and stuff. And he surely don't want no heavy music and hip-hop dancing in it. All that stuff got to go." But arguments like the deacon's do not necessarily persuade many of his church's younger members, youngsters who think that the church should keep up with the times (and maybe even get over a few of its more chauvinistic hang-ups) if it hopes to win black bodies and souls to the Lord.[15] During one Crown Heights Baptist congregation's weekly youth-outreach meeting, just five days before Shanita's spring concert, I listened to several church members, all women, debate the implications of musical innovation and high-energy dancing for the sanctity and reverential quality of their church services.

"Young folk need to be in the church," said Sister Daley, a twenty-seven-year-old, Jamaican-born nurse. She was addressing the small cadre of church members convened by their pastor specifically to determine ways of increasing youth attendance at their weekly worship services. These members met bi-weekly in their church basement, in the small room directly across from the padlocked storage space where members and community residents line up periodically for huge, government-supplied boxes of breakfast cereal, Ritz crackers, and cardboard-boxed blocks of American cheese. My chair was along the outer hallway, almost in another room entirely, closer to the bathrooms and the pastor's study than to the group, but I could still see and hear most, if not all, of what was said.

That day, Sister White, a spry seventy-four-year-old and honorary leader of this small, deputized group, shifted her weight atop an under-sized, metal folding chair pulled from the adjoining Sunday school class-room. As Sister Daley talked about reaching out to the young people in whatever way they could understand, Sister White loudly sucked her teeth in protest. She knew where Sister Daley was going with this. She had heard the argument before and preferred not wasting everybody's time going through it all again. Even as she huffed loudly, Sister Daley continued, undaunted: "They aren't here," she said, "and we got to bring them in. Cater the message to them. Give them good music and a welcoming spirit, and they will come."

"The church has good music," responded Sister Rosalind, who had been a deaconess in the church for more than twenty-five years. "You are talking about that drumming, drumming and all that worldly sound-ing music. Them things promote a certain kind of feeling in the church that doesn't lead to understanding the serenity of God."

"I'm not trying to say that we got to have only an organ in the sanc-tuary," Sister Madeline, a newly baptized member from Trinidad, chimed in. "We just can't be bringing all that bup, bup, bup into God's house. Once you start with the tump, tump, tump, your mind move from God, and your head start moving to the beat—then your backside sure to fol-low. Save all that for Saturday night. This here ain't no nightclub to be wiggling, wiggling your bamsy."[16]

"You can move your backside to the Lord though," Sister Daley replied. "King David's Psalms tells us to play all our instruments to the glory of the Lord. And some of y'all should be thankful you still got bamsies to wiggle." Everyone laughed.

Bamsies, backsides, and behinds have been wiggling praise to the Lord for centuries now, and these women all knew that well enough; a few might even support the careful use of a controlled liturgical dance to help spread God's message. The problem, however, was dance's potential connection to the Dionysian, to sinful and carnal lust of the Sodom and Gomorrah variety. Different kinds of bodily movements are said to imply very different kinds of spiritual states— some, the reverence of high holy days; others, the profanity of a Saturday night dance club. The rhythmic movements of the body proxy the inward states of the psyche, the interior landscaping of the spirit. Sisters White and Rosalind are hardly some modern-day Medusas turning all religious flesh into stone. The body can do all the moving it wants. Those movements just shouldn't be reminiscent of a religiously inflected Soul Train episode with a Reverend Don Cornelius delivering his remixed sermons to a bunch of scantily clad holy hipsters.

The church members who disagree paint dancing and gyrating church bodies in a much more generous light. They reclaim the expressive meaning of all dancing bodies from exclusive coalescence with the bacchanalian, from some kind of direct or implied correlation with sin and transgression—dressing those very same bodies up in new robes of heavenly white. These more positively viewed dancing bodies house heaven-bound souls signed up for that impending Christian Jubilee. Their names carved on the blood-stained cross, one can envision these fleshless, boneless, skinless saints marching their way right on up to the pearly gates, a path lined with disco balls of fire, mysteriously weeping tweeters and thunderously massive woofers, all placed strategically across the vastness of Club Eternity—where the party really never stops! Meanwhile, The Master of all Ceremonies is cutting and scratching and mixing souls to a celestial beat tapped out with an omniscient index finger on the proverbial Book of Life. Sister Daley might take issue with the imagery, but my point is simply to hint at the controversial connections between musicality and religiosity, connections that my Aunt Agnes, a retired nurse living in the Bronx, understands firsthand. She has been moving and grooving to that Godly beat for quite some time now.

"Every time the preacher say something in church," Uncle Rudy chuckles, "she get up to do the fox trot."

"And give me time," she says. "I'll do the boogaloo and the Charleston, too."

Sanctified Bodies

In any treatment of the mind, the spirit, the soul, and their connectedness to the human body (big-butted or otherwise), a complexity emerges from that confluence, a complexity that is almost indescribable, more of the Bataillean *impossible*. Like the rest of the academic world, Anthroman is very much into "the body"—literally and otherwise, his own and others'. It is the body, is it not, that holds and houses its aforementioned cohorts: soul, spirit, and mind? [17] The soul resides within the body, or, even better, is the body in a different dimension—on a different plane. The spirit permeates the body, informs and coats its physicality like magic mist or some celestial paint job. And the mind is quite inside of the body, a part of the pyrotechnicality of one's very body, the electrical cognitivity that helps power all utterly liquid bodies. Bodies, bodies everywhere, and not a drop to drink!

But what are the administrators at Shanita's high school saying about the souls, bodies, spirits, and minds of their young charges by attempting to ban any of them from "catching the Holy Spirit"? How could they hope to outlaw a phenomenon like that? Are they calling it fake, phony, forced? Like the BOSS jeans that Shanita buys from sidewalk vendors on Nevins Street? Like materialist responses to Feltonian whiteness? Or ever more fabulous versions of ghettodom? Do they not understand it? Do they not want to? If not, why not? Because "it's a black thang"? [18] A ghetto thing? How about a seventeenth-century Quaker thing? Whatever the case, the Lord sure does work in some mysterious ways. And yes, Anthroman knows from experience.

When my godmother, Lynette, took me to her small Pentecostal church in the Bronx for the first time some twenty-five years ago, the black bodies there all terrified me—mostly because of how emphatically and uncontrollably they were performing some Holy-Spirit-catching activities of their own. But that was hardly the only uncomfortable thing. First of all, there was no church bulletin for me to doodle on. There wasn't even (I thought at the time) an actual church really, just the second floor of her friend's home lined with rows of cushiony folding chairs that all faced some kind of makeshift, wannabe podium in what was (on other than Sunday mornings) somebody's humbly decorated living room. No pews. No organ. Only an electronic keyboard and Radio

Shack microphone—both plugged into a small speaker in the center of an oval, bright-red mat placed at the front of the room.

As someone who grew up in a rather large, brick Seventh-Day Adventist church furnished with a four-tiered choir loft, a carpeted rostrum, and a built-in baptismal pool, this home-cum-sanctuary seemed, at the time, more than lacking. It was profane! ("Is that a Jet magazine on the altar?") But that wasn't the worst of it. Even more horrifying than architectural and decorative concerns were the bodies of the dozen or so people who made up the collective church body. They were doing things that appeared, at least to my young Adventist sensibilities, anything but spiritual. They were moving like they were out of their minds, like those minds were disconnected from their bodies. Sure, I had long considered my mother's church far too staid, but this alternative was an even greater extreme in the other direction. It seemed sinisterly unsacred.

But not at first. The preacher's message began by sounding quite usual to me—normal, familiar. It was intermittently layered with the collectively ad-libbed punctuation marks of his twelve-member congregation, along with the occasional arm flying up into the air with an open-palmed handshake to the Lord at the end of it. None of this was new; I had seen it before—maybe not in church, but at least in movies and television shows that tried to depict black worship services. I even felt at home in it—less from firsthand experience than media exposure. Even my mother's church, with all its middle-class aspirations, was still used to a rousing sermon or two—and to a sometimes conspicuously responsive church audience. But Reverend Dickson, my godmother's preacher, brought on my horror quite simply and succinctly enough by saying something like, "Move spirit of God and move in me" and then chanting what sounded like "humdumalumla, hummunnala." At that point, a skinny man with a big, fat burgundy tie sitting to my right began verbalizing random sounds that amounted to something along the lines of "nocobononlacasa." And so the sweaty preacher was still going, "humdumalumumma humdumloohuma," and now this man was too, "nobolacada nobolacdada," and then a big-boned, bigger-bodied woman on my left, wearing a snake-skinned pill-box hat and a flower print dress, rang in with her own "oohhlooloonahsun." So all three could be heard —and then another, and another, one at a time, each playing his or her respective ditty. And then the burgundy-tied man's hands began moving. First just the right one. It was more like twitching initially; then the twitches got bigger, grander, the left hand joined in, around and around and around. And he nearly poked my eye out once or twice in the process.

(For a long time after that, the burgundy-tied man's hands plagued my nightmares, his open palms often appearing as five-fingered, double-jointed tormentors detached from their wrists—flexing and unflexing, clenching and unclenching, waving me off into eternal damnation.)

Did I think these folks were faking or playacting? Not in the least. If anything, I wished they were, but it all seemed terribly genuine, too much so. I would have pleaded for them to stop if my six-year-old self could have worked up the nerve. However, amid all this dynamic action, I was, ironically enough, utterly paralyzed—as though the sheer force of their movements precluded my own. I was catatonic, calcified. And so, trapped in my own frozen flesh, I felt jailed by these gesticulating bodies in the prison of my own bodily fears. They did not fit into my understandings of what bodies did anywhere, let alone at church, and so their unintelligible vocalizations worked like swords at my choked throat, verbal and somatic chains around my petrified limbs.

But I was horrified to an exponentially greater degree once I looked over to see what was happening three seats diagonally in front of me: tears flowing silently down my godmother's cheek. Her body, rock-hard, wholly still, looked as paralyzed as I felt. And that is when I figured that if my godmother's spirit possession came upon her so silently, so motionlessly, then maybe I too, at the selfsame moment, much like the rest of this spiritual chain-gang, was being possessed into paralysis. Maybe the Holy Spirit was occupying me, confining and controlling me, only I was so far gone that I didn't even know it. And with that admission, I held my breath, focused my eyes, and stared straight at a godmother who stared, it seemed, right back through me, her body's only sign of motion the tears escaping from the corners of her eyes. The spirit and/or soul of the body oozing out from within? Bodies, bodies everywhere, and not a drop to drink!

Hairy Bodies: From Corinthians to Judges

. . . and on that great judgment day, I hope to be there. *Praisejesus. Yeslord. Thankyoufather.* Bodies and souls reunited in full. I got to be there. *Amen. Yeslord. Takeitslownowpastor.* But do you all want to be there? *Yeslord. Yesjesus. Thankyoujesus.* I said, I want to be in that chosen number, do you want to be there? *Amen. Yessir. Teachpastor. Preachit. Amenthankyoujesus.* Does anybody, uhh, does anyone remember the story of Samson? *Amen. Yessir.* You remember the story of Samson? *Yessir. Preachitpastor. Goheadnow.* You can never read the story of Samson enough. *Youright. Goheadpastor. Amennow.* Samson with the long, flowing hair. *Praisegod. Thankyoujesus.* Samson with the heavenly strength. *Yeslord. Thankyousaviour.* Samson with a body from God. *Amennow. Yessir.* Oh, but Samson put a lady before the lord. *Yeslord. Wellnow.* Uh oh, I'm hitting too close to home for some of ya'll now. *Youpreachitpastor. Yessiramen. Preachthetruthpastor.* Ya'll saying *amen* now but some of you got stung by that last one. *Thatsalrightnow. Preachpastor.* Samson with the long, flowing hair and the heavenly strength and the body from God put something else before sweet Jesus. *Preachit. Amenow.* And that something else took away all that Samson had in this world, took away God's gift of strength. *Wellwellwell. Preachpastor. Amennowpastor.* See, his body lost its strength 'cause his spirit lost its strength. *Yessir. Preachpastor.* It was Delilah, in case you don't know, who took his strength and power from him. *Youbetter-preach. Goheadsir. Amen.* And God let that happen because Samson let the flesh, his love for the body, come before the Lord, before his love for the Lord. *Preachpastor.* So the Lord took that body back. *Yessir. Amen.* God took it back. *Amenlord. Yes.* But you know what? *Bringithome-nowpastor.* On judgment day, God has the power to give it all back. *Amenamenamen. Thankyoulord. Yesjesus. Yeslord.* On that day, *yes-lord, thankyoujesus,* you can bet Samson will have his hair. *Yeslord. Bringithomenowpastor.* His long, flowing hair. *Praisejesus, Thank-youlord.* Rapunzel ain't got nothin on Samson. *Amen!* I said, Rapunzel ain't got a thing on Samson. *Yeslord. Hallelujah.* On that day the Lord will be able to cry out, "Samson, Samson let down your hair!!" *Amen! Yespastor. Praisejesus. Thankyoulord. PraiseGod.*

Resurrected Bodies

As I drive my mother's recently paid-off, light-blue Mazda 323 to the high school gospel concert, my Aunt Agnes and Uncle Rudy keep me company on the ride. Aunt Agnes fills the time by telling one of her favorite personal stories about a near-death experience thwarted by the power of song. It is a story that I have heard, with different emphases and inflections, many times before. Still, she tells it again, as if for the first time, with all due awe and thanksgiving: "Back when I was real sick, you weren't even born yet," she says, "I was on my way to the grave; I was surely gonna die." She was lying sick in a hospital bed when Death himself tiptoed by her. Death snuck past the 24-hour nurse at her bedside and pinched her shoulder blade talking about, "time to go. You just about done." And her nurse-attendant had been daydreaming, or sleeping, or something when Death made its entrance, but was pulled

from her daze by auntie's mammoth wail. AAAAHHHH!! On cue, seeing
the shade of Death's shadow cover her patient's face, "the nurse moved
from the windowsill to my bedside, preparing to sing me into God's
open arms. And I heard her voice, and it sounded so beautiful, so warm
and loving, that I decided to sing along. Nothing too strenuous. I didn't
have the strength. I didn't even sing really; it was more like humming.
But I tell you, as God is my witness (along with Mrs. Covington, that
nurse by my side), I began to sing along with her in a way that made ol'
Death wait just a little while longer. I'll tell you that. Ssshhhheeeee, if
not for that singing, I wouldn't be talking now."

Surely, my Aunt Agnes's musically induced resuscitation is not the
only tale of black bodies moving toward the great beyond and then back
again. It is not even her sole example. And some bodies go so far as to
cross over that living/dead divide and then scuttle back to this world of
mere mortality. Anyone can read the newspaper advertisements placed
by such people, those who have escaped the sickle of death and returned
to life—usually with extrasensory gifts and supernatural abilities. One
of my Aunt Agnes's favorite stories is about when she made up her mind
to consult such a person.

"It was when I was much younger, more silly," she says. She found
out about him from some friend of hers. "He works good," her friend
assured her. At first Aunt Agnes was too spooked ("being a Christian
and all") to think about going to see this man. But then she got desperate. She didn't know what else to do. And so she finally decided to visit
this great man of all the many magical mysteries that were revealed
to him from beyond the grave. The person who removed the largest
of stumbling blocks from pathways, brought loved ones back from the
great beyond, removed the demons from around you, made many shat-
tered lives whole—and advertised said occult services in the back of local black weeklies. She had taken one of the newspaper advertisements
with her when she went to see him, just to make sure that she didn't forget the address, and to reread its lofty claims on the way, trying to keep
convincing herself that she had made the right decision. If he could do
just half of what the ad said, she thought, he would surely be able to help
her. And just like that, this Christian woman passed up prayers to Christ
for an alternative reading, or rather, did both.[19] "I figured that I might
as well cover all my bases," she says.

> Rudy was looking deathly sick you know, and I didn't know
> what to do. At first, when Alicia, that's my friend who told me
> about this fellah, gave me the ripped-out ad from the paper—

or maybe it wasn't a newspaper at all, it might've just been a flyer—anyway, I didn't want to hear nothing about some man who says he's come back from some grave. I figured that some crazy dead man didn't know nothing that could help me. But I always kept hearing my mother talking about miracles. And I had tried everything, so I asked God if it would be okay to go to this man to try to save Rudy's life ('cause he was real sick, folks thought he was sure to die), and I asked that if it ain't okay he should tell me so ('cause, you know, I just wanted an excuse to do it). I was young. I was desperate. And I went into this man's place, it was in Harlem, and I didn't even tell Rudy I was going. I didn't tell anybody. I knew most of my friends would think I was crazy, so I didn't tell no one. And Rudy was so far gone that he wouldn't have known what I was talking about anyway. Now, I'll tell you something. Some of these folks are just fakers. Others really do be conjuring. Like those Haitians who be messing with voodoo. And this guy was Haitian, so I figured he probably knew some of what he said he did. And I was just so scared for your uncle.

The place was not too far from where your Aunt Sandra used to live, her first house. So there was something consoling about being so close to someplace I knew. And the place looked so regular from the outside, like any other house on that block, nothing different or odd about it. I think I would've missed it if I didn't keep the number of the house in my brain: 462. You know, Alicia played that number a little while after that and won her a little something, like $500. Number 462. I don't know, I think I expected the house's number to be burning in fire on the door or something, just burning and burning. But it wasn't. The place looked normal. The only way I even knew it was the right place was by the small black numbers.

When I got inside, drawings and stuff were all over the place, monster-looking things, crazy-looking. And a small little woman asked me some questions and told me to go wait for a couple of seconds while she went upstairs to see about the guy. Long John was his name, or at least something close to it. The place was so big, but it felt small because of all the little dolls and pictures and trinkets crowding around one another and around me. The young woman who met me as I entered (she had a name like Rita or Linda or something) came down and told me that I could go into the next room and wait there for Long John to have counsel with me. My heart was beating so fast I tell you. I shook my head as if to say okay and walked toward the closed door she had gestured for me to use. The walls, lined with dolls and strange pictures, gave me the feeling that something was gonna jump out at me. But I kept singing "Precious Jesus" in my head and holding on to Rudy's old fishing hat I had brought with me, clutching that tired little brown thing as hard as I could, reminding myself that I was doing this all for him. I remember opening the door, a very heavy door, and thinking that I was just glad I had chosen this place over some of the other ones I had heard about. The woman in the front seemed so nice. It was at least in a neighborhood I knew. It was right near where your Aunt Sandra used to live. So it wasn't even too far from home.

Cummerbunded Bodies

Lucy, Shanita's mom, is already in the high school lobby when my aunt, uncle, and I arrive. Leaning against a far wall and flipping through a copy of the day's newspaper, she has come straight from her custodial job at a Manhattan hospital, her dark uniform visible beneath a thin brown overcoat. Lucy is alone tonight. Shanita's brother is sick at home (having caught his mother's flu), and Shanita's father, who lives in New Jersey, has already apologized to the family for not being able to take off from work. I introduce Lucy to my aunt and uncle, the three exchange pleasantries, and we all move quietly toward the packed and noisy auditorium. Squeezing our way through the throng of smiling parents, we pass students selling items to commemorate the event. They flank the auditorium doors hawking goodies of all sorts to raise money for their organizations—bits of chocolate, whole pies and cakes, novelty candies, long-stemmed roses wrapped in noisy, colored-foil paper. "Oh my God, look at the prices of these things," my aunt says. "Between that and the tickets, they want to take all our money." Moving through the gauntlet of goodies and into the echoing auditorium, we slowly find our row. We all sit together and chat, anticipating that the house lights will dim momentarily. Bodies, bodies everywhere!

The maroon curtains of the stage are drawn back to reveal four rows of young faces in blue choir uniforms. The conductor is a light-skinned man with a large midsection (magnified, it seems, by the red cummerbund around it). He takes slow and careful steps to the center of the stage, positioning himself in front of the choir, his back to the audience, his hands raised, his baton poised in midair. The cummerbunded man gives a nod to the instruments in the pit, and in a flash his arms drop. A huge, collective "Yes Lord!"—short, hard, staccato, all in unison—shoots out from the otherwise motionless and expressionless choir. Bits of the crowd begin to shout, clap, and "Thank you lord" in the comma of silence left behind by the choir's outburst. Immediately, the cummerbunded man's hands are up again. Then down. "Yes Loooord." More of the crowd responds. This is a teaser, and it goes on for about forty-five seconds before the choir allows the school's orchestra to join them. The concert has begun, and the room becomes charged with an almost suffocating energy, the type one only connects to through the primordialness of things like music.[20] Tyrone is going through tunes without a hitch, controlling his body with no problem at all, keeping that banned Holy Ghost at bay.

An hour into the performance, the audience is up, waving hands and singing along. A young woman in the choir begins to cry during her solo. But she holds her body steady, calm. If any Holy Ghost–induced gesticulations are welling up inside her, they are being repressed, dammed within, spilling out only in the tiny beads of sweat on her forehead. Just then, the cummerbunded man steps aside and allows Tyrone to conduct a song, which he does with long, strong arm movements. My aunt faintly mirrors his motions from her seat: hands up and out, up and down and out.

"What does the conductor really have to do?" my uncle asks her, "'cause that boy ain't conducting nothing but himself wildly."

But Tyrone is not really that wild, just emphatic in his motioning to the melody; there is self-control there. Could he catch the Spirit as he conducted? Anthroman waits, but nothing. After another song, the pot-bellied conductor takes over again, and the choir continues for about another half hour. As the last song is set to begin, Tyrone positions himself in front of one of the two soloists' microphones. By this time he has already been teary-eyed for a good while—along with the rest of the choir and crowd. The evening has been emotionally draining for most, wonderful but taxing. Tyrone, sniffling a bit now, is trying, it seems, to hold back some of his tears. Maybe even fighting off an encroaching Holy Spirit, fighting the Lord's attempt to take over his adolescent body, which could get him suspended and in trouble—just as signing a fake hall pass would land him in detention, or throwing food in the lunchroom might get his parents called.

Shanita's microphone is on the other side of the choir, and she is on fire in a solo of her own:

> SHANITA: And God said, "Let there be a firmament in the midst of the waters."
> CHOIR: Yes He did!
> SHANITA: And God made the firmament!
> CHOIR: Yes He did!
> SHANITA: And God divided the waters which were under the firmament from the waters which were above the firmament.
> CHOIR: Yes He did!

Lucy beams. She often boasts about Shanita's singing, about how her daughter could be a professional vocalist if she really wanted to be, "but she is just as good at so many other things that she hasn't devoted as much time as she could to this natural singing gift of hers." Lucy continues to smile as her daughter wows the crowd. When Shanita finishes, Tyrone piggybacks on her last note and takes the audience over from there.

Everyone is still clapping for Shanita as he begins. I look over at my aunt, who is clearly enjoying herself, her excited face shining with perspiration, so I am glad that I dragged her along. My uncle, however, is another story. He is fighting sleep and losing, his head bobbing up and down from the blows—up then down, up and down, his red eyes open for a second and then shut again. But he needed to get out of the house anyway, Aunt Agnes says, watching me eye her husband. He likes being cooped up too much. This is good for him.

The entire crowd is standing now. My aunt and I have to stretch our necks to their limits just to catch a glimpse of the singing bodies. And then, without warning, it starts! Tyrone's body begins breaking the high school principal's decree. First his legs twitch and then his arms. The caramel-colored choir conductor with the red satin cummerbund looks backstage and runs his right index finger across the front of his neck. The show is going to be over. Tyrone's legs continue to jerk and flex as the conductor calmly, slowly walks toward the wings, stage-left. The curtains begin to close. Tyrone flails his arms more wildly now. What were once twitches become swings. He almost falls but catches himself. "Thank you Jesus," he singsays. "Thank you Jesus. Thank you Jesus." As the curtains continue to close and the choir finishes the song, a few more singers begin to shake. It is contagious.

The conductor is still walking silently to the backstage area. The crowd is still clapping and moving with the choir. My aunt begins to complain about dizziness as she leans against her once-sleeping husband. More claps, hand waves, and hallelujahs fill the auditorium as the huge, maroon curtains are slowly drawn together. Before they completely close, however, the curtains stop—stuck on something. The musicians are still playing; some of them are crying, too. Tyrone has almost fallen again, but regains his footing. The red-cummerbunded conductor has now vanished backstage, undoubtedly working on that curtain problem. The music is still coming through to the electrified audience. The choir is still singing and crying to the Lord. The crowd is still standing and appreciating it all. Everyone claps and cries, singing in unison: *And I'm glad, and I'm glad, and I'm glad that God made man.* The curtains are unstuck and begin to move again. The choir and audience are still singing. The orchestra continues playing. But now, after much dancing and twitching, Tyrone has moved himself too far downstage, beyond the curtain's reach. It will close behind him, leaving his illicit, Spirit-catching body alone, uncovered, and exposed onstage. The music feels louder. The choir sings louder. Tyrone appears to have absolutely no control over his body now—bending, falling, and wailing, "Sweet Jesus. Thank you Jesus." One of the gospel singers in the front row, just to the right of Tyrone, catches his waving and lunging left hand, drawing him upstage, safely behind the curtain's plane. Within seconds, the curtains are finally closed—and all one sees is a sea of red velvet where only moments before were teenage bodies in blue choir gowns. The crowd, responding to the curtain's symbolic finality, reinvigorates its applause— with the curtain shooting out at points where Tyrone's body, on the other side of that velvet ocean, is still hitting up against it, but soon that too subsides. Right next to me, Uncle Rudy revives Aunt Agnes, who has just fainted and fallen back into her seat. Every body is different, but each can only take but so much spirit filling up its soul.

No Bodies

Anthroman bolts for the backstage area, questions ricocheting around in his head: Was Tyrone being reprimanded for his actions? Chastised for his bodily behavior? Would he get suspended or expelled for breaking the principal's command? Maybe even physically removed from the premises, a lesson for other fledgling Spirit-catchers: take note of the swift and sure-footed justice such infractions meet. However, none of that happened—at least not on this night. Backstage, people simply hugged and cried and continued to thank the Lord—Tyrone, Shanita, everyone (even the cummerbunded choir director who, only seconds earlier, had made the decision to close the curtains early). No censure. No criticism. No security guards carting students off in handcuffs.

The following week, Tyrone was called into the principal's office and mildly scolded for his spiritual excesses. "I would have been suspended," Tyrone tells me, "but since my grades are good, and I am about to graduate, they said that they were letting me off the hook. They just said that I can't have another solo—which doesn't matter anyhow 'cause that was the final gospel concert of the year! So they ain't really do nothing. And if they did, I wouldn't have cared. The Holy Ghost can't be stopped." Maybe not, but my question is, can it be measured, analyzed, interviewed?

Anthroman spends the subsequent months badgering Tyrone about his spiritual possessions, prodding him to describe the feeling he gets when he catches the Holy Ghost, even attending church services with him once or twice—all in an attempt to contextualize his practices. I want to know how he experiences it, but he cannot quite capture the thing. He can't find the right words, an idiom capable of accurate representation. After much prodding, he grudgingly offers terms like "happy" and "high" as incomplete and unsatisfying analogies. But they do little justice, he avers, to what it really feels like "inside." "Sometimes, I can, like, see myself," he says. "I can't feel anything, but I can see myself, like I'm looking down on myself and seeing what's going on. And I know it's me, but I can't control it. It's like not me, even though I know it is. It's hard to explain."

I start to think that Tyrone probably pities me—that he pities anyone denied access to such an inexpressible Holy Spirit feeling. Fighting the urge, I want to tell him about my own incessant channeling of Zora Neale, about my Anthroman exploits, about how they also take on a kind of out-of-body feeling, an almost self-alienating empowerment. But this attempt at an empathetic move is the height of desperation. It misunderstands Tyrone completely, which probably makes me seem even that much more pathetic in his eyes. But like the fictional realness of my own heuristic devices (these mobilizations of Hurston and scientific superheroism), catching the Holy Spirit is an embodied rendition of subjectivity that might help us to theorize racial realism. These possessed choir bodies allow us to think about the relationship between sincerity and authenticity, between beingness and thingification, between very different ways of calculating racial subjectivity. Ferdinand de Saussure is interesting, here, not so much because of how he talks about bodies, about the "thingness" of the human body, but for how he would seek to talk "the body" away, to defer it from analysis—almost indefinitely.[21] Saussure's semiotics help to highlight the epistemological significance of any switch from authentic to sincere *reals,* and I want to turn to this linguistic discussion as a way back to my main argument about sincerity's intersubjective excesses.

Saussure's linguistic sign does not deal directly with material bodies in the everyday world. It does not quite theorize physically frightening gospel bodies that sing, cry, and careen with the Holy Spirit. Any notion of a "referent," an actual material body, exists beyond the sign, external to his analysis.[22] His linguistic sign does not unite, say, a *thing* and a *name.*[23] Signs are the things themselves—self-referential, internally coherent. His system is self-contained, closed. Any changes in language, therefore, are due less to the actions of individual language users, possessed or not, than to the internal dynamics of a relational structure. By "ethnographizing" Saussurean linguistics, we can think more generally about the relationship between structural epistemologies and agential ones—while implicitly juxtaposing semiotic systems and their material constraints.[24] I imagine this as a way to emphasize the spaces opened up by closing down the objectifying presuppositions of "authenticity" and its contaminated critiques.

Charles S. Peirce, son of the last chapter's mystical mathematician, posits a tripartite semiotic system, incorporating the referent, the real, more decidedly into his linguistic equations, arguing that some signs have an actual "physical connection" to the objects they proxy, intrinsically resembling (iconicity) or spatio-temporally adjoining (indexicality) the real world.[25] He wants to gesture outside the sign, beyond its totalizing, networklike form, to the bodies that appear to be vessels for celestial spirits, the flesh that is spooked and sparked by heavenly ghosts.[26] Philosophers like Paul Ricoeur would most certainly and sympathetically set out a similar challenge to Saussurean closures, asking questions about existence and the real that are tabled by Saussure's structuralism—and only partially addressed by Peirce's additions. Human beings and their existence, Ricoeur posits, come before language (a representation of that existence), falling back on a metaphysical Heideggerianism of preexistent Being.[27] "Is it not philosophy's task," Ricoeur asks, "to ceaselessly reopen, toward the being which is expressed, this discourse which linguistics, due to its methods, never ceases to confine within the closed universe of signs and within the purely internal play of their mutual relations?"[28]

Ricoeur wants to open language up into being, into reality, into the world of big-butted, spirit-possessed bodies that jerk themselves beyond language, outstripping it. This is different from sheer deconstruction, different from what Jacques Derrida does when he dissolves the sign into more and more levitating signifiers, cracking it open not into the world, the referent, the real, but into the overdetermined fictions of further textuality, so that there is no Being to preexist texts—only naturalizations that fool us into believing the ontological hype about our own arbitrary conventions.[29] All claims to the real are so many more fictions and fakeries, Prada bags from illegal Chinese factories, Harlemites without an expressed racial commitment to community. This becomes the heart of an anti-essentialist gesture, the denaturalization-game that challenges any and all invocations of realness. But what then? What's the next step? Well, we can look at Derridean references to *différance, play, marks,* and *absence* in light of their connection to the symbolics of violence—a sneaky rerouting of our discussion back to human bodies themselves. Derrida's "différanced" man is akin to the one, in those old-time gangster movies, who knew his days were numbered (a numbering with unmistakably Lefebvrean implications) when the mobsters sent a package of wrapped fish to his home. We (the movie audience) knew that it was just a matter of time before the Mafia killed him. He was already ("always already") a walking corpse. With all its Derridean and Mafioso connotations, he was already a *marked* man, *authenteo,* killed by the external strictures of authenticity.

This gesture is not all that distant from the anxieties at the center of the Saussurean linguistic project, a project where the racialized body becomes nothing more than the phonological concatenation of the utterances "bah" and "dee"—flung from a speaker's tongue to the hearer's waiting ear.[30] To *mark* the *body* in and through language becomes an irreversible elimination of that *body* as referent and real, presaging and producing that *authenteo*-like death.[31] The body becomes mere corpse. For Saussure, language is a schema, an order, a structure composed of interrelated parts. Illusions of realness are a function of relationality within the system, not correspondence with its long-dark outsides. In fact, Saussure divides linguistic phenomena into a portion that is darkened, deferred, ignored, and precluded (*parole*—the individual, chaotic, heterogeneous, and performed speech acts) and another that is scientifically analyzable and classifiable, open to the searchlight of scientism (*langue*—that which rests behind those speech acts and anchors them). He is able to perform this metaphysical operation, this privileging of *langue* over *parole,* light over dark, this removal of *parole* from the linguistic body like some blighted organ, by arguing that *langue* "gives unity to speech."[32]

Therefore, he contends, without separating and isolating the analyzable/classifiable *langue* from the rest of language, linguistic phenomena would be beyond a certain kind of analytical comprehension.

To further highlight Saussure's vanishing of the linguistic body, it is important to take into account his belief in the arbitrariness of its basic components, the idea that any linguistic sign (the connection between a *signifier*, say, the written or spoken "n-i-g-g-e-r," and a *signified*, the notion of a brown-hued *Homo sapiens* creature actually making its way in the world) is unmotivated, and he uses this idea to reinforce the importance of the *langue*/schema/structure: for the value of the linguistic sign rests not in some natural and intrinsic bond between the sound-image and the concept, and especially not in some inherent link between the sign and a prelinguistic *real*.[33] For Saussure, the linguistic sign can only ever have value when looked at in (and locked within) the context of an entire sign system. The sign is a relational structure that only has meaning within the larger framework of which it is a part, and this is why "structure" is so vitally important to Saussure. It allows for the privileging of *langue* over *parole*, system over speech acts, the social over the individual, the homogeneous over the heterogeneous, the ordered over the chaotic, form over content, head over heels—and, what is most relevant to our present discussion, authenticity over sincerity. Authenticity is a way of spying the real by privileging structures over agents, hard and fast systems over slippery sensibilities. Sincerity is too unpredictable, potentially chaotic, and ultimately unfalsifiable. But what else is lost (disappears) in such a maneuver? Could an analysis of sincerity as *parole* hold any keys for competently understanding the everydayness of race in a way that does not seek to banish a large portion of the subject area beyond the bounds of understanding? If nothing else, might it help us to unpack the racial subject?

Imagine Saussure's system more nervous. What happens when we are not afraid to grope around clumsily in the darknesses of the real, a reality beyond our vain attempts at search-engine certainty and scientific transparency? How might we recognize the body in all its nervous materiality, all its sensual opacity? Saussure is only useful, and that by analogy, because he suggests our own worst fears about "the real," about the real body, about its utterly unknowable interiority. We would all prefer to cage that realness in some overarching frame or system, secure it with some kind of external anchor. Authenticity testing is an interpersonal master-form of just this predilection, this closed system of being and relating, but sincerity de-emphasizes that externality; it privileges the tenuousness of interpersonal knowledge. Sincerity highlights a willful subject who can always, of course, be faking it—an orgasm, a sympathetic hug, a corporeal visit from the Holy Ghost.[34] This potential demands the vulnerability of intersubjective trust, even as we simultaneously seek signs of authentication, empirical validation, the deeds that go with the words. But the primacy of sincerity's route to the real (over and against authenticity's) privileges an epistemology of uncertainty and ambiguity.[35] The real becomes a palpable darkness that flashlights simply blind us, all the more, from seeing.

This is a very different gloss on intersubjectivity than the kind to be found in some versions of postmodernity and/or digitized global post-humanity. For some, there is a fundamental permeability of the body (a permeability of the human self) that makes any "othering" gesture utterly inadequate. In her brilliant mixture of critical theory and spiritual incantation, Anne Weinstone uses Derrida, Gilles Deleuze, post(hero-ism), Michel Foucault, digital linguist Naomi Baron, Indian Tantra, and much more to think about the state of human relationships in an age of "millennial capitalism," to conceptualize the reemergence of unfalsifi-able faiths amid the scientificity of twenty-first-century hyperrational-isms.[36] She argues that there is a connection between bodies that makes a lie of their purported discreteness. We are not seeing into the alterity of the other, but the mimesis of the self.[37] One knows the other implic-itly, absolutely, confidently. However, as an intersubjective ethos, sincer-ity demands a flimsier grounding, a blinder faith. So, for instance, a Hol-lywood filmmaker's bloody Jesus story is read as a filmic testament to the centrality of sincerity.[38] Taken to its extreme, sincerity becomes the unflinching self-truth of the terrorist, which is part of what scares us so traumatically. Where Weinstone sees bodies permeable across selves and subjects, the primacy of sincerity maintains that we are not totally per-meable to one another (and most certainly not through our universaliz-ing attempts at authenticity testing). Maybe otherness is not really the bogeyman—or, at least, not the most frightening one in our cluttered social closet.

There is a dark continent to the soul—dark to self and other—that we cannot easily navigate, not with science, not with Tantric religiosi-ties, not with metatheories and mathematical calibrations, not with au-thentifications of any kind, no matter how seductive. To be human, sin-cerity demands, is to accept mutual impermeability. It means to grope around for the very impermeability of the other; it is to read the other darkly. There is a nervousness to our system, a nervousness that should be embraced, must be, even though we have been trained to believe that systematicity provides complete knowledge. A reality mined through sincerity recognizes that we can only ever read the other dialectically, accepting the partiality of our own intersubjective lenses—even as some are wrongheadedly tempted to test the sincere for insincerities.[39] An authentic model will ignore such impermeable differences to proffer transparent ones (of race, sex, ethnicity, etc.). A sincere alternative might say that such impermeable intersubjectivities are productive, even progressive, forces, as long as we do not let our fears of the dark make us catatonic.

For Shanita, Tyrone, and their high school gospel choir, there is a permeability at work, but it is of another order entirely: human bodies and Holy Ghost. This interpenetration helps to emphasize our mutual impermeabilities as human beings. Are they really being possessed? How do we know? How might we prove it?[40] These are all sacrifices to the gods of authenticity. We do not quite know if we can believe their sincerity, but this still leaves the possibility of a choice that reduces authenticity to irrelevance, remembering, of course, all the while, that it can be faked, it might all be a lie—to prove one's religious authority, to pass for a real Christian, or even just to thumb a nose at some clueless high school principal. Given that ambiguity, we can either clamor for authentification or accept the deferral of absolute certainty that sincerity privileges. This is different from Saussure's deferrals. We are not bracketing any discussion of realness, only its final adjudication. The unpredictability of the Holy Ghost and its impact on the gospel singing body is another way to think about what it might mean to mark realness as trust over proof, to theorize a notion of reality otherwise prematurely foreclosed by authenticity's cannibalistic machinations.

4 Real Jews

(for brothers fred hampton & mark clark, murdered 12/4/69 by chicago police
at 4:30 a.m. while they slept)
. . . were the street lights out?
did they darken their faces in combat?
did they remove their shoes to creep softer?
could you not see the whi-te of their eyes,
the whi-te of their deathfaces?
or did they just turn into ghost dust and join the night fog?   **Haki Madhubuti**

There was no deceiving him [the slavemaster]. His work went on in his absence
almost as well as in his presence; and he had the faculty of making us feel
as if he was ever present with us. This he did by surprising us. He seldom approached the spot where we worked openly, if he could do so secretly. Such was
his cunning that we used to call him, amongst ourselves, "the snake." When we
were at work in the cornfield, he would sometimes crawl on his hands and knees
to avoid detection, and all at once would rise nearly in our midst, and scream
out, "Ha, ha! Come, come! Dash on, dash on!" This being his mode of attack, it
was never safe to stop a single minute. His comings were like a thief in the
night. He appeared to us as being ever at hand. He was under every tree, behind every stump, in every bush and window on the plantation. . . . He seemed
to think himself equal to deceiving the Almighty.   **Frederick Douglass**

Overseer, overseah, oviseah, ofiseah, offiseah, officer. . . . They both ride horses.
                                                                    KRS-One

: : :

An Introduction to New World Orders, Officers, and Overseers

It is nighttime in Brooklyn, and law enforcement plays hide-and-seek in Crown Heights, hide-and-seek with itself. One moment all is silent, dank, darkly muted. The police, cloaked and camouflaged, surreptitiously pause before they pounce, waiting for some unsuspecting wrongdoer. And then, almost magically, like rabbits plucked from asphalt top hats, wailing sirens co-narrate the stories told by flashing lights of blue and red and blue and red and blue. This is Brooklyn, circa 1994: the same neighborhood that produced, one year prior, a disheveled and seemingly demented elderly black man, his voice trailing off into the distance, who screamed nonsensical numbers over his shoulder at me after his unprovoked, clench-fisted attack ("seven, six, four, nine, nine, four, nine, nine, four, six, seven, four, four, nine . . ."). Hearing my recap of that strange incident, local residents mostly shrugged their shoulders or shook their heads and advised me to use those exact integers in the next week's Lottery drawing, just in case.

This is the Brooklyn I know best, where and when I first picked up that undoubtedly annoying (to some) habit of singing myself into contemporary pop tunes: "*You Remind John of his Jeep . . . something like John's bank account,*" a habit I copied from a local weed dealer who could effortlessly fit his first name into the chorus of just about any song ever recorded.[1] My ethnographic séances with Hurston and Mead were inaugurated here, and I found my inner Anthroman on these same streets. From a forgetful perch in the twenty-first century, I look back now on this space and time with an almost intuited sense of history, a nostalgic chronology, something I can less safely prove than simply believe.[2]

This particular summer night in Crown Heights was sizzling, which meant that the tenants who lived in my mom's housing project complex, my informants, were hanging outside their stuffy tenement buildings in the moonlight, opting for the slightly lesser of two sweltering evils. Neighbors leaned their torsos against barred terrace openings. They dangled their legs from rusting fire-escapes, slouched backs against metallic folding chairs—all the while, fanning themselves with old magazines and newspapers, a mostly futile attempt to beat back some of that heat. I was also outside on this night, shuffling playing cards and fellowshipping with a few of the neighbors. Some of them I knew well; most I did not. Several other tables of card games were taking place at one and the same time; we all concentrated as much on the braggadocio from nearby contests as on the details of our own hands.

At midnight, while we continued fanning ourselves with an assortment of printed matter, an automobile loudly pealed past us from the direction of Eastern Parkway, stopping abruptly in the middle of an adjacent intersection. Collective eyes crawled up from their games to see, as Stokes asked out loud (and for the entire group), "Whah de fuck is goin' on out dere!?"[3] Stokes is a sixty-one-year-old man who has lived in Crown Heights for some fifteen years. Before that move to Brooklyn, he drove a cab in Harlem, where he was an occupational acquaintance (I would find out nine years later) of Bill and his clairvoyant wife, Gina. This was before Bill's vending days, when he drove a taxi full time. Even before I heard Bill's firsthand version of these events many years later, Stokes had told me about fellow cabbies getting held up at gunpoint—and even fired at by passengers. Fortunately, in Bill's case, the gun did not discharge, which he took as a sign, never returning to work again.

Stokes has been in the United States for more than forty years, but he was born and raised in Jamaica. In fact, most of the residents I came to know in and around this specific section of Brooklyn were no more than one or two generations removed from places like Jamaica, Barbados, Guyana, Trinidad, and Haiti. You almost trip over people's hyphenated identities whenever you pass them on the street—in this case, a thickly accented West Indianness that people drag around the neighborhood with them, diasporic crosses they most happily bear. These tiny sections of Brooklyn can feel like life-size replicas of, say, Kingston, Jamaica, only without a standing army or any of the bloody PNP/JLP conflicts.[4] This cultivates a sense of transnationality that is almost contagious. As a child, I did not visit Antigua, where my mother was born, more than a few times, and then only for a week or two during several summers. Even so, in certain stretches of Crown Heights and Flatbush, there are moments when I feel every bit as Caribbean as I do "Yankee" (by way of my biological father from the American south). But not even Antiguan really, just Caribbean, which is an even more curious awareness of self. And in the parts of Crown Heights where Caribbean-Americans play card games on sidewalk strips outside at midnight, such fanciful cosmopolitanism might just make sense, especially when people are sending themselves, their money, and other family members back and forth across nation-state borders every month out of the year. Stokes, who had only recently returned from his last trip to Jamaica a few weeks earlier, continued speaking as the now silent automobile remained motionless across the avenue.

"Whah de hell is goin' on in dis muddahfuckah?" he asks.

"You ain't really asking, 'cause you know we nah know!"

The quick retort came from Kyrle, a forty-something former attorney from Trinidad who drove dollar cabs up and down Remsen Avenue to make ends meet. He was the single father of a twelve-year-old girl, Darlene, and he also happened to be my Spades partner on that night—and not a very good one at that ("Bring out de dominos. I bet I'll bone all ya!" was his defensive mantra). Kyrle and Stokes began to theorize out loud about the identity of the car's driver. They first decided drug dealer, but then quickly figured that a hatchback Honda Civic was not nearly fancy enough; it would have to be a Benz or BMW—or at least a souped-up Honda Prelude. Maybe an undercover cop, someone else offered, but that suggestion was quickly dismissed, since it sounded reasonable to most within earshot when Kyrle claimed that government workers, undercover or not, have to use American cars, only a few skeptical naysayers silently shaking their heads to the contrary.

What happened next went very quickly. A man and woman, screaming and yelling at one another, spilled out of that vehicle and into the otherwise empty intersection. The unidentified man, pulling up the sleeves on a sky-blue Adidas sweat suit, slapped the woman across her face. From their perches on fire escapes above, folks yelled out for him to stop, or just yelled, and Kyrle stood up for a potential confrontation, but it would not happen, not today. Instead, the police must have been called as soon as the suspiciously screeching car made its entrance onto the block, because within a few seconds, cops arrived from what seemed like every conceivable direction, the once-silent block ringing out with sirens and flashing blues to reds to blues to reds. Officers surrounded the vehicle, put the man (now handcuffed) into the back seat of one squad car and the woman into another. They perfunctorily took statements from some witnesses and arranged, via walkie-talkie, for the now driverless car to be towed. After about thirty minutes or so, it seemed like their work was just about over, but the true criminal apprehending had only just begun.

The patrolmen slid back into their police cars, fastening seat belts and keying ignitions, when a deafening sound rang out in the dark night. It was a rap song, "Fuck tha Police," by the Los Angeles–based group NWA (Niggas with Attitude). The shocked officers, looking more than a little agitated, left their cars and started to scurry ("like chickens wit dey heads cut off," Kyrle said), falling over one another in an almost Keystone-cop-like attempt to locate the source of that musical disturbance. Once they determined its general direction, they moved in quickly—toward our set of tenement buildings. They dashed right past us, a blue flood flowing in almost poetic unison, and with a singular purpose. They shot by our card table, almost upending it, as they barreled into the dim bowels of an adjacent building.

"Whah de hurry?" Stokes asked, laughing and shuffling cards. "Dem can't take de troot?"

Ever Anthroman, my Anthrosense tingling, I made mental notes for myself about the number of officers (seven in all, two blacks), their body types, the configuration of their vehicles in the street (almost like an isosceles triangle), and specifics about the scowls and scars on a couple of their faces. As they passed, Stokes, Kyrle, and most everyone else simply continued playing cards: long after the police came back down the steps with their third handcuffed culprit of the night (Leroy, one of my childhood friends from junior high school in Canarsie), his now silent Aiwa double-cassette deck in one of the officer's black-gloved hands; long after the blue and white police cars, those hide-and-seek cars, had taken off their flashing lights and disappeared back into the night; and even after we stopped commenting about the night's festivities. Everyone continued playing card games and trying to beat the heat. It was summertime in the city, and the living had never been easy.

This chapter is about police and paranoia, about anxieties that breed cultural alienation. It evokes the real and imagined connections in time and travel that expose, say, officers who pass for overseers and local beliefs that confound commonsense assumptions about race, place, and cultural difference. These juxtapositions lay the groundwork for subjective distinctions between everyday sincerities and their authentic mirrors, between "crocodile tears" and the truest of sobs—even if parsing such a difference is only one more instance of that Bataillean search for "the impossible," a foregone failure as ethnographic mission.[5] In this case, I am talking about impossible surprises from a Pandora's Box of crosscutting and splintered spiritualities, ones not all that far removed from the ecstatic behavior of gospel-singing high school Hottentots. We are shifting, however, from spirit possession to secret societies, from concerts to conspiracies. Most specifically, I want to examine one variant of black Judaism as a particular slant on contemporary racial subjectivity, a tangible example of how racial authenticities fold in on top of one another, and on top of proffered sincerities, to rewrite our overly monolithic iterations of racial identity.

This chapter highlights some of the cosmological understandings that defined a particular version of black identity in a mid-1990s Brooklyn community of "Fuck tha Police" responses to excesses of the New York Police Department. In this case, I am talking about a Black Jewish identity codified into a loudly conspicuous and nationalist rhetoric of absolute racial difference. The Worldwide Truthful Understanding (WTU) Black Hebrew Israelites in New York City are somewhat famous for their cable-access television shows and sidewalk spectacles, where they blare antiwhite oratory from soapboxes set up on busy city streets. These are quite certainly displays of black *masculinist* spirituality. Only men take part in these public performances of Black Jewishness, black men with deep baritone voices, full beards, and Old-Testament-inspired garb.[6] In 1994 WTUers located spiritual subjectivities in *authentic* genealogies of racial reasoning, genealogies traced through anticop rap songs and conspiracy theories, conspiracy theories that ended up implicating the discipline of anthropology itself—and as much more than just a neocolonialist project.

For practitioners of this specific version of black Judaism, what you see is never what you get. The real is always, by definition, so much more than meets the eye, and they proffer an alternative method for understanding such a world, for mining its truths. Theirs is a method that nervously, even traumatically, models a way of seeing that operates at cross-purposes, I would argue, with some of the very techniques they used—at least in the second half of the 1990s—for reckoning the realness of human bodies, for determining "authentic" black (Jewish) identity, and for making sense of assumed racial differences. Their conspiratorial ways of seeing (stories about witches, warlocks, and worldwide cover-ups) are just a more extreme version of the general racial and cultural paranoia that threads itself through much of African American public discourse and highlights the profound inadequacies of sight—a seeing that demands believing and disbelieving at the same time.[7] This specific group's hard-and-fast assumptions about black Judaic belonging, assumptions linked unquestioningly to maternal genes and fatherly seeds, belie their more skeptical collective responses to supposed transparencies of the social world.[8] I want to examine this mixture of social skepticism and certainty, thinking specifically about how authenticities and sincerities erratically coexist—often in volatile equilibrium. The chapter's opening tale about hide-and-seek police cars and anticop rhetoric exemplifies the contextual fodder that sincere and authentic versions of reality use to make their cases—and to challenge each other's social claims. "Real Jews" looks at local police officers, conspiracy theories, and vernacular notions of genetic difference to make a case for why the sincerity/authenticity distinction helps to clarify the stakes of contemporary racial reasoning. Authenticity may appear to dominate here, but, as I show in the next chapter, sincerity can win some small victories of its own.

Toward an Authenticity of Black Jewry 101: A Quick Primer

The Black Hebrew Israelites of Worldwide Truthful Understanding, founded in the mid-twentieth century, share the designation "Black Jews" (even though they eschew that term for "Israelite") with several other organizations and religious denominations around the country and the world. Each version of Black Judaism exhibits a slightly different history and philosophy—although their cross-fertilizing linkages through time and space are undeniable. Some of the earliest African American identifications with Judaism date back to the beginnings of the nineteenth century, and William Christian founded one of the earliest self-professed Black Jewish congregations in the latter half of that century.[9] In the early 1900s, people like Prophet Cherry and William Crowdy started what many historians characterize as "Black Jewish" worship services—The Church of God in Philadelphia and The Church of God and Saints in Christ in Lawrence, Kansas, respectively.[10] Appealing to the metaphorical resonances between American slavery and the bondage of biblical Jews, these Black Jewish hubs extended outward to the north and west as congregants and ministers traveled far and wide with their Judaic teachings. Jamaican Rastafarianism is also associated with this diffusionist impulse as a function of its Jewish iconography, most conspicuously its ubiquitous Star of David.[11] The Nation of Yahweh in Florida is a Black Jewish group infamous for its links to crime and corruption, whose leader, Yahweh Ben Yahweh, is serving time in a Pennsylvania penitentiary.[12] Another sect, the Law Keepers, is a Torah-based organization that disavows the label Jew, spelling their self-designation with a capital Y: Yisraelites.[13]

Most famously, the Commandment Keepers of Harlem, ethnographically canonized by Howard Brotz in the 1960s, were founded in the early 1900s by Rabbi Arthur Wentworth Matthew, a black man believed to have come out of Marcus Garvey's Universal Negro Improvement Association, which was also the breeding ground, some historians argue, for several important religio-political leaders in mid-twentieth-century black America.[14] James E. Landing, one of the foremost American scholars on Black Judaic history, even goes so far as to argue that the Nation of Islam's institutionalization of self-help economic strategies is a direct outgrowth of earlier Black Jewish techniques.[15] The Commandment

Keepers seem to follow this tradition, and Matthew's group is usually considered one of the most closely related to Judaism proper, especially since Matthew allowed white Jews to visit his services and often consulted them on Jewish practices and rituals, something the WTUers would not imagine. Matthew mixed Judaism with a mystic Christianity, and this syncretism caught on, translating into new congregations all over the city and even the world.[16]

Presently, Commandment Keepers in Brooklyn, Philadelphia, and all across the country are carefully codifying the history of this particular Jewish organization.[17] Part of that project entails making it historically and cosmologically clear just how their own brand of Black Judaism differs from the kind practiced by contemporary WTU Black Hebrews, a group based not more than five blocks from the Commandment Keepers' Harlem synagogue. Making this distinction explicit is important because the WTU Black Hebrew Israelites are decidedly vocal about their hatred for whites—a hatred rooted in racialized readings of Genesis that interpret Rebekah's birthing of twin boys (Esau and Jacob) as the beginning of two mutually exclusive nations (read blacks and whites) destined to be at war with one another until the end of time. Understanding their gloss on pending race-war might begin with a richer contextualization of "Fuck tha Police" anticop rhetoric in contemporary black America.

The Art of Resisting Arrest

The *Village Voice* once characterized the now defunct and disbanded rap group NWA as America's Musical Enemy #1. The FBI hates this group, their cover read. And why not? The lyrics from their 1988 hit record "Fuck tha Police," the same song Leroy was ostensibly arrested for blasting into the Brooklyn night, put the entire Los Angeles police department on notice for their systematic brutalities against young black men—and all to the staccato accompaniment of heavy drumbeats and courtroom interludes. As critic Nelson George writes, "N.W.A., a/k/a Niggas With Attitude, were to the 80s what the Beach Boys were to the 60s and the Eagles to the 70s—the definitive California band. 'Fuck the Police' spoke to the fantasies of [L.A.'s] majority no less than 'California Girls' and 'Life in the Fast Lane.'"[18] In the mid-1990s, they were "the definitive California band" with a clearly national following. "Fuck tha Police" has undoubtedly blared at cops from windows in cities throughout the country, probably the world. And that was even before the Rodney King video and verdict, when the hip-hop tune became a kind of militant, grassroots theme-song. And who can forget rapper Ice-T's 1992 anticop controversies? His heavy metal band's album, *Body Count*, got him attacked by police associations and governmental officials, specifically for lyrics like "die, die, die! Pig, die"—complete with an intertextual reprisal of NWA's "Fuck tha Police" anthem.[19] Ironically enough, the selling of that record led not to an increase in cop murders or assaults, but to a string of death threats against the top brass at Warner Brothers, Ice-T's record label. Record company executives' lives were seen as less sacred, less important (at least to the thousands of participants in that particular letter-writing campaign) than the lives of the police officers these missives were written to defend.

At the same time, ubiquitous evening news stories described yet another kind of "cop killer": the street name for special bullets with hollowed-out tips, which allow them to pierce police body armor. Journalists emphasized that these bullets had become many criminals' projectiles of choice. Cop Killer bullets did not just go through vests and into bodies. As a hideous bonus, they splintered into a thousand tiny pieces, with fallout from shrapnel inside the body destroying far more organs than the bullet's initial entry, prompting many to cry out, even those leery of police abuses, "What officer deserves that?"

Maybe, some would answer, officers like Michael Dowd, someone made famous by New York City's Mollen Commission after admitting to hundreds of acts of brutality on the job. Dowd, the so-called cocaine cop who pled guilty to drug trafficking and racketeering in 1992, relayed a story of corruption and criminality running rampant among New York City's finest. The Dowding of law enforcement was not the sensationalist exception, he argued, but the everyday rule, a dysfunctional nervousness within the system. But how are everyday Dowds created? And where?

Internal Affairs investigators historically linked such serious corruptions to the "dumping grounds" phenomenon, a common practice of assigning young, rookie officers to the least desirable locations, which meant neighborhoods full of poor black and Latino residents. In these high-crime urban areas, the theory goes, suburban police officers usually could not have cared less about local residents, assuming that higher-ups did not either. If they did, why would they assign mere rookies to patrol them? That may just be part of the reason why, in the Crown Heights I know, an ethnographic Crown Heights of 1994, the term "flaking civilians" (planting drugs on them to make a bust) was a part of the everyday language residents used to characterize local policing. References to police flaking (and probable police flaking) were quotidian. Residents imagined themselves seeing more police flakes than dandruffed or snowy varieties. And, with only a few degrees of separation from the whiteness of dandruff flakes to the Satanisms of contemporary anthropology (and this chapter goes through the paces of those degrees—from dandruff flakes to Procter & Gamble's Head and Shoulders shampoo to television commercials to magical "Holly Wood" to Franz Boas's witchcraft-based anthropology), even these seemingly innocent dandruff flakes are an important, if ancillary, part of the tale to be told about how identities get determined through various allegiances to authenticity.

Silver Badges, White Ropes

Once, when I was all of eleven or twelve, I was sitting inside my mother's Mazda in the parking lot of a Key Food Supermarket in the Brownsville section of Brooklyn. I used to hate going into those huge grocery stores whenever they were packed with shoppers (as they usually were when we went), my mother making me hold a place for her at the back of one of the long checkout lines while she collected a few items. So on this evening, I pled my case (feigning sickness or something) and won: I stayed in the car, reading comic books and listening to music while she shopped. But I hadn't been alone ten minutes when two casually dressed white men (both in jeans, T-shirts and denim jackets) approached the car, one on each side, and tried the locked doors. The men then knocked on the car's windows, displaying their badges (hung neatly around their necks) and motioning for me to unlock the door. I froze. It was a preteen terror that, in retrospect, I often dismiss as ridiculous, irrational, unwarranted. Surely, they must have been undercover, caught my head bobbing inside a parked car in a dark parking lot, and immediately thought of vandalism. However, I never did unlock those doors.

If guns had appeared from behind the backs of those two badge-necklaced men, then surely their gestures to unlock the doors would have carried more weight with my eleven- or twelve-year-old self, no? But instead, I froze, could not respond, just as I had in my godmother's living-room church. And eventually, the two denim-clad guys simply turned around, vanished, faded back into the world, into the night, into the darkness from which they had so mysteriously emerged. To this day, I imagine that they were criminals with fake badges trying to take advantage of some unsuspecting soul. But maybe they were worse: real cops, Dowd cops, poised to abuse their state-sanctioned power.

Desmond Robinson was a black cop, an undercover black cop who was shot in 1994 for being too black and too convincing for his own good, someone able to go so deep undercover that a fellow police officer shot him five times on a subway platform after mistaking him for a criminal assailant. His bald-headed, bearded, and ear-ringed brown face was deemed so unlike that of an average police officer that he was said simply to blend into the fluid mass of commuters that swarm New York City's subway system daily. Officers who knew Robinson, and admired his careful crafting of an undercover persona, called him "The Phantom." He disappeared into crowds like a ghost, and this was the very skill that got him killed.

"They said he didn't look like a cop," says Clarence, Stokes's thirty-something son, as we walk into his apartment building. "Didn't look like a cop?! He sure didn't, but that was before he took off his uniform. He didn't look like a cop when he was born. He came out his momma's womb, and the doctor must've been like 'Damn, you don't look nothin' like a cop.' Got no business in that shit. Like fighting a war for these fuckers. Hell no!"

"What do cops look like?" I ask him, pressing the buzzer down in the halogen-lit lobby entranceway.

"Shit, not like us!"

The stories that make their way from person to person in Crown Heights about crooked police officers are often incredibly disturbing—scary examples of "cops gone bad," of bureaucratic corruption running wild, of us "all going to hell in a handbasket." Many of these harrowing police stories are offered up during card games in front of sweaty apartment buildings on hot summer nights. They are passed around at dinner tables, miniature versions of a Malinowskian-described kula ring, where I pass mom the tale of the cop who beat up Charles ("Yeah mom, Charles, the one you are always calling 'the pretty Indian-looking boy'!") for no reason at all, and she tells Aunt Rita (who's not really my aunt) about her friend's stepfather being framed by police in Manhattan twenty years ago for some crime he couldn't have committed because he had only stepped off the boat six minutes before.

And the tales passed on get bigger and bigger. More and more horrifying. A kind of storytelling potlatch always resupplied with newer and fresher tales to burn one's ears with. Long before the police shot an innocent Amadou Diallo and arrested a crooked Michael Dowd, before Phantom Robinson's mistaken identity, before Aunt Rita's friend's stepfather and the cops who arrested Leroy for playing a rap song, other officers from the Seventy-third precinct, within a siren's earshot of my mom's second-floor window, were convicted for conducting dozens upon dozens of illegal shakedowns, extorting drugs and money from neighborhood drug dealers. One cop even threatened to feed a drug dealer to pit bulls unless the dealer turned over hidden crack and cash for the officer's own private stash. Nefarious police exploits didn't need Judge Milton Mollen's commission to get police corruption onto the lips of Crown Heights residents. The Rodney King fiasco was just icing, not the cake itself. Former NYPD commissioner Raymond Kelly evoking Durkheimian notions of anomie at local press conferences (to describe a small, "rogue" section of the police force) was not necessary, either. Nor was the media's oversaturated coverage of other shakedown rings in the city, other beatings, other police abuses. Indeed, many folks in Crown Heights just assume that officers are corrupt. That is the norm. Even without all the hoopla and media attention, an entrenched skepticism provides fecund ground for, say, Johnnie Cochran's police-conspiracy defense. That may not always have been the case, and may not be in more middle-class neighborhoods, black or white, but in this small, working-class section of Brooklyn, it is. Even the good cop, some residents say, is ultimately just a mild variant of the crooked officer. There is no fundamental disconnectedness between the two.

"A good cop ain't but a little less bad than de bad one," Stokes says to me over another card game on another hot night in Crown Heights. "Don't be fooled. A good cop de rock, and a bad cop is de fuckin' hard place, as God's my witness." German theorist Walter Benjamin talks about how easily and readily government violence becomes a complicatedly self-perpetuating and self-justifying force.[20] For Benjamin, the police are exactly like poet Haki Madhubuti's "ghost dust" cops, periodically vanishing into and out of the thick white fog of night, repeatedly condensing to perform heinous acts (like killing Black Panthers Fred Hampton and Mark Clark while they sleep) only to disperse once again back into the white night from whence they came. Even the shiny, silver-colored badge is hidden in the fog, merges with the white opaqueness and ambiguity of the dark and foggy night.

Is the badge no longer sacred in Crown Heights? Was it ever? Are those who don it simply being possessed by some kind of police Pentecostalism? Should the badge be sacred? Must it be so for the good cops to do their jobs? To profane the badge, to have it thought of as less than sacred, to be de-badged—is that simply an exposing and unmasking of fraud? Is the police officer always already imagined as phony, fake, a charlatan, a Leo Felton waiting to be outed by an ever-persistent, watchdog public?

"You were put here to protect us," raps KRS-One, at a crowded hip-hop club on the elusive Crown Heights/Flatbush border, "but who protects us from you."

COINTELPROs and Cons

One bitterly cold Sunday afternoon in November, I organize a focus-group meeting with several of the young people I know in the neighborhood, providing space for them to talk about police brutality and other issues. I am really being the anthropologist now, I think to myself, or at least a sociologist, collecting data on people's subjective realities. The entire meeting will be taped, and I have a few laser-printed pages of what I believe to be carefully crafted, open-ended research questions—to be delivered with my best interviewer poker face.

Damon, twenty-two, a part-time construction worker and one of my most talkative informants, was not there. He was supposed to be, but he did not show. Shanita, the high school gospel singer, didn't make it either. Two others, Thomas and Carl, both students at Brooklyn College, did, along with a couple of their friends, Ray and Tic, guys I had never met before, one a janitor at an office building in downtown Brooklyn; the other, looking for work. The focus group met in my mom's one-bedroom apartment. As we talked, the tape recorder whirled and whizzed, but with an NBA basketball game muted on the living room's TV screen (per Tic's request), it picked up as much hooting and hollering as anything else. After the game, we decided to call it quits. The guys were tired from a long day.

"Yo, have you ever heard of COINTELPRO?" Thomas asks me, heading for the front door. "You need to check that shit out. You interested in the police and the government and shit, you gotta be checkin' that bad-boy out."

"I do have the book," I reply, walking over to my junky bookcase. "At least I think I do. I ain't read this shit, yet, though. Give me an overview!"

"It is, like, blowing shit up like the World Trade Center, on shit like the ways that the black leaders and groups and shit were fuckin' totally infiltrated and shit. Like how folks was like being framed by the government and the government be knowin' that shit but won't do anything about it. Deep shit!!"[21]

"Make a motherfucker go crazy," Carl stretches and yawns as he weighs in. "A niggah read that shit and start tweakin' out. Wanna Colin Ferguson motherfuckers and shit."[22]

"What ya'll think about that shit?" I ask, milking the last few minutes for all the ethnographic relevance I could get. "I mean, about that whole Colin Ferguson thing, yo?"

"Damn, that was a while back, hunh?" Thomas muses. "Shit, time be flyin'. That was like a year ago."

"More than a year, I think, but what do you think about it?" Anthroman persists.

"What do you think?" Charles asks, craftily employing the old informant-switcheroo tactic.

"I don't know," I respond. "Blood musta had some serious problems, kid."

"Nah, that niggah was just handlin' his business," Ray assures me. "Fuck around and lay me off, and I'll be a subway shootin' motherfucker, too."

Charles laughs. Anthroman, on the other hand, is haunted by thoughts of Franz Kafka, of his soon-to-be-decapitated Joseph K, of the differences and similarities between him and Colin F: that Colin may have known something that Joseph did not (or vice versa)—to escape the power of the law, if only for a second, is to transgress it. In the end, you still lose, but you go out with a big bang and not just the faintest whimper. In this scenario, resistance is futile, and everything is pre-ordained, a setup. But the more futile the situation, the harder they come. And the WTU Black Hebrews are not nearly the only ones who successfully exemplify this fact. When the focus-group guys finally leave my place, I finish watching the basketball post-game show, scribble a to-do list for myself, and then help my mother clear off the dinner table.

Black Maskulinity

If de-badging can be considered akin to unmasking in any way, what does the Colin Ferguson Long Island Railroad massacre unmask? What about the Desmond Robinson shooting? Not to mention the Rodney King extended beat-down? What does all this unmask about the police and their relationship to the policed? And whose masks are fooling whom?

> We smile, but, O great Christ, our cries
> To thee from tortured souls arise.
> We sing, but oh, the clay is vile

Beneath our feet, and long the mile;
But let the world dream otherwise,
We wear the mask.[23]

This excerpt from Paul Laurence Dunbar's most famous poem, "We Wear the Mask," distills and articulates his understanding of just what it means for African Americans to hide their feelings, their emotional and psychic identities, from a purportedly hostile and antiblack world. Dunbar's "We" stands as a proxy for black America—black Americans shielding their/our true selves from the rest of the nation-state. "We" smile and shuck and jive and laugh, he laments, even and especially when we are least happy. In fact, for Dunbar, happiness becomes a kind of racialized impossibility. The masks "We" wear may fool the rest of the country, but they cannot fool us. The wearers still feel the pain and misery of their duplicitous, costume-balled lives.

What might it mean, in this context, to unmask? Attorney William Kunstler appropriated the phrase "black rage" to describe Colin Ferguson's horrific act.[24] But if it is a race-based rage, is every black person, as a function of their unexpressed anger, prone to such pure and extreme rages in the dark recesses of their (our) "tortured souls"? Do we still, like Frederick Douglass, see an infamous slavemaster, that "snake," Massa Covey, behind every tree and stump and fire hydrant in view, hidden "like a thief in the night"? How much is masking ourselves, Dunbar's characterization notwithstanding, actually about fooling *ourselves*—first and foremost—not just other people? And does such self-delusion complicate claims to intentionality and willfulness? What if the image of the mask can sometimes, if even only fleetingly, fool the wearer, too? Can we look in the mirror and forget "we" sport a disguise, taking that hard and flat-footed reflection as the sure totality of our very being, a self with clear and unalienated features? What would happen if "we" took off those masks? If we no longer let them fool us? Would exposing the truth about oneself (by ripping off one's racial masks) mean gunning down innocent people on the Long Island Railroad and proclaiming, in a courtroom full of incredulous eyewitnesses, that someone else really did it—the legal tactic borrowed a decade later by Washington, D.C.'s serial shooter, John Allen Muhammad? How does one even do that—that is, take off masks so prosthetically and hermetically glued to a sense of selfhood?

Maybe rumors unmask!? Conspiracies? Like the one Damon told me (a fact, he says, not a rumor) about Snapple beverages being owned by the Ku Klux Klan? Or the other one I heard from my cousin Isaiah about a Procter & Gamble spokesperson appearing on a television talk show to tell the world that proceeds from their products go to Satanic cults— and that it doesn't really matter what people think about that newly revealed fact because their products are everywhere, all over the world, indispensable, and so Christians can't do anything about it anyway? Did you hear the one about Reebok sneakers being made by a South African company to support the Apartheid effort with African American dollars, a rumor so pervasive that Reebok had to launch a national advertisement campaign to dispel it? Didn't they? Or how about Camel cigarettes? Or was it Marlboro? Church's chicken?[25] Are rumors more powerful than facts? Are they more true than "the truth"? As counterintuitive as it sounds, might rumors provide some of the fastest routes into the inner structure of the real?

"I wouldn't fuck with Tropical Fantasy," Richard, twenty-two, who lives across the hall from me, advises as I go with him to the corner store and pick out one of the bright, multicolored bottles of fruit punch from the deli's refrigerator.

"Why not?"

"I heard that they be putting shit in there to sterilize us. Sterilize black men."

"Where you hear that shit?"

"Fucking all around. You know it's probably true. They only sell that shit in black neighborhoods. Like malt liquor and shit. If motherfuckers wanted to wipe us the fuck out, which you know they do, they know to hit us with the fried chicken and the fuckin' alcohol."

"White folk drink alcohol and shit," I reply, still holding the bottle of Tropical Fantasy in my outstretched hand—but keeping the freezer door ajar with my foot as I await his response.

"Yeah, but I bet they ain't drinkin' shit like this." He points to bottles of Old English and Red Bull malt liquors, both served up in forty-ounce portions. "And you damn well know they ain't got no Tropical Fantasy in they shit, either. Pepsi. Coke. That is the shit that they drink. And I ain't gonna be the niggah caught out there when the eleven o'clock news starts talking about some scandal at Tropical Fantasy and shit. By then it would be too late for you Muggs. Shit, and if that stuff ain't fucked with by whitey, it won't be by me. Sprite, Coke, and the regular shit tastes better than all them cheap shits anyways."

Not quite convinced, but wanting to be more safe than sorry, especially if Richard's late-breaking newscast comes true, I put the Tropical Fantasy back for a small Poland Spring bottled water. "I'm glad you ain't pick up that Evian," Richard adds as he drops some change on the countertop for a box of Philly blunts and some plantain chips. "You know what KRS-One said about that shit, 'it is *naive* spelled backwards.' You better recognize."

Evian sure is naive spelled backward, I think to myself. And, oddly enough, doesn't the Boston tea-party iconography on Snapple bottles look a little like slave ships landing on America's colonial shores? And what's to say that the *K* by the picture doesn't stand for, as the theory goes, Ku Klux Klan? I study my Poland Spring bottle even more carefully before finally deciding to buy it.

Rumors speak the unspeakable, of sterilization and Klan-based economics, of naive consumers and Satanist manufacturers. They talk about the world in ways that are unsettling, mostly because of what they claim to reveal, to unmask. And they have a wonderfully proficient way of co-opting more official truths to their cause. For surely, as many Brooklynites have told me time and again, the Tuskegee Experiments (where black men with syphilis were allowed, by World Health Organization Doctors, to die untreated in the name of science) were, in fact, real deaths.[26] And isn't there documented proof, Shanita asks me, real proof, that the first settlers gave blankets laced with small pox as peace offerings to the Native Americans? Didn't she hear that somewhere? Or read it in history class? If so, why would the idea of AIDS as a man-made, government-engineered, black-people-killing disease seem absurd—especially when AIDS rates in Africa are so astronomically high?

"Like Africans spend every day sitting around in their huts exchanging blood," Richard frowns, shaking his head in disbelief. "They trying to get rid of them folks," he declares matter-of-factly. "Us folks." And rumors use all of that stuff, sift through it, turn over the facts, and come out clearer, truer, stronger. They are the ultimate myths we tell ourselves about why someone else might want to kill us—and how they might try. In Crown Heights, at least the Crown Heights I knew in 1994, conspiracy theories helped to rewrite the contours of local community, national polity, and international concerns.

"When we steal, we take tangible shit," Damon says to me as we walk over to McDonald's for a quick dinner on me. "A TV, a stereo, and shit. Objects and shit. When white folks steal, they steal souls and shit, they steal cultures. We kill people, they kill people*s*. That's the difference. Look at all that shit they done did to us, and tell me they ain't evil."

Soulthievery

The soultheft Damon was talking about manifests itself in many ways. Not just Tropical Fantasy sodas and Reebok sneakers. Not just KKK-owned Snapple products and water-bottled sterilization. But the rumors are a good entry-point into this world of stolen black bodies, souls, and peoples, a world bubbling over and above that familiar one of more discrete and tangible things. Surely, there are treacherous ways into this world—extreme roads, rough tracks—like the path that leads from Derrick's apartment in a three-story brownstone to the Brooklyn Public Library.

"The Ankh is the important symbol." Derrick, nineteen and recently graduated from high school, carefully weighs his words as he stage-whispers to me from across the narrow library table. "It is the key, and the key is the knowledge. The key is the knowledge. The most obvious and straightforward proof we have of Christianity's patriarchal, Western, and devilish ways. Take the ankh and look at it. You have to really look to see the truth."[27] I stare at his drawing of the ankh and cross as he continues speaking from across the table.

"I'm about to teach you symbology," he continues, "you ain't gonna get this over there at Columbia. The ankh is male and female, man and woman. Do you see it? Penis and vagina, a coming together, a community, a family. That is what the ancient Egyptians realized, how they gained their power. Now go from there to the cross, and you will see Western, white supremacy's patriarchal axing-out of the female. She is gone. Cut out. The ankh is cut along the female half, so you only have the male portion left. What was once a heavenly unity and sexual to-getherness is now a warped picture of some male God birthing a man without a woman, kid. You see that sick, unnatural shit, son? That homosexual fantasy? See, whitey got it in for his bitches, too."[28]

Derrick demonizes a form of "patriarchal" power to validate an equally sinister sexism. Black Egyptians treated men and women equally, he says, but white supremacy marginalizes femininity, rejecting its symbolic power. With the non-sequitur invocation of homosexuality, this becomes another kind of Settepani moment. Sexual orientation is linked to whiteness and dismissed as part of a larger, antifemale conspiracy—and Derrick was making his case long before Dan Brown's controversial thriller.[29] This becomes another kind of soultheft, an antifeminist feminism, something that mirrors the larger stealing of "peoples" that is imagined to have long-term consequences for racial soulfulness and collective vitality.

Soultheft? How does one get away with that? And why do conspiracies help us find our answers? Because the truth is too lame? Too obvious? Do we have a hardwired need for explanations that are more complex? Derrick and I leave the library to get a bite to eat at a McDonald's on Utica Avenue, and he makes our culinary context an explicit theme of analysis.

"We have to eat either this nasty-ass McDeath," Derrick says, "or in these Chinese places and shit with two-inch thick bulletproof glass, like we are animals in a cage, 'cause they are afraid what we gonna do once we get sparks of the real truth of how they killin' us." Anthroman decides to play devil's advocate, saying stuff like, "What the fuck would we do, man?" and "Shit, if we ain't got the truth yet, when we gonna get it?" And Derrick mostly ignores me or counters with even darker truths—about the hidden secrets of the U.S. monuments, about the symbolic importance of obelisks as geometric form, about Washington, D.C., being designed and laid-out on the basis of an ancient Egyptian model, and about the powerful secret societies that really run our country. And Anthroman is jotting details down all the while:

> Notes on Derrick's Theory—
> 1. The Washington Monument (symbol of American what?), tallest structure in the Washington, D.C., area; no other building allowed to obstruct view.
> 2. Structured after African obelisk, symbolic of the regenerative powers of Godhead?
> 3. The design of Lincoln Memorial, patterned after a temple in honor of Ramses II (or III), pharaoh of nineteenth dynasty (?), Egypt.
> 4. Meridian Hill Park in D.C. made to align the city with the same pathway of sun passing through Ancient Egypt. What does it even mean to align sun-pathways? Go back to Howard dorm and verify?
> 5. Stealing cultures means stealing people's symbols.

Derrick gives me some book titles and challenges me to do my own research, to uncover "for myself" the ways in which the United States is very cryptically but obviously connected to ancient Egyptian Freemasonry. He shares a horizon of rationality with any social scientist, the careful cobbling together of purported historical facts.[30]

"But people don't really believe that stuff, do they?" one of my graduate-school colleagues at Columbia asks over some Ethiopian food at Massawa's in Upper Manhattan. "They don't believe that that is true, do they? They can't!" About as much as "they" believe the smallpox blankets, I reply. Or the Tuskegee experiments. Or the Atlantic slave-trade for that matter. Are the "paranoid" feared because they have an ultrafinalized view of the world that is not open to discussion or change? There is some kind of soulstealing going on in this land of wailing sirens, outlawed Holy Spirits, and the red/blue/red/blue ambivalences of flashing police lights, but where do we reasonably draw our epistemological lines in the sand?

Undoubtedly, there is power in conspiratorial finality. It is what the hard scientists look for: the chemistrial-conspiracy that makes all re-actions and equations clear, providing absolute certainty. It is what anthropologists long for: that metanarrative, master narrative, which explains all of mankind in a few sparse lines. They all want conspiracy. They want the power of paranoia. Conspiracy theories are simply structural functionalism on acid.[31] Structural functionalists would love for their analyses to read the way "Who shot JFK?" does, where everything fits snugly in its place and no rock is left unturned, no hand unsoiled. Everything has a function, a reason for being: in this case, to promote the status quo by dissembling and duping the masses into thinking that things ever change. For conspiracy theorists like Derrick, we are still in ancient Egypt, whether we know it or not. Edward William Lane's *Account of the Manners and Customs of the Modern Egyptians* could really be about us right now.[32] Current Afrocentric preoccupations with ancient Egyptian antiquity can be read as current events.[33] We are always reliving the same unfinished battles between Napoleon and the Egyptians, between goodness and evil, with evil reproducing itself, re-producing its coherent systematicity through lies and secret symbols. This is a kind of ultrasincerity that gives agency not only to people but to everything else. It is global animism, where things are given interior-ities and the most dastardly intentions, things like nation-states, multi-national corporations, fruit punch, anything. There is no passive-verb theorizing. Everything is about locating effective agents, even and espe-cially where one might least expect to find them.

When forty-ounce bottles of Old English Malt Liquor are poured, passed, and swallowed for the people not present (because snuffed out by the very real surreality of inner-city violence), conspiracy is more than a belief, more than a perspective. It becomes incontestable, as-sumed, a given. All else is added or taken away, but the disproportion-ality of death-rates remains beyond modification. The particularities and justifications are almost immaterial and unimportant—wholly unnecessary.[34] That Snapple *could* be owned by the KKK is as real as the death rates of young black men caught up in Harlem's version of Bangladesh.[35] And in a frantic and unfulfilling search for answers to horrific questions, the explanations chosen become as harrowing as the questions themselves. And Snapple, Reebok, or some other commodity-cum-traitor is as potentially reasonable a culprit as any other. Conspiracy theory becomes a populist technique that, much like the novelistic form, "organizes reality and knowledge in a such a way as to make them susceptible to systematic verbal reincarnation." [36]

The hyperreality of conspiracy theories reifies and fetishizes "the real" in ways that potentially unmake it, challenging its abilities to inconspicuously define our everyday social interactions. Mark Liechty's distinction between "reality" and "plausibility" among middle-class residents of contemporary Kathmandu is particularly operative here. Conspiracy theories, like middle-class Nepali readings of Hollywood films, are not simply about imagining or "organizing reality" in a way that privileges realism. Instead, they are about appreciating the powers of plausibility, of the merely possible.[37] They are less about what is, than what could be—what simulates the rules for constructing realities most persuasively. Conspiracy theories privilege this distinction between reality and plausibility, reversing their relative importance and fraying their intertextual edges.

Hollywood Spells

I first met Thomas through Derrick. A WTU Black Hebrew Israelite, Thomas is twenty-five and works as a security guard. Guys in the neighborhood don't seem to have any problem with Thomas, "no static," as they say, because everyone knows that "he is all about some serious shit, being a black Hebrew Israelite and all." Thomas reads the Bible daily, interpreting it to describe how the real Jews of God's covenant were displaced and replaced with impostors, those who, according to Revelation, "say they are Jews, and are not, but do lie." [38]

It is an Early Saturday morning in January. Thomas laughs heartily, approvingly, when he sees me, insisting that my Black Hebrew subconscious is trying as hard as it can to get me to accept my "true Israelite identity." I haven't trimmed my spotty beard for at least two months now, and the WTUers believe, on the basis of their literalist readings of the Old Testament, that African American men, the real Black Israelites, should not trim their facial hair. Thomas tells me that he wants me to read and study with the Israelites, to go to some meetings with him.

He wants to convert me "to the truth you already should know, do know, in the back of your soul."

"Black folk gotta realize they ain't Africans," he says. "We are from the twelve tribes of Israel. All that Egypt, Kemet, Africa shit is bullshit. We ain't got shit to do with Africa. But don't worry. I'm gonna show you the light!"

The Black Hebrew Israelites are usually labeled a black supremacist group, but if so, this is black supremacy with a difference. Whereas much black separatism is predicated on a certain embrace of Africanity (in terms of ancient Egyptian antiquity in its Afrocentric guise, or the presentist diasporic leanings of various Pan-Africanisms), these Hebrew Israelites are adamant about blacks in the New World not being African at all—they do not claim Africa as some kind of symbolic, cultural, or genetic ground for contemporary social identity in the Americas. The Black Hebrew Israelite diaspora is configured quite differently from conventional models of black diasporic possibility. Ties to Africa are completely severed.[39] There is still a notion of connection across the Americas, but these links have different significances. Each New World nation is associated (through particularized readings of history books, of the 1611 King James Bible, and of the controversial Apocrypha) with a particular Jewish tribe from the Old Testament: black Americans are the tribe of Judah; West Indians are the tribe of Benjamin; Haitians, the tribe of Levi; Dominicans, the tribe of Simeon; Puerto Ricans, the tribe of Ephraim; Guatemalans, Panamanians, Cubans, North American Indians, Seminole Indians, Argentineans, Chilean, and Mexicans are each designated as members of distinct tribes. And the contiguous Latin American countries between Colombia and Uruguay are lumped together as a singular tribal unit, Asher. This is a notion of diaspora (and a labeling of diasporic belonging) that cuts across racial categorizations (at least as they conventionally operate in a U.S. context) and allows for a Black Israelite diaspora that connects Chileans and Colombians with Cubans and African Americans, but disallows any inclusion of continental Africans. Indeed, the Israelites offer a corrective to what they consider Afrocentric excesses and historical misreadings of transatlantic travel. For Black Hebrew Israelites, "Arab Muslims" and African Muslims/Christians/pagans sold the Black Jews into bondage. And they did this, the Black Hebrew Israelites claim, because these "Africans" and "Arabs" knew that the Black Jews in Africa were an entirely different *people.*

"Yo, come here," Thomas yells, "and check this commercial out." The lone television in this two-bedroom apartment that Thomas shares with his friend and housemate, another Black Hebrew Israelite, Bigs, is tuned to a McDonald's commercial set in an apartment building full of black families.

"Yo, you know I been to Hamburger University, right?" I mutter over the television advertisement. "The McDonald's college for Hamburgerology or something like that."

"Where the fuck is that?" Bigs asks. "I think I have a boy who went there."

"Near Chicago," I answer, my eyes still glued to the commercial. Bigs's face signals a feeble acknowledgment.

"This commercial is a trip and a half," Thomas exclaims, nodding his head back and forth to the faint hints of a jingle forming the ad's musical bed.

The scenes depict bags of McDonald's food giving off a white mist that circulates through an apartment building full of black residents, forcing them all to hunger for those "two all beef patties, special sauce, lettuce, cheese, pickles, onions on a sesame-seed bun." The characters in the ad don't seem to know exactly why they suddenly crave McDonald's. And they aren't even smelling the food. Its manna-like power is simply hypnotizing them, a white mist spreading through their tenement building like curlicue smoke. All they really know is that they suddenly crave some Mickey D's.[40] Once the McDonald's spot ends, our discussion veers toward sitcoms, miniseries, and rap music. When the conversation focuses on contemporary cinema, Thomas decides to "school" me on Hollywood.

"It is, historically speaking," he assures me, "the name for the actual wood that witches and warlocks used in the olden days to make magic wands and broom sticks. Holly wood. Straight up."

"How you know that?" I ask.

"Man, we got mad info on these folk. They be tellin' on themselves left and right, and you can get that shit from they own books. Like I told you before, this shit is about wars. About good and evil. About God and the Devil and which side you choose. The founding fathers and shit was all Masons. Every one of them. From Washington on down. You heard of 'the skull and crossbones' shit that Bush was a member of at Yale or Harvard or some shit. That shit is all tied to the same thing. Satanism, man. These motherfuckers are about the Devil, man. They cast spells. That is why Hollywood has the name. It's one big broomstick, yo. They want to let you know without letting you know. You think this shit ain't real; you better do your own research. It is like I done told you. It ain't about converting and shit to a particular religion or being an African.

JACOB vs. ESAU

Who Were JACOB & ESAU? They were descendants of Abraham and Isaac (Gen. 25:19-26, 1st Chron. 16:16-17). JACOB and ESAU were Twins at birth (unidentical twins) Gen 25:24-26.

Who was Jacob? Jacob was the 3rd father of the Promise, meaning he & his seed (children) would be chosen unto the Lord as his people, which is the 12 Tribes of Israel, a nation in Egypt for 430 years (Exod. 1:1-14, Gal. 3:17). Jacob was a man of color (brown-skinned from melanin, so-called black man,) contrary to his brother Esau who was described as red & hairy (Gen 25:25, Gen 27:11) *Jacob is the father of the chosen race.*

Who was Esau? Esau is the father of the Greeks and Romans, who are the forefathers of the so-called *White* people, Caucasians or Europeans which they refer to themselves as today. "Esau" comes from the ancient Hebrew Word "I-Shaw," which means "wasted away is he," because his Brown color (Melanin) was taken away from him in his mother's womb (Gen. 25:25, Num. 12:9-12). At his birth, ESAU was described as being "**Red (so-called white), all over like an hairy garment,**" (Gen. 25:25) and he became the father of the Edomites (or "*Idumeans*", which means RED people: See Zondervan Bible Dictionary under "*Edom*". The descendants of Esau, called **Edomites** lived in Mount Seir (Gen. 36:1-end). Esau *despised* and *sold* his birthright (Gen. 25: 25-34 & Heb. 12:15-17) *even though he was the first-born between himself and his twin brother Jacob.* Esau's descendants, **so-called whites are a race cursed by God** (Isa. 34:5, Rom. 9:13 [Mal. 1:1-4] Ezek. 35:1-end, Ezek 36:5).

Did either of the parents, Isaac or Rebekkah understand that the CREATOR loved Jacob and Hated Esau? *Yes, Rebekkah Understood!* READ: Gen. 25:19-22 (1st Sam. 9:9),Gen.25:23-24,

Genesis 25:23 "And the LORD said unto her (Rebekah), Two NATIONS are in thy womb, and two manner of people shall be separated from thy bowels; and the one people shall be stronger than the other people; and the ELDER shall SERVE the YOUNGER."

Gen. 27:5-33(especially verse 13) and Gen. 25:23-24.

Does the *CREATOR* **still have a preference between the two?** YES! He still only loves JACOB's CHILDREN, the 12 Tribes (Rom. 9:1-5&9-21, Deut. 7:7-8, Zech. 2:8, Jer. 1:5, Rom. 11:1-4, Rom. 9:9-21[Mal. 1:1-5], Ezek. 25:12-14, Mark 7:24-30 [Greeks / Romans = Edom(ites) / Idumeans], Isa. 45:17-19, Amos 3:1-2, Psa 147:19-20, Isa 14:1-8, Ezek 35:1-end, 2 Sam 7:23-24, Isa 46:13, Amos 3:1-2, Acts 5:29-31, Matt 10:5-6, Rev 7:1-4 and Rev 21:10-12).

Why can't the descendants of ESAU (so-called whites) and JACOB (the 12 Tribes) get along with each other as two nations? First of all the Lord made them two (2) different nations (Gen 25:23-25) and all the prophecies concerning our two nations must be fulfilled. Enmity (or hatred) between the children of Esau & the children of Jacob (Gen 3:14-15) (Note: The Serpent=Edom / Red[or so-called white] people - Read: Rev. 12:3,9, Job 30:1-8 & The Woman=Israel[the 12 Tribes] - Read: Isa. 54:5-10). *The Creator, chose one nation over the other* (Ps 147:19-20, Amos 3:1-2, Deut 7:7-9, Rom. 9:11-14, Gen. 25:21-25, Isa. 14:1-3, Jer. 51:19). The nation of Edom has broken the brotherly covenant (Obad 10-15&18, Ps 83:1-6, Amos 1:9&11).

Is Edom still CONDEMNED? YES, Esau was condemned before he was born! (Gen. 25:25, Num. 12:9-12, Rom. 9:11-13, Heb. 12:6-8, Prov. 16:4, Isa. 34:5, (Apocrypha) 2nd Esdras 6:7-10), Isa. 26:10).

Even if they repent they will not obtain mercy from the CREATOR (Heb. 12:16-17, Gen. 25:29-end and Isa 26:10).

Why does the CREATOR love JACOB (the Israelites) so much? READ: Deut. 7:6-10, Zech. 2:8, Deut. 32:8-10, Isa. 43:21, Isa. 44:1-8 & v21-26, Isa. 45:v14-19 & v21-23&25, Ps 148:14, Ps.

(Apoc) 2 Esdras 6:7-9: " 7-Then answered I and said, What shall be the parting asunder of the times? or when shall be the end of the first, and the beginning of it that followeth? 8-And he said unto me, From Abraham unto Isaac. when Jacob and Esau were born of him, Jacob's hand held first the heel of Esau. 9-For Esau is the end of the world, and Jacob is the beginning of it that followeth."

THE 12 TRIBES OF THE NATION OF ISRAEL – ACCORDING TO THE KING JAMES VERSION OF THE HOLY BIBLE

1. JUDAH----------THE NEGROES
2. BENJAMIN----WEST INDIANS
3. LEVI-------------HAITIANS
4. SIMEON--------DOMINICANS
5. ZEBULON----GUATEMALA TO PANAMA
6. EPRHRAIM--PUERTO RICANS
7. MANASSEH----------------CUBANS
8. GAD--------------------------N. AMERICAN INDIANS
9. REUBEN----------------------SEMINOLE INDIANS
10. NAPHTALI-------------------ARGENTINA AND CHILE
11. ASHER-----------------------COLOMBIA TO URUGUAY
12. ISSACHAR-------------------MEXICANS

As well as the Scattered (Dispersed) Israelites in all Nations throughout the Four Corners of the Earth. In Places like Europe, Asia, the Middle East, Egypt & Africa, India, the Far East and More...

God has a chosen people, Jacob's seed. And he has people he hates: Esau's offspring, the children of Edom. And he describes who is who in the Bible. And God is gonna destroy these Satan worshippers. But for now they trying to fortify they ranks and shit. To cast their spells on the masses. Keep them stupid and ignorant. Hollywood is straight-up about casting spells, kid.

"Do you notice that every time some shit comes out in the movies, it is only a bit later and it is out in real life. They *create* that shit with movies. Movies are like their spells, son. They be using that shit to get us

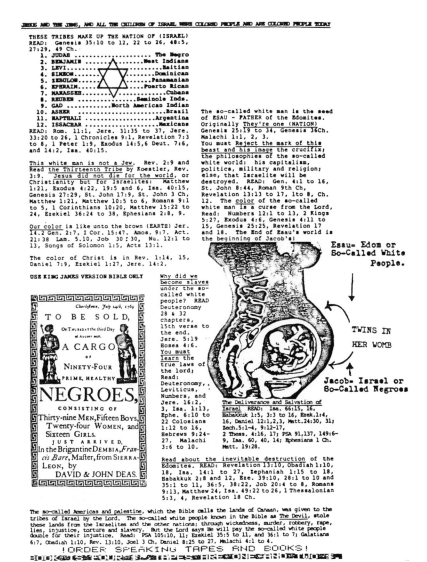

JESUS AND THE JEWS, AND ALL THE CHILDREN OF ISRAEL WERE COLORED PEOPLE AND ARE COLORED PEOPLE TODAY

THESE TRIBES MAKE UP THE NATION OF (ISRAEL)
READ: Genesis 35:10 to 12, 22 to 26, 48:5, 27:29, 49 Ch.

1. JUDAH .... The Negro
2. BENJAMIN .... West Indians
3. LEVI........................ Haitian
4. SIMEON..................... Dominican
5. ZEBULON................... Panamanian
6. EPHRAIM.................... Puerto Rican
7. MANASSEH.................. Cubans
8. REUBEN .... Seminole Inds.
9. GAD .... North American Indian
10. ASHER ....Brazil
11. NAPTHALI ....Argentina
12. ISSACHAR ....Mexicans

READ: Rom. 11:1, Jere. 31:35 to 37, Jere. 33:20 to 26, 1 Chronicles 9:1, Revelation 7:3 to 8, 1 Peter 1:9, Exodus 14:5,6 Deut. 7:6, and 14:2, Isa. 40:15.

This white man is not a Jew. Rev. 2:9 and Read the Thirteenth Tribe by Koestler, Rev. 3:9. Jesus did not die for the world, or Christianity but for Israelites: Matthew 1:21, Exodus 4:22, 19:5 and 6, Isa. 40:15, Genesis 27:29, St. John 17:9, St. John 3 Ch, Matthew 1:21, Matthew 10:5 to 6, Romans 9:1 to 5, 1 Corinthians 10:20, Matthew 15:22 to 24, Ezekiel 36:24 to 38, Ephesians 2:8, 9.

Our color is like unto the brown (EARTH) Jer. 14.2 Gen. 2:7, I Cor. 15:47. Amos. 9:7. Act. 21:38 Lam. 5.10, Job 30 : 30, Nu. 12:1 to 13, Songs of Solomon 1:5, Acts 13:1.

The color of Christ is in Rev. 1:14, 15, Daniel 7:9, Ezekiel 1:27, Jere. 14:2.

USE KING JAMES VERSION BIBLE ONLY

The so-called white man is the seed of ESAU - FATHER of the Edomites. Originally They're one (NATION) Genesis 25:19 to 34, Genesis 36Ch. Malachi 1:1, 2, 3.
You must Reject the mark of this beast and his image the crucifix; the philosophies of the so-called white world: his capitalism, politics, military and religion; else, that Israelite will be destroyed. READ: Gen. 4:1 to 16, St. John 8:44, Roman 9th Ch, Revelation 13:13 to 17, 1to 8, Ch. 12. The color of the so-called white man is a curse from the Lord, Read: Numbers 12:1 to 13, 2 Kings 5:27, Exodus 4:6, Genesis 4:11 to 15, Genesis 25:25, Revelation 17 and 18. The End of Esau's world is the beginning of Jacob's!

Esau= Edom or So-Called White People.

TWINS IN HER WOMB

Jacob= Israel or So-Called Negroes

Why did we become slaves under the so-called white people? READ Deuteronomy 28 & 32 chapters, 15th verse to the end. Jere. 5:19 Hosea 4:6. You must learn the true laws of the lord; Read: Deuteronomy,, Leviticus, Numbers, and Jere. 16:2, 3, Isa. 1:13, Ephe. 6:10 to 22 Colosians 1:12 to 16, Hebrews 9:24- 27. Malachi 3:6 to 10.

The Deliverance and Salvation of Israel: READ: Isa. 66:15, 16, Habakkuk 1:5, 3:3 to 16, Ezek.1:4, 16, Daniel 12:1,2,3, Matt.24:30, 31; Zech.5:1-4, 9:12-17, 2 Thess. 4:16, 17; Psa 91,137, 149:6- 9, Isa. 60, 40, 14; Ephesians 1 Ch. Matt. 19:28.

Read about the inevitable destruction of the Edomites. READ: Revelation 13:10, Obadiah 1:10, 18, Isa. 14:1 to 27, Zephaniah 1:15 to 18, Habakkuk 2:8 and 12, Eze. 39:10, 28:1 to 10 and 35:1 to 11, 36:5, 38:22, Job 20:4 to 8, Romans 9:13, Matthew 24, Isa. 49:22 to 26, 1 Thessalonian 5:3, 4, Revelation 18 Ch.

Charlestown, July 24th, 1769

TO BE SOLD,
On THURSDAY the third Day of August next,
A CARGO of NINETY-FOUR PRIME, HEALTHY
NEGROES,
CONSISTING OF
Thirty-nine MEN, Fifteen Boys, Twenty-four WOMEN, and Sixteen GIRLS.
JUST ARRIVED, In the Brigantine DEMBIA, Francis Bare, Master, from SIERRA-LEON, by
DAVID & JOHN DEAS.

The so-called Americas and palestine, which the Bible calls the lands of Canaan, was given to the tribes of Israel by the Lord. The so-called white people known in the Bible as The Devil, stole these lands from the Israelites and the other nations; through wickedness, murder, robbery, rape, lies, injustice, torture and slavery. But the Lord says He will pay the so-called white people double for their injustice. Read: PSA 105:10, 11; Ezekiel 35:5 to 10, and 36:1 to 7; Galatians 6:7, Obadiah 1:10, Rev. 13:10, Joel 3 Ch, Daniel 8:25 to 27, Malachi 4:1 to 4.

!ORDER SPEAKING TAPES AND BOOKS!

ready for what they gonna do to us. They want to get us prepared for what's coming, for the ways they gonna come out the closet with they wicked shit. Man, don't sleep on these motherfuckers, kid. This shit is real. They want us to accept anything as okay. You be watching those talk shows, you seein' how they are gettin' us ready for all kind of blasphemy against God, all kind of shit they about to bring on. It used to be that just being homosexual was wrong. Now that shit is accepted, and they got ya'll accepting that shit as normal so they doin' more and more crazy shit. Geraldo got shit like lesbian sisters in love, or men who turn into women and shit. 'Cause they want you ready for the perverted world of chaos they are gonna institute; their new world of chaos. That is the new world order they looking for."

Thomas promises to bring me the documentation for his Hollywood stuff. And he stands by its accuracy. He can prove it, he says, back it up, "back it all the way up." Thomas and Bigs insist that they understand what is going on with black folks in America today, and it has to do with a casting of spells on the populace, the way the mass media literally construct reality. The guys claim to have proof. We talk a little more about television shows and motion pictures, about the country's top-grossing movie at the time, *Stargate*. Jaye Davidson, the male actor who played a man who fooled much of America's movie-going audience into thinking he was a woman in *The Crying Game*, is Ra in *Stargate*, the god of ancient Egyptian fame. And the movie makes Ra an alien from outer space with a raspy and course ("devilish," says Thomas) voice and glowing eyes. Not a god, but a space alien. Thomas finds this alteration particularly meaningful.

"They want us to know they got folk comin' from outer space for our asses," he warns with a solemn grin. "And all day, man, all day, with their movies, their television and their music, they are trying to fatten us up for the slaughter."

New World Orders

As part of the fieldwork experience, Anthroman decides to read/study with Thomas, Bigs, and a few of their Israelite friends. We meet at least once a week for a little more than three months. From the middle of February to the beginning of June, we read books that they assign, getting together to talk about them afterward. I want to be the anthropologist, to get into their heads and hearts and souls, to find out not only what they think and feel, but why. After a couple of weeks, I even start to see myself making some headway, getting some data. I begin to know their points by heart, to get their dogma down. And as I try to do my ethnographic job, they are trying some heart and soul excavating of their own. They want to find out what I'm about, if I am one of those "sellout niggas not worth a shit" (a phrasing from Bigs), someone they are going to have to disavow sooner or later, like when "the war is on and we gotta paint a bull's-eye on your skull while Branch Davidians are dropping bombs from helicopters right over Harlem."[41] And so we talked; we read; we argued.

A month into the whole thing, I know their entire "new world order" argument inside out. They mention it constantly, the world-manipulating Illuminati, a secret society of Devil-worshipping families (Rockefellers, Carnegies, Rothschilds, etc.) trying tirelessly—and successfully!—to control the entire world. I know that these robber baron zillionaires of America's yesteryears were all, according to Bigs and Thomas, Freemasons, as were America's Founding Fathers, each one part of a secret society intent on wrenching the world from the hands of God and "his chosen people," the Black Hebrew Israelites: black, brown, and tan peoples in the Americas.[42]

I have heard these guys wax historical about the King James version of the Bible, the only translation "sanctioned by God and around for all these years." They emphasize the book of Revelation and its invocation of "fake Jews," people now commonly accepted as Jews, they say, embracing a complex kind of anti-Semitism that explicitly overidentifies with Jewishness while concomitantly denouncing it. They decode symbols, deciphering them with a plea to common sense. If Egypt was in Africa and the Egyptians were black, then the Jews had to be a dark-skinned people—even though, I am reminded, the Egyptians are anything but God's people. And "blacks in America are not African."

They want me to understand Black Judaic identity as something passed on by the mother. This is how you know whether someone is really a Black Hebrew Israelite, whether they themselves embrace that truth or not. You consult their genealogical tree—at least the closest branches of it. This is especially important, they stress, for biracial inquirers. If your mother is black, then you are a Black Hebrew. If your father is the black parent, the only black parent from one of the designated Black Hebrew nations in the Americas, then you are not. The difference is hard and fast; the status is rendered unilineally. They cite Ezra, where Shechaniah decides to disavow a non-Jewish wife and offspring, rededicating his life to God's absolute law. They refer to sections of Leviticus and Deuteronomy in the Old Testament. We read the passages; they explain the backstories of the persons mentioned. They even seem genuinely bummed that this matrilineality disqualifies some potentially interested people, but they also stick by what they've been taught—the importance of distinguishing real Jews from impostors—a difference that cannot just be parsed phenotypically.[43]

This version of unilateral descent is very important and does not lose

that significance simply because other Black Hebrew WTUers have offered me understandings of Black Jewish identity that are clearly predicated on a different genealogical reading—that is, the identity is passed
not through the mother, but through *the seed,* the father, a function of
reading identity patrilineally. Even Bigs sometimes seems to imply that a
black father is enough for inclusion—using the Bible's frequent grocery-
listing of males begetting males as a part of that paternal justification.
In either case, the Bible is imagined as final arbiter, and it is used to
read identity through the externally verifiable lens of ancestry: womb of
the mother; begotten by the father. Many people might call themselves
Black Jews, but if they don't fit the proper unilineal formulation, they
are summarily disqualified. This is an authentic model for reckoning
community and gauging the realness of social identity. We can shake one
another's family trees and authenticate/disqualify other people as a
function of what falls out: a white mother, a black father. For the Black
Hebrews, this serves as a kind of foundational belief, one that all of their
other arguments and considerations rest upon.

It will be another ten years before I realize the importance of this
fact, especially of subsequent Black Hebrew attempts to disavow this entire argument, but in 1994, I am less interested in the seed/womb debate
and more fascinated by their readings of the dollar bill: how money is
implicated in every facet of their theories, how everything neatly fits together; nothing innocuous, nothing left to chance. "Coincidence is the
Devil's lies," they tell me again and again. I commit their dollar bill details to memory: Why, Bigs asks, if the first pilgrims came from Europe,
wouldn't they put symbols on their money from the places that they
knew in Europe, "all those big monuments and landmarks and buildings and clocks they so proud of?" Did they use that? No. It is a pyramid and the eye of Horus instead: Egyptian symbols of Freemasonry.
The Illuminati and the Trilateral Commission know the symbolism on
the dollar, they argue, but that demonic coterie tries to keep it from the
masses, to keep it all hidden in plain view. Especially the truth behind
the important number thirteen—a truth as seemingly profound as Minister Louis Farrakhan's Million Man March speech organized around
the symbolic significance of the number nineteen, a nineteen that represents womb and secrecy. Thirteen, nineteen. Nineteen, thirteen. This
thirteen is the number of early American colonies and of brick-levels on
the pyramid in the dollar bill's left circle, and of arrows in the American
eagle's clutches, and of stars above its head. The eagle is also significant; it is the only animal, they reiterate, that can stare straight into the

blazing sun, which they chalk up to more Egyptian mythology, more sun-worshipping devilry. The sun is just a ball of fire, they tell me. Just like hell itself. If you worship the sun, they stress, you are worshipping hell. They make their case matter-of-factly. It is all so much more common sense.

And I hound them with questions, usually based on some of the very little I already half-know about Black Judaism: the Falashas are over in Ethiopia, right? Arthur Wentworth Matthew and those Commandment Keepers don't have anything to do with you all, do they? It's Noah, Abraham, Isaac, and then Jacob, right? And what is the history of the Apocrypha anyway? I even ask for clarification on the Sammy Davis Jr. question—just to be sure. The guys listen respectfully, correcting some of my many mistaken assertions ("Nah, we ain't got nothing whatsoever to do with Reverend Ike"). And as they do, every single thing in their world quickly dissolves into its proper place, reveals its hidden purpose. It is all internally consistent. And what is the end result of all this global dissolution? All this plausibility? It is none other than the highly touted "new world order," *novus ordo seclorum,* also written on the dollar bill. But that is really just another name for an "old hellish chaos," Bigs says. "All of what the Devil says means its opposite. You translate with the opposite."

Bigs keeps going back to A. Ralph Epperson's book *The New World Order,* one of his favorites (and mine too, especially with chapter headings like "Marx, Satanist").[44] His copy has many passages highlighted, words circled, pages dog-eared and worn from rereading. The book's back cover expresses Epperson's fear that his exposing of "the truth" may get him killed by the Satanist powers that be. (And many of the authors we read during those three months begin or end their manuscripts with similar invocations.) However, other than that huge apprehension, Epperson's tales of devilish conspiracies are written with calmness, coolness, an informal and casual style that belies his more paranoid musings. He affects the distant and sanitized language of a seasoned historian. He talks in sure and confident tones about these vengeful Satanists, linking most of the entire world's history to their hidden machinations: the rise of Russian Communism, the motivations of Adolph Hitler, President George Bush going to the Great Pyramid in Egypt in 1999 "to bring in the millennium reign of Lucifer." Inside the body of the theory, all of the elements fit tightly. They only make sense in relation to one another: Bush is ushering in Satanic rule because of his ties to Masonry, his popularizing of the phrase "new world order," his speeches about "a thousand points of light," a reference to the reign of Lord Maitreya. Like all conspiracy theories, it is conspicuous for its internal consistency—again, a would-be structural functionalism, global theory without a passive voice. In this theory, however, Satanism is the driving force: this is not a Durkheimian social solidarity, but a Satanic one.

"Remember, the founding fathers were Masons," Thomas reminds me again, "Children of the sun, and they worshipped the Devil. Most Masons don't know, but that is the truth."

For the guys in my WTU reading group, everything fits. "Nothing is innocent." The Satanic state has us all duped. Yes, a Satanic state, not a welfare state. Big Brother is really Beelzebub. And the truth is all right there in the monuments and on the dollar bill. Plain as day in the money we spend. All around us. The Satanic state is everywhere. It is the master in every tree. Present even when absent. Behind every door, in every object. One day it will pounce on us all: "Come, come! Dash on, dash on!" The Satanic state doing its bewitching thing right under our very noses—casting spells, using magic. The real magic of this state, then, is a literalized, spellbinding, and mind-altering witchcraft that, if anything, has the ability to conceal not its lack of realness, but its super-reality.[45] A state like a motherfucker. "Look at the dollar bill closely," Bigs reviews. "Money is the root of all evil, but not because of what we think." It isn't consumption and capitalism that are to blame, but conspicuous conjuring.

"And the secret society stuff is all over it," Bigs assures me. "Nothing is innocent." The Egyptians, the Freemasons, the Satanists are all there. Rumors and conspiracies and truths and lies all commingling for an instant in preparation for the next inevitable fission. Like the truth and lies and truth and lies in the police car's flashing blue/red lights. The hide-and-seek of the serpent state! A different kind of "snake" in the grass. Its thereness coupled with an equally powerful not-thereness, another "something else" entirely.[46] And I am listening to these guys talk and asking questions. Trying to unpack their stories, to punch holes in their analyses. And they love that. They eat it up. Debate is their forte. "Come on, Ivy Leaguer," they say. "Bring it on!"

"You up in Columbia, so you got access to crazy literature and shit," Tim, another Black Hebrew Israelite, proclaims. "You gotta have access to shit to blow up the spot on the Illuminati, on the Trilateral Commission, on all that shit. You just don't know what to look for, son. Let me up in that library. I'll find them folks telling on themselves. Just let me up in there. I'll blow they whole shit out the water like you wouldn't believe."

Drexler and Shamanism

"Brrrriiinnnnng. Brrrriinngg." The phone rings. I have to finish reading Kafka for class tomorrow, so I want to ignore it. Brrrriiinnnnng!!!! I pick up. It's Bigs.

"Yo, Johnny J. What's up, man?"

"Nothing, reading and shit."

"Yo, I got some shit to tell yo ass. You are gonna trip out, kid. Crazy shit."

"Like what?" I bookmark Kafka, pull out my fieldnotes, and open to a clean sheet.

"Yo, T brought home a tape about the Illuminati that I never heard before. By some ex-witch turned Christian or something. And this white blood was droppin' science on that shit.[47] Telling on folk. He was talking about when he was young. About how he was brought up as a witch and thought everyone was, too. And then he learned that wasn't true. He was from one of them old family of witches who came here with, like, the pilgrims, kid. And like check this out. He dropped a bomb, kid. You know the Salem witch hunts; you know what those really were about?"

"What?" I ask.

"Guess!"

"*Not* witch hunts?"

"Christian hunts! They were witches burning Christians and shit. And like he was taught that. And that the history was changed and shit. Blood was blowin' shit up about shit like actual spells he was taught to do for shit. And then he dropped the nuclear. He got busted for killing somebody, right? He got into a fight and shot some person or some shit, right? When he got to jail, this guy called his father, a major witch, a granddaddy witch, before his court date, right? He asked his daddy witch to say a prayer and cast a spell so that the jury would be lenient. And he says that he only realized how powerful they were when a senator or some shit came by the next day and let him out of jail and gave him cash, son. And told him to go on and do his thing. That was it. And this is gonna trip you out. Guess where he said that he studied most of his witchcraft shit! And from one of the highest warlocks, he said, in the whole fucking thing."

"Where?"

"Guess."

"I don't know, Egypt?"

"Columbia!" He exclaims jubilantly. "Columbia University. Ain't that some shit? The dude that taught his ass was named Arthur Drexler, and guess what the motherfucker taught?"

"Anthropology?" Anthroman responds, finally realizing where Bigs is going.

"Ain't that a trip, man. I told you you sittin' on a gold mine up in that bitch. The guy said that Arthur Drexler taught there and was in charge of the department of anthropology but that all the records were changed to cover it up, the history."

I write feverishly: Drexler: devil? Look up in clio. Witches and Legal Justice System. Chair of Anthropology. Get years. Get dates. Warn folks (hah, hah!).

"Anthropology?" I repeat, skeptically. "What years was he here?"

"I don't have the tape on me, but I'll find out. I'll let you see it, too. You'll bug out. But you are sittin' on some crazy shit, man. Look at that history. Damn! Yo, and like now, what kind of stuff are they teaching you there, kid?"

"I don't know, all kinds of shit, son. It's really about whatever you want to focus on, you know. So I choose my own courses. Sometimes in other departments and shit."

"But is anybody there, like, studying some weird stuff. Like the occult or witchcraft or something?"

"Not really. I mean people are talking about everything. But nothing that would seem like that."

"What kind of books they write?"

"Like on different things. I mean it really is all over the place. Like one professor does stuff on rituals in North Africa, another is like the only one really even remotely like writing about magic—violence and shamanism and stuff."

"Yo, T," Bigs calls out to Thomas, who must be off in another room. "You heard of . . . say that again."

"Shamanism," I say again.

"Spell it," Bigs requests.

"S-h-a-m-a-n-i-s-m."

"Sha-man-ism," he pronounces, "you heard of that shit, T?"

"Yeah, it is something like those witch doctors and shit," Thomas answers from a distance.

"Oh shit," Bigs returns to me. "You gotta be on the ball with that, J. Yo, I'm about to break. But don't blow up the spot about that shit. Just chill and shit. You are right there with that shit. You gotta let me know what's up. Let me read some of their shit. I know they tellin' on themselves. Keep your eyes open, alright?"

We hang up, and I pick up Kafka. I want to do more reading, but can't concentrate. I have full phrases written out from the phone conversation, so I create a transcript from memory for my ethnographic records. Tomorrow, I'll get that tape from Bigs and find out the dates of this Drexler's supposed stint. I turn off the light and try to fall asleep. The faster I go to sleep the sooner I can head out for the library in the morning. But my body is charged; I can't fall asleep. It's only 10:30 p.m., and the university's libraries don't close until midnight. I'm not in Brooklyn anymore, I think to myself. It was a big deal for me, two months earlier, when I finally decided to move closer to campus, three short blocks from the school's library—and for situations just like this. In a flash, my front door slams behind me, and I am sprinting down Amsterdam Avenue.

I look up Arthur Drexler on CLIO (Columbia's computerized library catalog) and find several books on architecture. I retrieve them from the stacks and check them out at the circulation desk, but not before skimming through them quickly, looking at the designs and photographs inside. I search for clues the way Thomas or Bigs might: How many floors in that building? And what is the shape of this other one? I want to have some information ready to go when I get to Brooklyn, when Thomas and Bigs examine the texts. I'll have to sleep on it; think about things. It's 11:55 p.m. by the time I retrieve my material from the stacks, and I struggle to keep them from falling as I scurry through the library doors and out into the darkness of the night.

Walking home with this Drexler information, an uneasy creepiness washes over me. I'm spooked. Scared. Just like that night with the badge-dangling police officers knocking on my mom's parked Mazda. I didn't realize it until right then, until just that second, walking through the pouring rain from Columbia's library, umbrellaless, hatless, with books of possibly Satanic architecture precariously stuffed under my armpits. Getting wet, I want to run home. Not to get out of the rain. The water was fine—tangible, physical, material. I want to get out of the meta-physicalities of the night. All this talk of spellcasting witches and Satanic subliminality has the Seventh-Day Adventist boy in me freaked. But no, not like in my mom's car with the badge-around-the-neck cop-alikes. Not like sitting in one of my graduate courses at Columbia—classes where I sometimes trembled at the thought of uttering a single word. Not even scared like I feel, almost a decade later, writing the chapters for this book—that they are nowhere, all over the place, nonanthropological. More than any of those things, walking through the rain that night, I am scared of my own rational uncertainties. I look all around me, asking Anthroman to protect my vulnerable soul. Invisible Satanic eyes might surely be plotting.

As a child, I was always scared of the dark, of ghosts and demons coming to get me from bedroom closets in the blackness of the night, of being possessed, against my will—just like that girl in the movie *The Exorcist,* losing my soul to some supernatural, bean-soup-regurgitating *other.* As far as I know, it has never happened, but the thought is harrowing enough. And besides the terror of demonism, it must also be rather embarrassing to get possessed. What do you say to people afterward, once you come to? How do you apologize for that, go on with your life as though it never happened? It would be just as bad, I think, if the "other" in question were "Holy," and I were sitting in my godmother's friend's tiny living room-qua-church on a sunny Sunday morning. But how much worse still if I were possessed by "something else"? Someone else? Some other kind of spirit? Demons, demons everywhere. I know that if there are demons, they must be all around me on Amsterdam Avenue this night, especially as I make my return from the library at midnight, the witching hour—evil architectural books in my grasp and demonically coded, crumpled-up dollar bills in my front pockets.

I start talking out loud to myself in the rain—first singing a song. It might have been an old Negro spiritual. Or maybe a gospel tune? "And I'm glad, I'm glad, I'm glad that God made John." But then my thoughts and words change drastically: "Is this white dude following me, the one with the green, oval glasses?" "That corner looks strange, weird. This alley, too." And I can't even begin to form thoughts about what kinds of wicked goblins lay waiting in the expanse of the park across the street from my new apartment building. I try to laugh myself out of it, walking briskly, almost jogging, my pulse strong and fast. Somehow, I eventually make it home. When I do, once I do, I bolt the door, sneak peeks outside from my guarded first-floor window, and wait the dark night out.

Maybe anthropologists have a hard time dealing with their own culture because it won't be quiet to criticism, won't quiet down and just be talked about, won't shut up and be studied, already. Forcing monologues into dialogues, or even glossalia-like conversational free-for-alls, it insists on talking back—and in a language that the anthropologist knows all too well. Like a real thing. Irrepressibly ethnographrenic. Too many voices, too much backtalk, can make one crazy, ethnographically speaking, especially when every voice wants to be on equal footing.[48] As a teenager, I used to sleep with the lights on at night. I still do—sometimes. I am still afraid of the dark, to write it, to read it, to even think it—especially when the darkness can speak back.

The next day Anthroman is writing tons of notes, even more than usual, scribblings about Satanism and how "The State" is made magical, fictional, and real all at once; about the WTU's distrust of government agencies, a distrust that is foundational for most conspiracy theories.[49] That same night, some eighteen hours after my midnight library trip, I bring the Drexler books to Thomas, Bigs, and their buddy Damon, who first introduced me to the idea of "soultheft." The three look the stuff over carefully. They all agree that "this has to be the guy," or at least a clue to his existence. And they bet that if we examine the buildings closely, we will "catch him telling on himself because," I'm reminded, "Esau always, always does."

After we talk for an hour about Drexler, architecture, and anthropology, I read them the title for an early draft of this very chapter, preliminarily titled, "The Satanic State: White Conspiracies and Black Prejudices." Immediately, Damon jumps up to take issue.

"Black folk can't be prejudice," he declares, shaking his head and waving his hands emphatically. "The way I see it, it's like this and shit: Prejudice means to prejudge. To judge before the facts. To prejudge someone is to judge before you meet them. Like what the Europeans did when they were on their merry way to Africa for slaves. They judged before they knew. Now, after four hundred years of living through slavery, and the slave trade, and all that shit, after seeing racism and genocide and all that, we can't ever be labeled prejudgers of shit. We are judging, but it is after over four hundred years of evidence has been rolling in on these motherfuckers. If we are anything, we are *postjudice*. We judge them based on their history. Based on knowing what they are capable of doing. Black folk can't be prejudice. We are postjudice, and that is just using your God-given common sense and knowing your damn history."

5 Real Publics

When the revolution comes, Jesus Christ is going to be standing on the corner of Lenox Ave and 125th Street, trying to catch the first gypsy cab out of
Harlem.   **The Last Poets**

Modern science— genetics and anthropology— continually affirms that modern
man descends from African origins, supporting the Biblical historical account. . . . To conclude then that the anointed messiah of God is/will be an African image is not a stretch of the imagination or a fit of "reverse racism." It
is the logical expectation.   **Ahmadiel Ben Yehuda**

Only God can judge me now.   **Tupac Shakur**

: : :

The Other Daughter

Bill doesn't discuss his eldest daughter, Denise, with
nearly the excitement and long-windedness that characterize most of his declarations about the difference between "sucking wind" and following racial destinies. Instead, he grows uncharacteristically silent. It was months
before I even realized that he had another daughter. Bill
would almost rather just shake his head, suck his teeth,
and shrug her off into some kind of silent nonexistence—
anything but talk at length about their difficult relationship. When he and I first met, Bill hadn't seen Denise for

several months. She, her mom, and her little sister still talked regularly, but she and Bill were estranged. It would take a few months for me to get the story and connect it to my own preoccupations with Black Judaism in New York City.

"Do you know any of the Black Hebrew Israelites up here?" I idly ask.

Harlem, 2003. Bill and I are sitting outside, along Frederick Douglass Boulevard, our backs pressed against the storm-gated storefront of that two-story walk-up precariously housing his eviction-threatened loft. Dozens of astrology and health books are splayed out on two flimsy tabletops in front of us. "I want to do some research with the Black Hebrews while I'm here this trip," I continue. "Do you know them, the group up the street? They used to be in the building with Sharpton's organization, but I think that space burned down or something. Do you know anyone over there?"[1]

"They can't tell you anything about Harlem," Bill dismisses, scanning the far corner of our block for any potential customers. "Why would you want to waste your time with them? They can't tell you anything about Harlem—nothing."

"Why do you say that?"

"Because they're mixed up. They don't know if they're coming or going. They are the worst thing that could ever happen to black people in Harlem. Just silliness."

"You don't think they're trying to be revolutionary?"

"Revolutionary? What revolutionary? Those uneducated dress-wearers? You seen them walking up and down here in their dresses? Men who wear dresses, what revolution is that? Give me a break. You not thinking about joining some nonsense like that? Don't make me lose what little respect I have for you. I'd rather you just got back to your momma's teat in North Carolina."

"I want to study them," I respond, "figure out how they see the world."

"Crooked."

A heavy-set black woman approaches the vending table. Bill stands up and hands her, unsolicited, a short "how-to" on fasting for weight loss and improved health. She takes the thin paperback from him and opens to an arbitrary page. Bill talks to both of us as she skims.

"This book is a great investment. It can save your life. *You need to stay with me and help save these people. Forget about that Black Jew nonsense.* Just give me whatever you want. However much you want for it. You decide. *We have work to do. We have a people to save.* Don't walk away from the table without this book, sister. Give me whatever you want for it, but don't go home without it. Not today. This guy here, he's an anthropologist studying Harlem, and he wants to see black people helping themselves. So you should help him out by doing that. Pay whatever you want to, but invest in yourself and your future."

After his persuasive appeal, the young woman turns a few more pages and fishes a dollar bill from her pocketbook. She hands it over to Bill and heads up the street. "Thank you, sister." Bill hollers at her back while she walks away. After squeezing the dollar into his pants pocket, he slaps his palms together exuberantly. "There's hope! There is hope. See that? That is what keeps me here. At least she had on a nice dress, no pants that don't fit her, even though she's a little big. But she knows she's big, and she respects herself by dressing appropriate. I did my job. I got her the knowledge. Now it's up to her. She has to do the work. I'll ask her about the book the next time I see her. I'll be able to tell you if she's read it. I'll see it in her eyes. And if she has, it'll open up her mind to want more. Knowledge does that. So I'm increasing my client base, too. That's how the math works. One at a time."

"What if she doesn't read it? If she comes by again, and you can tell she hasn't read it, do you keep selling her books she's not reading? How does that help her?"

"If her spirit's telling her to stop and look, I'll make sure I have something for her to take. If she won't read it now, she'll read it later. All I can do is lead them to water. They'll drink when they can't take the thirst anymore. They'll drink or die. That's the only law of the world: survival of the fittest. Survival of the fittest! Drink or die! No one can drink for you. You have to put your head down and take it for yourself."

"And you don't think some people save themselves by drinking what the Black Hebrews provide them with?"

"Get them out of your head, boy!" Bill scolds. "You're like the worst broken record. Let it go. You need to stop talking about them and start with how you can help me over here. You see all these books we have to get out there, all this knowledge. I can't do it alone. I need you here, helping me figure out what to do with these books, to help me do this the way it should be done. Then we'll be doing something—something powerful! This is the knowledge. I have it. I have it. I just need help getting people to see it. Getting people to wake up to their destiny. Think about how much better we'd be as a people if we just followed our own destiny and didn't just do whatever white folks told us to do. Think about it. Can you imagine that?"

"Isn't that what the Black Hebrews are talking about? Very differently, but still . . ."

"You are crazy," he interrupts. "All they do is shout nonsense at people who they hope don't know the difference."

"You ever had any run-ins with them?"

"You can't help but run into them, if you have half a brain and won't let them program it, brainwash it. But you can't even have a conversation with someone so far gone as that. They won't be able to hear what you say to them. They just say things and don't even know what they're saying. If that's who you want to speak to, you're worse off than I thought. You might as well go back to Duke University, because you don't know a thing about what black people need in Harlem."

With specters of soulthievery, postjudiceness and racialized social destinies suspended in the ethnographic background, this chapter looks at one specific version of the contemporary black public sphere, a gendered and decidedly religified rendition of the much-celebrated "marketplace of ideas" to which someone like Bill regularly contributes foodstuffs or books or just his own opinionated rhetoric.[2] The most famous intellectual discussant of the public sphere, Jürgen Habermas, imagines that space to be enabled by capital and ordered by principles of rationality and articulate debate.[3] He envisions a civil conversation hostile to authorities that are simply status-based, immune to irrationalities and unfalsifiable claims, purged of groundless, unexamined, or superstitious beliefs about, say, numerological predictions, Satanic Hollywood producers, wonder-working powers of the Holy Ghost, and worldwide conspiracies to sterilize already marginalized black men.

This chapter offers up a gendered and spiritualized black public sphere rife with rational discourses aimed at seemingly illogical or unreasonable ends: the decades-long accumulation of thousands upon thousands of unfiled newspaper clippings haphazardly strewn across a Harlem office floor; lengthy and heated curbside debates about supposedly Pangaeac forms of African American identity; swabs of trademarked genetic tests for determining African tribal particularities; and revisionist WTU ruminations on the impossibilities of identity-based genealogies. These moments help to trace the boundaries and interpenetrations that overdetermine any analysis of sincere and authentic racial ideologies. I want to examine this particular black public sphere as a counterpoint to more vulgar appropriations of Habermas, a counterpublic to mainstream assumptions about the hyperrational public sphere, situating the beliefs of WTU Hebrew Israelites in a wider context that highlights their attempt at a kind of anticipatory sincerity amid the confines of their own cosmological authentications. Just as "extreme" conspiracy theories mix postures of confident certainty with hints of ever-lingering doubt, so is the black public sphere shot through with almost seamless integrations of rational and irrational forgings of community, an occult-like economy that encapsulates all forms of racial thinking.[4] This is a black public sphere almost completely controlled and populated by men, marked off as a space of male agency and power, characterized by an idiom of rhetorical violence and competitive conspiratorial theorizing. It is also a place where sincerity meets up with authenticity on crowded city sidewalks, gesturing toward the "structures of feeling" that reinforce and outstrip discourses of external authority.[5]

AFRAM News

I schedule a noon meeting with Paul Wilson, someone who, in the late 1990s, used to share a tiny second-floor office with the Harlem Tenant's Council, Netta Bradshaw's activist group—that is, before Bradshaw and company moved into a new building three blocks east and just down the hall from the WTU Black Hebrews. A locally celebrated journalist, archivist, and "vernacular intellectual," Wilson is also a massive trafficker in public information.[6] Every square inch of his tiny office floor is always covered with newspaper clippings relevant to African American politics and culture, clippings he carefully cuts down to size, photocopies, and then forwards along to his national mailing list of academics, business people, and students. If anyone can find me a secular point of entry into this sacralized public sphere, especially with respect to the WTUers, this man most surely can.

Wilson started AFRAM, what he calls a "public service communication agency," in the late 1960s. He wanted to produce his own personal archive of black history through contemporary periodicals and their coverage of current events. Any time I had previously paid him a visit, announced or not, he was always hard at work, scouring newspapers (dailies, weeklies, monthlies) and clipping articles connected to African American life. While he did, an otherwise shrill and feedback-prone hearing-aid was invariably turned off, so I was forced to find creative ways of getting his attention, something besides uselessly calling out his name from the hallway—and without inadvertently stepping on any of the newspaper articles that carpeted his office floor.

On the few prior occasions when we have had lunch together, Wilson has walked me one block west to Manna's restaurant, fast becoming one of Harlem's most famous lunchtime institutions, especially since getting revamped in the mid-1990s, a gentrification-induced interior and exterior makeover that also bankrolled the restaurant's further expansion eastward to a second branch just around the corner from the WTUers and their new nightly meeting space. At Manna's, Wilson and I scoop fried fish and starchy side dishes from hot metal bins before walking upstairs to sit and talk. He usually regales me with his personal stories about Malcolm X, whom he knew well for many years. Wilson tells me about his own earlier academic years at Columbia University, about his youth activism, about the history behind his newspaper fetish, which began the day Malcolm X was assassinated, a kind of silent homage to his fallen friend. Wilson embodies the self-conscious historicity of a place like Harlem. He marks the tiniest alterations in its symbolic and demographic landscape—keeps track, assesses implications, passes on information. This is some of the reason why he seems to know everyone who has ever stepped foot in the neighborhood—and even has news stories on half of them. So if anybody could help me reconnect with the Black Hebrew Israelites, I thought to myself, listening to him describe the interpersonal charisma of Malcolm, it would be Wilson.

Putting aside my paper plate of ravaged fish bones and half-eaten potato salad, I give Wilson a little background on my work. Some of it I have told him several times before, but since he doesn't know me very well, or see me very often, he usually forgets the details between visits. So I summarize my first book on Harlem, which I had given him more than a year earlier, my current ethnographic interest in sincerity as a critique of authenticity discourse, and my past stint studying with the WTUers in Crown Heights, Brooklyn. I tell him about my Seventh-Day Adventist childhood, a religion-filled youth that organized my everyday social activities as a teenager and continues to subtly shape my understanding of physical and metaphysical questions.[7] The denomination's strict policing of bodily adornments (no jewelry, not even wedding bands, no makeup or pants for women, no beads in the hair) and cultural performances (no Christmas trees, no movies, no work or socializing on Friday nights and Saturdays) informed the kinds of idiosyncratic reactions I would later have to religious cults and spiritual sects, and probably helps to explain, I tell Wilson, my current fascination with the WTUers.[8]

After giving him more details about Seventh-Day Adventist practices, I describe how I used to borrow Columbia University library books for a few of those WTUers, how they would debate me on history and theology, prophesy and contemporary world events. I go into a long aside about Bigs and Thomas, the two Black Hebrews I knew best. I tell him more about Thomas, who grew up in East Flatbush, Brooklyn, during the deindustrializing 1980s of supply-side Reaganomics.

Wilson sits patiently as I recount how Thomas spent his childhood with a Pentecostal mother who spoke in tongues, attended church five times a week, read her Bible incessantly, complained to him about his lack of religious commitment, and demonized anything that was not a direct mandate from the Word of God. This was even a stricter religiosity than the Seventh-Day Adventist bans on movies and jewelry that I grew up with, and it helped Thomas and I to identify with one another in powerful ways. Thomas's mother explicitly marked linkages between worldliness and Satanism, a move that presaged Thomas's later philosophy as part of the WTU group.

As hip-hop music and culture became conspicuous on the streets of New York City, Thomas's mother's response to this musical genre was clear and harsh.[9] This is the Devil's music, she would say, music in service to Satan and his dominion. To deejay or emcee, to poprock or uplock, meant manifesting a Satanism not tolerated in her household. I explain to Wilson how Thomas spent his teenage years in classic youthful rebellion, smuggling hip-hop cassettes and turntables into their house, teaching himself how to scratch with the mixer and turntables hidden underneath his twin-size bed—bonding with the local hip-hop scene while challenging his mother on the extremism of her Satanist rants. Periodically, she would find a Grandmaster Flash album or a cassette tape of Mr. Magic's WBLS show (recorded straight off the radio), and she would scream and yell and call the minister to bless the house anew, all the while threatening to throw Thomas into the street for his Satanic predilections. This went on throughout his high school years, I tell Wilson. Sometimes Thomas was kicked out of their two-bedroom home and forced to live with relatives in New York—sent to stay with his father in Florida, or with an uncle in Washington, D.C. By the time he turned twenty, amid all of those battles, Thomas had given up his high-top fade for a full beard (as full as he could muster at such a young age) and became a WTU Israelite after attending a few informal meetings at a friend's Crown Heights apartment.

Indulging me, Wilson nods when I tell him that I first met Thomas while I was still a graduate student, only a few years after his conversion, and that Thomas was adamant about showing me why his Black Hebrew beliefs made so much more sense than his mother's "irrational" Pentecostalism. One of the first things he tried to "teach" me (and pedagogy became the defining dynamic of our interactions) was the fact that the word *religion* comes from a root that means "to bind or hold back." Religion holds you back, he would say. It binds you. Black Hebrew Israelites don't believe in a religion; they believe in "the truth." Only the truth can set you free, the truth that blacks in the Americas were actually not Africans, but the Israelites of biblical lore, a fact of history distorted and concealed by global conspirators hell-bent (literally) on deceiving God's "chosen people." I surprise myself with the amount of Thomas's story that I can remember so many years later—more, I am sure, than Wilson had wanted to hear. All the while, of course, as I go on and on about Thomas and Adventism and sincerity and my dissertation's thesis, Wilson constantly readjusts the vacillating volume on his faulty hearing aid, punctuating my overlong monologue with sharp whistling sounds from the speaker in his left ear. As I apologize for my verbosity, I also realize that I am talking as much for myself as for Wilson, in an attempt to dissipate my own ethnographic remorse, feeling guilty about abandoning Thomas for a subsequent Harlem project that became my dissertation. I end my spiel to Wilson by explaining how I eventually lost contact with Thomas upon relocating from Brooklyn to Morningside Heights in the mid-1990s.

"So I don't know where these guys are," I conclude. "I don't even know anyone in the group these days, but I see that they have a new meeting place on Madison. And since you know so many people in Harlem, I thought you might know someone over there who could introduce me around and help me to interview some of them."

"I know the group you're talking about," Wilson says, shaking his head apologetically, but he doesn't know anyone over there. He finds them to be very insular and not particularly friendly. He does have some contemporary articles about the group in Israel he says I should look at, and even some information about the Falashas from Ethiopia, but he doesn't know anyone who can introduce me.

For Wilson, the newspaperman, WTUers are an unconventional oddity that might merit a curious aside now or then, but they are hardly real news. He represents a hard and fast objectivity vis-à-vis the public sphere. His articles emphasize facts, specific details, evolving shreds of emergent history. This version of the black public sphere understands WTU machinations as atavistic ravings, more distraction (or disgrace) than valid sociohistorical reality.

I help Wilson down Manna's steps, and we stroll back to his office, where he gives me a few photocopied articles for the road and goes back to more newspaper clipping. Feeling thwarted, I head downstairs and out into the hot sun. I know enough to realize that the WTU Black Hebrews will be skeptical of my anthropological project unless someone they know and trust can vouch for me. A local patriarch like Wilson would have been a good bet—but even that might not have been enough. The WTUers inhabit a world of undeniably duplicitous realities; they can't trust anything; they take nothing at face value: the seen is only evidence for the real if read against the grain of its most adamant purported claims, against its own assumed authenticities. Remember that reality for WTUers is mapped along the conspicuously hidden signs and symbols of dollar bills, traced along the mere asides to dominant narratives of national history. The literal must be mined for the figural, the metaphorical, and these same metaphors are only ever useful, only every truthful, only ever *real,* once unmasked in the public sphere for all their popularly concealed literalities. Theirs is a world overrun by the materiality of, say, mass media's wooden weaponry, Satanic sunshine, and a planetary rotation fueled by governmental pronouncements about new world orders. The WTUers could not nearly take me at face value, even and especially when a proven warlockian institution like Columbia University—with its own Drexlered history—is the very place from which I'm vetted.

After leaving Wilson's office, I walk westward on 125th Street so as to pass the Harlem WTU's new space. I have made this walk dozens of times, usually to meet informants in front of Bradshaw's building or to watch the young black and Hispanic men and women congregate separately (by gender) outside on the street before their nightly WTU events. From the curb, I see that a Star of David dresses one of the group's second-story windows, along with a black Lion of Judah. A gold-trimmed awning frames it all. I nervously head upstairs, first walking past the group's closed door and down to the Harlem tenant activists' office at the end of the hallway. I ask Bradshaw about her new Black Jewish neighbors, and she responds positively, even if it is clear she doesn't quite get what they are about. She rarely sees them, she admits, but when she does, they are always polite and respectful.

"Sometimes, I'll have boxes or bags to bring up," she says, "and they'll say, 'We'll take that for you.' They never give us any problems. You hardly see them, really."

I return to the WTU's locked door. I stop and stare at its new world mapping of the Twelve Tribes and its posted operating hours: every evening from 7 p.m. until 10 p.m.—and just about all day and night on Saturdays. I copy the hours in my Anthropad, careful not to look too suspicious (in a COINTELPRO kind of way) and bound down the stairwell, four steps at a time, back into the sun-drenched street. I walk over to Bill's vending table to see what he is up to and to plan the rest of my afternoon. When I get there, he suggests that I accompany him to Queens in the morning.

"You should come along," he says, "if you want to."

"I will," I agree, "but I'll have to make sure to get back by 6:30 or so."

"We won't stay out there that late. Just a couple of hours. If you get to the church by ten, you can cut some watermelons with me in the morning, and then we can go."

"Sounds like a plan."

"What do you have to do afterward? I can take you to mid-town and show you some of the street photographers I used to work with when I took pictures down there of tourists and stuff. Most of the people I used to work with are gone, but some are still out there, a few."

"I'm going to see your favorite people tomorrow night," I say, smiling sarcastically. "The Black Hebrew Israelites. I've decided to just go to one of their nightly meetings and see what's up."

"What? We'll go to Queens," Bill says, shaking his head in disgust, "and then I'll take you to 42nd Street. Forget about that other nonsense. Not tomorrow."

"You have no love for them, hunh? None."

Bill finishes packing his books away and wipes some sweat from his forehead.

"You know, my other daughter, Denise," he says, "the one you haven't met; she married one of them fools. And now he has her brainwashed. Won't let me see my grandchildren. Won't let me see my daughter. He's filling her mind with all kinds of thoughts against me and how I raised her, what I do. Trust me when I tell you they are a waste of your time."

"I didn't know that about your daughter. How long has she been with this guy?"

"A while now. I can't remember. A couple years. I really messed up with that one, and now they have her. And I probably won't get her back. They try to hold on to you and dig you in deeper and deeper."

"And she just won't speak to you?"

Bill shakes his head and starts to rearrange a few books in his carrying case. We both remain silent for a few minutes until Bill sits back down on his red canvas stool and, with no segue, starts to tell me how great tomorrow will be in Queens. He thinks that we will get lucky, that maybe I will even have a chance to finally meet the twenty-five-year-old woman he always talks about, the one he says wants to join his family and help him run his business. He complains that the watermelon prices have been a little high for a few days now, and so he hopes they start dropping soon. He will probably buy two in the morning and then see how they sell. I sit with him for the rest of the day. As the sun starts to

set, I head home, leaving Bill by himself as he waits for Gina in the coolness of dusk.

Street Spiritualities

The Worldwide Truthful Understanding group is not nearly the most
provocative or exotic segment of Harlem's current spiritual landscape,
its idiosyncratic version of the black public sphere. Not even close. Every
day, around the corner from Bill's loft space, you will find a different as-
sembly of young black men debating philosophical and religious theories right out there on the sidewalk, just across the street from Wilson's
office and "the white man's Apollo" Theater.[10] The men hover around
one particular vending table where a thirty-something black man affiliated with the Nation of Islam, Brother Bey, a vendor and videographer,
sells informational VHS tapes about black history, culture, politics, and
religion. Bey helps cultivate this small, spiritually inflected public sphere
by videotaping these sidewalk discussions and marketing them for sale
as part of a series he calls *125 Street: Live, Raw, and Real.* His *125
Street* series is shot with a Canon mini-DV camera that he keeps under
the vending table, alongside extra copies of taped lectures by African-
centered scholars from a variety of religious and political perspectives,
people like Khallid Muhammad, Ivan Van Sertima, Ashra Kwesi,
Frances Cress Welsing, James Smalls, and Dr. Ben.[11] But his *125 Street*
tapes are particularly powerful. Tape 2 in that series, which I purchased
along with a videotaped lecture on Judaism's African origins, is organized around the laminated and enlarged copies of early twentieth-
century lynchings that Bey keeps taped to the front of his vending table.
Most prominent is the 1935 Ft. Lauderdale lynching of a homeless tenant farmer named Rubin Stacy, accused of attacking a white woman,
Marion Jones, and killed as a consequence.[12] A group of masked men
stole him from the local authorities and hung his body from a tree—that
is, after first riddling the black body with bullets (and before taking off
their masks for subsequent pictures besides the flaccid corpse).

The front of Brother Bey's table is lined with several laminated lynchings, eight in all, each one enlarged and binder-clipped to the kente
tablecloth underneath his neatly aligned VHS tapes. These images include the burned remains of Texan Jesse Washington hanging from a
telephone pole in 1916; a fancily dressed Laura Nelson dangling above
an Oklahoma river in 1911; Lige Daniels, killed in Center, Texas, in
1920; and John Richards, suspended from a tree in Wayne County,
North Carolina in 1916. During the first two decades of the twentieth

century, some of these same photos were callously used as postcards and mailed by white Americans to distant family members, often along with brief and indifferent details about the lynchings depicted on them. Bey makes sure some passersby realize this specific fact.

In volume 2 of his *125 Street: Live, Raw, and Real,* Bey uses the lynching images to start on-camera conversations with a random selection of passing pedestrians about the history of American racial violence. He videotapes their responses to his questions, along with just about anything else that transpires in front of the camera's lens, his handheld microphone intermittently thrust into the picture frame. The responses captured on video are varied and riveting: a French-accented tourist who uses the word *nigger* and gets called "the mother of all bitches" for chalking that error up to linguistic ignorance; a shouting, straw-hatted black man who proclaims that prayer is useless to black people, advocating the death of "black devils and white devils" alike, and praising nineteenth-century white abolitionist John Brown, "who loved niggers more than they love their God-damn selves." [13]

In *125 Street,* Bey's camera captures a wide assortment of Harlem pedestrians: An Australian man in a NYPD baseball cap confesses, after much prodding, that he learned black people were "niggers" by looking at television, but refuses to imagine his mother and father implicated in any of the laminated lynchings displayed—even though Bey assures him that the blood of the white people pictured at the lynching runs through his own Australian veins. Preteen Trinidadian boys and girls, when asked about the lynching photographs, smilingly agree—with a shy nod of their heads—that "the white man is the Devil." Hip-hop artists Stic.man and M-1, from the group Dead Prez, explain that their mainstream record company dropped them because of their race-conscious politics. Former Nation of Islam minister Conrad Muhammad is asked to justify his recent conversion "backward" to Christianity, a religion, Bey reminds him, that underpinned American lynching in the south. Crown Heights activist Richard Green is accused of being a "boot-licking, buck-dancing Uncle Tom," a "sellout" scared to call white people devils and paid off by Giuliani to condemn the Million Youth March in 1998.[14] A gray-headed Latino preaches on the World Trade Center. An irate, dread-locked Rastafarian yells at Bey for implying that black people cannot also be "devils"—and for moving around him with the camera instead of standing still and letting him talk. "You the white man's nigger," Bey screams back. "You ain't no real rasta, man. You ain't real. You an impostor." A husky, bald black man lectures Bey on the meaning of the word *devil,* which he says comes from the word *double,* and should be embraced by black people because the name Lucifer comes from Lucy, the ancient black fossil found in Africa. These are only the tip of the iceberg in terms of what one finds on Bey's three-hour tape—and what one hears during an average conversation at his packed vending table.

Most of the time when I walk past Bey's table, there is a crowd of some ten to fifteen men around it, often engaged in heated conversations—with or without Bey's mini-DV camera recording/prompting the proceedings. They debate the history of blacks in America, the fault lines of contemporary local, national, and international politics, the relative merits of particular religious denominations. Members from the Nuwaubian Nation of Moors (Yamassee Native America Nuwaubian), the Black Hebrew Israelites, the Black Muslims, the Five Percent nation, the Egiptian Church of Karast/Christ, and others debate one another right in front of Bey's table, a dramatic example of black male commitments to displays of intellectualism. And each group has its own setup within a block or two of Bey's: a Nation of Islam Mosque around the corner, the Black Hebrew Israelite school down the street, Nuwaubian pamphleteers at the nearest intersection, and Karast followers selling CDs and books at the end of the block.

Passing Bey's table one Saturday afternoon, I catch a former Nuwaubian debating a member of the Karast group, arguing that both communities were started by the same Nuwaubian leader, Dr. Dwight York, a thirty-something black man believed, by his disciples, to have arrived via UFO in 1970 from the Illyuwn galaxy—promising them that 144,000 Nuwaubians would be taken back to the planet Rizq.[15] York, whose group was famous for its 476-acre compound in Georgia's Putnam County, had recently pled guilty to seventy-five counts of child molestation, and Brother Bey (who has the confession on tape, but won't sell it) wonders aloud how the guest at his table could ever have followed an admitted pedophile.

"You don't know if he did it," the man defends.

"I have it on tape," Bey responds. "He's admitting it, with four- and five-year-old boys. I have it on tape. I own it. What kind of spiritual leader is that?"

"You have him on tape having sex with kids?"

"Not having sex," Bey clarifies, "are you listening? On the stand, in court, putting his hand on the Bible and admitting to raping children. That's your leader. And I thought you all weren't even supposed to put your hands on Bibles, isn't that what he teaches?"

"We don't."

"So why do I have him on tape with his hand on the Bible in the white man's court, the Devil's court, admitting that he raped young boys? What's up with that?"

"That is mind control," another black man chimes in, "mind control and hypnotism. That's how they got all these black people believing in space ships from other planets and whatnot. Mind control."

"Where do you think blackness comes from?" York's former follower responds. "Blackness, null and void, without light. That's outer space."

Six guys jockey for discursive space in a heated debate about the limits of space, about the lynching pictures, about the realities of racial difference. Another black man claims, to Bey's chagrin, that those are not his ancestors on the laminated sheets at all. There are some people, he says, like himself, who are indigenous to the United States. They may look like other black folks, but they aren't.

"What do you mean these ain't your ancestors?" Bey challenges. "You white?"

"No."

"So what are you talking about?"

"You might have come over on slave ships with slavery, but that is not the history of my people. Some of us, who look like you, were here before the continents drifted. We have always been here. And we are different from those brought over on the ships. We weren't made to work as slaves, and if we were it was a mistake. That [he points to the lynchings] is not *my* history."

"You Native American?" someone asks, which is met with a few dismissive chuckles.

"Not in the way you think. I was here before America was formed, geologically. I was here when the land was one. Before what they call *continental drift.*"

"Man, you just don't want to be black," Brother Bey dismisses, shaking his head. "That white supremacy has your mind." A few more guys join in the head shaking.

"No," the man responds, undaunted, "white supremacy is that your narrowness of being needs me to be what you need me to be for you to be you. White supremacy is your black shit." When I leave, two hours later, they are still going strong, and Bey is only then beginning to take out his camera. I decide to come back and buy the tape whenever I can.

African Ancestry

Brother Bey's vending-table debates are not the only rearticulations of racial discourse at play in contemporary black public spheres, not the only example of racial authentication at heightened levels of analytical complexity, levels beyond what we might take for granted as common-sense and everyday understandings of race. African Ancestry is a business based in Washington, D.C., that specializes in testing people's DNA for particular traces of African genetic material. Dr. Rick Kittles, the anthropologist co-owner, was working with bones found in the excavated African burial ground uncovered in lower Manhattan in the early 1990s and formalized a method to check those bones for genetic information about the geographical specificities of that disinterred population.[16] During an interview about the testing process, a journalist asked him if he could use the same DNA test on living samples, which he thought he probably could (even if the idea had never crossed his mind), and within a week, the national newswire services had picked up the claim, running stories about a Howard University anthropologist who could test people for "African DNA." Over the next few months, Kittles received dozens of e-mails a day from people requesting to take the test.

"It is a need emanating straight out of the community itself," Gina Paige says. She is the MBA-brain behind the operation, having left corporate America to help Kittles launch African Ancestry a couple years before. "There are very rarely new products. Just better brands of old products: new tartar control toothpaste, new and improved cleaning fluid. But this was a brand-new product altogether, something new that filled an almost ancient need. I jumped on it." That is why they don't publicize, she says. There is no need. They can barely handle the clients they get from word of mouth alone.

African Ancestry is housed in a one-room, third-floor office along the Washington, D.C./Silver Spring, Maryland, border, with a large, multi-colored map of Africa hung on its otherwise sparsely decorated walls. Kittles and Paige worked from their homes for the first six months of the business, with little more than cell phones and laptops to keep the operation afloat. They wanted to set African Ancestry up as a supplement to the genealogical work already being done by the many groups that chart family trees through archival and historical research.[17] Their method does not supplant such carefully culled research, Kittles maintains. It is only a minor extension of it. They say that they have to be very clear with people about what they can offer, genetically speaking. They are testing for far less than 1 percent of an individuals' genetic makeup, just a tiny sliver of the overall genome. So the test cannot, say, tell someone definitively and completely, once and for all, what part of Africa his or her enslaved ancestors came from, which is usually what people want to know. It only provides information about one specific ancestor from among hundreds or thousands that might have existed in different places at different times throughout Africa or around the world—one itty-bitty stalk of hay in a mountainous haystack.

African Ancestry has two distinct tests for two different pieces of transgenerational data, tests for Y-chromosomes and mitochondrial DNA. Both are clonally inherited—that is, they are transferred from parents to children without any major change to their genetic structure: Y-chromosomes from fathers to sons, and mitochondrial DNA (the same information that scientists use to justify the claim that all of life started in Africa) from mothers to both sons and daughters. So all African Ancestry clients can have at least two initial tests that provide them with two different, discrete, and mutually independent shreds of genetic data—information that is impossible to contextualize significantly (historically, genetically, or culturally) in anything other than the most abstract and symbolic ways.[18]

To take either one of the tests, you rinse your mouth out with water, roll two cotton swabs along the inside of both cheeks, let them dry, and then mail everything back to African Ancestry, where the materials are coded and then sent to an accredited genetics lab for testing against a database of twenty thousand African samples. After six weeks or so, you receive a letter stating what, if any, ethnic group in contemporary Africa shares the same tiny piece of DNA—along with a one-page representation of the chromosome polymorphism studied, a Certificate of Ancestry "authenticating" one's results, a shaded image of the African continent indicating the current group that shares one's chromosome DNA sequence, and a free Encarta Africana CD. My own PatriClan results matched samples of the same sequence found among the Biaka people of the Central African Republic. However, if the staff at African Ancestry cannot find a match among those twenty thousand samples from 130 different ethnic groups, they look through their European database—and an even smaller Native American one after that.[19] Using these procedures, they are able to find some kind of match for more than 90 percent of the people who take their tests. Many test-takers use both the PatriClan and MatriClan kits, getting different results for each one of the independently assorted traits.[20]

African Ancestry has about seven competitors worldwide, but none of them specializes in such a specific African database. "They can only barely begin to tell you if they can find any kind of African sequence," Kittles says, "and not what kind. It is really useless for black people. They only tell you if they find any African genetic material. They don't offer our detail." Kittles looks to expand his database with even more

African samples, which means increasing the test's resolution. So, for instance, if there are seven distinct Akan groups in terms of these bits of DNA data, he wants to be able to tell clients which one they are most specifically linked to. For now, the test can only flag genetic Akan-ness more generally. Eventually, they also want to offer more services in order to diversify their operation. For example, they might begin selling vacations to African countries, information about African cultures, or tours of important cultural sites. "The issue," Kittles warns, "is exploitation." He even invokes the Tuskegee syphilis experiments to ground his fears and apprehensions. Black people are always being exploited and manipulated in the name of science and profiteering, he says. And they do not want African Ancestry to be another scientific con, which is why he has turned down every potential investor interested in expanding their small enterprise too quickly. They hope that African Ancestry might even help to increase African American scientific literacy as a by-product of the genetic education that comes along with taking the tests and interpreting their results.

Kittles uses Craig Venter, founder of Celera Genomics, as his model for thinking about what genetic entrepreneurialism can look like.[21] Venter won the race to finish sequencing the genome by focusing on filling in what was not already in the public domain, quickly copyrighting that specific information as private scientific property. Kittles wants to slowly fill in the blanks in his own African samples, similarly copyrighting his database and blocking his competitors.[22] He therefore takes periodic trips to places like Cameroon and Ghana for more and more samples. At first, Kittles was not quite sure that the continental Africans knew what he was doing there. However, now they do, he says, and they are invested and supportive—mostly, he thinks, because they covet more tourist dollars. They want to make sure that their samples are in his database. They hope that African Americans who discover a specific genetic/national link to an otherwise purely symbolic Africa that is located in their particular nation-state might be drawn to contact their national tourist board and visit.[23]

At the same time, Kittles says, this kind of DNA specificity gives African Americans more of a tangible investment in Africa, not just broad-brushed commitments to an empty symbolism, but a specific point of entry. "Each person we test has a story," Paige says. "They have gone from New York to Cameroon to study a culture they feel connected to because they have a tiny genetic link. They have set up Sierra Leone societies in their hometowns. One woman invested money in Liberia. She started reading about the area, educating herself and her family about the history of the country and its current violence. She felt a connection to these people that was tangible, real. That's why people take the test. And they look at Africa in a totally different way now. They'll listen to something on the news and say, hey, that's where my people are. It is a powerful thing. When more blacks have a specific investment like that, they get more involved in world politics and African current events. It means something. It becomes personal."

African Ancestry thus calls upon genetic authenticity to justify renewed political sincerities and insincerities: African Americans are imagined to have a newly real stake in African issues, while Africans might be said to manipulate these rehabilitated African sentiments in the name of greater financial gain within otherwise truncated economic contexts. There is also a self-conscious recognition on the part of Kittles, an African American anthropologist, that science has a history of racialized exploitation, and he represents African Ancestry as a sincere alternative to other scientific authenticity tests, versions that have wreaked havoc on black communities in the past. Finally, we see genetics being used not only to deconstruct racial categories (African Ancestry calls race a "social construct" on its official website), but also to subtly mobilize racial affect (through biology) even as it denies any biological basis for race. This represents a complicated epistemological landscape that highlights the inadequacy of social constructionism as some kind of full inoculation for the contemporary biopolitics of racial reasoning.[24] Here, race is acknowledged as a social construction while simultaneously being activated in the service of arguably essentialized ends.

Thursday Night Service

African Ancestry's growing popularity within the black community notwithstanding, for the WTU Hebrew Israelites, blacks in America have nothing whatsoever to do with Africa—symbolically, historically, genetically, or personally. Black Jews are not African at all. Black Jews are Israelites, a drastically different people from the Canaanites, Cushites, Hagarenes, Hamites, and Philistines that make up Africans' biblically defined lineages. The WTUers offer a notion of diaspora that connects Haitians and Dominicans with Mexicans and African Americans, but disallows any inclusion of continental Africans—demonic heathens who sold Black Jews into captivity.[25]

In June 2003, I decide to start attending a few of the Harlem WTU group's 7 p.m. meetings, a nightly routine that is fairly standardized.[26] Getting to the WTU building, I stand outside among some forty people milling about on the sidewalk. The men and women line up separately, men along the curb, women against the side of the tenement building. The women dress in all white, the word *Noah* spelled in gold on headbands around their heads. The men don rimless caps with Stars of David cut into them and leather cords tied around their heads. While they wait, the guys read newspapers and talk among themselves. The women appear to do the same.

In an effort to break the ice, I ask one of the young men lined up next to me if he knows a Hebrew Israelite named Thomas, "a guy I used to hang out with in Brooklyn about ten years ago," I say. As I ask my question, I realize that I cannot remember Thomas's last name. Even worse, I am not sure I ever knew his "Hebrew name," which is what my interlocutor would really need to identify him. I tell them that I live in North Carolina but just wanted to check out their services before heading back down South at the end of the summer. They welcome me cautiously, letting me know that there are several WTU groups in North Carolina that I should visit when I get back home.

As I copy the phone numbers for the WTU's North Carolina branches, the women are quickly allowed up the stairs and into the meeting space, and it has suddenly become our turn to enter. Security guards, in similar WTU garb, pat down each young man one at a time in the building's tiny lobby entranceway. During my turn, they ask me for identification and closely examine my North Carolina driver's license. The WTUer searching me seems genuinely excited to have an out-of-towner in attendance. I tell him that I teach anthropology in North Carolina, and he nods his head approvingly. After going through my book bag and checking to make sure that my cell phone is functional, he welcomes me warmly with a handshake and gestures for me to head upstairs.

Once I reach the second-floor hallway, there are several forms to be filled out on an oblong table at the entrance, information about upcoming meetings and special holiday festivals. I pick up one form that is specifically for Men-in-Training, a support group and learning cohort for new male members. Once inside the meeting space, I see that guys sit together on one side of the center aisle and women on the other. There is a long, empty, rectangular table at the front of the room, by the gold-trimmed, second-story windows that look out over 125th Street. A group of men in the front of the space are fiddling around with a fairly elaborate video setup. There are two large video cameras on either side of the main table, along with a control panel and switching board in the front corner, from which several men manipulate the recorded video signals. The WTU are very good about videotaping their sessions—for their own institutional archives and for potential broadcast on New York City's public access channels.

It takes about thirty minutes for all of the men to take their seats after being searched in the lobby. As soon as they do, two older members enter, stride to the long table in the front of the room, and sit down— a third arrives much later. The men up front begin their session by denouncing "crackers" and "Edomites" for being minions of Satan, for practicing demonology under the auspices of science, and for being "abominations to God." One of the leaders spends thirty-five minutes on the biology of childbirth. He describes it as a miracle of God that "the red man's microbiology" cannot fully explain. For Black Hebrew Israelites, their rewriting of race even translates into a different interpretation of the epidermal body. They call whites "red," linking that recolorization to the ruddiness of Esau's depiction in the Old Testament and equating such redness with the disease of leprosy. One priest reminds everyone that such leprous skin is a prophesied curse from God. He then talks, off the top of his head, about the biological specificities of childbirth—and with such detail and particularity that he sounds like a well-prepared high school science teacher. He outlines the process from beginning to end, using technical terms for the biological elements involved—and then ends by declaring scientific attempts at cloning little more than feeble Satanic efforts to usurp God's regenerative powers.

We read scriptures throughout the evening, from both the King James Bible and the Apocrypha. At several points, everyone recites memorized passages using the WTU's specific Hebrew dialect (La-Sha-Wan Qa-Dash: Holy Tongue), partially a response to supposed Yiddish contaminations of contemporary Hebrew.[27] When the third priest arrives, he wants to focus on the similarities and differences between and among the twelve tribes. The Tribe of Judah is the head tribe, he says; most of the important teachers and leaders come out of Judah. He reads from Esdras 5:5 in the Apocrypha to make his point. The Tribe of Levi, he says, has its own special covenant with God: Deuteronomy 10. He then switches gears and reminds everyone that the Feast of High Fruits is coming up; it will cost $50 to take part in the festivities. On that note, they open up the evening's services for tithes and offerings, which last about thirty minutes. They make it clear from the outset that they will not stop the offering portion of the program until they raise at least $200 that night, money slated specifically for their building fund. They count the money once, twice, three times, waiting for everyone to give a little more, before eventually reaching their self-imposed goal and moving on with the class session.

After the offering, they open the floor for questions. Attendees ask for particular scriptures to be explained. The priests refer to Strong's Concordance (an annotated dictionary of individuals, places, and things from the Bible) and to one another for their answers. One Latino man in the back asks for the scripture he can use to explain (to the uninitiated) how one determines a real Black Hebrew Israelite, something about tracing their mother's line for two or three generations. He says that that is how he was taught. He once knew the exact passage, but he can't remember it. Whispering, the priests consult with one another for several minutes. Then one of them reads Titus 3:9 from the Apocrypha, which admonishes people to eschew any reading of genealogies: "But avoid foolish questions, and genealogies, and contentions, and strivings about the law; for they are unprofitable and vain." The priests tell the man that this verse from Titus teaches them to leave genealogies alone. "God does not want Israelites searching other people's genealogies." They then invoke 2 Timothy 3:16, which says that knowledge and understanding come from the Holy Spirit and can change once new knowledge is revealed: "All scripture is given by inspiration of God, and is profitable for doctrine, for reproof, for correction, for instruction in righteousness." This means, they tell the young Latino man, that even if the Black Hebrews used to teach people to check for the race of people's fathers or mothers to determine whether or not they are really Jews, they have changed that teaching because they now know it to be false. They focus on the "correction" portion of that aforementioned Timothy passage. In renouncing their former genealogical practices, the priest says, they have corrected their former errors. This genealogical method is exactly the kind that Bigs and Thomas had used to reckon authenticity in the mid-1990s. Between then and 2003, the Black Hebrews had drastically changed their technique for understanding identity.

The priests insisted that WTUers should instead determine the true Black Hebrew Israelite simply by seeing if the Spirit moves in his or her soul. As it says in John 16:13, another priest reads, when the "Spirit of truth" is in someone, it will be evident in what they say and do. "The Holy Ghost," he continues, "will sift all houses of Israel." Leave it to the Holy Spirit, the priests say. The Holy Spirit will sift Israel's houses (Amos 9:9), and we should not seek to usurp the Spirit's power and mandate with our own paltry genealogy tests.[28] "So contrary to what you might have once been told," a different priest makes clear, "it is not your job to judge another Israelite based on anything." The Holy Spirit alone will judge. "Someone can come in here looking like George Bush," he says, "and if they can hear the truth, hear the Spirit, that is all there is. Spirit knows Spirit. It is not for the flesh to decide. We have nothing to do with it."

This exchange stuck in my mind because it provided a way to think about the differences between Black Hebrew authenticities of the 1990s and their newfangled sincerities of 2003, between balanced and unbalanced intersubjectivities, between externally verifiable and internally controlled access to real Judaism. Within a decade, the WTUers had moved from a prior framework of genealogies and ancestries to a new one of inner spirits and sifted souls, of unverifiable Holy Ghosts. They interiorized attributes of Black Judaic validity so as to privilege ambiguity, even and especially in the face of a conspicuous lack of certifiable racial markers like skin color to provide ostensible clarity.

Where Thomas, Bigs, and the Puerto Rican questioner were all trained to test identity through seemingly hard and fast external criteria, in 2003 the priests offered up a definition of Black Judaic belonging that was more difficult to disprove. And the invocation of George Bush was not idle, not innocent, especially given that Bush is often explicitly connected in WTU literature to the Satanist secret societies that seek to wage war against God. Now even someone who could pass for George Bush cannot be dismissed from the Judaic fold as a function of genealogical verifications. The key is internal, interiorized. The real Jew is to be found inside the body's soul and spirit, not its flesh and skin.

The entire myth of Esau and Jacob defines difference through ancestry, through blood and familial ties. Rebecca has two sons, brothers who represent two distinctive peoples destined to wage war against one another until the end days. The ideas are tied to understandings of filiation—all the way down to Mary and her immaculately conceived son, Jesus. The Old Testament fetishizes such genealogical ties: Acts 7:8, "Abraham begat Isaac, and circumcised him the eighth day; and Isaac begat Jacob; and Jacob begat the twelve patriarchs." The connections are clear.

The WTUers I knew in 1994 used matrilineality to ground Judaic difference. The new Latino initiate wanted to know why, if the Bible also uses patrilineal links, he was taught, as he was, to reckon authenticity matrilineally. The priests, however, made it clear that the group's early interpretations of the Torah were mistaken, rotating around the hermeneutic circle with recourse to alternative verses, each one implying a slightly different significance to matrilineality, a significance separating real Black Hebrews from fake ones. But they also declined to privilege patrilineality.[29] In 2003, they still imagined a line between real and fake Jews, between Black Hebrews and Edomites, a line still grounded in the mythical story of Jacob stealing Esau's birthright for a bowl of porridge. The difference, however, was that now they disavowed some of the explicit genealogical trappings they once used to define such distinctions, forcing themselves to trust the workings of the Spirit, to leave adjudication and authentication up to the Holy Ghost, the same Holy Spirit that Tyrone experienced during his high school gospel concerts. Again, the invocation of George Bush is very important here. He represents the ultimate Drexlerian stand-in for a demonic and hyperfetishized state. In this new, nongenealogical formulation, however, even a Bushalike's Jewishness cannot be opened to external genealogical review. This new notion of Black Judaism pivots on an unfalsifiable internality, a way of rendering self that cannot be externally disproved by a human authenticator. In some ways, authentication is utterly beside the point. Once it was important to determine Judaic authenticity as part of an effort to distinguish Black Hebrews from, say, continental Africans—or to figure out if a mixed-race person should be counted as one of the fold. The new model says, instead, that you need not bother to look—that, actually, it is not even your place to check. It assumes not an object to be validated, but another's intentional subjectivity, a wholly internalized realness, a spiritually sifted agency that only God can judge.

The *black* White Supremacist, Leo Felton, who, with a white mother, would have been disqualified from Black Judaism on strictly matrilineal grounds, is echoed in this newfangled spiritualism. This model of sifted souls without genealogical corroboration is akin to Leo Felton's Varange-inspired critique of racial materialism, a critique that also made racial identity less about authenticity (at least not an authenticity verifiable with recourse to simplistically materialized criteria like blood, skin, matrilineality, etc.) and more about a slippery and internally constituted sense of racial intentionality fully backing a notion of willful and sincere subjectivities. In that sense, it becomes a particular form of racial humanism. This does not imply some kind of ultimately final word on questions of racial identity, but only a more contentious, ongoing, daily conversation on racial specificity, a conversation that might potentially be as much about the subversion of authenticity as its capacities for cooptation. That is, even if we were to read the WTU's change cynically as a technique for including more converts (and raising more building funds every night), it still provides the tools necessary to confound much of what is most profoundly troubling about essentialized notions of racial difference. Moreover, if the issue with humanism as practiced in the West has always been its partial constitution by the seeds of anti-humanist degradation and xenophobia, then racial humanism as one of sincerity's organizing principles must be victim to some of the same kinds of internal contradictions.[30] Remember, sincerity can kill, too. Just ask Bill: "We're too sincere, and its killing us." Yet that young, Puerto Rican WTUer is challenged to imagine race anew, to think differently about racial belonging, and in ways that contest some of authenticity's claims to absolutist and externally verifiable power. After getting his answer, the Latino Israelite takes his seat, visibly stunned, and I notice, for the first time, a heavy-set young woman directly across the aisle from him, a woman who looks like a younger version of Bill's wife, Gina. Catching her eye momentarily, I smile and never look back.

6 Real Natives

I know, you got your eyes on me. I feel you watching me. But it ain't hard to see that you can't see me. You try, but what you think you saw, ain't what you thought you saw. You're better off not looking at all.

Truth Hurts, "The Watcher 2"

Hope and desire are always in uneasy relationship. . . . We often use hope to mean desire. We are less prone, I believe, to use desire for hope, though we sometimes do. That the social and psychological sciences have ignored "hope," both as a descriptive and an analytic category, suggests mistrust.

Vincent Crapanzano

Man, in his most intimate reality, is a profane being. Here, where he appears both to himself and to others as a real individual, he is an illusory phenomenon.

Karl Marx

: : :

Sylvia's Finest

Like other big and small Harlem landmarks/institutions (the Apollo Theater, Brother Bey's vending table, the Adam Clayton Powell State Office Building, the Greater Harlem Real Estate Board, Bill and Gina's psychic fairs, etc.), Sylvia's restaurant exemplifies the presentational self-consciousness and self-referentiality that defines prevalent forms of black visual culture today. In the main lobby of that soul food establishment a multitiered glass case on the right wall displays an assortment of mass-produced Sylvia's merchandise manufactured for a national retail and wholesale market: Sylvia's hot sauces and salad dressings, powdered pancake mixes and canned collard greens, glossy cookbooks and silk-screened t-shirts, prepackaged candied yams and black-eyed peas, even moisturizing shampoos and men's colognes—and just about all of it marked with the same photographic portrait of an iconic Sylvia Woods donning a chef's hat and offering up her best motherly smile. Along the walls of the central dining room, autographed publicity photos of various international celebrities hang interspersed with candid shots of other famous patrons posing inside Sylvia's with their arms wrapped around the back of its locally mythical owner, the "Queen of Soul Food." Each photo is signed to either Sylvia or Sylvia's and expresses appreciation for the existence of such "an important local institution," one that "does Harlem proud!"

On this particular day, a group of tourists from a double-decker bus crowds the sidewalk space in front of the restaurant. Disembarked sightseers mill about along Lenox Avenue, snapping pictures while recording Hi-8 and mini-DV footage of themselves and their friends grinning eagerly beneath Sylvia's flickering yellow neon sign. Inside the dining area, two young Asian women tap Sylvia on the shoulder to ask if they can take a picture with her. She graciously obliges, adjusting her hair and blouse as one of the women removes a small digital camera from the dark-blue *Harlem USA* knapsack strapped to her back.

Two tables away, I am eating fried chicken under the framed, frozen gaze of former Mayor Rudolph Giuliani and talking casually with tenant-activist Netta Bradshaw. I've taken Netta to Sylvia's so that I can finally pin her down for an upcoming film shoot. I am coproducing an ethnographic film on gentrification with a local Harlem filmmaker, Diana Bailey, and we are trying to finish principal photography by capturing the energy and activity of Netta's daily grind; we want to spend a few weeks trailing her with a mini-DV camera as she visits local tenants who complain of landlord harassment and unlawful eviction attempts.[1] But Netta has a request for me, too. Her organization, the Harlem Tenant's Council, has just been given the go-ahead to use local community-access cable equipment to produce its own documentary program, and Netta wants to put together a video guide for senior citizens that explains their rights as tenants and outlines clear-cut strategies for tenant organizing. Her busy schedule leaves her little time to produce such a video herself, and so she offers a deal: I can film some of her activist work in Harlem ("No problem," she says), but she wants me to help put together this short documentary for elderly Harlemites. "That's the way we have to get these things done," she declares. "We have to share our skills and expertise so that we can make the most out of the resources we have. There are tons of talented people here in Harlem. We just have to learn to make use of one another's skills. Pool our resources. That way, we all win. Harlem wins."

This short ethnographic scene helps to concretize contemporary connections between so-called visual anthropology and native anthropology, connections that overdetermine the kinds of exchanges and interactions deemed possible for an African American filmmaker/anthropologist working in black America today. The questions that these two subfields put to the center of the discipline they share are fundamental; however, these questions are predicated on certain renditions of ethnographic subjectivity and praxis that beg for (and usually receive) unrelenting criticism and deconstruction: Who is a "native anthropologist," and how does knowledge produced by such a researcher compare with the so-called non-native variety?[2] What are the intradisciplinary limits of "visual anthropology" (i.e., what on earth would *not* be considered *visual* anthropology), and how might that institutionally policed and explicitly labeled subfield be understood in the context of traditional anthropological inquiries that have always been organized around a certain ocularcentrism, a privileging of what anthropologists *see* as the basis for what they can be said to know about the social world?[3]

Continuing to use fieldwork in contemporary black America as an ethnographic rehearsal space for my own attempts at theorizing racial sincerity and its challenges to academic emphases on racial authenticity, I want to analyze just a few of the ways in which the "native" and the "visual" intersect in contemporary anthropological discourse, an exercise that parses sincerity's contribution to contested discussions of social identity. Disentangling nativity from visuality serves to further thematize the blurred relationship between sincerity and authenticity, highlighting instances when their assumed transparencies break down—natives as iconic instantiations of primitive nature, and seeing as transparent window into the realness of the world. This breaking down allows us to rethink the imagined certainties of our own understandings about race and intersubjective difference.

Moreover and more generally, there is much that "visual studies" can specifically bring to bear on a place like Harlem, a place where tourist technophiles take still and moving images of community landmarks, where local business owners authenticate their establishments with recourse to signed and wall-mounted celebrity snapshots, where street vendors sell tapes of themselves taunting passersby about early twentieth-century lynchings, where fringe religious groups use multicamera setups to record their nightly classes, and where anthropologists flout neutrality by agreeing to coproduce activists' documentaries about tenants' rights, unabashedly and complicatedly "participating in the processes of cultural objectification."[4] I would like to place these visual matters in conversation with traditional concerns about the politics and pragmatics of native anthropology.

Anthroman's investment in these seemingly antiquated concerns is specifically sparked by the fact that his/my relationship to Harlem as an ethnographic field site is usually understood (by academic colleagues and Harlemites alike) as an example of just such nativist research. Some serious assumptions are at play here, and I am interested in how they affect ethnographic fieldwork—as well as in complicating any possible misconceptions about such nativity providing clearer and easier access to the terrain of the real or the safety of social sincerity. If anything, a so-called insider-anthropologist must work harder to mark the mutual impermeabilities and uncertainties that are usually elided by assumptions of sameness and fictive kinship, ethnographic authority and authenticity.

Anthropological Nativity Scenes: The Basic Fault Lines

One way to start a discussion about what lies behind the production of anthropological knowledge is to argue the obvious: that Western anthropology's epistemological project is predicated on displaying an intimate and exhaustive understanding of divergent cultural landscapes. The point, for the anthropologist, has been to master the lifeways of faraway cultures so thoroughly and completely as to be able to understand them as surely as though one were looking through the natives' own eyes. Traditionally, such a perspective was labeled *emic* and likened to an approximation of nativist self-understanding.[5] Of course, were that maneuver ethnographically sufficient, the so-called natives could just speak for themselves (provided we first conceded the representativeness of *any* specific native as stand-in for *all* natives from a given community). However, instead of reducing anthropological processes to such a narrowly mimetic faculty, we place an analytic (and *etic*) layer of explanatory scaffolding atop these *emic* understandings and use it to elucidate the deeper significance of foreign cultural worlds—deeper meanings that are not necessarily apparent or even recognizable to the native practitioners themselves. It is this secondary impulse, the move from *emic* to *etic* comprehension, that grounds anthropological claims about scientific knowledge production.[6] Anthropological truths are not reducible to knowing the other as if one *were* an other; they also entail translating those local understandings into a more general theory of translocal factuality and objectivity—Georg Simmel's oft-invoked "stranger" reimagined as Nigel Barley's "innocent anthropologist" capable of examining a foreign land with much less prejudicial bias than any overly invested native could possibly muster.[7]

This is where tensions between the native and the non-native in anthropology begin to tug at each other's heuristic limits, loosening the knotted ties between sincerity and authenticity. The scientific researcher engages in intense and long-term participant-observation so as to understand a culture from "the inside out";[8] however, that is just the first part of a two-step process. The conventional Western anthropologist, remember, is not really a native and, therefore, finds it necessary to determine when enough is enough, when it is finally time to emerge from the fray of the field and write up the results.[9] Such writing allows space (in a literally geographical sense) for a certain critical separation between *native* and *re*-civilized anthropologist, a crucial distance that permits the anthropologist to see not just *through* the native's eyes, but also to examine what those natives' eyes see through a much more powerfully scientific pair.

Even if the native anthropologist might be said to understand his or her native population more intimately and intensely than the foreign researcher, the native anthropologist is still assumed to be less adept at creating the kind of objective detachment needed to properly interpret the *emic etically,* to turn humanistic rumination into true scientific fact. The native anthropologist can be sincere, is marked as such, but that same heartfelt sincerity is believed to foreclose the possibility of true ethnographic and etic authenticity. As some anthropologists argue, "[t]his attitude strongly implies that native and female [women working on feminist issues] anthropologists are seen as potential 'tools' to be used to provide important information to the 'real,' white male anthropologists."[10] That is, unless those "*real,* white male anthropologists" go, à la Frank Cushing, "native"—developing the anthropological equivalent of a Tarzanian complex wherein Western anthropologists unlearn their ability to speak (i.e., to publish) and apingly overidentify with the behavioral alterity of that researched other.[11] Here, such sincere overidentification undermines true ethnographic authority and legitimacy.

Native ethnographers are believed to begin from this overly identificatory position, relinquishing some of their ability to create the requisite dissociation from the field that "writing up" is supposed to encapsulate. The hunters and trappers conquer the wild other; they don't, like Tarzan and Cushing, become it. Native anthropologists are assumed to be agential extensions of this same wildness; they don't, like real anthropologists, stand above and beyond it in a posture of laboratorial scrutiny—even when these anthropologists are American citizens working in minority communities in the United States.

Since at least the early 1970s, this argument about native anthropology's implications and limitations has been rehearsed and re-rehearsed in various guises.[12] The personal investments and community-shared histories of native anthropologists may provide a richer *subjective* knowledge of a given social group, but that subjectivity compromises attempts at the objective disinterest necessary for anthropological neutrality and scientificity. Of course, once the hardest and fastest scientific claims of anthropology were thrown into doubt with meta-ethnographic arguments about ethnography's fictionalized constructedness (about how truth-claims are secured through rhetorical, narratological, and textual strategies), the earth began to shake and crumble a bit beneath the impartial ground of non-native anthropological inquiry.[13] Some of the most compelling renditions of native anthropology start with the premise that it provides much-needed "correctives" to traditional ethnographic representations, representations reread and reinterpreted less as scientifically objective than orientalistically fantastic.[14] Anthropology's claims to detached impartiality were said to mask very biased and stereotypical presuppositions that the native anthropologist felt chosen—even anointed—to dispel.

Once scientistic and objectivist claims for privileging the outsider anthropologist over the insider began to fall away, however, another political project became even more important to the native anthropological cause: the use of ethnographic research for the explicit political benefit of those co-natives under study. This meant changing the epistemologies and methodologies that were operative in the field, requiring due diligence on the part of the native ethnographer: "[T]he native anthropologist, the insider, must be ideologically conscious during her study [or] else her research [may] become co-opted."[15] Doing native anthropology became doing an entirely different kind of anthropology. It meant embracing a certain brand of "native politics."[16] Delmos Jones put it quite forcefully: "A Black Man in this century cannot avoid identifying with his people. I am an intrinsic part of the social situation that I am attempting to study. As part of the situation, I must also attempt to forge a solution."[17] This was a notion of native anthropology that was not simply an epistemological or methodological corrective; it was also a distinctively political intervention: "[F]oregrounding *native* in relation to anthropology, or oneself as a native anthropologist, can act as an empowering gesture and critique of the positionings of natives in the stagnant slot of the Other." [18] Here, ethnography is not just a research method; it is also a new work ethic, a new scientific policy, a new kind of salvage ethnography, one that saves natives from the many abuses of feigned neutrality.

These same sentiments rest at the center of Netta Bradshaw's aforementioned cable-access request, speaking directly to anthropological debates about nativity, politics, authenticity, and ethnographic practice. When she asks me to help produce her documentary film for seniors, Bradshaw is operating under the reasonable assumption that my engagement with her (and with the discipline of anthropology) extends beyond claims to scientific impartiality. I am presumed to em*body* a racial politic, a presumption based, at least partially, on commonsense acceptance of my nativity as an African American working in Harlem—someone who surely stands to benefit whenever "Harlem wins," with victory in Harlem often translating into a decidedly racial winner's circle.

Alongside these same concerns/assumptions about nativist solidarity, one can locate equally valuable theoretical arguments that deconstruct the discreteness and mutual exclusivity of categories like "native" and "non-native" as adjectival parsings of anthropologists and their sociopolitical locations. As the title for Kirin Narayan's important 1993 article asked, "How native is a native anthropologist" anyway? [19] That is, if middle-class African Americans are the advancing front guard for a gentrification push that threatens to displace poorer Harlem residents (the very same tenants that Netta Bradshaw wants to educate through media technology), how can it be assumed that my own professionally middle-class status will not compromise my commitment to keeping poorer black Harlemites housed, especially when some of the residents most interested in my Harlem research (and probably most likely to purchase my books) are these newly arriving, black, middle-class community members?

Discussing this very dynamic, John Aguilar and Donald Messerschmidt have characterized academia's professionalization process as socializing a certain kind of elite difference within all of its initiates, regardless of their supposedly nativist beginnings. [20] This same problematic guided poet and feminist Audre Lorde's often-invoked discussion about the limits of nativist reappropriations—that is, whether slaves actually could use their master's tools to dismantle their master's homes. [21] How clean is a methodological baby formerly washed in Westernized bathwater? And how can anthropology ever be "decolonized" from within its own ivory-towered and institutionalized comfort-zone?[22] Revolutionary Martinican scholar Frantz Fanon also made this point when he argued that metropole-trained natives are just as foreign (vis-à-vis the colony) as the foreigner—if not more so—and certainly just as potentially detrimental to the revolutionary project, donning Dunbarian masks that hide themselves from themselves in a brutal form of self-alienation.[23] As an African American anthropologist working in urban black America, one tiptoes gingerly along a tightrope hoisted high above and between the Scylla of racial belonging and the Charybdis of class-based cooptation. According to some, the script is already written, the roles cast: one can play only sellout or savior. In this tight scripting of racial roles, authenticity and sincerity are graphed far too perfectly (and simply) atop one another.

Narayan eschews the binaries of native/foreigner, insider/outsider, colonizer/colonized, sellout/savior for the idea that "we might more profitably view each anthropologist in terms of shifting identifications amid a field of interpenetrating communities and power relations." She calls for "the enactment of hybridity in our texts" and an understanding of all anthropological authors "as minimally bicultural."[24] All ethnographers are asked to embrace the native and the foreigner inside them. For some, this might sound a little like "Zen and the art of identificatory voluntarism." As Karla Slocum points out, this particular argument, however ultimately compelling, somewhat sidesteps the issue of power differentials that make certain embraceable identities more or less valid than others, more or less native than others, more or less marked than others, more or less real.[25]

These questions about the precarious possibility of unproblematically being native and the political implications of embracing nativity, speak to some of the important fault lines that define how native anthropology is understood in contemporary contexts, especially when the relationship between informant and researcher is often inherently hierarchized no matter how closely the native fieldworker identifies with those studied in the field. This is a hierarchization that is recognized from across both sides of the ethnographic track, a recognition that Brackette Williams flags as comprehension of the differences between "skinfolk" and true "kinfolk."[26] Some of these kinds of s/kinfolk distinctions are a function of class differences between the middle-class native anthropologist and the less-well-off informant being studied—a reminder that class differences exist even among members of marginalized communities and that one can also "study up" within racially stigmatized groups by examining the lives of people like Sylvia Woods or Netta Bradshaw rather than focusing exclusively on Harlem's poorest residents.[27]

German philosopher Walter Benjamin might offer some of the best routes of escape from both simplistic dismissals of native naïveté and countervailing essentialist excesses about native authenticity when he declares that the storyteller (as much the *ur* anthropologist as Simmel's "stranger" ever was) can hail from both faraway lands and the very center of the teller's own community.[28] If anthropology is a powerful technique for telling stories about the stories we tell ourselves about ourselves, then the so-called native must offer up a tale that compels us all to huddle that much closer around the scholastic campfire. And how much tighter the yarn gets spun when the anthropologist/storyteller is also able to use media technology to peer over that flame and catch the native looking at the anthropologist looking at the native watching back.[29] This mutual gaze, this seeing and being seen, maps sincerity's distance from authenticity's assumptions about social transparency. Where authenticity fools itself into scopic certainty, sincerity can't help but recognize its gaze as the feeblest attempt to visualize the invisible: the dark insides of the subjective, intentional, and willful social other.

From Nativizing to Visualizing the Anthropologist

Visual anthropology has constantly asserted and reasserted itself as a vibrant and valuable subfield within the discipline. In fact, visual technologies played an important role in ethnographic research from quite early on.[30] Just as the Lumière brothers unveiled their crowd-pleasing filmic invention in the 1890s, scientists and naturalists (proto-anthropologists) were using that same equipment on ethnographic excursions to Europe's Oceanic "other" as well as in internationally attended exhibits of Europe's African "others" presented right in the middle of Paris—and all before the twentieth century.[31] From the very beginning, theorizing the relationship between this new media form and a still relatively new (and newly institutionalized) disciplinary practice (academic anthropology) entailed making claims about film's scientific pedigree and usefulness, which meant likening it to the microscope, telescope, and thermometer in terms of realistic specificity.[32] Again, the point was greater scientific objectivity, neutrality—and the cinematographe, it was argued, would surely assist in that cause.

As film's grammar was refined and reformulated by filmmakers like Eisenstein, Vertov, and Griffith in the first and second decades of the twentieth century, anthropology redefined its relationship to this new medium.[33] In the early 1920s, as Malinowski was reconfiguring the nature of anthropological research, Robert Flaherty conjured the formal beginnings of ethnographic filmmaking, and he did this by telling an overly romanticized story about a character he renamed Nanook and depicted alongside a fictitious Inuit family.[34] In the 1930s and 1940s, the Mead-Bateson filmic collaborations helped to continue the discipline's fascination with the prospect of using visual data as potential ethnographic data—combating the literary and textual fetishizations of an anthropology that Mead would later disapprovingly label "a discipline of words."[35] In 1950s Europe, Jean Rouch continued the kind of fiction/ nonfiction boundary-blurring that Flaherty utilized for *Nanook of the North* (and even more self-consciously), engaging in what he labeled "shared anthropology" and offering viewers "ethnofictions" (films purposefully drawing on fictional techniques to tell their ethnographic truths). "Fiction," Rouch argued, "is the only way to penetrate reality," and he claimed to actually produce his films for the very Africans depicted in them—what might be called a spectatorially native cinema.[36]

In the United States over the past forty years, just as questions of the visual in anthropology were beginning to gain a new kind of theoretical significance, academic spaces were opened up for the codification of visual anthropology as an officially sanctioned subfield within the academy, with its own section in the American Anthropological Association and its own refereed journals. Wenner-Gren funding in the 1960s created the Program in Ethnographic Film out of an initiative spearheaded by a group of New England–based anthropologists and filmmakers. This was followed by institutions like the Society for the Anthropology of Visual Communication in the 1970s and the Society for Visual Anthropology in the mid-1980s.[37] At Temple, Penn, USC, and NYU, Sol Worth, Timothy Asch, Jay Ruby, and Faye Ginsburg further institutionalized the pedagogical purchase of this burgeoning field and its pressing questions.[38] How can visual matter (found in the field or created by the fieldworker) tell stories about the cultural other? How truthful and scientifically useful will such stories be? Visual anthropologists attempt to answer these questions by examining the processes behind the productions, placing mass media texts in the context of social mediation itself.[39] A film becomes read not just as a particular story about the social world, but also as a text occupying an extradiegetic and pro-filmic space, another cultural character in a larger ethnographic tale about the wider social world of which that film is a part. This marks a move from what some might think of as mere "ethnographic film" to a more substantive engagement with the cross-fertilizing links between "media and culture."[40]

Even in visual anthropology, the native has arrived to challenge the legitimacy of conventional ethnographic films and the ethnographers who make them. If anthropologists use films to write stories about the other, what do those projects mean in a contemporary context where relatively cheaper digital video cameras and nonlinear editing systems have made the once cost-prohibitive practices of the ethnographic film-maker more feasibly useful to those *others* themselves? To tourists at a Harlem landmark. To vendors producing their own merchandise. To Black Jews recording their own worship services. With the democratization of video production comes the increased vibrancy of indigenous filmmaking. But will this lead to a more "participatory cinema" or just an already doomed "bargaining with Mephistopheles"?[41] Moreover, what do these new media offerings mean for the traditional ethnographic films made by the non-native anthropologist—the aforementioned skepticism about that dividing line between native and non-native notwithstanding? Some anthropologists interpret "native" use of visual media as the disqualification of non-natively produced ethnographic film.[42] The anthropologist-filmmaker loses all claims to the film/video camera as a tool for writing the other once these others have gained the technical skills to speak for themselves through film. What could be more authentic than a native making a film about his or her own nativity? This is another point at which the *native* mirrors the *filmic* in anthropology's implicit epistemology: both entail assumptions of immediacy—the native anthropologist as direct extension of some native ethos, and the film image as realist, transparent index of a concrete, physical world.[43] Then there is the concomitant push for "reverse anthropology," for the native to turn the camera around and create a filmic subject out of the erstwhile ethnographic filmmaker, yet another mechanism for blurring the borders between those two categorical designations.[44]

The influx of more and more indigenous film and video offerings creates the need for an ethnographic cinema that recognizes the importance of what Faye Ginsburg calls the "parallax effect" in contemporary visual anthropology.[45] The parallax effect becomes a way to explain how both conventional ethnographic films and indigenous ones can be placed in complementary conversation, taking seriously what they have to say to one another as forms of cultural critique and ethnographic representation. Looking at the same cultural material from slightly different positions creates a more holistic and multidimensional understanding of the world than either vantage point would produce alone, which explains the profound value of a parallax effect for the future of visual anthropology. This parallaxing project is another way to think through the ethnographrenic multivocalities, the ethnographrenias, that complicate both written and filmic anthropological representations of the real world.

Toward a Rigorous Reflexivity

Ginsburg's parallax effect says that different kinds of subjectivities can tell different kinds of truths about the social world, truths that don't negate one another but fill in some of each other's unavoidable lacunae. Jeff Himpele uses Michael Taussig's notion of "mimetic vertigo" to argue that a parallax effect also takes place whenever unwitting anthropologists get "drawn into the projects of other cultural producers." [46] By showing the uncanny similarities between his own anthropological appropriations and the tactical maneuverings of a Bolivian talk-show host, he argues that an appreciation of the parallax effect reinforces a need for reflexivity in the dizzying give-and-take of anthropological research (and I want to come back to this dizziness later).

The parallax effect asks for very specific kinds of reflexivity in the collaborative conversations between anthropologists and subjects. This same call for collaboration and intersubjectivity is at the thematic center of a recent article on reflexivity by two urban ethnographers working in contemporary Chicago, Reuben A. Buford May and Mary Pattillo. [47] Even when doing qualitative research in the same place at the same time, these two ethnographers see quite different things in the field. What complicates matters even further is that both of these social scientists would equally be labeled native researchers. They are studying black Americans in Chicago, and they are black Americans (one from Chicago, the other from a city not more than an hour away). What makes their article so interesting is that May and Pattillo show that even with all of their demographic similarities, they still often observe very different things in the field, even during exactly the same ethnographic encounters. As with Ginsburg's parallax effect, they attempt to highlight the necessary complementarities of differing ethnographic perspectives —further complicating the native-foreigner dichotomy by showing the importance of divisions within the native category itself. There is never a single unproblematized native; rather, there is as much variety in the categorical other as there are actual others themselves. How does one imagine native authenticity with such rampant internal differentiation?

In their attempt at a critical reflexivity, May and Pattillo describe demographic differences between the two of them (in terms of gender, class, and even marital status) to explain the intraracial divergences in their respective ethnographic visions in/of the field.[48] They argue that a determination of one's social standpoint begins to explain one's social viewpoints. This maneuver is necessary, but along with it we might want to provide more "vulnerable" forms of reflexivity, forms more closely related to Himpele's suggestion of parallax as vertigo. Here, I mean to invoke Ruth Behar's notion of the vulnerable ethnographer whose vulnerability is predicated on a reflexivity that is not reducible to simple social taxonomies.[49] Scholars who theorize reflexivity are often making a case for how the social slots that researchers occupy shed light on the kinds of presuppositions and biases they bring with them to the ethnographic moment. In this context, social identities are listed as a technique for exposing ideological cards. To write or make a film about race, class, gender and/or sexuality, makes it imperative for researchers to reveal their own particular inhabiting of such categories, especially since such occupancy can determine what they will and will not be able to see as social scientists. However, that is just the beginning (not the end) of the reflexive impulse, of what's important about such self-revelatory maneuvers, of why reflexivity has theoretical and heuristic purchase. To stop there is to come dangerously close to making little more than empty autobiographical gestures, feebly recuperating simplistic empiricisms. Surely, there are better and worse ways to invoke the "I."[50]

Behar's notion of vulnerability says that these same sociological categories into which we fit ourselves can obfuscate as much as they enlighten. Thus, we are charged to dig deeper, to find out how differently (and maybe even idiosyncratically) we inhabit these overly reified social categories. Reflexivity for Behar is not reducible to easy sociological classification in its final instant; instead, true reflexivity troubles the very categories themselves. In this context, marking oneself as black and a researcher doesn't simply make one *native* in the context of urban Afro-America; it merely provides some of phenomenological pretext for the fraught social interactions one will necessarily experience in the field.[51] Self-reflexivity is not an attempt at greater authenticity, a truer representation of self. It is, more importantly, an instantiation of authenticity's utter impossibility.

Being a middle-class African American scholar (in May and Pattillo's case—as in my own) does not only mean deconstructing notions of "race" that would have it operate as some kind of all-encompassing mechanism for supergluing assumed connections across the material chasm of class differences, and neither is it simply about axiomatically accepting a certain kind of social alienation from non-middle-class black informants. It mandates understanding how both differences and similarities infuse every moment of the intersubjective ethnographic project —even for black anthropologists working in black America. These are moments we cannot control, moments we will never totally predict, and moments that force us to revel in the partiality of our windows on the world. A rigorous reflexivity says that answers don't come automatically with the admission of one's social location vis-à-vis race, class, gender, and so forth, but that such an admission is only a more sophisticated way to begin asking the same important questions about the kinds of knowledge-producing interactions possible out there in the world—and about the necessary trust and blind faith that define those interactions in the first place.

In effect, for the so-called native anthropologist working in visual media, this is an important difference between reflexivity as a kind of double vision and reflexivity as a truly Du Boisian manifestation of "double consciousness." [52] While Du Bois does not invoke "double-vision" per se, he does use an optical metaphor to ground his psychological point. He talks about the African American being "a seventh son, born with a veil, and gifted with second-sight." [53] That second sight is similar to what Ginsburg wants to call a parallax effect. It is the ability to see from at least two different locations at once. For Du Bois, the distinction is between black and white, but that color-coded logic quite persuasively mirrors the scopic distance between informant and anthropologist, native filmmaker and non-native filmmaker, savior and sellout. This Du Boisian twoness makes ethnographic vision more layered and multidimensional. However, superficial invocations of reflexivity are less like Du Boisian double-consciousness-as-doubled vision than they are headache-inducing instances of seeing double, instances predicated on, say, a sharp whack upside the head. In the latter case, seeing double is hardly seeing better, or even seeing at all—and a far cry from the kind of social "stereoscopy" that Du Bois talks about, even if it might still resonate well with Himpelean notions of vertiginous reflexivity. [54] The multiple voices of ethnographrenia become more operative here. Stereoscopic fictions can sometimes be less useful than vertiginous ones, especially when overheard and interviewed voices in the field are never as seamlessly coherent as their retrofitted textualizations imply.

For a truly rigorous reflexivity, simply flashing one's social categories is not nearly vulnerable enough. There is a difference between vulnerable reflexivities and mechanical ones, differences in levels of self-

transparency, differences in methodological rigor, differences in susceptibility to authenticity's seductions.[55] Here, distance becomes important
in placing space not just between the anthropologist and the cultural
other, but also between anthropologists and their own presuppositions,
especially presuppositions about what critically defines the self in the
first place, distinguishing between postpositivisms and truly honest invocations of subjectivity.

A filmic double-vision (half stereoscopy, half vertiginous blurriness)
and rigorous reflexivity (much more than claiming identity categories)
can emerge out of collaborations between indigenous and conventional
ethnographic filmmakers, or even take place within a singular filmmaker
herself. I am thinking here of Fatimah Tobing Rony's notion of "mobilizing the third eye" to eschew simplistic, zero-sum equations about the
categorical difference between objectivity and subjectivity, replacing that
with a model of seeing that looks past such simplistic reifications for moments of practical deconstruction and even small-scale transcendence.[56]
Rony mounts Zora Neale Hurston to make her case, using Hurston's
powerful raw film footage as a prime example of how such third eyes
function. This is a way of "showing seeing" to ourselves so that we can
look at how we look at the world—and maybe even craft slightly new
ways of viewing it.[57] For Ruth Behar, this showing of how we see, this
vulnerability born of critical reflexivity, sometimes takes on a kind of
psychoanalytic tinge, offering readers a way into Behar's anthropological self through the return of her own psychological repressions.[58] Admittedly, many of the spaces between the lines of Behar's *The Vulnerable
Observer* reek of a self-psychologization. That may be a degree of personal confessionalism (and even psychological reductionism) that others
are simply not up to—and it need not be the only way to think about
how we might problematize overly coherent and authentic selves through
self-distancing maneuvers that still try to avoid solipsistic excess. Even
though they also explicitly liken reflexivity to confession, Jay Ruby and
Barbara Myerhoff offer it less as ethnographic penance than as an example of scientific rigor, social empathy, and political commitment.[59]

Reading Amos and Andrew

During my field research in New York City, the visual and the native
were both operative as important nodes of ethnographic understanding.
I can hardly overstate the extent to which televisual and filmic images informed my readings of local residents like Netta, Thomas, Shanita, and
Bill—not to mention local residents' readings of one another and of me.

With that in mind, I want to invoke the 1993 Nicolas Cage and Samuel L. Jackson film *Amos and Andrew* as one last example of the mutually constitutive relationship between nativity and visuality. *Amos and Andrew* is an obviously self-conscious play on the *Amos 'n Andy* radio/television serials of the earlier parts of this century, complete with Nicolas Cage's provocative blackfaced scenes foregrounding that explicit connection.⁶⁰ The first time I watched *Amos and Andrew* (a comedy about a racist American town's misreading of a black cultural anthropologist as criminal intruder and their bumbling attempts at rectifying that mistaken assumption), it was in the one-bedroom apartment of a Harlem resident, Tina, who offered the film up as her way of clarifying what it meant for me to be a black cultural anthropologist, the only black cultural anthropologist she claimed to have ever met. The copy of the tape Tina screened for me was important as an entry into a discussion of how films are used to communicate both parasocially (between spectators and television characters) and socially (among specific spectators)—as well as because of what its actual acquisition can tell us about local political economies of the visual (as determined by video sales and rentals) in underserved black communities. At the time, Blockbuster was only beginning to think about making its way into Harlem, and so a community of more than three hundred thousand residents was served by smaller, local, mom-and-pop video providers, often corner groceries and bodegas with video tapes displayed on metal racks behind their checkout counters.

But this particular copy of *Amos and Andrew* was picked up at one of the neighborhood's self-consciously visual local institutions (a store around the corner from Bill, up the block from Sylvia's, and just across the street from Brother Bey's vending table). This institution is a local video store that is playfully and hyperbolically famous among neighborhood residents for having any and all race-related (or martial arts) films ever made in the history of humankind. These are not official copies, mind you. Instead, they are dubbed versions, complete with dot-matrix-printed titles of each film on the VHS tape's spine label. Before you purchase your film, the owner (or his employee) pops it into one of the two VCRs stationed in front of the counter so that you can see the image quality before handing over the money. Indeed, part of what defines many urban city streets is the ease with which pedestrians can find such bootlegged and/or stolen copies of all sorts of pop cultural fare—from films to CDs and audiocassettes to hardcover bestsellers and fake Prada bags, all sold right on the sidewalk space itself, a sprawling, com-

mercialized and unapologetically ghetto-fabulous version of that same "black public sphere." [61]

Any talk of visuality and urban ethnography in contemporary Harlem must also take note of the brick and mortar changes to the landscape that are part of the same gentrification process that Netta Bradshaw critiques—and yet another obvious site for marking mutations in the visual vis-à-vis urban America. This is an empowerment-zoned context where storefronts change rapidly. Stores set up shop and get moved

out almost overnight—transformations that create palimpsestial Harlems, one on top of the other, like those most conspicuous eyesores: the abandoned and dilapidated buildings with their huge billboard advertisements. When I started to take still photos of such ads in the mid-1990s, I was chronicling the ironies and oddities of contemporary urban landscape commodification. But not only did I take still photographs, I also used a mini-DV camera to capture video footage. Some of these images were shot for my eyes only as video fieldnotes; others were earmarked specifically for future ethnographic films. It was this imbrication of the visual and the ethnographic (taking stills and shooting videos in Harlem) that brought home the complicated ways in which certain forms of visuality pressed me closer to (or farther away from) notions of nativity, to the occupation of a native anthropological positionality.

Walking the street with my video camera, I am more conspicuously the tourist, or even worse, the carpetbagger: still phenotypically black, but not assumed to belong unproblematically or preternaturally. In the context of contemporary gentrifying forces (and with the black gentry leading a multiracial residential charge), being a tourist of any kind links one to the calculus of that incoming threat. Hostile questions abound, suspicious stares: "What'cha taking pictures for? Looking to buy something around here?" Such queries are offered less out of pedestrian curiosity than suspicious exasperation. In some ways, my own "native" status becomes troubled by such a mobilization of visuality by way of "prosumer" video equipment; I lose some of my ability to effortlessly blend in. With the video camera around my neck or taking pictures of billboards atop empty buildings on Harlem's main thoroughfare, I am marked as an outsider, and this feeling of outsiderness vis-à-vis the unfamiliar Harlemites I pass on the street (even in the context of assumed, skin-based similarity) becomes quite palpable.

However, a second way of using the video camera was also operative. Following Rouch's claims about "shared" anthropological movies produced for the people depicted in them, there is another visual and native ethnographic instant wherein one is not making an "ethnographic film" for colleagues and a wider audience (or even, per Netta Bradshaw's request, coproducing an activist documentary for political mobilization), but simply documenting an important social event for the people being videotaped. This is a more specifically intended audience for those canonical social rituals that anthropologists often emphasize as important sites of sociocultural production: baptisms, birthday parties, baby showers, dance recitals, gospel choir rehearsals, and so on. In a world where the televisual is an imperative mode for capturing, disseminating, consuming, and mediating all kinds of cultural fare, appeals for assistance in recording personal events for private viewing are understandably frequent.[62] This is not just making films that equate subjects with audience members. It means making films intended exclusively for the people in them. No fancy editing into an anthropological narrative for professional or popular consumption. Just documentation—for familial memory's sake, in service to someone else's attempt at self-archivization.

How many times have I been asked to do just that? Far more than I can count, with no "ethnographic film" as the final endpoint, just a giving back (through the visual), an obligated reciprocity. I awkwardly stand, say, in the back pew of a local Baptist church, my mini-DV camera hoisted above my shoulder, while a congregant's son is warmly welcomed into the spiritual fold. Since a bedridden grandmother is unable to attend, this anthropologist's shaky footage will be as close as she comes to witnessing the event. I get the request two days before. "Of course," I say. "It would be my pleasure." And so I shoot, trying to stay out of the way of peripatetic ushers and deacons—and of mothers shuttling crying babies back and forth to the lobby. His grandmother wants the sermon, too; so they get permission for me to shoot that as well. The next day, I transfer the footage to VHS, place a label on its spine, and drop it off with the new congregant.[63]

This is a gift, an imagined instantiation of digital and electromagnetic sincerity, with all due Maussian intonations—cementing social bonds, redefining and reproducing the contours of community, insisting on interdependencies.[64] After all, the first gift was a willingness to trust me with their precious thoughts and personal stories. "What imposes obligation in the present received and exchanged," Mauss writes, "is the fact that the thing received is not inactive. Even when it has been abandoned by the giver, it still possesses something of him." [65] In this case, the video also "possesses something of" the gift's receivers, capturing, at the very least, their physical likenesses—and maybe even, according to some, their very souls. This exemplifies a different brand of "total prestation," one where the totality of reciprocity is not just a function of the gift's ability to simultaneously implicate all social spheres in the exchange (politics, economics, kinship, religion, etc.), but also its uncanny capacity "to partake in something of the personality of the giver," and (with video) of the receiver, too.[66] Such a video-gift may possess the filmmaker's aura, but it is also literally the receiver's image.

And how vulnerable is such a personal gift given to "the other"? What if they don't like it? What if they can't use it? What if several of the zooms or tilts or pans or tracking shots destroy the cosmological gravity of the baptismal moment? Or maybe his grandmother just wants something framed a little differently—to show her friends, to play for her neighbors, to enjoy over the holiday season with family members in from out of town. But in this instance at least, I am simply thanked and told that granny will love it no matter what—and with clear implications for the gift I get back in return: a quasi-familial relationship to her, to them, to these people that I *study*.

All anthropologists give gifts (as signs of gratitude, as incentives, as bribes), and they often feel such familiarity and familiality in return. For the so-called native anthropologist in particular, gifts are also attempts to negotiate informants' assumptions about community and co-nativity with respect and generosity, assumptions that use reciprocal sincerity as a proxy for native authenticity. Here, the gift is a probe into the unknown (but hoped for) other. This very hope provides a key for understanding sincerity's distance from authenticity proper. Vincent Crapanzano's position on the analytical usefulness of distinguishing hope from academia's more commonly invoked *desire* differently rehearses a similar de-cobbling gesture, one that he uses to talk about the terrifying prospect of intellectual "mistrust." [67] It is fear born of a similar mistrust that grounds authenticity as discursive formation, anchoring its cynical efforts to foreclose intersubjectivity's unknown and necessary partialities. The ethnographic project can be interpreted as another way to dance both in and out of the preconceived social boxes that lump and splinter us into varying renditions of the *real*: some we see, some we cannot; some we perform, others get performed on us; many can kill, and many more we are willing to die for. In such a fundamentally schizophrenic context, the careful use of a video camera can help to provide epistemological *hope* for how we might imagine forms of mutual impermeability as interpersonal intimacy—and not just so much more objectification and alienation.

Like the aforementioned baptismal footage, such personalized filmmaking demands something more, something else, from a visual anthropologist. Of course, that something else is potentially compromised if the anthropologist asks for (and receives) specific permission to show clips or stills of this same personal footage at talks around the country (or to reference them as part of articles or book manuscripts). If this move (to film something solely for the people being filmed) can be said to bring me a bit closer (as native) to my own nativity (to mutuality and gifting as a member of an assumed social grouping), my recontextualization of that same material is, indeed, the other side of an opaquely ethnographic flimflam, an ethnographic *film*flam that we, as anthropologists, hope might still be ethically sound—if not theoretically helpful. It at least marks what might be imagined (following Marxist theoretical formulations) as a transformation of consumptive emphasis: from the *use-value* of video images (captured for the viewing of those being represented) to their *exchange-value* (replete with surplus symbolic import parlayed into academic capital or film festival awards). As with all gifts, the potential for exploitation is endless; however, film production is especially valuable as a teaching tool because of this exploitative potential. By this I mean to say that film is a constructive medium through which to think about the ethics of participant observation, of ethnographic representation as discursive form, and of sincerity as a de-authenticating political act. And it is all the more important for the so-called native anthropologist writing self and other (and thinking self as other) through the democratizing technologies of contemporary film and video production.

We know that the hard and fast dichotomy between natives and anthropologists is fundamentally false; however, it obviously has real productive force. But this is a discursive and practical productivity that emerges not only from performances given in front of the camera, not just from cultural representations per se, but also as a specific consequence of the very wielding of video-recording equipment. It is as much about the extradiegetic as the diegetic, as much about pro-filmic excesses as the filmed proscenium. The question is not just how others represent themselves through their own indigenous film offerings. It is not even reducible to an easy anthropological reversal whereby the perennial subjects make filmic subject matter out of the anthropologist's cultural landscape. It is a mistake to imagine that the only important questions here are those predicated on degrees of representational authenticity, with concomitantly unjustifiable assumptions about intrinsically more authentic self-depictions. Theorizing the connections between nativity and visuality requires an engagement with the inescapable changes to self and other wrought by film/video as a process that is photochemical/electromagnetic at one end and discursive/performative at the other. We might begin to rewrite nativity and visuality at the crossroads where these two ends meet. Bea Medicine puts the possibilities best:

> I am part of the people of my concern and research interests. Sometimes they teasingly sing Floyd Westerman's song "Here Comes the Anthropologist" (1969) when I attend Indian Conferences. The ambiguities inherent in these two roles of being an "anthro" while at the same time remaining a "Native" need amplification. They speak to the very heart of "being" and "doing" in anthropology. My desire to be an anthropologist has been my undoing and my rebirth in a very personal way.[68]

The "ambiguities inherent in these two roles of being an 'anthro' while at the same time remaining 'Native'" can be provocatively theorized when we use film/video to show us some of how we see the *real*—and how others see us seeing them eyeing it. It provides ways of rethinking nativity through visuality, Medicine's *desire* through Crapanzano's *hope*, and racial authenticity through its cognate, sincerity, while at the same time offering the beginnings of a conceptual framework for the construction of more vulnerable and rigorous reflexivities that challenge anthropologists to mobilize their many gifts (including third eyes, parallax effects, shifting stereoscopies, and inexpensive digital video technologies) to reinvent themselves into the emergent future of ethnography.

7 Real Emcees

I love KRS-One for two reasons: 1. He's real. 2. He keeps it real by constantly keeping pace with the speed of our challenging and ever-changing times.

Tavis Smiley

On the road to riches and diamond rings, real niggas do real things.

The Notorious BIG

Black male hip-hop artists who receive the most acclaim are busy pimping violence; peddling the racist/sexist stereotypes of the black male as primitive predator. Even though he may include radical rhetoric now and then, the hip-hop artist who wants to make "a killing" cannot afford to fully radicalize his consciousness. Hungry for power, he cannot guide himself or anyone else on the path to liberation.

bell hooks

: : :

The Decepticons: "More Than Meets the Eye"

A few weeks after attending Shanita's high school gospel concert, the one where Tyrone caught the Holy Spirit during his final solo performance, I met a classmate of theirs, Jeffrey, who exemplifies the kind of hip-hop impulse that foregrounds both sincerity's vernacular powers and its limitations. Jeffrey was not a member of the gospel choir. In fact, he barely attended any of his mandatory classes, let alone extracurricular activities after hours. Jeffrey's school-wide fame was predicated on his purported connection to a violent, citywide street gang, the Decepticons, a notorious crew whose very name, as an explicit pop-cultural reference, hints at the widespread significance of skepticism vis-à-vis our perceptions of everyday reality.

The Decepticons were an army of ruthless mechanical villains from a famous cartoon serial of the 1980s, *The Transformers*.[1] These Decepticons waged a civil war against the heroic Autobots in some distant world called Cybertron, a war that subsequently spilled over onto Earth, threatening humanity. Both factions, the evil Decepticons and our planet's benevolent new protectors, the Autobots, shared the same defining feature: they were self-conscious and thinking machines that could transform themselves from ordinary vehicles (trucks, jeeps, cars, and planes) into simulations of mechanical human bodies, complete with arms, legs, torsos and expression-filled faces. By the time the Decepticons transformed themselves again in the 1990s—from colorful cartoon characters to infamous city nuisance—the deception was about blending in not as seemingly inanimate motor vehicles but as otherwise inconspicuous high school teenagers, unmarked youth that could violently disrupt the city's public schools from within, blending into the masses much like Madhabuti's ghost dust or the NYPD's murdered undercover "phantom."

I probably met Jeffrey all of three times during the mid-1990s, but I will never forget how he made sense of his own interiorized and differently verifiable humanity. This teenager spent most of his time (by all accounts) selling drugs on the corner, car-jacking automobiles, and beating up fellow students. In terms of most commonsense measures, he was clearly "bad news." Shanita even described him as such. However, she also claimed to realize that he was really a "nice" person underneath it all. Leaning against their high school's back wall, his right leg folded upward, the bottom of his rubber sole gripping the building's beige-painted brick, Jeffrey puffed on a cigarette as Shanita playfully teased him for not joining the gospel choir with her. He had promised to attend their end-of-year performance, but something came up, he mentioned ambiguously, which was why he didn't make it. Before hugging Shanita goodbye and heading off to the subway, Jeffrey offered one last justificatory salvo: "God knows my heart," he said to her. "God knows my heart."

"God knows my heart" is a common refrain within certain segments of contemporary African American culture—so much so that it gets lampooned by comedians on Black Entertainment Television and canonized by hip-hop artists—think Tupac's musical mantra, "Only God can judge me now." It finds one of its closest corollaries in the WTU's newfangled sifting of souls: only the Holy Ghost can determine who is or is not a genuine Black Hebrew Israelite. Only God judges, not genealogists or even geneticists. Moreover, even for the WTUers, hip-hop is key. In fact, one of my earliest introductions to WTU's cosmology came in the form of a hip-hop CD, "Revelation," which was billed as "written and produced by The Most High and Christ through" the WTU duo Sons of the Power, priests Hamanatazachahmath and Shayarahwar, who represented for their Philadelphia-based WTU group (as well as for "all the Brothers & Sisters of all the Israeli Churches Scattered abroad") with songs like "Wake Up Israel," "Say Your Name 3x," and "Here We Come, Esau." [2]

In this chapter I want to examine how we can use hip-hop music to think critically about traditional and innovative iterations of identity politics and politicking, examining how sincerity might resist some of authenticity's hegemony. Beginning with a discussion of the kinds of laboring divisions that balkanize hip-hop cultural production along various (and variously politicized) lines, I examine how these differently divided laboring practices make up a kind of material baseline for negotiations about identity and belonging in contemporary hip-hop discourse. Drawing on the work of hip-hop artists like Wyclef Jean, Biz Markie, Lauryn Hill, 50 Cent, Kanye West, R. Kelly, and especially Mos Def, I argue that these divisions of musical labor within hip-hop provide performative space for rewriting the assumed ontological boundaries surrounding and separating hip-hop's racial selves.

Divisions within the modes/means of hip-hop production chart potentially fruitful paths for analyzing the ins and outs of identity production more generally. I want to argue that sincerity is sometimes used to police and subvert entrenched expressions of hip-hop authenticity. Since nothing is innocent, least of all singing, I look at how male emcees' attempts to sing can be mined for sincerity's cross-fertilizing connection to authenticity, rewriting authenticity through an invocation of the sincere that can be imagined as more than mere lapdog to authenticity's powerful mandates. Just as Jeffrey makes clear that only God can really know his heart (i.e., can adjudicate interiorized realnesses irreducible to empirical validation), hip-hop artists attempt, however fleetingly and unsuccessfully, to challenge external categories of social authentication. Sincerity is never just another way to pass other people's authenticity tests. Instead, it provides justification for redrafting—and maybe even eliminating—the tests themselves, at least as presently formulated.

Hip-Hop Habitats

As both a larger cultural system and a popular musical genre, hip-hop is predicated on adamant and explicit links between race and place, senses of self and other: Esau vs. Jacob and Israelite vs. African in the aforementioned WTU version; Brooklyn vs. Queens and New York vs. California in more commonplace hip-hop circles. As one of its foundational gestures, hip-hop demands of its fans and practitioners alike a geographical grounding for all identities—be that grounding neighborhood-specific, citywide, regional, national/istic, or even post-imperial.[3] Whether debating hip-hop's origin stories or presentist impulses (i.e., distinguishing between where people are "from" and where they are "at"), mooring selves firmly to particular locations has become a way for hip-hop artists and fans to translate their individual experiences into culturally intelligible narratives.[4] These self-conscious spaces provide seemingly transparent windows for peering inside one's social interlocutors.

One small example of such a space-based organizing principle is concretized in what I have tried to previously theorize as Harlemworld, a naming of place within hip-hop discourse that purposefully emphasizes the symbolic and metaphorical over strictly literalist readings of racial geography.[5] Harlem (a mythologized localization of African American cultural and historical specificity) is reconfigured and relegitimized as Harlemworld (a larger-than-life audiovisual landscape) and placed in explicit, often contentious, conversation with differently reimagined and similarly renamed social spaces like Illidelphia, Shaolin (Staten Island), Bucktown (Brooklyn), Amityville (Detroit), and The CPT (Compton, California)—not to mention hip-hop production sites outside of the United States, foreign communities that create their own specific versions of local globality.[6] Ethnicity, race, gender, class, sexuality, urbanity, and artistic proficiency are all enlisted to complicate others' claims to hip-hop authenticity in a geomusical game of cultural one-upmanship, a kind of high-stakes "musical chairs" where participants scramble—once the beat stops—to shove themselves safely atop one or another seat of definable, identity-based certainty.

This same fraught investment in certainty is part of the reason for hip-hop's obsessive preoccupations with locating and presenting *realness:* real gangstas, real playas, real ballers, and real thugs. In hip-hop, realness is the most valuable form of cultural capital; its mandates frame most internal debates. For hip-hop artists, realness is always at stake, even in seemingly innocent contexts. Like conspiracy theories about rewritten Columbian histories and sterilizing fruit juices, nothing in hip-hop is innocent, nothing—which is one of the reasons why KRS-One would be just the perfect person to point out that Evian is actually naive spelled backward.[7] Hip-hop's preoccupation with realness is predicated upon deep-seated doubts about what usually passes for *real*, skepticism toward social performances/presentations offered up as indexical links to realness. If anything, hip-hop reads the *real* upside down, also sharing that particular propensity with conspiracy theories: bad means good, cold means hot, and new world orders are anything but.[8] This reading of realness is contingent upon the overdetermined significances of otherwise innocuous everyday things. It emphasizes mutuality between form and content, a mutuality that allows appreciation of both the phonetic materiality of language and its discursive force. The focus is equally about what you say and how you say it; where you are from and where you are at; public presentations of self and the private autobiographies underpinning them.

For many hip-hop scholars, academic or vernacular, the pivot point for such hyperrealities is racial identity. Hip-hop is considered a rendition of performative blackness with roots in everyday urban struggles against marginalization. It is supposed to be black cultural practice par excellence, and so when hip-hop artists battle over one another's access to the real (real gangstas vs. studio gangstas), they are also carving out the fault lines around a more general understanding of authentic African American identity. Some hip-hop scholars reduce these maneuvers to an all-too-easily essentialized essentialism, dismissing them out of hand.[9] Others search out more redemptive readings of these very same hip-hop debates, lobbying for less monolithic renderings of the contemporary hip-hop community and its polyphonic discourse.[10]

For Bill, someone who would dismiss hip-hop as little more than black pathology and amusicality, this equating of hip-hop with black racial difference exemplifies the very problem of contemporary black life. "Some of these hippity-hop fools need to have their heads examined," he says. "Some of the ugliest things my ears have ever heard in life. You know what it is? A wail before we die. I knew we were at the end of our rope. It's just a matter of time. It makes me sad to hear it."

Bill's cynicism about hip-hop music is mirrored in other intergenerational squabbles about, say, the relative value of hip-hop vis-à-vis jazz music or the blues. Jazz is deemed improvisational and expansive; hip-hop, myopic and contrived.[11] For many of these naysayers, hip-hop narrowly predetermines black identities; it does not provide the kind of improvisational wiggle-room that jazz demands. The assumption here that hip-hop's realness is summed up simply and completely by the fact that it places a premium on violence, materiality, and sexual conquest is rather unfair. As much as these themes are prevalent in contemporary hip-hop, they do not nearly exhaust the terms of the debate for how hip-hop constructs its notions of the real. For example, there are as many references to movies in hip-hop songs as to anything else (including guns and womanizing), and although these movies are often violent (*Scarface, The Untouchables, The Godfather, New Jack City*, etc.), the very fact that glossy Hollywood fictions would operate as the bewitching foil for hip-hop's rhetorical flurries should begin to complicate some of our presuppositions about what hip-hop even means by *real*. Most hip-hop songs have as many references to movie characters and sappy dialogue as they do to "pimps and hos." Jay-Z provocatively rhymes about living life as if it's his last movie, a very different rendition of the "art imitating life" discussion.

Hip-hop's realness skids along a slippery pathway between sincerity and authenticity, which means that its *real* is almost always contradictory and internally conflictual—regardless of superficial consistencies and patterned coherences. So, for instance, even though the shiny, diamond-studded "bling-bling" of materialism is often invoked as a way to imagine spirituality completely evacuated from hip-hop music, invocations of Christianity and Islam are actually ubiquitous in the genre— and not just from the WTUers or Holy Hip-Hoppers. DMX, MA$E, KRS-One, and Tupac are emcees who come out of a hard-core "gangsta" mold to espouse various forms of African American Christianity in their music.[12] Groups like Dead Prez, Brand Nubian, Black Star, and Poor Righteous Teachers, whose street credibility is rarely challenged, choose Islam as the spiritual centerpiece for all their lyrical proclamations. Regardless of how, say, Thomas's mother might reduce hip-hop to utter Satanism, it is more often about Christian and Muslim self-assertion than anything else. These mobilizations of motion pictures and religiosities are cues, among other things, for how sincerity is used to constitute and challenge hip-hop's vernacular authenticities.

Hip-Hop's Divisions of Labor

Émile Durkheim is most often invoked within certain social scientific circles for his theory of social cohesion and its relationship to the dynamics of intragroup labor relations. Although Durkheim is considered one of the forefathers of a sociological and anthropological functionalism that operated as direct rebuttal to conjectural evolutionist excesses, it is clear that his early writings about labor and solidarity take on their own decidedly evolutionary guise—charting a path from simplicity to complexity, from criminality to cooperation. According to Durkheim, societies with little to no internal divisions of labor, societies based on "solidarity by similarities," are organized around a preeminent and constitutive propensity for punishment.[13] The investment of individual group members in the legitimate authority of a transcendent collectivity (that sui generis "collective consciousness") must necessarily be enforced and overpoliced, according to Durkheim, by harsh group reactions.[14] Although not usually formulated in exactly the same terms, this becomes a way to think about the germinating kernels of future social authenticities. The eventual replacement of "repressive laws" with more "cooperative" and "contractual" varieties helps Durkheim explain the post-Athenian emergence of less criminally prone social groupings wherein the internal divisions of labor give a tangible materiality to interpersonal mutuality and commonality. Ironically, even contradictorily, this casting of things seems to be one part Rousseau-like romanticism (enviable primitivity) and one part Hobbesian Leviathan (where social contracts save us from the worst of ourselves). Durkheim's evolutionary and evaluatory slant comes through in the terms he uses to distinguish between these two social options: "mechanical" vs. "organic" solidarities. For Durkheim, this transformation from mechanical to organic forms of sociality is a function of changes in the nature of productive labor itself: intragroup, subsistence-based reliance on comembers reanimates and reenergizes the quality of social relationships themselves. This helps to explain the more all-encompassing authority that individuals cede to collectivities in so-called "complex" societies, an authority primed for expropriation by "the state."

Without fetishizing or resurrecting functionalism wholesale, I want to take this Durkheimian framework as a theoretical starting point, arguing that questions of group authority and racial solidarity within the hip-hop community help explain the purchase of various divisions of labor within hip-hop music and culture. Durkheim's discussion about the solidary implications of labor specialization cast an evocative theoretical light onto contemporary discussions of hip-hop musical production, especially when creating hip-hop music is read (by many younger African Americans) as (1) a privileged site of black racial performative difference and (2) one of the most viable forms of "work" left inside deindustrialized urban landscapes, leaving young people with little choice but "to put culture to work" as professional possibility, no matter how genuinely unrealistic the occupational prospects.[15]

Hip-hop is about work, but it is not just that. It has also usurped past apotheoses of racial capital. Diesal, webmaster for one of the Internet's several "ghetto fabulous" websites and former VHS-tape bootlegger (with a yield of $50,000 per month) in upper Manhattan, argues that in the 1980s, when he was growing up in Harlem and hanging out with the neighborhood's most famous drug dealers, all the other kids wanted to be like them. In fact, some even took part-time jobs to earn the start-up capital.[16] "Everyone wanted to be a drug dealer," he says. "It wasn't even just about the money." It was about the local prestige and glamour of it all. Twenty years later, he laughs, "even the drug dealers just want to be emcees." They'll take their chances on the street to save up enough money for some studio sessions and a demo tape. Even the erstwhile cultural capital of the formally idolized drug dealer must bow to the new cultural dominance and secular worship of the hip-hop entertainer.

Reading the creation of hip-hop culture as a kind of work (i.e., musical production as actual production) could begin to justify an analytic framework that examines the consequences of specialization within the production of hip-hop as a musical form. We might then activate this examination by highlighting the four most agreed-upon cornerstones of hip-hop's expressive edifice: emceeing, deejaying, breakdancing, and graffiti tagging. Many scholars of hip-hop and hip-hop artists themselves have argued for years that these four foundational elements of the subculture have been diverging more and more radically since their combined explosion onto the pop-cultural scene in the 1970s and early 1980s. So, for instance, when hip-hop first surfaced in pop-cultural discourse, its representatives were labeled "rapping deejays" and likened most directly to "Jamaican deejays talk[ing] over the heavy dub instrumentation of reggae."[17] The distinction between rapping (rhyming on the mic) and deejaying (spinning records) had not yet achieved social salience. Moreover, rapping, deejaying, bombing (spraypainting public places), and breaking (street dancing) were all read as parts of the same aesthetic project, usually performed by the same practitioners—and definitely occupying the same spaces in terms of parties, clubs, roller rinks, and so on.[18]

Early filmic representations of hip-hop (*Beat Street, Style Wars, Krush Groove, Breakin',* and *Wild Style*) clearly captured the simultaneity of these related expressive forms, highlighting their points of intersection even as each set of filmmakers focused on one or another specific practice. For instance, *Breakin'* took its title (and narrative thrust) from breakdancing, but placed such breakdancers squarely in conversation and practice-based cross-fertilization with emcees, deejays, and graffiti artists—each group adding something artistically valuable to the others. These films depicted cultural practices that, at the time, still had much more street capital than occupational/market value (there was barely even the dream of becoming rich and famous—and few examples of what such fame might look like). The practitioners were self-consciously and purposefully improving their talents for art's sake, pocket change, and/or intragenerational community building between would-be deejays and fledgling emcees. Even after the self-sustaining "rapping deejay" became the pairing of rapper *with* deejay, hip-hop creativity was still predicated on a certain productive symbiosis and interdependence between the two.

With the subsequent ascension of the untethered emcee (1985's *Krush Groove* begins to document this story most clearly), the deejay (whose initial job entailed both spinning records and periodically hyping up the crowd with a microphone) gradually ceded power. Whereas the emcee was once dependent on the musical largesse of a deejay (who knew the records, who owned the records, who provided the sound system), the current centrality of the emcee as hip-hop icon has taken the musical reins from the traditional deejay and handed them over to "the hip-hop producer," simultaneously catapulting some deejays into an alternate universe of turntablist experimentation.[19] If the 1970s, 1980s, and early 1990s were marked by hip-hop acts containing recognized, celebrated and public deejays (Grandmaster Flash, Terminator X, Jazzy Jeff, Jazzy Joyce, Scott La Rock, Jam Master Jay, Spinderella, etc.), the late 1990s produced the ostensibly deejayless hip-hop act. In a twenty-first century where emcees reign supreme, how many fans, even the most ardent, can name deejays for multiplatinum contemporary acts like DMX, Ja Rule, 50 Cent, Outkast, Jay-Z, and Nelly?[20] We know producers (Swiss Beats, Timbaland, Jermaine Dupri, The Neptunes), but not the deejays. Gone are the days when deejays headlined their acts (Philadelphia's Jazzy Jeff and the Fresh Prince; New York's Eric B. and Rakim).[21]

If the once-sacred relationship between deejay and emcee has become attenuated, the chasm that presently separates both musical roles from breakdancing and graffiti art is wider still—especially in popular representations of these subgenres. Graffiti art and breakdancing are still arguably vibrant subdisciplines within hip-hop, but their continuing productive connections to emceeing and deejaying dwindle by the hour. Many of the "old heads" of hip-hop culture, as well as current hip-hop periodicals like *The Source* and *XXL,* proffer a decidedly four-field approach, an all-inclusive representation of the subdisciplines as if they have remained in productive conversation for all these years, as if it were actually possible to reinvigorate the dormant connective tissues between them.[22]

Of course, many other important internal divisions and special-izations shape the contours and define the fault lines of hip-hop today. For instance, the division between recording artists and record labels frames a long history of struggles over the alienation of musical labor-power. Calls for artistic ownership of publishing rights (the creation of a recording-artist petite bourgeoisie) is one version of how this division becomes charged with politicized potential.[23] Hip-hop recording artists, learning their lessons from the exploited musical labor of mid-century black soul singers, have upped the ante on artistic business acumen with an almost fetishistic impulse to own, and own everything—from pub-lishing rights to subsidiary record labels, from production companies to clothing lines, from soul food restaurants to bookstores, perfume brands to hair-care products. Many have given up on the increasingly futile dream of subverting their own commodification, demanding in-stead a share of the residual proceeds and boardroom respect born of a new sort of corporate power held by late-capitalism's superstar celeb-rity moguls, especially those with their own reality-TV shows (Donald Trump, Oprah Winfrey, P. Diddy, Russell Simmons).[24]

The vibrant field of hip-hop emceeing, most specifically, harbors several notable binaries of labor: between the male emcee and the fe-male rapper, between the black rapper and the white rapper, between the "gangsta" and the neo–black nationalist, between the "bling-bling" lyricist and the conscious rhymer. These same divisions mirror hip-hop's larger cultural project: constructing *and* deconstructing the social, cul-tural, and political boundaries placed around black bodies, boundaries that prop up the very category of blackness itself, but in situation-specific ways. Such divisions help to define the parameters of con-temporary black aesthetics—as well as explaining some of the *dis*-communications between a so-called "hip-hop generation" and older African Americans like Bill, folks unable to identify with the music or appreciate its assumed centrality to contemporary black cultural life.[25] I want to talk about a slightly different kind of division here though, the salient vocal distinction between rapping and singing, theorizing this as a division of labor within hip-hop music that has powerfully productive force. For hip-hop, this seemingly harmless divide underpins many of the mechanisms powering hip-hop's most defining elements—policing categories of race and sexuality while foregrounding a slightly different connection between solidarity and divisions of labor, between authentic acoustics and sincere sounds.[26]

Mos(t) Def(initely) Black

In a move that combines ethnography with annotated discography, I want to explore hip-hop's singer/rapper bifurcation through a close reading of the genre's celebrity front-man Mos Def. As the epitome of a certain hip-hop eloquence in rhyming, one that extends far beyond musical recordings (to Broadway theater, made-for-MTV movies, HBO poetry series, and Hollywood films), Mos Def's offerings underscore the high-stakes implications of this singing/rapping distinction. His stint as a hip-hop recording artist covers the same time period as my ethnographic fieldwork, from an early emergence in the mid-1990s to a continued significance and authority maintained in the early decades of the twenty-first century. And although Anthroman might fancy himself more the Jay-Z of this ~~rap~~ academic game,[27] it is probably Mos Def who most directly and explicitly exemplifies the challenges to racial essentialism/anti-essentialism that Anthroman partially personifies. I want to look at Mos Def, then, as my alter ego's alter ego, as a distillation of the careful negotiations necessary in an indeterminate social context where, again, like conspiracy theories, nothing is ever innocent or simply what it appears.

As is usual for the genre, Mos Def's selfhood is rooted within a very particular originary place, Brooklyn, New York, about twenty-five blocks from the same Brooklyn community where I began my ethnographic research on high-school spirit possessions and Black Hebrew Israelites, where Anthroman became my anthropological ruse. Mos Def's commitment to Brooklyn (where he grew up, for instance, working in a black bookstore that, as an adult, he purchased to save it from closing, turning it into a community center only a short bus ride from Shanita's apartment) is also closely tied to his accompanying commitments to race, his own explicit brand of "post-soul" black pride.[28] Mos Def's racial project has been consistent, starting as soon as he first made an appreciable impact on the music scene in 1994 with singles from hip-hop compilation albums performed by his early group Urban Thermo Dynamics, formed with siblings and neighborhood friends in and around that same Brooklyn bookstore. A few years later, as a member of the Native Tongues hip-hop crew (which included innovative acts like De La Soul and Da Bush Babees), he formed (with Talib Kweli) the hip-hop duo Black Star, a direct invocation of Marcus Garvey and the Universal

Negro Improvement Association's repatriation efforts in the early twentieth century—and an unequivocal nod to blackness as a politically and historically important identity for the anchoring of contemporary hip-hop musical productivity.

From the very beginning, questions of blackness were central to Black Star. The group's 1998 offering was itself a multientry definition of such blackness, a lyricized lexicon that likened blackness to several evocative racial figures, among them: "the veil that the Muslimina wear," "the black planet that they fear," and "the slave ships that later brought us here." Each and every invocation of blackness on the album indexes representations of racial difference, as in the instances above: (1) black veils as metonym for an Islamic religiosity Mos Def embodies, an Islam most intelligible to African Americans through the Nation of Islam's separatism;[29] (2) black planets as metaphor for the racially differential reproductive rates of American citizens; and (3) slave ships as a shorthand history lesson on the transatlantic slave trade, the same genesis story for contemporary African American sorrow and New World difference that the WTU Israelites have slightly revised.

The bulk of that 1998 album is an ode to Brooklyn-based racial identities. The songs are purposeful and self-conscious re-citations of old-school hip-hop classics—literally, rewritings of identifiable hip-hop lyrics formerly set in the Bronx and Manhattan (when first delivered by the likes of KRS-One and Slick Rick in the 1980s) and re-*placing* them inside new Brooklyn-based retellings used to demonstrate Black Star's emceeing skills and authority. Brooklyn becomes a racial "contact zone" of resignifying potential that allows Mos Def and Talib Kweli to redefine blackness by reconnecting it to the Brooklyn of their youth, a blackness that is "blacker than the nighttime sky of Bed-Stuy in July."[30] Place is connected to race and mobilized as part of a larger evidentiary effort to explain the authorial and authentic ground from which the rappers speak.

Mos Def's fin de siècle solo project, 1999's *Black on Both Sides,* takes this definitional preoccupation with blackness and a particularly mapped cultural geography of Brooklyn even farther than Black Star's 1998 iteration. As Mos Def's title indicates, he wants to offer up a Janus-faced blackness, less contradiction than paradox. Here, his album's title does double-duty. It invokes a kind of essentialist discourse of racial authenticity at the same time that it troubles these same essentialized understandings of black cultural specificity by, among other things, challenging hip-hop's singerly exclusions.

In a move that seems to easily ontologize race, Mos Def demonizes

whiteness in several sections of the album, most clearly in his opening track, "Fear Not of Man." In that song, he argues (*speaking* instead of rapping) for a Welsingesque, psychological deep reading of white racial difference: "They wanna create satellites and cameras everywhere and make you think they got the all-seeing eye. I guess The Last Poets weren't too far off when they said that certain people got a God complex. I believe it's true."[31] Mos Def's invocation of the 1960s proto-hip-hop-poetry group The Last Poets (who delivered fiery, pro-black, spoken-word lyrics over "African drums") and their famous "the white man got a God complex" anthem, offers a strict black/white dichotomization of contemporary racial space. Blackness and whiteness are clear, distinct and operate at cross-purposes. Moreover, this gesture to The Last Poets is itself far from innocent. It highlights the historicity of a racialist rhetoric Mos Def draws upon for his own brand of racial reasoning. Mos Def places himself in the tradition of black-on-white critique that begins with the premise that blackness veers off from whiteness in hard and fast ways—colonizer/colonized, master/slave, watcher/watched, Esau/ Jacob, native/anthropologist, saint/Satan, Man/God. The rest of *Black on Both Sides,* however, does an intricate job of de-essentializing this same, clear-cut, racialized difference, redefining hip-hop credibility and questioning assumptions about black cultural validity in two ways: (1) reclaiming the singerly and (2) opening up hip-hop music to allow for the inclusion of seemingly separate (and racially specific) musical genres.

Mos(t) Def(initely) a Hip-Hop Singer

Although starting from a decidedly *speakerly* place (and invoking the often-quoted spoken words of The Last Poets), Mos Def quickly moves from speaking to the more proper delivery of the hip-hop artist: rap- ping/rhyming. That change from speaking to rhyming marks Mos Def's difference from the poetry of the 1960s, and it is also the staccato pre- sentational excess that distinguishes rapping from merely talking "the King's English." [32] But Mos Def does not stop there. He spends a good portion of the album not just speaking and/or rhyming, but also *sing- ing*—and taking that singing, it would appear, quite seriously.

One common and recurring trope in hop-hop music is for the rapper/ emcee to purposefully sing badly and playfully, canonized in the 1980s with Biz Markie's "Just a Friend" (taken from Freddie Scott's equally parodic 1968 version), a classic chorus memorable for its unabashedly out-of-key delivery. It is the very ethos that informs my own attempts— borrowed from that Brooklyn weed dealer—to write my name, loudly, unapologetically, and unmercifully, into any contemporary pop song I sing: "You, you got what John nee-eeds, and you say he's just a friend, and you say he's just a friend, oh baby, you, you got what John nee-eeds." This trope of hip-hop's untrained/bad singer continues all the way up to the present—one of the most popular 1990s versions is Jay-Z's "I Just Wanna Love U (Give It 2 Me)," where he croons "and I wish I never met her at all"—his voice almost cracking, decidedly off-key, purposefully deformed. [33] The bad-singing-emcee motif seems to foreground hip-hop's acoustic and aesthetic distance from well-seasoned vocal musicianship, a parodying that privileges hip-hop lyricism over its singerly counter- part. In hip-hop's rendition of presentational possibility, the instances of rhyming on a hip-hop song always outnumber those of singing, with that purposefully unprofessional singing relegated to the chorus and/ or a one-line reference to some popular R&B tune (the example from Jay-Z above referred to "I Wish" by R&B singer Carl Thomas). Or the emcee will allow another trained and professional singer to come in with a cameo performance—a common strategy for those hip-hop artists who need a catchy chorus to sell their songs but cannot risk singing themselves.[34] In every instance, the singing-rapping divide is explicitly marked. It draws attention to itself. It is what energizes the sing-songy difference of a Snoop Doggy Dogg lyric, a difference redoubling the dissonance that Nate Dogg's soulful crooning creates when juxtaposed with its "gangsta" content. It is Biggie Smalls's playful recasting of a classic soul tune about love into a cover song chronicling the attitudes of playas and pimps.

Hip-hop artists have always referenced the singerly, but they could never perform it—not with genuine musical sincerity. Hip-hop polices the borders between singers and rappers quite stringently. Thus, for example, although controversial singer/musician R. Kelly is undoubtedly one of the premiere male embodiments of hop-hop masculinity, he must approach the possibility of rapping quite gingerly.[35] He is not a rapper; he is a singer. Singers are not rappers just as much as the reverse—except when making specific moves to increase the distance between those two forms by crossing that line in recognizably ironic and parodic ways. Again, such border-crossings are made carefully—only a few bars at a time, sung with obviously mocking playfulness, nice and smooth.

Mos Def's 1999 hip-hop project reclaimed singing for the male hip-hop artist. He spent much of the album singing, and singing sincerely— only possible, some might argue, in a post–Lauryn Hill hip-hop landscape, where she *showed and proved* that an emcee could both sing and rap with gifted proficiency. However, in the decidedly gendered world of hip-hop (and of pop culture more generally), Hill only gave female emcees such license.[36] They alone were able to fully access this multi-genred world. Undoubtedly, the male hip-hop artist's disarticulation of sincere singing from skilled rapping is tied to notions of black masculinity that are not directly challenged when Lauryn Hill, Queen Latifah, or Eve sing *and* rhyme passionately in their songs. The distance between singing and rhyming (between an exclusive rhymer and someone who both rhymes *and* sings) might be even further extended for the male hip-hop emcee in a discursive universe where a male hip-hop artist's sexuality is continually connected to the behavioral particulars of self-presentation. In such a context, Lauryn Hill's adept combination of rapping with singing only further feminizes the singerly—and casts masculinist doubt on any male rapper who attempts to emulate such vocal syncretism.

In the 1990s, MC Hammer's attempt to reconnect dancing with rhyming created an analogous threat to hip-hop coherence by blurring the distinction between those two musical elements. Dancing was always undoubtedly important to hip-hop, but it was relegated to the marginalized exploits of background dancers. An emcee could dance a little (again, approaching the space gingerly), but there was a dancerly line that was quite difficult to cross. MC Hammer threw himself into the sweaty corporeality of his breakbeats so unabashedly, so sincerely, that he faced hip-hop censure and constant challenges to his authenticity.[37]

Similarly, Mos Def's balancing act between singing and rapping is an important rearticulation of authenticity and black masculinity in contemporary hip-hop. His singing is an intervention that recasts the popular template of a masculine hip-hop artist. Mos Def opens up space for the black, male, hip-hop body to sing itself anew, to destroy the categories of expressive difference that make an authentic male rapper different from an authentic male singer (or an authentic female rapper/singer). Wyclef Jean, who made his name with the hip-hop group The Fugees, has also made an effort to connect the male rap artist to his forsaken singerly side, forging those connections through an invocation of ethnic specificity, that is, a Jamaican reggae intensity borrowed from Bob Marley and a Haitian creole nationalist project linked to a diasporic rendering of place's connection to race in contemporary hip-hop's mobile cartography.[38] Wyclef and Mos Def are able to negotiate the split between singing and rhyming by linking these practices to specific locations (for Clef, Jamaica and Haiti; for Def, Brooklyn, New York) and mobilizing their efforts to create yet another related argument about race, music, and diaspora.[39]

Mos(t) Def(initely) Don't Walk This Way

Mos Def's heartfelt singing is noteworthy and theoretically interesting in and of itself, but the second important feature of this rearticulation of black male musicality is what it says about the racialization of genre differences, about where blackness can be said to begin and end. As mentioned before, Mos Def totes many of the same kinds of racial and racialist lines in *Black on Both Sides* that Black Star offered up a year earlier. For instance, he makes it clear that his central concern is with finding ways to realize one specific goal; he wants "black people to be free, to be free, to be free." And this aspiration is predicated on a very specific understanding of what constitutes liberation.

In the song "Rock N Roll," Mos Def proffers a recognizably racial argument ("Chains on they ankles and feet / I am a descendent of the builders of your street / tenders to your cotton money / I am hip-hop"),[40] but he also provides an argument that redefines race, authenticity, and aesthetic practice. He wants to open up the category of hip-hop, extending the term to include a more expansive vision of black performativity, allowing elements that narrower versions of blackness might dismiss out of hand. One of Mos Def's central interventions on this score is in terms of the assumed division between hip-hop and rock and roll—where hip-hop bodies are epidermalized as black, and rock-and-rollers get counterfactually read as unequivocally white.[41] Mos Def sings, but not just R&B tunes. He belts out the clear distinctiveness of "rock singing."[42] As an already racialized practice, performing rock and roll can be dangerous for an African American artist, which is precisely why many black rock musicians based in New York and Los Angles maintain that, more often than not, record executives, fans, friends, and even their own relatives treat them as less than legitimate *black* musical artists because they choose to play a genre of music that has been linked exclusively with whites—that ever-popular imagining of the quintessential rock musician as "a white man with a guitar."[43] Instead, Mos Def rewrites rock and roll as black, and this definition cuts against the grain of such commonsense assumptions about the a priori *white* masculinity of rock music and musicians.[44]

Mos Def, whose hip-hop credibility (partly as a function of his articulated Brooklyn childhood and masterful lyricism) is beyond reproach, uses his credibility to make a case for black musicality being rooted in rock musicianship. In doing so, he develops a notion of black musical possibility that has space for black rock musicians, as well as R&B, jazz, and hip-hop performers:

> I said, Elvis Presley ain't got no soul
> Chuck Berry is rock and roll
> You may dig on the Rolling Stones
>
> . . . .
>
> But they ain't come up with that shit on they own
>
> . . . .
>
> I ain't tryin to diss
> But I don't be tryin to fuck with Limp Bizkit
>
> . . . .
>
> When I get down in my zone
> I be rockin Bad Brains and Fishbone
>
> . . . .
>
> Say, James Brown got plenty of soul
> James Brown like to rock and roll
> He can do all the shit fo' sho'

> That Elvis Presley could never know
> Said, Kenny G ain't got no soul
> John Coltrane is rock and roll
> You may dig on the Rolling Stones
> But they could never ever rock like Nina Simone.[45]

He privileges black rock groups Bad Brains and Fishbone over white ones like Korn and Limp Bizkit. He folds Otis Redding, James Brown, Nina Simone, Chuck Berry, Little Richard, Bo Diddley, Jimi Hendrix, and even John Coltrane into his notion of rock and roll, but would eliminate Elvis Presley, The Rolling Stones, and saxophonist Kenny G as charlatans taking credit for and exploiting musical genres they did not create.

Mos Def makes this case not only rhetorically, but also musically—by (1) again, singing as much as rapping and (2) shifting registers from a folksy-bluesy lament to the hard-lined screeching of heavy metal screams. He relays the same lyrics in both registers, translating across genres that many litmus tests of racial legitimacy would discount: "Who am iiiiiiii?! Rock and Roll! / Who am iiiiiiiiiii?! Rock and Roll!" This project is still about black freedom, but this is freedom not merely from the racist and supremacist structures of white people and their God complexes; it is also about destroying notions of blackness that would disqualify certain musical identities from the realm of racial legitimacy.

His entire album makes this case—by switching musical genres within and between tracks and by returning to the strategy of citationality found in the earlier Black Star album. Yet this time around, his citations are not nearly as dominated by invocations of older hip-hop fare.[46] For instance, in an ode to Brooklyn, Mos Def expands his earlier use of past musical hits. As the song starts, he continues to sings his lyrics—sincerely, not mockingly. Moreover, Mos Def explicitly cites white punk-rock group the Red Hot Chili Peppers (and their song "Under the Bridge") in this heart-felt tune about belonging, community, and home.[47] It is important, I would argue, that Mos Def references a white rock group here as the way to make a case for his own place-based and race-based links to Bucktown and its residents. The Red Hot Chili Peppers are undoubtedly an atypical white rock band on many scores, which might help to explain Mos Def's use of their classic tune in his "Brooklyn" song. However, this choice speaks to the slipperiness of easy, anti-essentialist assumptions about how race is mobilized in contemporary hip-hop discourse. Hip-hop's hybridity has always been fundamental, manifested in sampling choices that never once hesitated to pilfer selections from various genres (and not just those conventionally defined as black and played on R&B radio stations). Mos Def's invocation of songs originally sung by white rock groups makes this founding hybridity central to his acoustic arguments. Mos Def ends this song by telling black folks, "Let's unite and all get down," a unification that allows for an understanding of blackness that is more inclusive than exclusive, able to mobilize all kinds of cultural productions under its racial rubric—a flexible and fluid building block for future black identities and solidarities.

What marks this moment as different from, say, Run-DMC's breakthrough song with rock group Aerosmith ("Walk This Way" in 1986) is the extent to which Mos Def implodes the hard and fast boundaries propped up between hip-hop and rock, boundaries that police the borders constructed to predetermine where hip-hop ends and rock begins. In that Run-DMC/Aerosmith collaboration (and other rock-rap offerings ever since), the musical event is understood as a concatenation of two distinct and mutually exclusive forms: rock on one side, rap on the other. The rock band meets the hip-hop artist, and the two genres combine their still-discrete styles. Run-DMC, for instance, was understood as rapping over a white musical mode that only more clearly concretized and reaffirmed its difference in juxtaposition with hip-hop alterity. Even Harlem's own P. Diddy followed the same recipe in his 1998 hit "It's All about the Benjamins," which was remixed as a rock song and featured Puffy shouting the chorus over heavy-metal music by rockers like Dave Grohl, of Nirvana and the Foo Fighters, along with Rob Zombie, founder of the heavy metal megaband White Zombie. Here, Diddy is still going for the novelty of a rap-rock remix, not making the case for their inherent instability vis-à-vis one another.

In Mos Def's conception of that relationship, rock and roll is merely a subgenre of hip-hop and a further instantiation of black musical sophistication. In this context, white rock musicians are deemed illegitimate practitioners (especially if they don't explicitly acknowledge their debt to black forebears) of a specifically black genre that is only subsequently rewritten as white, unfairly foreclosing black participation as full-fledged insiders. Run-DMC rapped over rock music. P. Diddy bumrushed a still-white rock world. Mos Def, however, conflated rock and rap into the selfsame musical form. This difference marks another important and emergent significance within a genre that often serves as final arbiter on public discussions about what blackness can and cannot be, about what authentic racial performances should really look like.

Changing Metaphors

Mos Def's intervention has opened up a veritable floodgate of singing emcees in the new millennium. From Murder Inc.'s Ja Rule to Outkast's Andre 3000, G-Unit's 50 Cent to rapper K-Os, contemporary male emcees
are now unabashedly singing—and not only in histrionically comedic
tones. They are able to pull this off, I would argue, because of hip-hop's
much-maligned nihilism, its "don't-give-a-fuck" sensibility (a colloquial
phrasing of undeniable importance in contemporary hip-hop). 50 Cent
is a particularly good example of this. 50's fame rests on a combination
of Dr. Dre's producing muscles, his often-cited story of escaping death
after a barrage of point-blank gunshots, and a sing-songy style that
mixes gangsta lyrics with a syrupy-sweet tone. 50 Cent epitomizes hard-
core masculinity, down to the bulletproof vests and pimp strut, but his
twenty-first-century gangsterism is much more confident in its presentational style than its twentieth-century antecedents. He's so hard-core, he
so doesn't "give a fuck," that he can sing whenever he damn well pleases
—and who's gonna tell him otherwise? 50 Cent takes his nihilism very
seriously, a seriousness that anchors his ability to sing as an emcee.

Moreover, we can wire hip-hop's nihilistic impulse to a discussion of
the social stakes implicit in sincerely and authentically rendered racial
"reals." Hip-hop is preoccupied with realness, but it also demands each
subject's individual ability to determine the contours of the real, regardless of social pressures and norms. If anything, bucking social standards
is intrinsically valuable in and of itself, outlawry for self-determination's
sake. To be real is to be true to oneself, in that old-fashioned, Polonius
sort of way. As Queen Latifah put it, "I'm not buying mansions or yachts.
I want to be as real as I can. That's all anyone can expect from me."[48]

However, for hip-hop, the real self is still partially figured mathe-
matically, through assessments of financial gain. The more cars and jewelry and cash one has, the more real one can purport to be—even and
especially if the rapper can also claim a Horatio Alger trajectory that
mixes the right measure of bling-bling success with clear remembrances
of where s/he came from. In twenty-first century hip-hop, one's nihilism
applies to everything but money, the ultimate medium of exchange, the
very mechanism for calculating degrees of realness.

Of course, it is never that simple, and there is also a realness imagined as outside of this calculation (that aforementioned realness of where
one comes from). And herein lies the juggling act: privileging money as
ur-category for evaluating the *real* while also avoiding criticism that one
has crossed some shifting line and, therefore, compromised an internal

and interior *real* self in slave-like service to others in the music business. The only options seem to be *pimp* or get *pimped,* and the difference is less about conspicuous displays of gold and platinum, and more about not-giving-a-fuck while proving one's money and material possessions to be exclusively one's own (and not just some movie-set prop rented by the record company as part of a glitzy music video shoot). Given this tricky context, when 50 Cent sings, he is asserting an indifference to conventional hip-hop standards (and to others' policing of singerly/rapperly impermeability), while also maintaining that his singing is his own choice (and not some marketing department's mandate)—or some more individually concocted act of Top-40 desperation.

Outkast's Andre 3000 sings, it is said, because he really doesn't care: "That boy is crazy." "He doesn't give a fuck." That's why, the argument goes, Andre wears those crazy outfits and swats aside gendered expectations. This indifference (usually glossed as nihilism in the context of, say, gangsta rap) is an asserted indifference to social mandates. Why "give a fuck" about what other people think when only God can judge you, and God knows your heart? If authenticity gives power to the social world as final arbiter on realness, hip-hop (though in a clear pact with such authentic commands) shows how sincerity reverses that power dynamic. The real is determined by a self that supposedly could not care less about external decrees. Although we know this unfettered subjectivity to be a discursive fiction, it also does a good job of providing some traction for the influence of the singular subject, the gangsterish and thuglike hip-hop subject, to mobilize its own interiorized inaccessibilities.

The emergence of the singing hip-hop emcee, then, is a small-scale iteration of sincerity's disconnect from authenticity. Its codification would be authenticity's frightened externalities reasserting themselves over the dark unknowability of the internally willful real. To know this real in hip-hop, we cannot simply look at bank accounts and conspicuous displays of largesse. We need to not even look at all, to not even care about others' criteria for authenticity. The Most High will sift all houses. Even if this were considered merely a self-delusional ruse for deeper hegemonies, this lip service to individual, internal, and interiorized realness is a potentially provocative counterweight for simple acquiescence to externally predetermined realities.

Sampling Durkheim

The kinds of divisions within contemporary musical production that I have highlighted here (between singing and rapping, between rock musician and rap artist, between internal and external reals) bespeak a different function of labor-based differentiations within social bodies. Durkheim explained how the divisions of labor within groups influenced the degree of solidarity and interdependency possible among group members. These divisions created a more organic form of commonality that furthered the collective's authoritative sway over individuals. Moreover, Durkheim's distinction between organic and mechanical solidarity mirrors the analytical disconnects between intersubjectivities predicated on sameness vs. difference. An intersubjectivity based on difference (interactions between two distinctly interiorized and discrete social subjects) can be just as powerful as any kind based on visible similarities (seen, transparently, through the skin and bones of the other), even if the former is also a little scarier as a function of admitted epistemological uncertainties. A realness linked to this same kind of darkened unknowability is exactly what sincerity can provide. At the same time, these increases in labor differentiation and specialization within any social group (i.e., hip-hop culture, religified public spheres, all of black America, or anything else) can also serve as the beginnings of a fetishization process that overdetermines the connections between group identities and specific social practices.

If everyone in society does different things, those same actions can be variously placed along a continuum of social value. The actions themselves become no more or less important than the boundaries constructed around them, separating them, however arbitrary and unimportant those actions (and their strict separation) may appear: nothing is innocent. Once the move is made from a kind of mechanistic to organic solidarity, we've institutionalized an avenue for potentially enlisting particular actions to shore up specific social identities. We move from repression and coercion to subtler hegemonies. Even in looking at specializations within hip-hop music, we can begin to see signs that authenticity tests may be little more than proof-positive that organic solidarities long for (even fantasize) their mechanistic beginnings. Another (not quite satisfying) way to formulate this would be to offer up a model that moves from mechanical to organic to cyber/virtual forms of solidarity: simple (primitive), complex (modern), and hypercomplex (postmodern) states of the real. In this framework, interdependencies born of labor specialization fossilize into atavistic traits made to seem superfluous by the fluidity and excesses of late capitalism. Durkheim demands interdependency through difference, and this move helps to explain sincerity, authenticity, and their heuristic divergences. Sincerity calls this organicism on its fictionalizations and will not simply bow to the will of any social group.

Hip-hop artists are constantly challenging the borders within which they operate. Mos Def's Brooklyn-based racial identity is not completely anti-essentialist (as if any kind could be), but it does open up space for discussions of black racial identification that are much broader than some people might expect. While Mos Def draws strict lines between black and white to clearly demarcate racial difference, his notion of blackness is also soaked through and through with various elements (singing, heavy metal) that many other versions of racial policing would discount. Several important musical divisions (used to shrink, as opposed to expand, performative possibility within hip-hop) are redefined within Mos Def's musical scaffolding: rock as encompassed by hip-hop's aesthetic reach and singing as not hazardous to a male emcee's authentic hip-hop credibility.

At a 2001 concert in Boston, Massachusetts, Mos Def spent as much time on a heavy metal set at the end of the performance as he did with his hip-hop tunes in the beginning. His song "Ghetto Rock" found him screaming lyrics written about everyday life in poorer sections of Brooklyn, singing and screaming over deafeningly loud electric guitar squeals. In the back corner of the club, the b-boy posse of young black men in goose-down jackets and baseball caps who had recited Mos Def's hip-hop lyrics along with him all night (and let out feigned buckshots— "buck, buck, buck"—at each and every lyrical mention of Brooklyn) bopped their heads reverently to this heavy-metal offering, a heavy-metal tune that they did not know. This was only possible because sincerity and authenticity are only ever strategically collaborative, which makes their relationship wholly susceptible to rewiring.

The authentic in hip-hop plays off of the sincere (and vice versa), most notably in a nihilistic Don't-Give-a-Fuckness and the courting of death found in many instances of so-called gangsta rap; Biggie Smalls and Tupac Shakur only embody its most extreme and sadly literal hip-hop incarnations. In these cases, celebratory and fearless nihilism is as absolute, unwavering, and totalizing as any Satanist conspiracy theory. With Mos Def and 50 Cent and other hip-hop emcees, what normally passes for real is disputed and disavowed incessantly—mirroring the constant, everyday negotiations between authenticity and sincerity. Authenticity models the real on what is observable, empirical. It is the real as phenotypic expression, a realness verifiable by the eye. It is the hip-hop of gesticulations and genealogies: do you come from the street or the suburbs? Do you have the walk? The talk? The swagger? The verifiable experience (Jimi Hendrix's or any other)? Sincerity, however, privileges the real as inside, ambiguous, and ultimately unverifiable—except, for some, by "the Most High." To be real is an attribute of the inside, an immanence, that authenticity wants to place outside, trying to domesticate it through a topsy-turvy externalization.

Mos Def's heartfelt hollering of heavy metal lyrics over electric guitars at a hip-hop club across the street from Fenway Park is an example of how sincerity can challenge the straightjacket of authenticity's requirements, its Decepticonlike deceptions. The moment serves as a small yet significant instance wherein the boundaries of black authenticity have been successfully reshaped and manipulated—even just a little—to include what would seem to many as irreducibly foreign. To fold hard rock and heavy metal into hip-hop, to perform a black musical masculinity that sings, and sings sincerely, of love and loss, of racial theft and freedom, is to recalibrate not just hip-hop music but blackness itself, a darkly interiorized blackness that is only acceptable (and possible) once hip-hop's emcees pull out their own authenticity cards, their own ghetto passes, to challenge institutionalized foundations.

Sincerity is hip-hop's most dominant interpretation of the real. And just as authenticity can possess an underlying "ideal" and ethic that particular adherents may or may not fully satisfy,[49] sincerity also has a laudable ideal (flatfootedly glossed as nihilism in its most destructive form), even if the structured and shared sexisms and homophobias of contemporary hip-hop culture show that artists continually fall short of that principle. Still, in a hip-hop where nothing is just what it seems, where all literal readings have several metaphorical references, where everything is a play on words with multiple meanings, a semiotics running completely amok, the smallest sincere attempts to reimagine race might be the closest back male emcees can carry us, theoretically and politically, to "the path of liberation." But it might also be a little closer than we think.

8 Real Names

Moses never changed his name from his Egyptian one. Shadrach, Meshach, and Abednego did not change their names from the one given them by their Babylonian masters. They didn't, neither should we. Unless you see yourself as a little god.   **Elder Shadrock**

A small, brown, bowlegged Negro with the name Franklin D. Roosevelt Jones might sound like a clown to someone who looks at him from the outside, but on the other hand, he just might turn out to be a hell of a fireside operator. He might just lie back in all of that comic juxtaposition of names and manipulate you deaf, dumb, and blind— and you not even suspecting it, because you're thrown out of stance by his name!   **Albert Murray**

50 Cent is a metaphor for change.   **50 Cent**

: : :

After 9/11

"I mean, look at how they've treated us," Kevin declared, reclining across a brown leather couch in his family's East Harlem apartment building on 119th Street. "Look how they've always treated us. I ain't fighting no war for them. Those people [the terrorists] ain't got no beef with me. They got beef with Bush and them, with white people. I do, too. And I ain't gonna go down there and fight them, not me. You crazy. They ain't mess with me. They ain't up in our community uninvited and whatnot. Call me when they bomb the Apollo, or one of the projects. Then I'll go fight."

As I was conducting ethnographic research in and around New York City over the past ten years, national and international events differently contextualized and redefined the significance of my project, changing the nature of its everyday and not-so-everyday implications. The research for this project was tragically bookended by Colin Ferguson (on a train in 1993) and John Allen Muhammad (perched along a highway in 2002) separately gunning down innocent commuters and then creating litigious circuses around similar demands to defend themselves in court. O. J. Simpson, Mark Fuhrman, and Johnnie Cochran turned the realities of a racialized legal justice system into another kind of courtroom sideshow. Janet Reno and ATF agents zealously raided former Seventh-Day Adventist David Koresh's Branch Davidian compound in Waco, Texas. There were Unabombers and new European currencies, the false-starts of Israeli-Palestinian peace accords and NAFTA's controversial ratification. South Africa conducted its first national election with unfettered black enfranchisement, and almost two hundred people were killed in the Oklahoma City bombing of a federal office building by a pair of would-be antigovernment survivalists. Former President Bill Clinton found himself scandalized and publicly censured for adulterous sex, and the Columbine shootings changed the way Americans talked about youthful alienation and outsiderism.

Of all the newsworthy events to take place over this time period, however, clearly September 11, 2001, stands out for many New Yorkers as the most jarring and life-altering of them all—at times, the weight of its social significance allowing little excess space for any otherwise unconnected collective memories. Subsequent incidents continue to get funneled through that day—defined against it. Obviously, September 11 changed this country substantially, even and especially in terms of how the federal government imagines its relationship to the rest of the world and to certain racially profiled segments of its own citizenry. Almost four thousand people were killed that day—in Pennsylvania, at the Pentagon, and in the dramatic collapse of the World Trade Center's Twin Towers, a World Trade Center less than an hour's subway ride, in opposite directions, from Harlem and Brooklyn, New York, and the people I've come to know in both places.

Americans' initial shock and fear on 9/11 have gradually given way to a slightly calmer sense of helplessness. American flags still mark reinvigorated patriotisms, even as a new color-coded national alert system highlights lingering fears, taking constant temperature of our continued

vulnerabilities. Immediately after the attacks, children stuffed their quarters, nickels, and pennies into firefighters' helmets for the relief effort.
Hollywood celebrities (including hip-hop's own deejay cum producer,
Dr. Dre, of NWA and "Fuck tha Police" fame) donated seven-figure
sums to the nationalist cause.[1] Eighteen-year-olds lined up at their local
Armed Forces recruitment offices to "fight for freedom," with Afghani-
stan and Iraq becoming mass-mediated theaters for American-led of-
fenses. Amid all this resuscitated nationalism, Kevin, a nineteen-year-
old African American born and raised in Harlem, could still find space
to voice a quite different post-9/11 sentiment, one not nearly as soaked
in unapologetically revanchist patriotism. His ideological position, I
think, helps to provide another entry point for discussions about analytically productive sincerities and the contentious pathways in and out
of complicatedly racialized terrain.

I want to use this chapter to theorize these sincerities somewhat
orthogonally, through an examination of naming practices that demonstrate their indebtedness to productive fictionalizations. This is an inves-
tigation of how one might rename contemporary racial realities, recon-
sidering what renaming principles imply for disputes about the parsing
of social reality. Nothing is innocent, least of all our names. What we
call ourselves, call our circumstances, and call our concocted "others"
determine the rhetorical grounds for collective fantasies we share about
the possibility of social transparencies, the kinds of transparencies that
are made to distinguish, say, nightclubs from sanctuaries, Harlemites
from gentrifiers, Esaus from Jacobs, spirit possession from adolescent
shenanigans, natives from anthropologists, singers from emcees, and the
Real McCoy from "authentic fakes."[2] Authenticity is usually the wedge
we use to pry open such seductive binaries; however, I have offered this
book, and this chapter's particularly conspiratorial rants, as a challenge
to some of authenticity's assumed usefulness on this score, to some of its
analytical hegemony. Briefly offering Kevin's take on 9/11 as a powerful
starting point, along with a short discussion about the history (and
almost-history) of the Adam Clayton Powell State Office Building in
Harlem, I want to discuss some of the ways in which naming can help
us to recraft our social *reals*—and to rethink sincerity as a powerful alternative to authenticity's embedded essentialisms, to its unquestioned
primacy within most strains of identity studies.

Let us imagine *naming,* then, the same way hip-hop artist 50 Cent
defines his own name, playfully, as a literalization of the metaphoric:
"50 Cent is a metaphor for change," he claims, for his own "change,"
that is, marking just how far he has traveled from his previous life of

violence on the street. This self-naming gesture succinctly encapsulates one of hip-hop's most ubiquitous moves: using language's semantic multivalency to juxtapose dissimilar elements in contiguous time and space, to pun ad infinitum: "Ya'll do it ya'll way; I'll do it Yahweh" (MA$E); "I pack heat like I'm the oven door" (Jay-Z); "They say hip-hop is dead, I'm here to resurrect me" (Common); "I dust them off like Pledge" (Lil' Kim). "50 Cent is a metaphor for change," but the kind that gets stuck in the bottom of linty pants pockets, not the versions that hint at massive recalibrations of life trajectories. This difference can help us to ask questions about what manner of faith naming demands, about what fears it tries to conquer, and the *hope* it allows us to short-circuit through *desire*.[3] Starting with Kevin's reading of 9/11, I want to turn form's assumed transparency into the opaqueness of content, arguing that names like Kevin and 50 Cent and Shanita and Anthroman organize ongoing battles between sincere and authentic accounts of racial realism. What sincerity suggests about the limits of authenticity discourse, about its ultimate inability to name and contain the limits of social reality, can supply new tools for thinking about social difference and labeling intersubjective human experiences.

Building Names

Once Kevin finished making his case about why he didn't want to fight a war for America, even on the heels of 9/11, his mother, Marla, sitting at the kitchen table across from him, looked mortified, visibly shaken by his anti-American comments. A fifty-year-old office assistant who has lived in Harlem since the late 1960s, Marla first arrived from the West Indies with her two sisters while they were all still teenagers. As an adult, attending night school part-time, she also worked directly across the street from the World Trade Center when the towers were hit. Her office was evacuated that morning, and she joined the mass pilgrimage of ash-covered New Yorkers forced to walk home on that fateful day.

Marla thought that Kevin was wrong, wrong-headed, and that he should be more than willing to enlist and serve. She actually *wanted* her son to join the armed forces, to fight for his country, to do something with his life, almost anything, as long as it was productive. What wouldn't be better, she asked rhetorically, than his breakdancing for change (the pants-pocket kind) in Times Square during the dead of winter, which is what he did for money the year before, just as he was preparing to officially drop out of high school? And Kevin knew she felt this way, which is why he wanted to be clear about his position, to make sure she really understood him. He was, of course, happy that his mother wasn't injured and that the death toll ended up being lower than initially expected. If he had the power, he said, he would make all such suicide-bombing stop (and not just in America, all over the world), but he was still not willing to fight a war for America—even a war billed as some kind of coalitional and antiterrorist effort. And Kevin used an image of the Apollo Theater to anchor his racial argument against participation in the War on Terror. Kevin's Apollo Theater, which is racialized very differently from "the white man's Apollo" summarily dismissed by the emcee who introduced Brother Bey's *125 Street: Live, Raw, and Real* video, is invoked to problematize the newly circulating narratives about necessary and automatic patriotisms.[4] For Kevin, the World Trade Center and "the world famous Apollo Theater" represent very different versions of racial urbanity: one spoke to him and his interests, the other did not.

Marla asked Kevin how he couldn't see that his Apollo rested on the same material and symbolic soil as the World Trade Center. And how, with a Nigerian father, he couldn't identify with the Twin Towers victims, especially since "the same people" bombed the embassies in Africa first. "Where your father is from!" He shrugged his shoulders, and she looked at him incredulously. Marla kept emphasizing the Africa bombings, but Kevin remained unconvinced. He acknowledged the African connections, but he remained devoutly skeptical.

This is a skepticism, I would argue, that permeates discussions in contemporary black America, especially in its more vernacular idioms, and not just vis-à-vis conspicuous forms of conspiracy theorizing. Harlem, for instance, seems soaked in it, which, in Kevin's case, begs the question of how his post-9/11 response might have played itself out if the World Trade Center were actually located there, where it quite possibly could have been—that is, if certain advocates had had their way. In 1966, an election year, Governor Nelson Rockefeller (whose famous name clearly marks him as a member of the world-dominating Illuminati's secret society) announced that a portion of the state offices slated to be the World Trade Center would be located in Harlem, demonstrating his desire to do something for black citizens in his state—and, at least, to capture them as a voting block in his reelection bid. But many Harlem politicos and elected officials dismissed this move as little more than "crumbs to placate blacks."[5] Whitney Young, head of the Urban League, then-Assemblyman Charles Rangel and State Senator Basil Patterson were among the most outspoken supporters of a proposal to move the entire WTC project uptown. They made passionate pleas in the black press. They held news conferences and public meetings. They wrote up proposals and opinion pieces. The State Office Building that presently stands at 163 West 125th Street was a pared-down compromise—and even that might not have been built.

In 1968, Governor Rockefeller created the New York State Urban Development Corporation (UDC), conceived to help expedite infrastructural improvements throughout the state. One of the UDC's first orders of business was to overcome a political battle with local community members that threatened to derail the construction of the State Office Building—let alone any more ambitious WTC proposal. The UDC cut through the red tape and quickly built the State Office Building—over adamant public protestation about alternative uses of that space.[6]

The World Trade Center went up, as planned, downtown, and the State Office Building became a humbler, twenty-story design uptown. Plans for another building somewhat similar to the WTC in Harlem were revived in the late 1970s, as Congressman Charles Rangel lobbied with the Harlem Urban Development Corporation (a subsidiary of the state's UDC) to create the Harlem International Trade Center, which, had it gotten off the ground, would have been twice as large as the State Office Building, dramatically increasing commercial connections among African American, African, Caribbean, and Asian markets. As of this writing, however, that building, too, has not been built.

With all the vectors of hypothetical modeling and alternative universes possible here, *naming* becomes a hidden but important mechanism for unpacking the historical roads almost traveled (the "What ifs?" of Harlem history), for distracting us from the obvious, the explicit, and toward some of the concealed conspiracies lurking underneath all theory making. Analyzing names/naming assists our examination of the intersecting "almost-histories" surrounding the World Trade Center towers uptown—along with its downscaled and renamed expression as the *Adam Clayton Powell* State Office Building. Unearthing this imaginary and alternative history takes an "excavation" of names, like those invoked by famous Harlem novelist William Melvin Kelley when he playfully placed himself in the twenty-third century as a character named Professor Lechsher-Hall (pronounced Lecture Hall) in a twenty-eight-minute "mockumentary" he gave me as a gift when we first met in his Harlem home during the summer of 2003.

In the 1988 video, Kelley (as Professor Lechsher-Hall) takes us on an archeological/museological tour of a newly discovered neighborhood that "had been land-filled over," a futuristic tour of the present that begins and ends in front of the neighborhood's iconic and newly excavated Adam Clayton Powell State Office Building. Lechsher-Hall explains that this ongoing excavation project is an educational attempt to uncover the hidden history of "ancient nativos" from the twentieth and twenty-first centuries. "Legend holds they came from China in boats," he authoritatively states, "under the command of King Half-Bull, and settled a colony on upper Mantan island, then known as Mantan-Moreland Island, shortened to Mantanland, and finally to Manhattan," just north of "Upperton National Park" (Central Park).

From the Adam Clayton Powell Building, our academic tour-guide walks us around this newly discovered and mostly deserted archeological site, explaining partially decipherable hieroglyphics (hip-hop graffiti), tin can artifacts supposedly "from the state of Campbell," and "totems" of thirty-foot-high basketball hoops (designed by artist David Hammonds in the 1980s) that Lechsher-Hall surmises must have been vital parts of elaborate religious rituals. This material represents definitive evidence, he claims, that the mythical "Africamerigos" once lived in Upper Mantan Island, "in a section known as Harleem." The fanciful history of Harleem gets more and more exotic as the story unfolds, with all its elements renamed as proxies for more standard historical figures and commonplace objects.

Ostensibly a critique of cultural degeneracy (the ultimate archeological find is a copy of Thoreau's *Walden*,[7] proving that twentieth-century humans actually had a literary culture, something they are just relearning in 2288) and racial expropriations (marked by Lechsher-Hall's elitist British accent), Kelley's short film highlights naming and renaming as a powerful form of self-expression and external authentication. The film makes it clear that all naming is performative, that it includes productive force and not just descriptive detail.[8] Kelley's filmic attempt to theorize naming processes as forms of knowledge production, identity construction and historical revisionism highlights the issues at stake in my own attempt to thematize naming/renaming as productive and performative fictionalizing moves par excellence—similar, in many ways, to the other fictional gestures exemplified in this monograph and the research that informed it (the sporadically novelistic dialogue, the anthropological alter-egos of Anthroman and Zora Neale Hurston, etc.). Invoking Jean Rouch's embrace of fictional techniques as a means of telling ethnographic truths, I want to use the idea of renaming as one important ethnofictional device with which to theorize the limits of ethnography—and the value of sincerity as authenticity's renamed surplus.

Naming Things

Anthropologist Ann Stoler has spent much of the last few years showing how we construct our social worlds through the naming of imperial categories, subsequently forging those names into real social things.[9] That is, naming begins the entification process (and with the resulting thingification as part of our existential problem). Stoler talks most explicitly about *mixing* (what Caribbeanists might call *creolization*), not just renaming,[10] when she makes her case, but it might be helpful to think of renaming as a kind of mixing ethos, a mixing up, a remix—of past with present, of new with old, of specificity with ambiguity. Harlem's State Office Building, say, was renamed (as was the street on which it stands) after Adam Clayton Powell Jr., Harlem's first black congressman. As such multinamed connections increase, however, the thingified and nameable details of geographical space expand in ever-unwieldy ways.

Again, we are talking about a Harlem with many names. It is East and West and Central. Morningside Heights and Manhattanville. Soha, Noha, and Spaha. Mantanland and Harlemworld. 125th Street becomes Martin Luther King Jr. Boulevard. Lenox Avenue is Malcolm X—as are we all, not just Denzel Washington in the eponymous Spike Lee biopic.[11] Adam Clayton Powell runs parallel to Frederick Douglass (this time, without his snake-like master, Covey) and intersects Reverend King at what's called African Square. I want to talk about names and renaming so pointedly and obsessively here, even conspiratorially, precisely because they generate alternative symbolic dimensions for the selfsame physical space, far more Lechsher-Hall's Harlem than Melvin Kelley's. Surely, it takes a very different kind of mathematical modeling to locate oneself in such a multinamed landscape, to find one's place in this nominally shifting world.

Literary theorist Henry Louis Gates described naming in Afro-America as "a metaphor for black intertextuality," as a rich rhetorical, even resistive, trope connected to traditional Yoruba mythologizing.[12] His interest was in naming and renaming as processes of signifying, what he would have us repronounce—or at least rewrite—as "signifyin(g)," a language of trickery used to arrive at direction through indirection, the front sides through the back ends, the semiotic rearticulation of a musician's attempt to get up on the down stroke. Gates invokes the name of Legba to make his folkloric and diasporic case—Legba or Eshu Elegbara, or even Elegba, that is, more naming, renaming. At this particular crossroad, yet another kind of African Square, there are so many different names to choose from.

Anthropologists have always thought seriously about naming/renaming as cultural practice, starting most conspicuously with names for kinship terms and degrees of relatedness. Terms for mother's brother's father, and father's brother's son. Terms for so-called cross cousins and parallel cousins. Honorific terms of address. Balinese birth-order names. And so on. Such naming didn't just pin down identificatory possibilities, it loosened them—problematized and reconfigured them. It allowed for gaps and slippages, emptied and opened up "spaces on the side" of the nomenclatural road.[13] Names gesture at the impossible, at the remembered and the forgotten in one and the same instant—necessarily rigid while remaining irremediably ambiguous.[14]

And we are all preoccupied with names, not just anthropologists and literary critics. It begins early in the prenatal process. Boys' names? Girls' names? Catchy, shortened nicknames and pet names? There is our overfamiliarity with celebrity names, even warping them to the dictates of our own preoccupations: J-Lo, Bennifer, Wacko Jacko. There is the obvious embarrassment of forgetting names attached to social acquaintances—the uncomfortable silences, the apologies after mnemonic lapses. For the social scientist, however, names are about all this and more. They open up some methodological spaces and keep others firmly closed. For ethnographers, informants' names are incredibly important, and so I would like to reinvoke Kevin, not to further interrogate what such a WTC-in-Harlem might have done for his connectedness to the happenings of September 11, but to offer his name's very invocation as fuel for my argument's fire. By that I mean to say that Kevin is not even Kevin. Kevin is not *really* Kevin. That is, Kevin is not Kevin's real name. Likewise, I have no aunt named "Agnes." No Uncle "Rudy."

It is a common anthropological convention to rename informants so as to protect their privacy and anonymity. Anthropologists may even sometimes have fun fabricating alternative names for the people they have worked with (and talked to) under the auspices of ethnographic research. I, for one, generally use an alliterative key to remember my own made-up research names, keeping first letters consistent as a way to organize the pseudonyms in my head, usually in combination with syllabic consistency, in which case Kevin could just as easily have been Kirkland or Kirby. That way I can remember the people my made-up designations stand for many, many months down the line. Kevin's mother, Marla, might really be, say, Margo or Martha, except for the fact that in this case I deferred not to alliteration but to the uncanny similarity between this particular informant's style and the soft, kind mannerisms of an anthropological colleague. And so Marla is not "Marla." Not even close.

And I could continue with these distinctions. Bill, ever-dying from sincerity, is not really "Bill." And Gina, his wife, is hardly "Gina." Moreover, I don't even think that I ever knew their eldest daughter's name, or at least I have never found it in any of my notes/transcripts, so I just made "Denise" up out of whole cloth, a severe ethnofiction. Netta Bradshaw's NB does, however, hold the place for her real names, as does Veronica Boynton's VB—unlike the BB of Brother Bey, an ethnographic pseudonym that is pretty much completely arbitrary and absolutely ignores the Islamic resonances of this videomaker's actual name, the one centered on the red, black, and green business cards that he hands out at his vending table.

So far, these are mostly Harlem people, all relatively recent interlocutors. At the start of my Brooklyn work in the mid-1990s, I had not yet devised this simplistic mnemonic technique, and so although I can, in fact, still remember Kenneth and Bigs and Shanita by their actual names, I can hardly retrieve names for anyone else—except Tyrone, whose first name, for some reason, I never bothered to change.[15] I cannot nearly recover all the names of those many Brooklynites, the majority of whom I have not seen in close to ten years. They are people I can now remember only through their renamed entries in my notes and previously published articles.

Of course, not only individuals' names are changed in social science research; entire neighborhoods or towns get renamed, too. We have fictitious Ghanaian communities named "Ayere,"[16] and "Plainville" for Wheatland, Missouri.[17] Made-up Papua New Guinean ethnic groups like the "Sambian."[18] There's the proverbial "Middletown" of Muncie, Indiana; "Village" and "Norton," two concealed neighborhoods in "Eastern City."[19] Carol Stack writes of middle-America's "Jackson Harbor" and "The Flats";[20] and we have renamed business institutions like Katherine S. Newman's "Burger Barn" fast-food joint.[21] These conceits are usually about anonymity (protecting the confidentiality of subjects) or generalizability (places purported to stand for a variety of communities—and hence their utilitarianly named everywhereness: The Flats, Middletown, The Village, Plainville). The latter names suggest that such field sites could be almost anywhere. One doesn't necessarily need to obsess about spatial specificity, because the findings can be applied to towns that readers might already know, the places they sound and look like. Such made-up names can be fun and particular, like the alliteration of Mango Mount, a small rural outpost of Kingston, Jamaica, where mangoes overrun the town's roads.[22] Or, as Linda Green makes clear in her ethnography of violence in Guatemala, renaming (and hiding the faces of) informants can be terrifyingly serious business, protecting folks from state-sponsored disappearance in a context where "fear" constitutes a palpable and everyday "way of life."[23] Here, renaming is not just about privacy; it is also critical for safety amid social scientific attempts at political interventionism.

Even so, several sociologists and anthropologists have jettisoned the fictionalities of pseudonyms for the hard, objective truths of real names and unmolested biographical details. Sociologist Mitchell Duneier's Lower Manhattan sidewalks are represented by book vendors with their parent-given names entirely intact. And anthropologist Steven Gregory's Corona, Queens, is peopled by political activists who do not shun public recognition for their mobilizing efforts. In fact, they may even use such publicity to assist their cause.[24] In these latter instances, renaming fictions are believed to obstruct the search for scientific accuracy or ethical, research-based intersubjectivity. The names themselves, in all their prefictional certainty, are part of the very epistemological point. To make up names, they argue, is to already miss out on the ethnographic real.

Hip-Hop's Names(t)akes

In hip-hop's symbolism, renaming works in ways that are very similar to the ethnographic landscapes just outlined—and similar to the everyday racial renaming of streets and roads. Think of hip-hop's place-names: the Harlemworlds, Shaolins, New Jerusalems, Illidelphias, North Cackalackies, Strong Islands, and Amityvilles, some of the most well-known examples of the kind of name-changing hip-hop uses to re*place* space. The Boogie-Down Bronx, Bucktown. Even if the name was not changed (Long Beach, Farmer's Blvd, Queensbridge), the name itself demanded continual citation, a fetishization that got subtly revamped with every single new reference.[25]

One thing that was clear about hip-hop from the very beginning was its emphasis on renaming practices. Back in 1979, right when hip-hop started its pop-cultural ascent, renaming was certainly front and center: Roxanne Shante vs. The Real Roxanne. Grandmaster Flash, Afrika Bambaataa and Kool Herc. The names themselves possessed a materiality and self-consciousness that still defines the signifyin(g) ethos of hip-hop practitioners today. And it wasn't just the deejays and emcees; there were also the breakdancers (Crazy Legs), the graffiti artists (Taki 183).[26] The entire culture was about renaming as act an act of rejection, renewal, and self-definition. When Kevin showed me shaky VHS footage of his crew's breakdance moves on 43rd and Broadway, he explained how his own crew-name had morphed several times—from Big-K to Kicks to BK to Daddy Long Legs.

In hip-hop, a masterful genre of epoynymical excess and rhyming reinvention, just one renaming is usually not enough. So, as in Dwight York's many nominal incarnations (or a Knowledge's occasional Knowledge *Allah*), Sean Combs has gone from "Puff Daddy" to "Puffy" to "P. Diddy" in only a few years. Shawn Carter became Jay-Z became Jigga became J-Hova became Shawn Carter again.[27] Before he died, Ol' Dirty Bastard announced on broadcast television that his name was no longer Osirus, but Big Baby Jesus, a far cry from previous incarnations as Joe Bannanas, Dirt Dog, Dirt McGirt or Unique Ason—let alone his more staid government name, Russell Jones.[28] There is significance, then, when the Fresh Prince, Big Willie, reverts to Hollywood's more mainstreamed Will Smith—less government name, less slave name, than the name on a million-dollar bank account. For Tricia Rose, renaming in hip-hop is about obtaining "status from below," especially in the face of limited access to legitimate forms of economic success—before Big Willies ever make it big.[29] For others, it might also be an obvious instantiation of that proverbial Du Boisian problematic, double consciousness, ethnographrenia as a function of already-mentioned parallaxed and doubled visions: "an American, a Negro, two souls, two thoughts, two unreconciled strivings, two warring ideals in one dark body, whose dogged strength alone keeps it from being torn asunder."[30] Du Bois argued that "one ever feels [t]his twoness,"—and, we might add, ever *names* it as well. Two names demand, at minimum, two viewpoints, a "seeing twice."[31] Maybe even thrice, with that "third eye," a way of continuing to split and splinter Du Boisian binaries—to challenge older black/ white racial designations in a differently cosmopolitanized, post–civil rights American landscape.[32]

For some analysts, this penchant for renaming should be linked to black masculinist expressions that predate hip-hop, especially within other genres of musical production (for instance, the Muddy Waters, Bo Diddleys, and Howlin' Wolves of the blues tradition). It also extends far beyond music to other spheres of cultural politics, to the renaming of, say, Cassius Clays and Malcolm Littles. In these latter instances, religious conversion represented a powerful impetus for renaming self, instantiating Nina Simone's heartfelt declaration, "I told Jesus it would be alright if he changed my name."[33] For Nation of Islam converts, renaming occurs in at least two stages: the first signals ignorance about one's own hidden and unknown past (and concomitant surnominal appropriations of the letter "X"), and the second celebrates a brand new name in Islam. Afrocentric reclamations (Asante, Karenga, even Baraka) have the same proclivities, as does Philadelphia's MOVE organization, which literalizes the Afrocentric call for taking up new names by using "Africa" as familial last name: Mike Africa, Rhonda Africa, Vincent Africa, etc.[34] A charismatic Nuwaubian leader also experienced many spiritually inflected renamings: from Dwight York to Malachi York to Melchizedek to Yaanuwn to Amunnnubi Rooakhptah to Chief Black Eagle. Thomas and Bigs both used new Hebrew names around their WTU brethren, names that I could not recall some ten years later, names like Andre Lavon Hicks's Priest Hamanatazachahmath and Thomas Cherry's Priest Shayarahwar.[35] And everyone has something to say about these name changes, too. Conrad Muhammad, former youth leader of the Nation of Islam, was read the riot act by the person I've called Brother Bey for changing his name back to Conrad Tillard, his "slave name," after converting from Islam to Baptist Christianity. Tillard is also his "government name," which is some of the reason why so many of the anti-government conspiracy theorists are really big on name changes, code names, nicknames, family names, and so on. If the government is illegitimate—and maybe even Satanic—one must reclaim the right to name oneself. Of course, there are also all the many names that are said to mark Satanism with their careful rereadings—like adding up the Roman numerals constituting the Pope's official name, Vivarius Filii Dei (Vicar of the Son of God), to get 666.[36] Numbers and names were just as important for sniper John Allen Muhammad, whose esoteric letters to police demanded they "Call [him] God" and use his bank account numbers, PIN numbers, and Visa Card numbers to provide him with millions of dollars.

Naming becomes a way to distinguish the real and unreal, the profane and the sacred. Of course, these gestures have historical precedents galore: biographical journeys from George Baker to Father Divine; the Daddy Graces, Noble Drew Alis and Elijah Muhammads of the black religious world. In colonial America, there was Gustavas Vasa's autobiographical twoness with Olaudah Equiano.[37] Later, Booker claimed "Washington" before learning of an earlier "T" (Taliaferro).[38] As in this latter case, the surnames of American presidents became popular in black communities quite early on: Washington, Lincoln, Jefferson, Jackson. There is my own long-standing anguish about *John Jackson*'s lack of singular specificity (I personally know five—and hip-hop emcee Fabolous is but one of several particularly famous John Jacksons), an anguish that only partially subsides when I think of Ralph Waldo Ellison lamenting his nomenclatural debt to Emerson,[39] or when I recall the voluntary reclamation of grandmotherly voice that accompanied bell hooks's replacement of Gloria Watkins.

In a recuperative gesture analogous to the ones just described, many of the young people I grew up with in Canarsie, Brooklyn, in the 1970s and early 1980s used to throw up two fingers, index and middle, to punctuate their omnipresent salutation, "Peace, God." "Peace, God" was a direct address, and the Five Percent Nation was known for making gods out of young black men.[40] And these gods took renaming to high art's outer limits in the inner city with offerings like Born Light, Freedom Knowledge, Wisdom Divine, Worship True. Clarence 13X and the Five Percent Nation moved Islam into America's backstreets, and young black kids' old names were the first things to go. And God forbid one of the uninitiated slipped and offered up a discarded Jeffrey or Anthony instead of the newly chosen Wisdom Eternal. I personally saw many a limp young body propped up against a brick building to be revived after a World Wrestling Federation "sleeper hold" had been applied for such an offense.

In a discussion of his life as an aide to New York's mayor John Lindsay in the 1960s, at around the time of Rockefeller's WTC decisions, Barry Gottehrer describes how Five Percent Nation members would add and subtract "Allah" from their new names, depending on whether Clarence 13X was present and within earshot. "Most of the young people," he writes parenthetically, "had names like Be Allah or Knowledge Allah or Wisdom Allah, reflecting the universality of godliness. When the leader was present, however, no one pressed the point. At these times there was only one Allah [Clarence 13X]."[41]

Those of us who were not Five Percenters, who had not changed our names or memorized their sacred "mathematics" (quoted verbatim on the sidewalk street whenever called upon by another Five Percent member), offered up the same two-fingered hand gesture (that sixties atavism known as a peace sign), tweaking the phrase to "Peace in the Middle East"—as much because it rhymed as anything else. The Middle East became less a marker of geographical conflict and more a nod to the hip-hop cultivated primacy of rhyme. It was also the closest some of us would ever get to the coolness of cliques like the Five Percenters, and to the exotica of their new names.

Names, in turn, can mask and unmask, both through Dunbarian or Fanonian rubrics, fooling others and/or ourselves into an overreliance on the certainty of dividing lines between native and anthropologist, savior and sellout, black and white.[42] If Louis Dumont is right, binaries always entail a hierarchization, but not necessarily in the direction we might imagine.[43] The fake, in fact, may determine the real as much as dissimulate, which helps make ghetto fabulosity so crucial to questions of realness and racial sincerity. It might explain the inventive names often lampooned in the popular media for their polysyllabics, their highly imaginative combinations of consonants and vowels: Shinanae, Anfernee, Sheloweethena, Antoneeka, Shaqueeta. These same ghetto fabulous names, something like the nominal equivalent of knockoff Gucci flip-flops on a busy city sidewalk, highlight the power of naming as a practice put on display, like the ID belt buckles that were all the rage in a Reaganized 1980s of Lee Jeans (with the then-coveted name, Lee, branded on their cowhide patch) and Izod alligators (an early version of ghetto fabulous stylings that are now making a comeback, especially on fancy fashion-show runways, spectacular examples of the fact that even the rich want to be ghetto fabulous).[44] At the same time, of course, you would have a hard time fitting a name like Shaneequa on those brass buckles of yore, and economists have argued that these names can actually translate into hindered job prospects for otherwise qualified applicants, because they conspicuously mark a racial identity that triggers employers' racial biases.[45]

Clearly, names expose our differences. They can disadvantage, maim, even kill, just like authenticity's etymological roots in *authenteo:* to kill—and, at least partially, by simply giving one's power over to a foreign authority, the social death of truly organic solidarities.[46] This threat is most literally illustrated in the 1992 horror film *Candyman,* directed by Bernard Rose and based on Clive Barker's *The Forbidden.* In the film, Helen, a University of Illinois anthropologist/folklorist (played by Virginia Madsen), studies urban legends, the kinds not too far removed from the ones that circulate through Brooklyn and Harlem and elsewhere about, say, Tropical Fantasy, Snapple, or Procter & Gamble. The story revolves around a specific Cabrini Green housing project legend of this ghostly African American figure, Candyman, who mysteriously appears and kills tenants whenever they say his name five times in a row while looking into a nearby mirror. *Candyman* functions like an allegory for the dangers of inflexible naming, even when the name itself might sound misleadingly innocuous, innocent: Candyman. As his murder victims pile up and the police increasingly suspect Helen of the crimes, the biggest issue for this ethnographic researcher becomes a hyperversion of ethnographrenia, where the epistemological murkiness of schizophrenia meets the experiential inadequacies of an ethnographic method that fetishizes access to the real. Helen's most significant and enduring dilemma, it seems, is less about whether or not Candyman will ultimately kill her—or even if the state will wrongly convict her for his crimes. Rather, she grapples with her angst and uncertainty about trusting the seductive and seemingly tactile indisputability of Candyman, a Candyman that seems all too real but (as the social scientist in her demands) must not be.

With Candyman, the name does not change upon continued recitation—no Candyman to Can Do-Man to Big C. Just Candyman, Candyman, Candyman, Candyman, Candyman, five times in a row, and then bloodshed and mayhem, mirrors and lightening-punctuated darknesses. And this nominal inflexibility/redundancy may be part of the problem, some of the reason for this specter's violent agitation. There is no space for renamed possibility, from Conrad Tillard to Conrad Muhammad and back to Conrad Tillard again—naming as circularity and not just the charting of linear frontiers or the rigidity of nominal sameness. Names that pin down but also open up. Such names and renamings do not simply mark a change; they also presage and portend it. And the name changes are coming from everywhere. This is not just African American exceptionalism. There is Branch Davidian David Koresh's former incarnation as Vernon Howell. The white black supremacist Leo Felton's Ulick Varange, that inspirational author of spiritual (nonmaterial) raciality, is also Francis Parker Yockey, his name-change bespeaking a certain political paranoia.[47] Such paranoia is often central to millennialism, revivalism, militias, and conspiracy theories, which is also why names become so central in that sphere, an overly speculative rumor-mongering space of "unnamed sources" that, according to more measured critics on the left and right, only drains limited resources away from serious and useful political projects.[48]

Hip-hop indisputably knows the conspiratorial power of *nomos,* the powers intrinsic to that naming process—Stoler's naming as entification, Gates's naming as intertextualization, Rose's naming as status acquisition.[49] Naming becomes a way to think about the resistances within such power. These naming choices are not just about individualism or idiosyncrasy. They also mark important social struggles. In the 1970s, the television miniseries based on Alex Haley's *Roots* broadcast a rendition of slavery's fundamental stake in controlling the naming process itself.[50] Naming was important for Haley's Kunta/Toby and, by extension, for the symbolic liberation of all African American descendents of slaves. Over the last four hundred years, the moves from nigger to Negro to colored to Afro-American to black to black American to African American to nigger to nigga have all been struggles over self-naming as a collectively empowering practice.[51] "The long history," Vincent Wimbush writes, "of the changes and attendant controversies around the designations by which persons of African descent refer to themselves and have been referred to by others—including the double nature of the current most popular designation ('African American')—reflects much about the drama of the collective experience of the people at issue. Who are they? Whence do they come? How is it that they do not have one name throughout history? Why would they refer to themselves, and others refer to them, in so many different ways throughout history? Do they have history?"[52] This collective renaming becomes just as purposeful as any alternate sobriquets taken up by individuals: George Burns (Nathan Brinbaum), Bo Diddley (Elias Bates), Mos Def (Dante Terrell Smith), Queen Latifah (Dana Owens), Dr. Dre (Andre Young), Lil' Kim (Kimberly Jones), KRS-One (Kris Parker).

Naming creates social and psychological reals, "not some nominalist's fancy but . . . something that might determine belief and action."[53] Some might call it primordial, this need to name, connected to a species-based will-to-classify.[54] Think of Adam's prelapsarian naming of plants and animals in the Garden of Eden; of Linnaeus and his still-extant, eighteenth-century classificatory schemas, a great chain of beingness tied together by a naming impetus that leaves no unknowns unnamed, no deferred X's awaiting some celestially named finality. Naming also becomes a way to think about the presuppositions of cultural politics—about whether one calls things, say, riots or uprisings, unlawfulness or civil disobedience. With the international "war on terror," are we dealing with "enemy combatants" or "prisoners of war"?[55] Such differences between terms bespeak variations in epistemology and ethics: slave names vs. names of freedom, individual names vs. group names, an X marking the impossibility of ever recovering former names, demanding the present efflorescence of names, along with a promise of new ones to come—a "letting go and letting God," or, in this case, Allah. Names of the present, past, and heavenly future codify concomitant temporal changes in materiality and sensibility.

Naming Sellouts

The names we call ourselves in self-censure or to denigrate others (curses, slurs, and epithets) are just as important as the nominal celebrations that mark our attempts at self-reclamation. For example, there used to be "sellouts" in the African American community; black people called "Uncle Toms" or "House Negroes" and considered beyond the

pale of authentic racial belonging. Sellouts were black Americans believed to selfishly put themselves and their personal interests above the
collective struggles of their race—and who got their identities challenged (or, more colloquially, their "Ghetto Passes" revoked) as come-
uppance. I am not nearly too young to recall some of that history: CBS
News clips of black radicals in sunglasses dismissing the activist work of
Rosa Parks for its assumed accommodationism; critiques of Booker Taliaferro Washington's economic efforts as an acceptance of white superi-
ority; even rap group Public Enemy's staccato pledge to "get the hell
out" of the music industry before they, too, fell victim to its consumerist
seductions and sold out black people. What Public Enemy showed was
that even as late as the 1990s, there were still sellouts in the black community, and being outted as one was the ultimate in racial disownership
and disavowal. It was to commit high-racial treason and get called on it.

Contemporary rhetoric around Clarence Thomas can serve as a
good example. There was a time when the second black Supreme Court
Justice would have been unequivocally deemed a sellout for consistently
ruling against the kinds of legislation that many blacks consider to be in
the group's collective self-interest. For instance, Thomas voted against
the University of Michigan's affirmative action methods in both their
hard (undergraduate) and soft (law school) incarnations, quoting
none other than abolitionist Frederick Douglass to explain his opinions.
Thomas's judicial antics, and his appropriation of abolitionist Douglass,
would once have been considered the epitome of selling out. But not any
more. People might call him conservative, hypocritical, even fascistic,
but they do not dare label him a sellout. Calling someone a sellout bespeaks too-easy confidence in external adjudication.

The era of the black sellout is over, gone the way of other obsolete
and outlived fare: matrilineality among WTUers, World Trade Centers
in Harlem, the nonsinging male emcee. The word *sellout* seems hope-
lessly antiquated now. Sure, a few racial diehards, a Brother Bey, may
still try vainly to invoke it from time to time, but that is only nostalgia
talking, a throwback to the not-so-distant past, some quaint recollection
of a bygone moment when Afros and Dashikis were the norm, and Black
Power was a street-politic of African Square, at 125th Street where Frederick Douglass and Martin Luther King crisscross. In the twenty-first
century, no one takes the notion of selling out seriously anymore, at least
not in black America. It is a putdown that no longer disparages, a naming without any teeth. That's because the sellout has been replaced in
contemporary African America's cultural parlance by the equally demonized playa-hater, the sellout's newfangled place-holder.

The playa-hater is the sellout's accusatory rejoinder. If the playa embraces the capitalist and individualist ethic of contemporary American culture with a vengeance (racking up cars, homes, and the proverbial "bling bling" of South African Diamonds), the playa-hater is the jealous loser who disingenuously invokes anything (including and especially racial solidarity) to explain his own failures and to delegitimize the playa's success. In a ghetto fabulous social world, the playa's usual response to such charges is swift and sure: "Don't hate the playa; hate the game." And the game is global capitalism, a global capitalism writ ethnic with the success of black entrepreneurs in entertainment, finance, politics, and corporate America who are rewriting the terms of Black Power so as to fling it all the way from the street corner to the boardroom.[56]

Even someone like Jayson Blair, the most recent fabulist at the *New York Times,* would have once been considered a sellout, pelted with such accusations both on his way up the journalistic ladder (for choosing to work at the *New York Times,* over, say, the *Amsterdam News*) and back down again (for embarrassing black folks, what people used to call "letting down the race"). Now everyone just waits longingly for a TNT biopic and his autobiographical tell-all.[57] In the age of the playa, he's our ultimate leading man.

Of course, accusations of selling out were always unfairly (even misogynistically) applied, allowing O. J. Simpson, Mike Tyson, and former Washington, D.C., Mayor Marion Barry protective cover from much internal, community-based criticism during their media-saturated bouts with infamy. Details of the more recently revealed Kobe Bryant sex-assault charges presage more of the "changing same."[58] Of course, Clarence Thomas also benefited from such racial wagon-circling vis-à-vis the public castigation of Anita Hill. The moral of all these stories is that men's racial laundry should always be discreetly dry-cleaned, never hand-washed and air-dried out in the open for all the world to see.

But that was the late twentieth century. The closest we get to sellouts these days, the last tiny remnant, is the oft-quoted notion of "acting white," an empty name-calling leveled at blacks not deemed black enough because of their everyday behavior and interpersonal style. Social scientists have used this idea of "acting white" as a major explanation for underachieving black schoolchildren. Getting good grades, they say, is equated with "acting white," and so black kids distance themselves from such allegations by being intellectually disinterested and underperforming.[59] Regardless of whether or not this thesis is true, "acting white" is still not the same thing as "selling out," at least not as we've traditionally understood it. And the difference is telling. Accusations of "acting white" criticize an aesthetic (how people dress, walk, talk, etc.) not a political stance (racial commitment, solidarity, etc.)—and that distinction is analytically crucial. The superheroic playa is a playa because he has the money, the success, and the pimp-strut, and he can immunize himself against the Kryptonite of "acting white" without recourse to any discussion of politics or important social issues.

You will rarely hear black people call Clarence Thomas a sellout, but you might catch folks—especially younger African Americans—saying that he sounds white, wants to be white, wishes he were white, married a white woman, and so on. These critiques are only tangentially about the slant of his judicial decisions. They are mostly issues of racial style dressed up to replace any real engagement with racial ideology. All Clarence Thomas needs to do is work on his striding gait—and maybe even pick up a cool pimp name (like Archbishop Don Juan or Prettyboy Clarence) while he's at it.[60]

Acknowledging Nominal Capital

Such name-games are very serious business—for the researchers as well as the researched, in terms of naming practices aimed both at the cultural analysand and the anthropological analyst. The anthropologist is often the one who gets renamed, primed for newer "roles" within anthropology's changing "morality plays."[61] One important aspect of this mobile process has to do with conventional performances of social capital, the demonstration of professional ties, friendships, and pedigrees concretized in the naming of intellectual interlocutors and friends. The first thing a student learns in graduate school is to read acknowledgments like some mixture of gossip-page and genealogical chart. The names listed are far from innocent. They mark out turf, appease intimate relations, and place the author along a continuum of academic importance.

One thanks generous and loving partners (Deborah Thomas) for putting up with the manuscript's incessant nightly clarion calls, embodying a selfless love that confounds linguistic prison-houses; immediate family members (Ethlyn Roberts, Robinya Roberts, Jason Roberts) for no other reason, really, than that they'd just want to see their names in print; extended relatives (Aunts Marilyn, Voicelyn, and Roslyn, uncles like Jerry, cousins Calvin, Elijah, Cheryse, etc.) who will probably never see the book except when the abovementioned "immediate family members" show it off to them at the next holiday function. One mentions a few nonacademic friends who won't allow academia to take all of one's soul (Larry Shields, Cora Daniels-Evans, Rondai Evans, Khari Wyatt, and Jaxon Jarrod); colleagues at one's home institution, faculty and students, especially those who graciously read early excerpts of the work (Anne Allison, Katherine Ewing, Ralph Litzinger, Diane Nelson, Attiya Ahmad, Charlie Piot, Dwayne Dixon, Andrew Janiak, Wahneena Lubiano, Bianca Robinson, Karla FC Holloway, Tina Campt, Priscilla Wald, Justin Izzo, Netta Van Vliet, Naomi Quinn, Jenny Woodruff, and Rachel Gelder); advisers/mentors (Katherine S. Newman, Kathryn Dudley, Patricia J. Williams, and Lee D. Baker); friendly intellectual interlocutors (Martha S. Jones, Kerry Ann Rockquemore, Crystal Feimster, Daniel Botsman, Maureen Mahon, Ajantha Subramanian, Caitlin Zaloom, Donald Robotham, Eric Klinenberg, Jackie Brown, Robert Adams, Kamari Clarke, Karla Slocum, Lanita-Jacobs Huey, Nicole Fleetwood, Marla Frederick, Carolyn Rouse, Velma Love, Cathy J. Cohen, Tavia Nyong'o, Roxanne Varzi, Celeste Watkins, Daryl Scott, Devin Fergus, Marcy Morgan, Stanford Carpenter, Lawrence Jackson, Jeffrey Forbes, Grant Farred, Prudence Carter, Randy Matory, Jeff Dolven, Noah Feldman, Barış Gümüş, and Jim Dawes); a warm and inspiring editor (Doug Mitchell); an assortment of professionals who made the book presentable and helped shepherd it to market (including Timothy McGovern, Peter Cavagnaro, Nicholas Murray, and Christine Schwab); big-name scholars you kind of know, or met a few times, or had lunch with, who you hope would not be too insulted by an explicit mention that implies inaccurate amounts of closeness and familiarity (Skip Gates, Leith Mullings, Robin D. G. Kelley, Manning Marable, Faye Ginsburg, William Julius Wilson, Setha Low, and Herman Gray); and all those, inconsistently recollected, who commented on aspects of your work during public talks and panels (Andrew Ross, Richard Sennett, Grey Gundaker, Angela Zito, Ann DuCille, E. Patrick Johnson, Jennifer Brody, Roderick Ferguson, Tommy DeFrantz, Richard C. Green, Jason King, Anna Scott, Annemarie Bean, Melissa Checker, Awam Amkpa, Marya Annette McQuirter, Anita Gonzalez, Melissa Fisher, David Graeber, Alondra Nelson, Anne-Maria Makhulu, Frank Romagosa, Daphne Brooks, Carolyn Rouse, Noliwe Rooks, Eddie Glaude, Valerie Smith, and others). Much of this naming is still about fictionalization, even without the pseudonyms, about concocting a network-based rendition of one's intellectual standing and significance. All of these names, never anonymous (except, of course, for the University of Chicago Press readers and the informants who signed confidentiality agreements), hint at the performative force of the seemingly innocent acknowledgment, the textual citations not codified in bibliographies and endnotes, which form still other categories of name-dropping potentiality. In this context, it becomes unreasonable to bracket such naming from the theoretical and ethnographic discussion at hand, from the conjuring powers of the well-placed nominal reference. It is all part of the same impulse—and continues with the writer's attempts to rename himself.

Naming Self

Like the incantations of acknowledgment pages, Anthroman attempts to think naming as a form of performative magic, even while staring down the superscientific needs of an empiricism that appears petrified by its own partialities. How do we see the real? Write it? Read it? And especially in the darkness of our own interiorized opacities? What do we lose and/or gain by imagining realness out there, external to us, and ultimately with so much more agency? What is the compromise we make when intersubjectivity necessitates transparent sameness through and through? All machines and organs outside the body—or all utter mutuality and somatic permeability.[62] How does authenticity name, and might sincerity rename, un-name, code-name? And toward what theoretical and/or practical end? In this hyperrealized and biologized moment, a biotech world of African Ancestries, cloned sheep, banned stem-cell research, and race-specific drugs for heart disease, what kind of intellectual intervention will work? How do we name it, and in what ways might it need to rename us, too?

One point of entry into the world of newly named anthropological sincerities is through the work of anthropological renamings of self. For instance, there is Michael Taussig's engagement with the magical powers of a reified state apparatus, an engagement that seems to necessitate his invocation of an equally mythical figure in response: Captain Mission.[63] Captain Mission leads Taussig's ethnographic voyage into an unnamed South American never-never land of Spirit Queens who valiantly guard portals to other worlds. The magicality of his unnamed nation-state is met with the revisionist efforts of Captain Mission, a superhero who tackles "both material and alma, body and soul." With his Nietzschean guide, Captain Mission searches, "as on a pilgrimage," for "any 'real' Indians" in that strange and mountainous land where "magical images [of Indians] bore not the slightest resemblance to the 'true' Indians but were instead lifted from the fantasy world of the US frontier as the war-bonneted figure of the plains warrior." Taking on Herman Melville's "Benito Cereno," Marx's commodity-form, and the ecstasies of spirit possession, Captain Mission circuitously shows that "[l]ike money, the state is thick with soulstuff." [64] And for the satanic state, a sterilizing state, a conspiratorially organized and hyperreified witchcraft state (full of soulstealing as much as soulstuff), Captain Mission marks the Herculean feats of renamed braggadocio that hyperrealities demand of their ethnographers.

Another good example of how this might work is FemaleMan, a self-consciously copyrighted and genetically engineered "modest witness" and cyborgian post-anthropologist (along with trademarked sidekick, OncoMouse) that Donna Haraway offers up as a way to complicate narrow renderings of contemporary extrahuman relations. Using everything from standpoint theory to science fiction, Haraway and FemaleMan perform critical science studies that open up space for the counterintuitively "nonmodern conversations we need to have about figuration and worldly practice in technoscience." [65] Like Captain Mission, FemaleMan marks an attempt at an ethnographic rendition of the wholly impossible.

I end this chapter by highlighting Captain Mission and FemaleMan for what they say about the playful power of renaming in anthropology, of renaming the anthropologist, and how that negotiates our impasses between methodology and epistemology, objectivity and subjectivity, authenticity and sincerity. It is in this very space that I would also insert Anthroman, another superscientific crusader. He can't fire steel-slicing laser beams from beneath his eyelids—or bend that steel to meet the whims and wishes of his spandex-covered arms. Indeed, neither can his aforementioned colleagues. He's not a guru or griot or witch doctor or Rosicrucian or Freemason—or any other such fancifully esoteric a thing. Anthroman is more like something of a cultural confectioner, a Pez-dispenser of social critiques across the ever-shrinking and commodity-consolidating sweet tooth that is our world—a world where nothing, remember, is ever innocent (least of all sugar).[66] Anthroman is a kind of embodied punch line, a figure representing the assumptions of emic intuition and nativist insight expected of black spokespersons asked to pontificate loudly and definitively on black folks and their troubling ways. Such requests are predicated on an implicit racial authenticity that grants the anointed (state-named) spokesperson authority to explain what is real, and really true, about all of black America.

What do we say about an ethnographic practice predicated on new names, superheroic names, seemingly fake names? Anthroman is an attempt to draw our attention directly to this make-believe naming—as should the pseudo-channelings of Hurston and Boas. What do we make of these fictions? These renamings? What reals do we access through these falsehoods? I am Zora Neale Hurston. I am Anthroman. I am Malcolm X. The latter is not just the new name of Lenox Avenue or of a Black Nationalist offshoot from Duke University (Malcolm X University).[67] It is everyone, everyname. What kind of schizophrenia is this, such incessant naming and renaming of self? How many names will do? How many selves? Does this nomofrenzy map onto the kinds of ethnophrenias that plague fieldwork and fieldnotes—if only to be smoothed over and repressed in our tamer published monographs?

"I got styles, all of them sick," raps Clifford Smith, aka Johnny Blaze, aka Tical, aka Ticallion Stallion, aka Shakwon, aka Methical, aka Hott Nikkels, aka MZA, aka Method Man, aka Methodical Man, yet another superheroic renaming. This is like the many styles of ethnographic writing and practice, all contested and hotly debated. It is not just semantics, this changing of names: anthropology, ethnography, mere journalism. The stakes are incredibly high, clear, ubiquitous. When Eminem breaks onto the scene with the song "My Name Is . . ." (Slim Shady and Marshall Mathers as well as Eminem), it is an interracial rehearsal of naming's centrality to contemporary culture and practice. It bespeaks his own legitimacy, which is tied not just to his Dr. Dre connections, but also to what Mark Anthony Neal parses as the difference between "white chocolate" and "blue-eyed soul," between long-term investments across racial lines and the shortcuts of exploitative appropriation.[68] White chocolate is a particularly useful metaphor for thinking about this difference because it indicates a realness predicated not on what you can see, but what you can taste, a different phenomenological starting point entirely. It is tactile, potentially messy, like the candy his name is a homonym for (Eminem/M&M). The chocolate inside is independent of the colors outside, and it all melts in your mouth, vanishes ephemerally anyway.

Dismissals of Zora Neale's crafting of vernacular English (as sincere but not authentic—that is, not about the business of what others consider to be true racial uplift) highlight sincerity's relegation to the backwaters of an oppressively externalized authenticity. Sincerity is potentially cute, at least for a little while (think of Sergeant Water's early sweetness before his venomous hate is revealed for guitar-picking "geechees" like C. J. in the Pulitzer Prize–winning "A Soldier's Story"), but it is always considered binding, constraining, disabling. Like the WTU's etymological critique of religion, it holds one back.

What's My Name?

If Kevin, whose real name isn't Kevin, can tell the mother I've called
Marla that he'd fight for the Apollo Theater over and against the non-
Apolloed white world, he is making an argument about place and race
that has serious implications for all African diasporic subjectivities.
How much more complicated this all becomes when America's military
might is significantly signified around the world by, as much as anything
else, a black man and woman. "Down with the USA and Bush" accompanied by "Powell go home" and Condoleezza Rice as the dark-skinned
embodiment of imperialist Americana. There are Harlemworlders (not
a majority, but still a hard-lined few) who believe that it wasn't Muslims
at all on September 11. They offer the white militia or even Uncle Sam
himself as the true terrorist culprit. Kevin's stance isn't quite as extreme,
at least not usually, but it does get the point across about presumptions
of place and racial purpose that underpin our conceptions of political
and cultural possibility. Cornel West likened America's newfound feelings of post-9/11 vulnerability to what he calls the "niggerization" of
America. He maintains that all Americans are learning what it actually
feels like to be systematically "unsafe, unprotected, and subject to arbitrary violence." [69]

   Does this niggerized landscape also mean that white America has access to the double binds, the veiled visions, the stereoscopic third eyes,
and the newest names we might associate with the so-called black experience? Might this be the upside to niggerized vulnerability? This is the
space where Anthroman meets not just Captain Mission and Female-
Man, not just Mos Def's Boogie Man or even Michelle Wallace's Superwoman, [70] but also where Anthroman meets his heuristic match—the inability to see with certainty and confidence across (or even within) the
socially constructed chasms of race. When social theorist Albert Murray
says that it is a mistake to assess someone named Franklin D. Roosevelt
Jones "from the outside," he is making a related argument about the
not-totally-empirical difference between authentic name-calling and sincere renamings, between sellouts and playa-haters, between superheroes
and their arch rivals. The legitimacy of outsiderly, external authenticity
testing doesn't work, and not even Anthroman can get at an absolute
real from some vantage point outside, beyond the otherness of the other.
The intersubjective moment demands an appreciation of inside's primacy, opacity, impermeability. Where authenticity imagines (as do some
characterizations of Sartre's *Being and Nothingness*) that we can only
confront one another as subjects against objects (an intersubjectivity

predicated on such incommensurate relations), sincerity counterposes a world where subjects can be mutually constituting and retain their respective and discrete subjectivities as a function of their ability not to *see* but to *listen*.[71] They are listening for the darkened, interiorized insides of the other, à la Merleau Ponty's renditions of the body as constructed through phenomenological personhood and sensate interpersonalities. They are listening to doubt, through doubt, and not just trying to beat it back. Descartes' foundational discussion of doubt (rendered through ever-widening circles from dreams to insanities to the evilest supreme deceivers,[72] with the latter reminiscent of WTUers' understandings of a global, Satan-led conspiracy) marks an even bigger trap: The more massive the doubt, the more concretized and certain that doubt, the more we use it to merely reconstitute the kernels of our own imagined certainties. Sincerity's self-doubt, its acceptance of interpersonal uncertainty, is most hermeneutically valuable when it doubts any version of doubting that eases into a certainty of doubt itself, another bankrupt version of ontologized ambiguity.[73]

Both of these possibilities (an authenticity vouched for from outside and a sincerity half-trusted through the darkest doubts of never truly knowing) constitute the realnesses we avoid, create, perform, televise, film, write, and live everyday. Authenticity is one form of realness, of the way we constitute our fictions of reality, but sincerity is its analytic cognate, often in cahoots (put in the service of authenticity's objectifications), but not always. Our distrust of the real should mean more than tighter straightjackets for tying our hands away from epistemological and existential worries. Anthroman is a concretization of that fret, of that fear, a renaming of the anthropological project through an emphasis on our repressed phobias about the slippery and shifting borders between reals and simulations. We are constantly battling over the insides and outsides of our racial reals, and authenticity tests are not nearly the most productive method for naming how they inform our individual and collectively wrought social selves. Rather, we need to find ways of reimagining racial politics, ways that privilege substance over style, reasoning over rhetoric, and actual politicking over posturing. And the names we use for this are crucial—and demand more than just old-fashioned name-calling.[74]

The loudest invocations of authenticity, the loudest iterations of racial discourse, the ones demanding impoverished and singular versions of identity, are those voiced by the very authenticity testers most haunted and tormented by their own inescapable doubts. However, these aren't simply people who are duped by the rhetorical powers of authenticity.

They stand in for authenticity's inability to craft any surefooted realities, racial or otherwise, its ultimate failure to name purported reals—with God-like absoluteness—into unquestioned actuality. Even when they hear those reals parroted back to them with exacting detail, they still have no other recourse than to trust that such discourse is emanating from dark subjective insides that can never be perfectly tested. This requisite trust, this reliance on pure faith (even when finessed through the watching of other people's "works") is the enabling node that authenticity dismisses and necessitates at the very same time. It is sincerity's silent but inescapable whisper over and against authenticity's much louder roar.

9 Real Loves

This boy Lebron James, $90,000,000 contract for Nike, and he ain't never played an NBA game. We look at stuff like that, and even though it's real— that's real money going into real pockets, and he's driving a real car down a real block, and he got on real clothes, and he bought his momma a real house— when you look at it, it's still an illusion because it's not quite real. And the reason why it's not quite real is because we are looking at the image and not the work. And we need to start raising up a generation who are willing to do the work.

Reverend Darren Ferguson

It is important that we all pay attention to the presence or absence of love and affection in our scholarship— at all stages of the production of our scholarship. If it is not there, it is important to ask ourselves why and what we should do about it. If it is there, we owe it to our readers to show it, to enable them to evaluate its role in the nature of our work. **Virginia R. Domínguez**

Mimicry is an art in itself. If it is not, then all art must fall by the same blow that strikes it down. When sculpture, painting, dancing, literature neither reflect nor suggest anything in nature or human experience, we turn away with a dull wonder in our hearts at why the thing was done. Moreover, the contention that the Negro imitates from a feeling of inferiority is incorrect. He mimics for the love of it. **Zora Neale Hurston**

: : :

What might the notion of sincerity, racial sincerity, add to academic debates about identity, authenticity, and the real? How can its interventions possibly extend the arguments already laid out along such well-worn intellectual pathways? And why enlist a sincerity like this one, described variously as opaque, interiorized, nervous, dark, and impossible to verify? In other words, how do we gain anything from relinquishing our ability to test the real, to authenticate it—especially when the realnesses in question are about the very taxonomies we use to understand ourselves as human beings inextricably caught up in complicated, hierarchical, loving, violent, friendly, and fraught relationships? Trying to think through potential answers to those questions, I have attempted to play a bit of the *bricoleur,* the "sauntering *flâneur,*" splicing the same ethnographic elements into differing configurations, combining the pieces into what I hope to be productive juxtapositions.[1] I wanted to work recursively, centripetally, emphasizing our mutual inability to look inside one another, to ever fully reach the unknown recesses of social interlocutors. And so, alongside illumination through "thick description" and ethnographic detail, I have opted for another kind of "deep play," a groping around in the darknesses of impermeability.[2]

I have done so because this impermeability, this opacity, is productive—and not merely comprehensible through the otherwise important critiques of authenticity testing. Such critiques are predicated on powerful indictments of false naturalizations, the same false naturalizations that prove integral to affective investments in the destructiveness of race—the sexisms, racisms, xenophobias, and homophobias that anchor racial essentialism. However, readings of race that rely exclusively on such de-authenticating gestures may already have conceded too much ground to the mandates of authenticity itself, an authenticity that imagines racial subjects as always already trapped within an inanimate, unthinking, and thinglike objecthood. But even these *things* have insides, a sharp "black interior" usually blunted by the dictates of begged questions ("What is inside?") that authenticity tests try, vaingloriously, to answer.[3] Sincerity recognizes these racial subjects as impermeable but not simply objectified. Instead of creating some authenticating puppeteer who predetermines the movements of racialized marionettes, sincerity sees racial identity as a continual debate between culpable subjects (even if those subjects' own fears would wish *others* into some kind of petrified and mute materiality).

The problem is not opacity, a belief that might propel some into a metaphysics of mutuality—where all is knowable to all and subjectivity implies the profoundest understanding of the selfsame other, the interconnected and permeable other.[4] Opacity here passes itself off as diaphanous, easily seen through, convincing us to think that we can peer beyond it and into the real, which is little more than the painted-over hillside that Wile E. Coyote assumes must be roadway—and not just because it looks like one, but also because he has already seen the Road Runner dash straight through and into it, into the rocky mountain's insides. Of course, for Wile E., the undeniability of that real reasserts itself as soon as his cartooned flesh meets a hardness unwilling to budge for his optical illusions. Were he just to look at the perfectly scaled mountain-portrait from a distance, with its well-proportioned convergences to some imaginary vanishing point, he might still not be sure about its trickery, but Wile E. does not rely on that alone. He tries it out, and that, I want to argue, is how race functions in people's everyday lives, how it internally deconstructs its own objectifying maneuvers. I want to label these intrinsic self-critiques a form of racial sincerity, a way of reasserting humanity through the demand that one's dark opaqueness and unknown interiorities be acknowledged. Sincerity's organizing principle maintains that the erstwhile racial object always knows more about itself, its insides, than the external authenticator—even while granting the incompleteness and partiality of all such attempts at self-knowledge.

When race operates in the world, authenticity and sincerity engage in daily jostles, ceaselessly antagonistic negotiations. Authenticity would imagine sincerity as one more test question, one more variable to be operationalized and measured, clarified and codified. Sincerity, however, stresses its excesses, its visible and invisible overflow, the elements of self not totally expressed in social phenotype. When Jeffrey (a cold-blooded, school-skipping, Decepticon gang-member) tells Shanita that God knows his heart, he is asserting just that interior irreducibility. It is what "Catching the Holy Spirit" dramatizes: an inside that those on the outside, "unborn-again readers," cannot quite understand and legislate, no matter how hard they try.[5]

Numbers don't work with sincerity, which flouts and nullifies them, confounding conventional mathematical solutions to problems of sociality and community. Sincerity's math is mystical; it is a journey from the real to the ideal, a journey that can only be caricatured with percentages and degrees. It is Zora Neale Hurston walking around Harlem, calipers in hand, determined to count and measure every single black head she can find. Sincerity exposes a science of the absurd. Certainly, there is something to all this counting, and something else, even an Ellisonian "something else," usually counted out—ghetto fabulousness, the spiritual whitenesses of Leo Feltons, conspiracy theorizing, "thingless names and nameless things," and so many more realist fetishizations of hip-hop music.[6] That sincerity can be faked, mimicked, is only all the more reason to accept its value and efficacy, privileging subjectivity's ability to wriggle out from the chains we use to hold it down, to hold it still. If our desires for realness are frantic attempts to fill our own imagined lacks (a Lacanian capacity for self-delusion that describes larger discursive formations as well, i.e., the inside-out network and its preoccupations with "perfections of form"),[7] then all these nods to realness deserve more than just poststructuralist laughs at the data-collector's expense.

Performativity warns us against ontologizing interiority, against presuming some "abiding interior depth" that comes before our "reiterated enactments."[8] Insides are "learned" through actions. Masking (Dunbarian, Fanonian, or otherwise) is not just a fake performance of self, but also a mechanism for its very constitution, through and through.[9] Conspiracy theories remind us that nothing is innocent, not even these aforementioned insides. So we remain skeptical, and racial sincerity accepts this wholeheartedly. It takes vulnerability as a necessary condition for social analysis, the ethnographic flimflam/filmflam that troubles our ability to think through all the dizzying implications of fieldwork—along with the opaque fictions of cross-cultural (or seemingly nativist) representations. We can suspiciously call out "acknowledgments" and the intertextuality of citations as little more than cocktail party name-dropping, naming for intellectual authority and authenticity's sake, a politics, poetics, and posturing of representation. Can we mine these naming practices for fakes, phonies—citations of texts not fully read, acknowledgments of colleagues not substantively known? Can we read these formalities as contaminated content, a placing of the formerly sidelined footnote into one's thematized main text? We cannot ultimately and finally know for sure, which is why Clarence Thomas can still be imagined (even now, so many ultraconservative verdicts later) as the spook ever-patiently seated by the door—seated, like us, in the dark.[10]

This groping around in the darkness is scary. It demands trust, accepting susceptibility to the persuasive liar, the subtle conjurer, the sense-memory actor. We say that "actions speak louder than words," but they too are imperfect, contingent. So what's the upside? Sincerity's purchase? Whatever else sincerity is, it should be described as tactical rather than strategic, the work of "guerilla ontologists," anarchic insurrectionists, happy with the ever-fleeting "natural anthropology" of temporary autonomous zones.[11] It posits an ephemeral user over the absolute utilizer. The user, a "fairly repulsive character who soils whatever is sold to him new and fresh, who breaks, who causes wear," is the perfect model for the sincere racial subject.[12] She does not *just* essentialize.

Her actions necessitate a double reading, a "dialectical critique," one that relishes identitarian paradoxes and contradictions.[13] Sincerity reads authenticity dialectically, against its grain, which also means critiquing in ways that do not harden "doubt" into a different kind of certainty: the antiauthentic, the worst brands of dismissive, elitist, and hubris-filled anti-essentialism.[14]

Real Black is not meant as a comprehensive compendium of authenticities and sincerities, a substantial listing of all their manifold instantiations. It only scratches at the epistemological sutures that link "biological citizenship" to "soul citizenship," false consciousness to false pretense—from the commodified biopolitics of African ancestries to the soulstealing "necropolitics" of worldwide racial oppression.[15] These muddled combinations bespeak the murky, impenetrable subjectivities of Bill's deadly sincerity. And gospel-induced ghosts, like ghetto-fabulous conspiracies and numerology, like parallax anthropologies and singing emcees, help to parse some of these particulars.

In a cameo appearance on Jay-Z's retirement CD, *The Black Album*, MC Threat exemplifies sincerity's sharpest edges. "Yo once a pimp gets threats," he says, "that's right, that's the—the that's, that's threats them / And I'm serious about mine, I'm so sincere[16] / And I, nigga I'll kill ya, I'll chop ya up / put ya inside the mattress like drug money nigga." MC Threat's sincerity marks itself as other, as different. It literally *threat*ens to slice us up into the ultimate opacity, death. One thinks, then, of that colloquial decree, "to stay black and die," a mantra of dense and vulnerable defiance.[17]

With such looming threats in the background, sincerity can be scary, but the racialized subjects do not back down, do not simply acquiesce. Instead, there is an ebb and flow, a back and forth, from sincere to authentic and back, from real illusion to fake one. When further graphed onto the critical geography of Lefebvrean directives, this vacillation looks unwieldy, chaotic. "The urban illusion," he writes, "culminates in delirium. Space, and the thought of space, leads the speaker down a dangerous path. He becomes schizophrenic and imagines a mental illness—the schizophrenia of society—onto which he projects his own illness, space sickness, mental vertigo."[18] This is the vertiginous mimesis of the ethnographrenic, of manic renamings, where the meaning of schizo (which should provide the "phrenia" its semantic twoness) is palimpsestial, erased but implied. It is the material language of hip-hop, the realness of sincerity. Not solely contingent on good or bad intentions, it is a way of experiencing the world in all its improvised and fractured wholeness. It finds a small, ephemeral victory in "being willing to do the work," recognizing, of course, that some of the work has already been done on us. On me.

Surely, I could have offered up many more stories of sincerity's wonder-working power. Tales of, say, disputed and fictitious Harlem mayorships, of homegrown tigers raised in tenement apartments. I've left out so much that might have furthered my case: zoological arguments that configure all communication as hard-wired deception, "cultural poetics" that expose the constitutive fluidity of "apparent fixities."[19] But Bill and Gina's sincerity suggests, I think, a powerful model for how we can imagine our necessary vulnerabilities, the kinds opened up by relegating exclusively authentic critiques to critical conspicuousness. Even now, writing in my Durham apartment, I can see the two of them in my mind's eye: Bill and Gina, sitting at their vending table in the hot July sun. She watches the watermelons; he chats with a friend. I am standing off to the side, changing the batteries in my tape recorder and taking note of Bill's conversation. He is showing his friend a copy of my first book, even as he shakes his head contemptuously about academia being a waste of my time. The first thing I need to do, he says, is leave Duke. I don't even have to call them and let them know. Just don't go back. And then I can begin the business of helping him to save black people, to find their collective destiny. Part of me, even the Anthroman part, really thinks he might be right, but I quickly reject this as romantic "oversincerity," maybe "Super Sincerity"—"sincerity, with a motive."[20] Shaking my head at myself dismissively, I catch Gina's eye and smile. She smiles back, watching me in silence for several more moments. "This is real love right here," she finally says, softly, almost to herself. "This is the real thing." I kept smiling, sheepishly, awkwardly, not really sure what she meant. Even now, many months later, I remain unsure. But still, I want to believe her. And so today, on this day, I simply do.

Notes

CHAPTER ONE

1. What I am calling the "ethnographic face" is one of the first points of conflict/contestation between ethnographic sincerities and authenticities. We cannot talk about qualitative fieldwork without thinking through the implications of our many ethnographic faces: performances mapping gestural differences along a continuum of affective postures—from the careful listener to the inviting friend to the confused outsider and so on. For a discussion of "calculated dimness" as a useful solicitation tool in ethnographic interviews that clearly mandates concomitantly solicitous facial expressions, see Grant D. McCracken, *The Long Interview* (Newbury Park, CA: Sage, 1988).

2. For a general overview of the nature/culture debate within anthropology and its relationship to gender analyses and social hierarchies, see Sherry Ortner, *Making Gender: The Politics and Erotics of Culture* (Boston: Beacon, 1997), especially chapter 2.

3. I am thinking here of the representations of disciplinary crisis and reconfiguration usually invoked with recourse to James Clifford and George E. Marcus, eds., *Writing Culture: The Poetics and Politics of Ethnography* (Berkeley and Los Angeles: University of California Press, 1986).

4. There is a tradition of humanistic anthropology that embraces the kinds of narrative strategies employed by fiction writers and poets, defining those gestures within the definitional boundaries of ethnography—maybe even questioning the very need for such boundaries. For a few of the important instantiations of this kind of genre-blurring and experimental work, see

Gregory Bateson, *Naven: A Survey of the Problems Suggested by the Composite Picture of the Culture of a New Guinea Tribe Drawn from Three Points of View* (Cambridge: Cambridge University Press, 1936); Claude Lévi-Strauss, *Tristes Tropiques* (New York: Atheneum, 1974); Kirin Narayan, *Storytellers, Saints, and Scoundrels: Folk Narratives in Hindu Religious Teaching* (Philadelphia: University of Pennsylvania Press, 1989); Alma Gottlieb and Philip Graham, *Parallel Worlds: An Anthropologist and a Writer Encounter Africa* (New York: Crown, 1993); Michael Taussig, *My Cocaine Museum* (Chicago: University of Chicago Press, 2004). For a historical analysis of irony and the "persuasive fictions" that have defined anthropological writing from Frazer to the postmodern present, see Marilyn Strathern, "Out of Context: The Persuasive Fictions of Anthropology," *Current Anthropology* 28, no. 3 (1987): 251–81.

5. For further explication of these terms, see Arjun Appadurai, *Modernity at Large* (Minneapolis: University of Minnesota Press, 1992); David Harvey, *The New Imperialism* (Oxford: Oxford University Press, 2003); Michael Hardt and Antonio Negri, *Empire* (Cambridge, MA: Harvard University Press, 2000), and *Multitude: War and Democracy in the Age of Empire* (New York: Penguin, 2004). For a useful ethnographic analysis of street vending in lower Manhattan, see Mitchell Duneier, *Sidewalk* (New York: Farrar, Straus, and Giroux, 1999).

6. For a description of such an "argument of images," see James W. Fernandez, "The Argument of Images and the Experience of Returning to the Whole," in *The Anthropology of Experience*, ed. Victor W. Turner and Edward M. Bruner (Urbana: University of Illinois Press, 1986), 159–87. For an important caveat predicated on the idea that "images murder the real," see Jean Baudrillard, *Simulacra and Simulation* (Ann Arbor: University of Michigan Press, 1994), 5. For a related discussion about the cannibalistic powers of media images as spectacles, see Donald Nicholson-Smith's translation of Guy Debord, *The Society of the Spectacle* (New York: Zone Books, 1995).

7. For popularized claims about the seemingly irreconcilable differences between Western and non-Western cultures in supposedly postideological contexts, see Samuel Huntington, *The Clash of Civilizations and the Remaking of the World Order* (New York: Simon and Schuster, 1996); see also Philip Jenkins, *The Next Christendom: The Coming of Global Christianity* (Oxford: Oxford University Press, 2002); and Robert D. Kaplan, *The Coming Anarchy: Shattering the Dreams of the Post Cold War* (New York: Vintage, 2001). For an accessible philosophical discussion of subjecthood, human rights, and geopolitics, see Jacques Rancière, "Who Is the Subject of the Rights of Man," *South Atlantic Quarterly* 103, nos. 2/3 (2004): 297–310. For a postcolonial take on the othering of Africa vis-à-vis Europe (an important division for current theorizations of "blackness"), see V. Y. Mudimbe, *The Invention of Africa: Gnosis, Philosophy, and the Order of Knowledge* (Bloomington: Indiana University Press, 1988); and, more recently, Paulla A. Ebron, *Performing Africa* (Princeton, NJ: Princeton University Press, 2002).

8. When the name-calling gets reversed, the right-winger becomes a racist, sexist, disingenuous Christian with un-Americanly fascistic and hawkish tendencies.

9. See Jim Sleeper, *Liberal Racism* (New York: Viking, 1997), especially chapter 6, for a discussion of "civic culture" and an analysis of how and why legal scholar Randall Kennedy distinguishes racial solidarity from nationalistic patriotism, privileging the latter.

10. Though some may argue that President George W. Bush gains a great deal of political traction from public jokes about his purported ignorance, the flipside of this humor traffics in certain concomitant assumptions about his own deeply southern and Christian sincerities, even as Joan Didion, "Mr. Bush and the Divine," *New York Review of Books* 50, no. 17 (2003), expresses the possibility that he may just be passing for Christian. For a discussion of Bush's handling of September 11 as an example of a "dignified authenticity" that Americans "trusted," see Gary L. Gregg II, "Dignified Authenticity: George W. Bush and the Symbolic Presidency," in *Considering the Bush Presidency,* ed. Mark J. Rozell and Gary L. Gregg II (New York: Oxford University Press, 2004), 88–106. It is also important to remember arguments about such binaries (sincerity vs. authenticity) being relatively evaluated and hierarchized; see Louis Dumont, *Homo Hierarchicus: An Essay on the Caste System* (Chicago: University of Chicago Press, 1970). This book is an attempt to exercise the implications of such an idea through race theory and not simply by maintaining the binary and turning it on its head. Moreover, staying on the theme of religion, one could read the Reformation as a replacement of formal religious authenticities (mediated through high priests, opaque ceremonies, and ancient languages) with vernacular religious sincerities (wherein every person becomes his or her own priest, responsible for his or her own individual salvation).

11. In chapter 2, "Real Bodies," I talk in more detail about what linguistics and semiotics provide for the parsing of these two related concepts.

12. Kwame Anthony Appiah, "Race, Culture, Identity: Misunderstood Connections," in *Color Conscious: The Political Morality of Race,* ed. Kwame Anthony Appiah and Amy Gutmann (Princeton, NJ: Princeton University Press, 1996), 97. For other powerful discussions of racial authenticity vis-à-vis blackness, see Todd Boyd, *Am I Black Enough for You? Popular Culture from The 'Hood and Beyond* (Bloomington: Indiana University Press, 1997); and, highlighting its historically classed nature, J. Martin Favor, *Authentic Blackness: The Folk in the Harlem Renaissance* (Durham, NC: Duke University Press, 1999). For a provocative and autobiographical discussion of his dismissal by Jim Brown and Amer-I-Can (Jim Brown's social justice foundation) for being "too clean cut" and not authentically black enough, see Renford Reese, *American Paradox: Young Black Men* (Durham, NC: Carolina Academic Press, 2004). Glenn C. Loury, *The Anatomy of Racial Inequality* (Cambridge, MA: Harvard University Press, 2002), reminds us that racial categories themselves grease the wheels of oppression—that categorization necessarily precedes hierarchization. In the new millennium, he uses this position not to dismiss the validity of race, but to argue for the continued importance of remedies like affirmative action.

13. Appiah, "Race, Culture, Identity," 99. For a discussion of anthropological scripts that are also "too tightly scripted," see Micaela di Leonardo, *Exotics at Home: Anthropologies, Others, and American Modernity* (Chicago: University of Chicago Press, 1998).

14. See Paul Gilroy, *Against Race: Imagining Political Culture Beyond the Color Line* (Cambridge, MA: Harvard University Press, 2000); see also Kwame Anthony Appiah, *In My Father's House: Africa in the Philosophy of Culture* (New York: Oxford University Press, 1996); and Walter Benn Michaels, *Our America: Nativism, Modernism, and Pluralism* (Durham, NC: Duke University Press, 1995).

15. For two formative collections on essentialism's many pitfalls, see Wahneema Lubiano, ed., *The House That Race Built* (New York: Pantheon, 1997); and Kwame Anthony Appiah and Henry Louis Gates Jr., eds., *Identities* (Chicago: University of Chicago Press, 1995). Two powerful and performatively different ethnographies on essentialism and authenticity are E. Patrick Johnson, *Appropriating Blackness: Performance and the Politics of Authenticity* (Durham, NC: Duke University Press, 2003), and David Grazian, *Blue Chicago: The Search for Authenticity in Urban Blues Clubs* (Chicago: University of Chicago Press, 2003). For a philosophical critique of anti-essentialist excesses vis-à-vis race, see Lucius T. Outlaw Jr., *On Race and Philosophy* (New York: Routledge, 1996).

16. See Marshall Berman, *The Politics of Authenticity: Radical Individualism and the Emergence of Modern Society* (New York: Atheneum, 1970); and Doug Rossinow, *The Politics of Authenticity: Liberalism, Christianity, and the New Left in America* (New York: Columbia University Press, 1998). For Berman, the work of Rousseau and Montesquieu help explain how and why "authenticity" moves from psychological escapism to political activism. (He also highlights Rousseau's case for modern selves being incapable of insincerity, which would attach a degree of realness to modern identities that they do not, in fact, possess.) Rossinow examines the therapeutic undertones to New Left calls for authenticity, calls that offered African Americans in the late 1960s as quintessential authentics. Charles Taylor, in *The Ethics of Authenticity* (Cambridge, MA: Harvard University Press, 1992), unpacks the communal ideals (glossed as a common "horizon") that form the basis for calls to individualism and authenticity, steeping them inextricably in sociality.

17. For a summary of social constructionism and a recent critique of its excesses, see Peter Berger and Thomas Luckmann, *The Social Construction of Reality: A Treatise in the Sociology of Knowledge* (New York: Anchor Books, 1966), and Ian Hacking, *The Social Construction of What?* (Cambridge, MA: Harvard University Press, 1999).

18. See Lionel Trilling, *Sincerity and Authenticity* (Cambridge, MA: Harvard University Press, 1971).

19. Trilling, *Sincerity and Authenticity*, 6. Moreover, to bring up performances means marking the fact that "sincerity" is also important for the successful execution (and the very definition) of performatives themselves; see John Langshaw Austin, *How to Do Things with Words* (Cambridge, MA: Harvard University Press, 1962). For an explicit discussion of race in Austinian terms, see Louis F. Mirón and Jonathan Xavier Inda, "Race as a Kind of Speech Act," *Cultural Studies: A Research Journal* 5 (2000): 85–107. There are also Lacanian notions of the real to be distinguished from the symbolic or imaginary realms. For an overview, see Philippe Julien and Devra Beck Simiu,

Jacques Lacan's Return to Freud: The Real, The Symbolic, and the Imaginary (New York: New York University Press, 1994). For a Lacanian reading of how the body gets racially marked, see Kalpana Seshadri-Cooks, *Desiring Whiteness: A Lacanian Analysis of Racial Visibility* (London: Routledge, 2000). For a discussion of Freud and Lacan in the context of postcoloniality and the search for global justice, see Ranjana Khanna, *Dark Continents: Psychoanalysis and Colonialism* (Durham, NC: Duke University Press, 2003).

20. Trilling, *Sincerity and Authenticity*, 10–11.

21. For a witty examination of faking as a foundational frame for understanding everyday social life, see William Ian Miller, *Faking It* (Cambridge: Cambridge University Press, 2003). For recent controversies in psychology around, among other things, faking mental illness for the sake of experimentation, see Lauren Slater, *Opening Skinner's Box* (New York: W. W. Norton, 2004).

22. For an analogous discussion of how sincerity demands a similarly public and "ceremonial" expression among Sumbanese Dutch Calvinists, see Webb Keane, "Sincerity, 'Witchcraft,' and the Protestants," *Cultural Anthropology* 17, no. 1 (2002): 65–92.

23. One should add the proviso that *things* and *objects* are not necessarily the same. Bill Brown, in *A Sense of Things: The Object Matter of American Literature* (Chicago: University of Chicago Press, 2003), argues for a specific, pre-objectified thingness to things and asks what it might mean to engage them under something other than the rubric of objecthood (which seems to presuppose a seeing subject) or the already economized and fetishized commodity. Even so, it is the critic who is attempting to make such distinctions, not the re-thingified things themselves. Brown is trying to compose a criteria for thingness that is not reducible to its "social life"; see Arjun Appadurai, *The Social Life of Things: Commodities in Cultural Perspective* (Cambridge: Cambridge University Press, 1988).

24. For a different version of this discussion about thingification and silencing, see Gayatri Spivak, "Can the Subaltern Speak?" in *Marxism and the Interpretation of Culture*, ed. Cary Nelson and Lawrence Grossberg (Urbana and Chicago: University of Illinois Press, 1988).

25. This very debate (about subject-subject vs. subject-object relations) was philosophically rehearsed in the work of Sartre and Merleau-Ponty. Jean-Paul Sartre, in *Being and Nothingness: An Essay on Phenomenological Ontology* (New York: Philosophical Library, 1956), insists that "the champion of sincerity" turns people into things—ironically, "precisely no longer to treat [them like] a thing" (65). It is an essentializing gesture that freezes someone in time and space. In similar "bad faith," any person likewise turns herself into a thing in trying to achieve such sincerity, especially with knowledge that the goal is unreachable. As a logical extension of this argument, Sartre maintains that human mutuality and dialogue are predicated on subject-object relations. One person must become the object of the other's subjectivity. Maurice Merleau-Ponty, in *Phenomenology of Perception* (New York: Routledge, 1991), holds out the possibility of mutual subjectivities amid radical uncertainties and inevitable interdependence. The fault line of this debate roughly mirrors the sin-

cerity/authenticity divide offered here. Of course, as social beings, we all need and want recognition from others. This recognition need not relegate us to sheer objectification. However, in a reasoned defense of affirmative action, Loury, in *Anatomy of Racial Inequality,* argues that racial categories themselves are the problem, with racial hierarchies merely a logical extension of that classificatory base. According to Loury, racial recognition is not a neutral party to social marginalization; one cannot have the latter without the former. They are truly inextricable.

26. For a historical treatment of race-based chattel slavery as a form of "social death," see Orlando Patterson, *Slavery and Social Death: A Comparative Study* (Cambridge, MA: Harvard University Press, 1982).

27. See Ralph Ellison, "A Very Stern Discipline," *Harper's,* March 1967, 76–77.

28. John L. Jackson Jr., *Harlemworld: Doing Race and Class in Contemporary Black America* (Chicago: University of Chicago Press, 2001). For an overview of kinesics, see Ray Birdwhistell, *Kinesics and Context: Essays on Body Motion Communication* (Philadelphia: University of Pennsylvania Press, 1980). Where kinesics imagines a broadly cultural basis for bodily movements, I tried to make an argument for a particularly racial lens through which people interpret the body's everyday actions. *Harlemworld* also makes an almost existentialist claim for racial experiences over and against racial essences. I argue that vernacular notions of race define it as what people "do" more than what they "are" in some sweepingly ontological sense.

29. I am interested in the real as "that created consistency, that regular constellation of ideas as the pre-eminent thing . . . not to mere being, as Wallace Stevens's phrase has it" (Edward Said, *Orientalism* [New York: Pantheon, 1978], 5), or, as even more provocatively and famously put by Jean Baudrillard, "Disneyland is presented as an imaginary in order to make us believe that the rest is real, whereas all of Los Angeles and the America that surrounds it are no longer real, but belong to the hyperreal order and to the order of simulation" (*Simulacra and Simulation* [Ann Arbor: University of Michigan Press], 12).

30. For a discussion of the political and legal agreements among whites (offered up as universal) that have historically served as a hidden underside to institutionalized racial oppression, see Charles W. Mills, *The Racial Contract* (Ithaca, NY: Cornell University Press, 1999). On identificatory opacity, see David Murray, *Opacity: Gender, Sexuality, Race, and the "Problem" of Identity in Martinique* (New York: Peter Lang, 2002).

31. This move is always, as Foucault reminds us, a certain kind of power play, even if we dispute his capillary organizing principle and opt for more clearcut, agential heroes and villains. For a discussion of Michel Foucault's usefulness to anthropological theory-building and colonial studies, see Ann Laura Stoler, *Race and the Education of Desire: Foucault's History of Sexuality and the Colonial Order of Things* (Durham, NC: Duke University Press, 1995).

32. Frantz Fanon, *Black Skin, White Masks* (New York: Grove Press, 1967), 112–13.

33. For an articulation of "anti-anti-essentialism," see Paul Gilroy, *The*

Black Atlantic: Modernity and Double Consciousness (Cambridge, MA: Harvard University Press, 1993), particularly chapter 3. James Clifford, *On the Edges of Anthropology: Interviews* (Chicago: University of Chicago Press, 2003), applies this idea to his work in Native American advocacy.

34. See the dialogue between Peggy Phelan, in *Unmarked: The Politics of Performance* (New York: Routledge, 1993), and Philip Auslander, in *Liveness: Performance in a Mediatized Culture* (London: Routledge, 1999), for debates within performance studies about the metaphysical and epistemological question of mediation.

35. For an almost magisterial treatment of the ethics and politics of "doubt," see Jennifer Michael Hecht, *Doubt: A History* (San Francisco: HarperSanFrancisco, 2003). I also want this written ethnography to embrace the uncertainties of doubt. Ronald Petias, in *Writing Performance: Poeticizing the Researcher's Body* (Carbondale: Southern Illinois University Press, 1999), is especially suggestive in terms of his comments about "the poetic essay": "I want to write in another shape. I seek a space that unfolds softly, one that circles around, slides between, swallows whole. I want to live in feelings that are illusive, to live in doubt" (xi). Indeed, he wants to write stridently and courageously even from a position of irredeemable doubt.

36. For a discussion of Evans-Pritchard's work with the Azande in the 1930s (and an articulation of this Azande quotation's philosophical significance), see Veena Das, "Wittgenstein and Anthropology," *Annual Review of Anthropology* 27 (October 1998): 171–95.

37. Staring down negativity is reminiscent of the call in Michael Herzfeld, *Cultural Intimacy: Social Poetics in the Nation-State* (New York: Routledge, 1996), to take stereotypes seriously as windows into political and cultural processes of state-making.

38. In the 2001 film *The Believer,* written and directed by Henry Bean, Ryan Gosling plays Danny Balint, a neo-Nazi skinhead who tries to hide the fact that he is actually Jewish.

39. Paul Tough, "The Black White Supremacist," *New York Times,* May 25, 2003.

40. Tough, "Black White Supremacist."

41. Ulick Varange, *Imperium: The Philosophy of History and Politics* (Sausalito, CA: Noontide Press, 1948), 294.

42. For a discussion of how blood gets quantifiably linked to identity in a Native American context, see Circe Sturm, *Blood Politics: Race, Culture, and Identity in the Cherokee Nation of Oklahoma* (Berkeley and Los Angeles: University of California Press, 2002).

43. Tough, "Black White Supremacist."

44. Cornel West, *Race Matters* (Boston: Beacon, 1994).

45. For a general overview of passing as both political practice and literary conceit, see Elaine K. Ginsberg, ed., *Passing and the Fictions of Identity* (Durham, NC: Duke University Press, 1996). Also, John L. Jackson Jr. and Martha S. Jones, eds., *pass•ing,* issue no. 28 of *Women & Performance* (2005).

46. See Richard Handler, "Authenticity," *Anthropology Today* 2, no. 1

(1986): 2–4; also, Eric Gable and Richard Handler, *New History in an Old Museum: Creating the Past in Colonial Williamsburg* (Durham, NC: Duke University Press, 1997).

47. See James Clifford's influential essay entitled "On Ethnographic Authority" in *The Predicament of Culture: Twentieth-Century Ethnography, Literature, and Art* (Cambridge, MA: Harvard University Press, 1988).

48. See George Marcus and Michael Fischer, *Anthropology as Cultural Critique: An Experimental Moment in the Human Sciences* (Chicago: University of Chicago Press, 1986).

49. See Bronislaw Malinowski, *A Diary in the Strict Sense of the Term* (New York: Harcourt, Brace, and World, 1967); David Stoll, *Rigoberta Menchu and the Story of All Guatemalans* (Boulder, CO: Westview Press, 1999); Derek Freeman, *Margaret Mead and Samoa: The Making and Unmaking of an Anthropological Myth* (Cambridge, MA: Harvard University Press, 1983); and Patrick Tierney, *Darkness in El Dorado: How Scientists and Journalists Devastated the Amazon* (New York: W. W. Norton, 2000).

50. Lee Clarke, *Mission Improbable: Using Fantasy Documents to Tame Disaster* (Chicago: University of Chicago Press, 1999).

51. Anthropology often relegates the spatial/cultural other to a mere symbol of the West's prehistoric past. For the definitive argument about this temporal othering (yet another form of thingification), see Johannes Fabian, *Time and the Other: How Anthropology Makes Its Object* (New York: Columbia University Press, 1983).

52. See Adam Kuper, *The Invention of Primitive Society: Transformation of an Illusion* (New York: Routledge, 1988) and di Leonardo, *Exotics at Home,* particularly chapter 1.

53. Michael A. Elliott, *The Culture Concept: Writing and Difference in the Age of Realism* (Minneapolis: University of Minnesota Press, 2002).

54. Intersubjectivity is an incredibly complicated issue for anthropologists. This begins with disputes about subjectivity itself, its dissolution or reinforcement. One can read, say, Claude Lévi-Strauss's structuralism as a major example of the former and the "anthropology of the senses" school as reclamation of the latter. One can map most of the major theoretical currents in cultural anthropology along this same continuum, even so-called postmodernist attempts to keep both options in a kind of critical and productive tension. For a powerful anthropological argument about the centrality of intersubjectivity for dialectical relationships between particulars and universals, see Michael Jackson, *Minima Ethnographica: Intersubjectivity and the Anthropological Project* (Chicago: University of Chicago Press, 1998).

55. This reference to "the real thing" comes from Richard Handler, "Authenticity," *Anthropology Today* 2, no. 1 (February 1986): 2–4. Moreover, ethnographobia is meant to gloss both (1) the fears of inherent corruptions intrinsic to ethnography as genre and (2) related dread about the vulnerable intersubjectivities demanded by the fieldwork experience itself.

56. For a discussion of *fluidarity* and its implications for leftist political certainty, see Diane Nelson, *A Finger in the Wound: Body Politics in Quincen-*

tennial Guatemala (Berkeley and Los Angeles: University of California Press, 1999).

57. In some ways, this notion of channeling may also be a useful metaphor for how we use citations. Citationality involves a politics, a poetics, and a psychology that shares some important elements with New Age channeling techniques. Calling on the power of other anthropologists during fieldwork is a kind of a literalization of the metaphorical calling forth of the citation, or might be interestingly reimagined in that light.

58. *Blankman* is a 1994 comedy directed by Mike Binder. Anthroman©®™ is a caricatured (re)presentation of the methodological underpinnings that support fantasies about objectivism in the social sciences. I use him to articulate the scholastic desire for social scientists to perform almost superhuman explanatory feats. The ©®™ symbols (which I will not append to every instance of the term) mark the politico-economic issues involved in contemporary knowledge production in the late twentieth century, which has almost reached the level of absurdity in its pervasiveness. The commodification of knowledge (through high-priced book deals, six-figure salary negotiations, and academics with rock-star followings) is almost better described as a kind of *comedy*fication, where the powers of a hyper and ludic capitalism reign supreme—and the invisible hands of the marketplace grasp its own belly in uncontrollable laughter.

59. This positing of friendship also needs serious interrogating, especially when couched (at least partially) in terms of pragmatics.

60. For a discussion of "blurred genres" as a writerly response to the call for interdisciplinarity, see Clifford Geertz, *Works and Lives: The Anthropologist as Author* (Cambridge: Polity Press, 1988). This ethnographrenia is the ethnographic equivalent of what Kenneth Gergen calls "multiphrenia." For a discussion of multiphrenia as a way to define the newness of contemporary life and the dissolutions of contemporary social selves, see Kenneth J. Gergen, *An Invitation to Social Construction* (London: Sage, 1999).

61. Of course, this is a version of the disorder that will never specifically be recognized in the DSM-IV. For an example of the kind of theoretical arguments that have helped to lead anthropology into a discussion of multivocality, see Mikhail Bakhtin, *The Dialogic Imagination* (Austin: University of Texas Press, 1981). For a discussion of autoethnography and progressive anthropology, see Irma McClaurin, "Introduction," in *Black Feminist Anthropology: Theory, Politics, Praxis, and Poetics,* ed. Irma McClaurin (New Brunswick, NJ: Rutgers University Press, 2001). Also see Deborah E. Reed-Danahay, *Auto/ethnography: Rewriting the Self and the Social* (Oxford: Berg, 1997), for a look at autoethnography's earlier predecessors—as well as an attempt to explain its epistemological and political import.

62. Judith Butler, "Force of Fantasy: Mapplethorpe, Feminism, and Discursive Excess," in *The Judith Butler Reader,* ed. Sara Salih (Malden, MA: Blackwell, 2004), 183–203, argues that "the real is positioned both before and after its representation; and representation becomes a moment of the reproduction and consolidation of the real" (185).

63. Discussions in performance studies have been foundational for me and my understanding of realness and writing. *Real Black* is an attempt to tangle with realness through the ever-important lenses of performance and performativity. I find Della Pollock's notion of "performative writing" highly suggestive here. She describes it as "an analytic, a way of framing and underscoring aspects of writing/life" as well as "an important, dangerous, and difficult intervention into routine representations of social/performative life." See her "Performative Writing," in *The Ends of Performance,* ed. Peggy Phelan and Jill Lane (New York: New York University Press, 1998), 75. I also take performance to be an important corrective to elitist academic preoccupations with textualization. For a critique of textualist emphases in social scientific writing and research, see Dwight Conquergood, "Performance Studies: Interventions and Radical Research," *Drama Review* 46, no. 2 (2002): 145–56. For a discussion of how "a radical performative social science" can be used for progressive political ends, see Norman Denzin, *Performance Ethnography: Critical Pedagogy and the Politics of Culture* (Thousand Oaks, CA: Sage, 2003).

64. For a description of "heritage" as replacement for a strictly biological notion of race, see Kamari Maxine Clarke, *Mapping Yorùbá Networks: Power and Agency in the Making of Transnational Communities* (Durham, NC: Duke University Press, 2004).

65. For two very differently pitched critiques of statistical abuses/misuses, see Tukufu Zuberi, *Thicker Than Blood: How Racial Statistics Lie* (Minneapolis: University of Minnesota Press, 2001); and Joel Best, *Damned Lies and Statistics: Untangling Numbers from the Media, Politicians, and Activists* (Berkeley and Los Angeles: University of California Press, 2001). For an invocation of the "mathematical frock coat," see Georges Bataille, *Visions of Excess: Selected Writings, 1927–1939* (Minneapolis: University of Minnesota Press, 1985), 31.

66. For an analysis of this connection between the primitive and the filmic, see Rosalind C. Morris, *New World in Fragments: Film, Ethnography, and the Representation of Northwest Coast Cultures* (Boulder, CO: Westview Press, 1994).

67. As mentioned before, this relationship between realness and representation is fraught with many conceptual pitfalls and contentious points of disagreement. In *Orientalism,* Edward Said (by way of Foucault) warns us that all representations are always already not real; however, Robert Young, *White Mythologies: Writing History and the West* (London: Routledge, 1990), calls this a kind of circular trap, a tabling of the real, characterizing Orientalism as a kind of neo-Kantian argument that reduces the real to little more than what we make it, a totality with no actual reference/referent, a floating signifier upon which we are all shipwrecked (135).

68. For a discussion of "free indirect discourse," see Henry Louis Gates Jr., *The Signifying Monkey: A Theory of Afro-American Literary Criticism* (New York: Oxford University Press, 1988).

69. The connections between race and the writerly voice connect quite specifically to broader issues of ethnographic writing and performativity. According to Diana Taylor, "Ethnography not only studies performance (the rituals

and social dramas commentators habitually refer to); it is a kind of performance" (*The Archive and Repertoire: Performing Cultural Memory in the
Americas* [Durham, NC: Duke University Press, 2003], 75). She goes on to
state that "[t]he ethnographic Other, like the dramatic character played by an
actor or like Columbus's 'Indian,' is part 'real,' part 'fiction'; that is, real bodies
come to embody fictional qualities and characteristics created by the ethnog-
rapher/dramatist/discoverer. Nonetheless, the ethnographer insists that the
spectacle is 'real.'" Any written performance of race should take such a critique seriously. How much do we want our performative writing to stand in
unproblematically for the realness of racial difference?

70. For a discussion of "thick description" and its parsing of winks,
twitches, and nods, see Clifford Geertz, *The Interpretation of Cultures: Selected Essay* (New York: Basic Books, 1973), 3. Geertz also memorably described the law simply as "one distinct manner of imagining the real," in
Local Knowledge: Further Essays in Interpretive Anthropology (New York:
Basic Books, 1983), 184.

71. "Annayya's Anthropology" is the title of a short story by A. K. Rama-
nujan, where the main character, a foreign student studying anthropology in
Chicago, comes upon an anthropological text in the stacks that shockingly
depicts scenes of his family back home—indeed, even the death of his father,
which Annayya knew nothing about before discovering the photos in the ethnographic account.

72. For a reading of Gramscian traces and their need for inventorying, see
Said, *Orientalism*, 25.

73. It is not enough to use Gramsci's distinction between civil and political
institutions to argue that sincerity's difference from authenticity is merely another pernicious doubling within power and control—exercised by coercion
or consent, by domination or the complicity of hegemony. I argue that racial
sincerity, as much as it can be marshaled toward such hegemonic ends, also
produces an ambiguous and interiorized subject (maybe even an agent) that
potentially challenges the reach of both hegemony and outright exploitation.

CHAPTER TWO

1. The terms stand for North (of) Harlem, South (of) Harlem, and Spanish
Harlem. These names, along with older designations—like Manhattanville,
Hamilton Heights, and Morningside Heights—often operate as everyday eu-
phemisms for a Harlem that connotes oversaturation with African American
difference and danger. Neighborhoods throughout New York City splinter off
from one another with recourse to such name changes, often fleeing from popular stereotypes about particular proximate locations. When the split becomes
sufficiently acknowledged, residents may even petition for different zip codes,
a more official and numerical form of spatial differentiation.

2. See Henri Lefebvre, *The Production of Space* (Cambridge, MA: Blackwell, 1991).

3. Lefebvre's distinction is reminiscent of Walter Benjamin's argument
about the anthropological significance of social spaces being predicated on

negotiating those locations from the inside out, less scientifically than absent-mindedly and functionally. See Walter Benjamin, "The Work of Art in the Age of Mechanical Reproduction," in *Illuminations* (New York: Harcourt, Brace, and Jovanovich, 1968), 217–52. Benjamin's argument is reworked and refined in Michael Taussig, *The Nervous System* (New York: Routledge, 1992), especially "Tactility and Distraction." For a similar discussion about how the Cross Bronx Expressway is best understood while driving on it (as opposed to examining it from a building nearby), see Marshall Berman, *All That Is Solid Melts into Air: The Experience of Modernity* (New York: Penguin Books, 1988), especially "In the Forest of Symbols."

4. Lefebvre, *Production of Space*, 362.

5. In this chapter, I almost cringe with any numerical invocation offered up as a mechanism for locking the transparent facticity of Harlem into its realistic place. Instead, I want to use numbers to trouble the waters of our own dreamed-of ratio-realisms. Still, readers have certain expectations about contextualization that it would behoove me to meet, even as that meeting place is the very pivot point for my own flawed disavowals. For other recent ethnographic engagements with contemporary Harlem as a demographic site, see Paul Stoller, *Money Has No Smell: The Africanization of New York City* (Chicago: University of Chicago Press, 2002); Monique Michelle Taylor, *Harlem: Between Heaven and Hell* (Minneapolis: University of Minnesota Press, 2002); John L. Jackson Jr., *Harlemworld: Doing Race and Class in Contemporary Black America* (Chicago: University of Chicago Press, 2001); Sabiyha Prince, *Constructing Belonging: Class, Race, and Harlem's Professional Workers* (New York: Routledge, 2004); and Katherine S. Newman, *No Shame in My Game: The Working Poor in the Inner City* (New York: Russell Sage and Knopf, 1999). For a serious analysis of what these same numbers might mean for local life-chances, specifically along class and gender lines, see Leith Mullings and Alaka Wali, *Stress and Resilience: The Social Context of Reproduction in Central Harlem* (New York: Kluwer Academic/Plenum, 2001).

6. Arjun Appadurai, *Modernity at Large: Cultural Dimensions of Globalization* (Minneapolis: University of Minnesota Press, 1996), 182.

7. For a discussion of how things are "hidden in plain sight," see Micaela di Leonardo, *Exotics at Home: Anthropologies, Others, and American Modernity* (Chicago: University of Chicago Press, 1998). Her rubric of anthropological "morality plays" is particularly instructive here.

8. Paul Ormerod, *Butterfly Economics* (London: Farber and Farber, 1998), xi.

9. For a discussion of these earlier incarnations of mathematical anthropology, see Michael Burton, "Mathematical Anthropology," *Annual Review of Anthropology* 2 (1973): 189–99; and Paul Kay, ed., *Explorations in Mathematical Anthropology* (Cambridge, MA: MIT Press, 1971).

10. Counting people and their movements through census-data collection and related procedures is only one way to mark the ends of nationhood and the tentacles of transnationality.

11. For a critique of statistics on race, racism, and difference, see Tukufu Zuberi, *Thicker Than Blood: How Racial Statistics Lie* (Minneapolis: Univer-

sity of Minnesota Press, 2001). For a discussion of anthropological roots in realism, see Michael Elliott, *The Culture Concept: Writing and Difference in the Age of Realism* (Minneapolis: University of Minnesota Press, 2002). For an argument about what a different kind of visualization might add to the use of multivariate statistics, see Lothar Krempel and Thomas Plumper, "Exploring the Dynamics of International Trade by Combining the Comparative Advantages of Multivariate Statistics and Network Visualizations," *Journal of Social Structure* 4 (2003): 1–22. For an overview of "rule-bound systems" analysis as a mechanism for using math to test certain cultural characteristics and trait frequencies among social groups, see Paul Ballonoff, "Notes toward a Mathematical Theory of Culture," *Mathematical Anthropology and Cultural Theory: An International Journal* 1 (2000): 3–20.

12. For a discussion about the slipperiness, interpretive flexibility, and embodied uncertainty of numbers in the context of global finance, see Caitlin Zaloom, "Ambiguous Numbers," *American Ethnologist* 30, no. 2 (2003): 258–72. For a more general discussion about how we seduce ourselves into certainty, from the embellishments of classic rhetoric to the self-evidence of numeracy, see Mary Poovey, *A History of the Modern Fact: Problems of Knowledge in the Sciences of Wealth and Society* (Chicago: University of Chicago Press, 1998). Of course, using numerology as a way to think numbers is a potentially dangerous thing—open to some obvious criticisms and downright dismissals. Think, for instance, of how Adorno made fun of astrology from the 1930s to the 1950s, critiquing it as a form of "semi-erudition" and fascism, something only believed by those not intellectually equipped to really understand the intricacies of science. For Adorno, it is just another absolutist appeal—and another way to craft people into mere consumers. He likens it to "other irrational creeds like racism" and reduces "number-mysticism" to little more than "preparation for administrative statistics and cartel prices." See Theodor Adorno, *The Stars Down to Earth and Other Essays on the Irrational in Culture* (New York: Routledge, 1995). Karl Popper criticizes astrology and numerology as methods of inquiry on the grounds that they would claim to be unfalsifiable, the very trait that I want to rethink as part of their hermeneutical strength. See Karl Popper, *Conjectures and Refutations* (London: Routledge, 1963).

13. For a rendition of this story, see Louis Menand, *The Metaphysical Club: The Story of Ideas in America* (New York: Farrar, Straus, and Giroux, 2001).

14. Charles Eliot, "Reminiscences of Peirce," *American Mathematical Monthly* 32 (1925): 3; retold in Menand, *Metaphysical Club.*

15. Gilbert Osofsky, *Harlem: The Making of a Ghetto* (New York: Harper and Row, 1971).

16. For a differently pitched discussion of this racialized history, see Osofsky, *Harlem;* Winston James, *Holding Aloft the Banner of Ethiopia: Caribbean Radicalism in Early Twentieth Century America* (London: Verso, 1998); Stoller, *Money Has No Smell.*

17. Michel de Certeau, Luce Giard, and Pierre Mayol, *The Practice of Everyday Life,* vol. 2, *Living and Cooking* (Minneapolis: University of Minnesota Press, 1998), 11.

18. This is a kind of global biopolitics that does not simply assume some postracial future once the human genome project is completed. As genetically unreal as race may be, it can still use genetics to justify nation-building and other absolutist work. I expound on this idea in chapter 5. For a gesture toward genomic biopolitics as an indication of postracial possibilities, see Adriana Petryna, *Life Exposed: Biological Citizenship after Chernobyl* (Princeton, NJ: Princeton University Press, 2002), 14.

19. See Michael Hardt and Antonio Negri, *Empire* (Cambridge, MA: Harvard University Press, 2000); and David Harvey, *The New Imperialism* (Oxford: Oxford University Press, 2003). For a discussion of Amiri Baraka's notion of "the changing same," see Paul Gilroy, *The Black Atlantic: Modernity and Double Consciousness* (Cambridge, MA: Harvard University Press, 1993).

20. For seminal discussions of globalism and modernity, see Appadurai, *Modernity at Large,* and Frederic Jameson, *Postmodernism, or the Cultural Logic of Late Capitalism* (Durham, NC: Duke University Press, 1991).

21. As Margaret Mead once put it, "Skin color can't be ignored. It is real." See James Baldwin and Margaret Mead, *A Rap on Race* (New York: J. B. Lippincott, 1971), 8.

22. For instance, the chapter by George Grier and Eunice Grier, "Urban Displacement: A Reconnaissance," in *Back to the City: Issues in Neighborhood Renovation,* ed. Shirley Laska and Daphne Spain (Oxford: Pergamon Press, 1980), 252–68, provides an early operationalization of dislocation; Barrett A. Lee and David C. Hodge, "Spatial Differentials in Residential Displacement," *Urban Studies* 21 (1984): 219–31, exempts occurrences like natural disasters from its definition of displacement and comes up with a national rate of 3 percent. David Ley, "Gentrification in Recession: Social Change in Six Canadian Inner Cities, 1981–1986," *Urban Geography* 13, no. 3 (1993): 230–56, compares six Canadian cities in the 1980s. Michael H. Schill and Richard P. Nathan, *Revitalizing America's Cities: Neighborhood Reinvestment and Displacement* (Albany: SUNY Press, 1983), focuses exclusively on rates of dislocation in gentrifying neighborhoods, while Rowland Atkinson, "Measuring Displacement and Gentrification in Greater London," *Urban Studies* 37, no. 1 (2000): 149–65, compares gentrifying neighborhoods with nongentrifying ones. Winifred Current, "Evicting Memory: Displacing Work and Home in a Gentrifying Neighborhood" (unpublished paper presented at Upward Neighborhood Trajectories Conference, University of Glasgow, 2002), looks at more than residential displacement, examining both "industrial displacement" (job loss) and "social displacement" (historical invisibility). Raphael W. Bostic and Richard Martin, speaking at the same conference, look specifically at intra-racial conflicts in "Black Homeowners as a Gentrifying Force? Neighborhood Dynamics in the Context of Minority Homeownership."

23. Ruth Glass, "Introduction: Aspects of Change," in *London: Aspects of Change,* ed. Centre for Urban Studies (London: MacGibbon and Kee, 1964).

24. See Kenneth Jackson, *Crabgrass Frontier: The Suburbanization of the United States* (Oxford: Oxford University Press, 1985); and Neil Smith, *The New Urban Frontier: Gentrification and the Revanchist City* (London: Routledge, 1996).

25. For one of the most famous sociological articulations of suburbanization's racial implications, see William Julius Wilson, *The Declining Significance of Race: Blacks and Changing American Institutions* (Chicago: University of Chicago Press, 1987).

26. George Gilder, *Wealth and Power* (New York: Basic Books, 1981).

27. For an example of these arguments, see Lawrence Mead, *The New Politics of Poverty: The Non-working Poor in America* (New York: HarperCollins, 1992); Charles Murray, *Losing Ground: American Social Policy, 1950 to 1980* (New York: Basic Books, 1984).

28. Criticisms of the "culture of poverty" are discussed in Adolph Reed, *Stirrings in the Jar: Black Politics in the Post Civil Rights Era* (Minneapolis: University of Minneapolis Press, 1999); and Wilson, *Declining Significance of Race.*

29. Richard Murnane and Frank Levy, *Teaching the New Basic Skills: Principles for Educating Children to Thrive in a Changing Economy* (New York: Free Press, 1996).

30. This "born again" rhetoric created optimism and newfangled strategizing among many Harlem residents, and by the 1990s (1) the Harlem Strategic Cultural Initiative had appeared, a group of nine local institutions (including the Studio Museum, the Dance Theater of Harlem, and the Harlem Boys Choir) that attempted to pool their resources in an effort to attract more tourism dollars; (2) a preservationist was preparing to publish a glossy coffee-table book about architectural revitalization; see Michael Henry Adams, *Harlem Lost and Found* (New York: Monacelli Press, 2002); and (3) Mayor Rudolph Giuliani was on a mission to sell off newly desirable city-owned buildings in Harlem.

31. Working with Boston data from the late 1980s, Jacob Vigdor, in "Does Gentrification Harm the Poor?" (unpublished paper, Duke University, 2002), finds that "low-status families" in gentrifying neighborhoods have lower rates of displacement than other families in the same gentrifying circumstances. Lance Freeman and Frank Braconi make a similar point based on New York City data from the 1990s in "Gentrification and Displacement," *Urban Prospect* 8, no. 1 (2002): 1-4.

32. See Smith, *New Urban Frontier.*

33. These quotations are all from the organization's in-house pamphlets, posters, and other literature—as well as an article about the fair in a free local weekly, *Harlem News,* July 21, 2003, 9.

34. Ibid.

35. The quotations are from organization pamphlets. Another flyer noted that local residents owned about 10 percent of the housing stock in the neighborhood, whereas the city average was said to hover at around 30 percent.

36. This interethnic and interracial coalition of tenant activists is a clear example of contemporary urban politics' demand for cross-ethnic mobilization. For an anthropological argument about just such current political realities, see Roger Sanjek, *The Future of Us All: Race and Neighborhood Politics in New York City* (Ithaca, NY: Cornell University Press, 1998).

37. See Taylor, *Harlem: Between Heaven and Hell.*

38. See Irma Watkins-Owens, *Caribbean Immigrants and the Harlem Community, 1900-1930* (Bloomington: Indiana University Press, 1996).

39. Mullings and Wali, *Stress and Resilience.*

40. For a discussion of Disneyfication, see Sharon Zukin, *The Cultures of Cities* (Cambridge, MA: Blackwell, 1995).

41. For "quality of life" policing, see James Wilson and George Kelling, "Broken Windows: The Police and Public Safety," *Atlantic Monthly,* March 1982, 29–38. For an alternative articulation of these issues about urban improvement, see the discussion on "collective efficacy" in Robert J. Sampson, Stephen Raudenbush, and Felton Earls, "Neighborhoods and Violent Crime: A Multilevel Study of Collective Efficacy," *Science* 277 (1997): 918–24.

42. This is reminiscent of the evocative notion of "private landmarks" in Colson Whitehead, *The Colossus of New York: A City in Thirteen Parts* (New York: Doubleday, 2003).

43. Certeau, Giard, and Mayol, *Living and Cooking.*

44. David Harvey, *The Condition of Postmodernity: An Enquiry into the Origins of Cultural Change* (Cambridge, MA: Blackwell, 1989), and *Spaces of Capital: Towards a Critical Geography* (New York: Routledge, 2001).

45. Frederic Jameson, "Notes on Globalization as a Philosophical Issue," in *The Cultures of Globalization,* ed. Frederic Jameson and Masao Miyoshi (Durham, NC: Duke University Press, 1998).

46. Appadurai, *Modernity at Large.*

47. See Deborah A. Thomas and Kamari Maxine Clarke, eds., *Globalization and Race: Transformations in the Cultural Production of Blackness* (Durham, NC: Duke University Press, forthcoming 2006).

48. These ads on buildings, which force pedestrians to look up at them in awe, create the gesture toward a "vertical city" amid the relative horizontality of Harlem.

49. I mean to invoke two different rehearsals of *ekphrases* (i.e., vivid descriptions of visual imagery), the latter of which is specifically racialized: W. J. T. Mitchell, *Picture Theory: Essays on Verbal and Visual Representation* (Chicago: University of Chicago Press, 1994); and Maurice Wallace, *Constructing the Black Masculine: Identity and Ideality in African American Men's Literary and Culture, 1775–1995* (Durham, NC: Duke University Press, 2002).

50. Put differently, "the margins are not inherently marginal"; see Lawrence Grossberg, *Dancing in Spite of Myself: Essays on Popular Culture* (Durham, NC: Duke University Press, 1997), 3.

51. Pierre Bourdieu, *The Logic of Practice* (Stanford, CA: Stanford University Press, 1990). This particular example is glossed from Philippe Bourgois, *In Search of Respect: Selling Crack in El Barrio* (Cambridge: Cambridge University Press, 1995).

52. For a Caribbean version of this "radical consumerism," see Deborah A. Thomas, *Modern Blackness: Nationalism, Globalization, and the Politics of Culture in Jamaica* (Durham, NC: Duke University Press, 2004).

53. These are descriptions of two websites named for ghetto fabulousness: ghettofabulous.com and ghetto-fabulous.com.

54. Houston Baker, *Turning South Again: Re-Thinking Modernism/Re-Reading Booker T. Washington* (Durham, NC: Duke University Press, 2001); Bill Brown, *A Sense of Things* (Chicago: University of Chicago Press, 2003);

Claire Alexander, *The Art of Being Black: The Creation of Black British Youth Identities* (Oxford: Oxford University Press, 1996).

55. For a discussion of how members of the middle class in Katmandu calculate forms of citizenship that "count," see Mark Liechty, *Suitably Modern: Making Middle-Class Culture in a Consumer Society* (Princeton, NJ: Princeton University Press, 2003).

CHAPTER THREE

1. Sing Sing, located just north of New York City, is one of the largest and most notorious prisons in the state. It is where, for instance, Thomas Alva Edison's electric chair was first demonstrated at the beginning of the twentieth century. Before that, in the early nineteenth century, prisoners at Sing Sing, and just about any other American prison, were forbidden to sing, dance, or cavort with one another in ways interestingly resonant with the tale retold here. For a discussion of Sing Sing's controversial history, see Scott Christianson, *Condemned: Inside the Sing Sing Death House* (New York: New York University Press, 2000), or Ted Conover, *Newjack: Guarding Sing Sing* (New York: Random House, 2000).

2. This is a reference to the 1984 film *Brother from Another Planet*, written and directed by John Sayles, starring Joe Morton. The movie is about a space alien who lands in Harlem, New York, and passes for an African American. At the risk of digressing into some kind of vernacular dictionary, "bigupping" means to give someone "props," that is, to show respect for another person's abilities in a particular sphere—in this case, singing. This theme comes up again later vis-à-vis hip-hop emcees.

3. Dwight Conquergood, "Rethinking Ethnography: Toward a Critical Cultural Politics," *Communication Monographs* 58 (1991): 180.

4. For a philosophical discussion of this kind of subject-forming subjugation, see Judith Butler, *The Psychic Life of Power: Theories of Subjection* (Stanford, CA: Stanford University Press, 1997).

5. On one side of the debate, Molefi Kete Asante, *Afrocentricity* (Trenton, NJ: Africa World Press, 1988), espouses a degree of ancestral, cultural, and even biological realness for race that many social constructionists would dismiss out of hand. Walter Benn Michaels, in *Our America: Nativism, Modernism, and Pluralism* (Durham, NC: Duke University Press, 1995), imagines that these same social constructionists merely cloak an equally biological grounding for race.

6. Such a naturalizing move is critiqued by all comers. One of its most recent incarnations, indebted to Marilyn Strathern and hinging on an abstract discussion of organizational forms irreducible to race, is Annelise Riles, *The Network Inside Out* (Ann Arbor: University of Michigan Press, 2000).

7. Vincent L. Wimbush, *African Americans and the Bible: Sacred Texts and Social Textures* (New York: Continuum, 2000), 21.

8. Wimbush, *African Americans and the Bible,* 22.

9. Kathleen Stewart, "Conspiracy Theory's Worlds," in *Paranoia within Reason: A Casebook on Conspiracy as Explanation,* ed. George E. Marcus

(Chicago: University of Chicago Press, 1999), 13, 14. Stewart's characterization becomes even more important in the next chapter, which examines such conspiracy theories as alternative ways of rendering the real.

10. See Michael Taussig, *The Nervous System* (New York: Routledge, 1992), especially chapter 8. Peggy Phelan's *Unmarked: The Politics of Performance* (New York: Routledge, 1993) is another attempt to challenge the hegemony of visuality in contemporary cultural criticism.

11. For an anthology that walks the same tightrope, see Monique Guillory and Richard C. Green, eds., *Soul: Black Power, Politics, and Pleasure* (New York: New York University Press, 1998).

12. For a discussion of Seventh-Day Adventist history and contemporary practices, especially as inflected by racial difference, see Calvin B. Rock, *Institutional Loyalty versus Racial Freedom: The Dilemma of Black Seventh-Day Adventist Leadership* (PhD diss., University of Tennessee, 1984).

13. For a more general discussion of the way similar sacred/profane distinctions have shaped the larger history of gospel music in American culture, see Jerma A. Jackson, *Singing in my Soul: Black Gospel Music in a Secular Age* (Chapel Hill: University of North Carolina Press, 2004).

14. For a dismissive critique of doctrinal changes within the Seventh-Day Adventist church (along with a much broader criticism of the denomination's cosmological foundations), see Paul K. Freiwirth, *Why I Left the Seventh-Day Adventists* (New York: Vintage, 1970).

15. For a larger philosophical and historical discussion of "gendered theology," see Kathy Rudy, *Sex and the Church: Gender, Sexuality, and the Transformation of Christian Ethics* (New York: Beacon, 1998).

16. I don't think Sister Madeline was advocating dance clubs but merely making a categorical distinction between venues—much like the spatial distinction implicit in the principal's ban.

17. Edward Tylor, in *Religion in Primitive Culture* (Gloucester, MA: P. Smith, 1970), was one of the first American anthropologists to distinguish "spirit" from "soul" analytically.

18. "It's a black thang. You wouldn't understand" is a popular and often-silk-screened slogan that is ubiquitous at most historically black colleges and universities.

19. For a recent and nuanced discussion of religious hybridity (a kind not simply reducible to commonsense notions of syncretism), see Joel Robbins, *Becoming Sinners: Christianity and Moral Torment in a Papua New Guinea Society* (Berkeley and Los Angeles: University of California Press, 2004).

20. For an ethnographic analysis of how such musical primordiality gets racialized/Africanized, see Paulla A. Ebron, *Performing Africa* (Princeton, NJ: Princeton University Press, 2002), especially chapters 1 and 2.

21. When I wrote an early draft of this chapter (in the mid-1990s), I was actively struggling with Saussurean semiotics as a heuristic tool for theorizing race. Since then, I have moved far afield of those earlier semiotic preoccupations, but I still find it useful to maintain the kernels of this earlier Saussurean discussion in this piece's current form. I was fascinated with Saussure when I originally conducted the research for this chapter, and I want to keep some of

NOTES TO PAGES 83–85

the theoretical integrity of that early moment while also connecting Saussure to my current concerns about authenticity.

22. See Ferdinand de Saussure, *Course in General Linguistics* (New York: Philosophical Library, 1959).

23. This *sign*'s relationship to naming is also an implicit part of chapter 8, "Real Names." For useful overviews of semiotics' theoretical purchase, see Roland Barthes, *Elements of Semiology* (New York: Hill and Wang, 1967), and Robert Innis, ed., *Semiotics: An Introductory Anthology* (Bloomington: Indiana University Press, 1985). For an explicit analysis of the sign's relationship to materialism and the commodity, see Jean Baudrillard, *For a Critique of the Political Economy of the Sign* (St. Louis, MO: Telos Press, 1981).

24. For a discussion of this structure/agency impasse, see Pierre Bourdieu, *Outline of a Theory of Practice* (Cambridge: Cambridge University Press, 1977), and *The Logic of Practice* (Stanford, CA: Stanford University Press, 1990); and Michel de Certeau, *The Practice of Everyday Life* (Berkeley and Los Angeles: University of California Press, 1984). For a discussion of practice theory's relevance for contemporary anthropology, see Sherry B. Ortner, *Making Gender: The Politics and Erotics of Culture* (Cambridge, MA: Beacon, 1996), especially chapter 1.

25. See Charles S. Peirce, *Peirce on Signs,* ed. James Hoopes (Chapel Hill: University of North Carolina Press, 1991).

26. In Riles, *Network Inside Out,* geopolitical reality (for NGO "focal points" in Fiji) is an effect of the formal and stylistic perfections/preoccupations of the "networks." Riles argues that realness is an imaginary outside proffered to hide the deeper realities of an all-encompassing Network-form. One might graph this interestingly atop Baudrillardian hyperrealities.

27. Taylor Carman, *Heidegger's Analytic: Interpretation, Discourse, and Authenticity in Being and Time* (Cambridge: Cambridge University Press, 2003), examines the philosopher's commitment to "ontic realism."

28. See Paul Ricoeur, *The Conflict of Interpretations: Essays in Hermeneutics,* ed. Don Indie (Evanston, IL: Northwestern University Press, 1974).

29. See Jacques Derrida, *Of Grammatology,* ed. Gayatri Spivak (Baltimore: Johns Hopkins University Press, 1997).

30. For a discussion of sound as a mechanism for racial theorizing, see Fred Moten, *In the Break: The Aesthetics of the Black Radical Tradition* (Minneapolis: University of Minnesota Press, 2003). Moten is also fascinated with theorizing thingification through aurality.

31. This *authenteo*-based death might be fruitfully read against a backdrop of the "sacred man," someone who might be killed but never socially sacrificed, not reappropriated postmortem by the body politic for its own collective reproduction. For a discussion of death, space, and the logics of sovereignty, see Giorgio Agamben, *Homo Sacer: Sovereign Power and Bare Life* (Stanford, CA: Stanford University Press, 1998).

32. Ferdinand de Saussure, *Course in General Linguistics* (New York: Philosophical Library, 1959).

33. Here, again, naming becomes less than legitimate; it does not mark a

real real. It has no power above and beyond the social contract. This position is complicated further in chapter 8, "Real Names."

34. For a discussion of virginity and orgasms as gendered fakery, see Marjorie Garber, "The Insincerity of Women," in *Desire in the Renaissance: Psychoanalysis and Literature,* ed. Valeria Finucci and Regina Schwartz (Princeton, NJ: Princeton University Press, 1994).

35. Ambiguity is not a silver bullet. For a discussion of ambivalence's political inadequacies (especially for anthropological theorizing), see Rosalind Morris, "'All Made Up': Performance Studies and the New Anthropology of Sex and Gender," *Annual Review of Anthropology* 24 (1995): 567–92. Also see Jennifer Michael Hecht, *The End of Soul: Scientific Modernity, Atheism, and Anthropology in France* (New York: Columbia University Press, 2003), for an examination of how doubt can be codified into an explicit form of certainty.

36. See Ann Weinstone, *Avatar Bodies* (Minneapolis: University of Minnesota Press, 2003); and John Comaroff and Jean Comaroff, *Millennial Capitalism and the Culture of Neoliberalism* (Durham, NC: Duke University Press, 2001).

37. This is also a rearticulation (on different terrain) of Donna Haraway's long-term project, an attempt to de-essentialize our understandings of species and speciation.

38. Bill Maher (during his HBO show *Real Time*) and other reviewers consistently labeled Mel Gibson's *The Passion of the Christ* (2004) a "sincere" film immediately after its release.

39. For a definition of "dialectical criticism," see Steven Caton, *Lawrence of Arabia: A Film's Anthropology* (Berkeley and Los Angeles: University of California Press, 1999).

40. For critical race studies, it might even be important to ask if bodies are possessed by a black or white ghosts. Think of the sincerities and insincerities of Jean Rouch's *The Mad Masters* (1954), practitioners possessed by former white colonial officers and administrators, which can be read as a religiously inflected postcolonial critique. Tyrone's move might likewise be seen as resistive, an everyday practice of religiosity that challenges the powers that be— that fights hegemonic discourses with dizzying tactilities and re-embodiments.

CHAPTER FOUR

1. "You Remind Me of Something" is a 1995 song from R. Kelly. Even as a Top Ten hit, it was lampooned by many listeners who thought it odd (and offensive) that Kelly penned a love song explicitly equating women with Jeeps, other cars, and bank accounts. It is also explicitly rehearses the human/thing dialectic that the sincere/authentic distinction further thematizes.

2. "Evanescent forms are becoming clearer, and confusion is being slowly dispelled. What has happened is that time has passed. Forgetfulness, by rolling memories along in its tide, has done more than merely wear them down or consign them to oblivion. The profound structure it has created out of the fragments allows me to achieve a more stable equilibrium, and to see a clearer pattern." This counterintuitively productive aspect of forgetting (of going back

to old fieldwork after many years), can be found in Claude Lévi-Strauss, *Tristes Tropiques* (New York: Penguin Books, 1993), 43–44. For another poignant version of self-remembering, see Samuel R. Delaney, *The Motion of Light in Water: Sex and Science Fiction Writing in the East Village, 1957–1965* (New York: Arbor House, 1988), especially "Sentences: An Introduction." For a more substantive discussion of Brooklyn's history, including the creation of its racial ghettoes, see Craig Steven Wilder, *A Covenant with Color: Race and Social Power in Brooklyn* (New York: Columbia University Press, 2000); and Walter Thabit, *How East New York Became a Ghetto* (New York: New York University Press, 2003). For a specific look at Crown Heights in the 1950s (as West Indians were just beginning to make inroads into the neighborhood), see Mark D. Naison, *White Boy: A Memoir* (Philadelphia: Temple University Press, 2002).

3. When I wrote the first draft of this chapter in 1994–95, I used a heavy-handed form of "eye-dialect" (representing ethnic speech phonetically) to textually (and unscientifically) render the pronunciational differences of West Indian accents. Although I employed this technique inconsistently (and with less than optimal linguistic rigor), I decided to keep most of the instances intact from that earlier, published draft—if for no other reason than to mark my thought processes and representational predilections at one particular moment in ethnographic time. For a more substantive discussion of eye-dialect, see Michael Toolan, "The Significations of Representing Dialect in Writing," *Language and Literature: Journal of the Poetics and Linguistics Association* 1, no. 1 (1992): 29–46.

4. For a discussion of Jamaican politics in a transnational perspective, see Laurie Gunst, *Born Fi' Dead: A Journey through the Jamaican Posse Underworld* (New York: Owl, 1996).

5. See Georges Bataille, *The Impossible* (San Francisco: City Lights Books, 1991).

6. Equally noticeable is the public invisibility of black female WTU members, which is not surprising, given the gender inequalities usually inherent in conservative interpretations of traditional religious mandates. This is related to the Pauline pronouncements I mentioned in the last chapter. In a future project, I want to examine how the WTU's gender differences work themselves out once the group's cable-access cameras are turned off, their display tables folded up, and their very public performances complete.

7. For a discussion of "cultural paranoia" and "the performance of paranoia," see Patrick O'Donnell, *Latent Destinies: Cultural Paranoia and Contemporary U.S. Narrative* (Durham, NC: Duke University Press, 2000), particularly "Entry: The Time of Paranoia." Also see Peter Knight, *Conspiracy Culture: From the Kennedy Assassinations to the "X-Files"* (London: Routledge, 2000); and Peter Knight, ed., *Conspiracy Nation: The Politics of Paranoia in Postwar America* (New York: New York University Press, 2002).

8. For a discussion of contemporary rhetorics of global transparency and their skeptical critiques, see Harry G. West and Todd Sanders, eds., *Conspiracy and Transparency: Ethnographies of Suspicion in the New World Order* (Durham, NC: Duke University Press, 2003).

9. For a substantive discussion of early Black Judaism, see James E. Landing, *Black Judaism: Story of an American Movement* (Durham, NC: Carolina Academic Press, 2002).

10. See Arthur Huff Fauset, *Black Gods of the Metropolis: Negro Religious Cults of the Urban North* (Philadelphia: University of Pennsylvania Press, 2002).

11. For a canonical study of Rastafari, see Barry Chevannes, *Rastafari: Roots and Ideology* (Syracuse, NY: Syracuse University Press, 1994).

12. See Sydney P. Freedberg, *Brother Love: Murder, Money, and a Messiah* (New York: Pantheon, 1994).

13. For a historically contextualized anthology on Black Judaism, see Yvonne Chireau and Nathaniel Deutsch, eds., *Black Zion: African American Religious Encounters with Judaism* (New York: Oxford University Press, 2000). For an ethnography of Black Judaism in contemporary Israel, see Fran Markowitz, Sara Helman, and Dafna Shir-Vertesh, "Soul Citizenship: The Black Hebrews and the State of Israel," *American Anthropologist* 105, no. 2 (2003): 302–12. See also, Rudolph Windsor, *From Babylon to Timbuktu: A History of the Ancient Black Races Including the Black Hebrews* (Philadelphia: Windsor's Golden Series Publications, 1988). Furthermore, there are also versions of Sabbath-keeping in Africa (Shembeism in South Africa and "Saturday God" worship in Ghana) that lend themselves to analytical discussion in this context. For a discussion of the latter, see Kofi Owusu-Mensa, *Saturday God and Adventism in Ghana* (Frankfurt, Germany: Peter Lang, 1993).

14. Howard Brotz, *The Black Jews of Harlem: Negro Nationalism and the Dilemmas of Negro Leadership* (New York: Schocken Books, 1964). James Landing, in *Black Judaism,* disputes several of Brotz's claims about this group. For a contemporary ethnographic discussion of conflicts between WTU Jews and Lubavitch Hasidim, see Henry Goldschmidt, *Peoples Apart: Race, Religion, and Other Jewish Differences in Crown Heights* (PhD diss., University of California at Santa Cruz, 2002), especially chap. 5.

15. Landing, *Black Judaism,* especially chaps. 2 and 3.

16. Ibid., chaps. 9 and 10.

17. Ibid., chap. 10; and see the Web site for the Beth Elohim Hebrew Congregation in Queens: http://members.aol.com/Blackjews/. Rabbi Sholomo Ben Levy, the "spiritual leader" of the group, received his doctorate in history from Columbia University while I was finishing my own doctoral program there in anthropology.

18. Nelson George, *Buppies, B-Boys, Baps, and Bohos: Notes on Post-Soul Black Culture* (Cambridge, MA: Da Capo Press, 2001), 157.

19. For a discussion linking Ice-T's "Cop Killer" to "Bush Killa," a 1992 hip-hop offering from West Coast emcee Paris, see Mark Anthony Neal, *Songs in the Key of Black Life: A Rhythm and Blues Nation* (New York: Routledge, 2003), especially 186–88.

20. Walter Benjamin, *Reflections: Essays, Aphorisms, Autobiographical Writings* (New York: Schocken Books, 1986), especially "Critique of Violence."

21. Thomas was referencing the earlier World Trade Center bombing of 1993, not September 11. For a discussion of COINTELPRO (the government's

infamous counterintelligence program) see Ward Churchill and Jim Van der Wall, *COINTELPRO Papers: Documents from the FBI's Secret Wars against Domestic Dissent* (Boston: South End Press, 1990).

22. In December of 1993, Colin Ferguson, thirty-five, a Jamaican-born New Yorker, opened fire on a Long Island Railroad car full of whites, allegedly waiting until the train left the city, not wanting to embarrass New York's first black mayor, David Dinkins. With notes to himself expressing hatred for Asians, whites, and "Uncle Toms," Ferguson killed six people and injured nineteen others. He was finally subdued by passengers when he tried to reload his gun with hollow-point bullets for another round of shooting.

23. Paul Laurence Dunbar's "We Wear the Mask," first published in *Lyrics of Lowly Life* (New York: Dodd, Mead, 1896). Adam Lively uses the mask motif as a guiding metaphor for his historical discussion of racial reasoning in *Masks: Blackness, Race, and the Imagination* (Oxford: Oxford University Press, 2000).

24. See William H. Grier and Price M. Cobbs, *Black Rage* (New York: Basic Books, 1968).

25. For a discussion of these very conspiracies and their circulation within the black community, see Patricia A. Turner, *I Heard It Through the Grapevine: Rumor in African-American Culture* (Berkeley and Los Angeles: University of California Press, 1993); and Gary Alan Fine and Patricia A. Turner, *Whispers on the Color Line: Rumor and Race in America* (Berkeley and Los Angeles: University of California Press, 2001). For a paradigmatic analysis of the "paranoid style" in American culture as a response to imagined communist infiltrations of the 1950s (and even earlier), see Richard Hofstadter, *The Paranoid Style in American Politics and Other Essays* (London: Jonathan Cape, 1966).

26. See James Jones, *Bad Blood: The Tuskegee Syphilis Experiment* (New York: Free Press, 1993).

27. The hip-hop group Brand Nubian has almost the same rendition of the ankh in their song "Dance to My Ministry," from the album *One for All* (Elektra, 1990): "come, into my laboratory / I'ma take you on a tour / An ankh is the key and the key is knowledge / which unlocks my lab's door / Kemet lets you enter, heat generates from the center / Lord Jamar's an inventor. . . . To the Right is where I keep my fuel / The Qu'ran and 120 lessons." They hint at an entrenched discourse based on popular versions of Egyptology and Islam.

28. Derrick goes back to several texts as his main reference material (in this conversation and others we share), most especially Anthony T. Browder, *From the Browder File: Twenty-two Essays on the African American Experience* (Washington, DC: The Institute of Karmic Guidance, 1989), which analyzes everything from the significance of Egyptian iconography on the dollar bill to "the mysteries of melanin" and the keys to healthy eating.

29. See Dan Brown, *The Da Vinci Code* (New York: Doubleday, 2003), a fictional thriller that unravels a global conspiracy to marginalize the iconic status of Mary Magdalen within Christianity (and her fictionally posited marriage to Jesus Christ).

30. For an anthropological anthology that places conspiracy theorizing within a certain, expanded notion of rationality (and does not just dismiss it as a mechanism for avoiding real discussions about social issues and their potential amelioration), see George E. Marcus, ed., *Paranoia within Reason: A Casebook on Conspiracy as Explanation* (Chicago: University of Chicago Press, 1999).

31. For an accessible overview of structural functionalism as theoretical orientation, see George Ritzer, *Sociological Theory* (New York: McGraw-Hill, 1992).

32. Edward William Lane, *An Account of the Manners and Customs of the Modern Egyptians* (New York: American University in Cairo Press, 2003). First published in the mid-nineteenth century.

33. I am thinking here of texts like, Molefi Kete Asante, *Kemet, Afrocentricity, and Knowledge* (Trenton, NJ: Africa World Press, 1990).

34. For a discussion of networking systematicity and totalization and how it short-circuits conventional causal modeling in the social sciences, see Annelise Riles, *The Network Inside Out* (Ann Arbor: University of Michigan Press, 2000).

35. Many people in the community often compared the two places, referencing a 1990 *New England Journal of Medicine* study arguing that men in the poverty-stricken country of Bangladesh live longer than those in this Northern Manhattan neighborhood (Colin McCord and Harold P. Freeman, "Excess Mortality in Harlem," *New England Journal of Medicine* 322, no. 3 [January 18, 1990]: 173–78).

36. Edward Said, quoted in Robert Young, *White Mythologies: Writing History and the West* (New York: Routledge, 1990), 133. For a discussion of conspiratorial populism and paranoia, see Mark Fenster, *Conspiracy Theories: Secrecy and Power in American Culture* (Minneapolis: University of Minnesota Press, 1999).

37. See Mark Liechty, *Suitably Modern: Making Middle-Class Culture in a New Consumer Society* (Princeton, NJ: Princeton University Press, 2003), especially chaps. 6 and 7.

38. See Revelation 3:9—"Behold, I will make them of the synagogue of Satan, which say they are Jews, and are not, but do lie; behold, I will make them to come and worship before thy feet, and to know that I have loved thee."

39. To complicate matters even more, the group of approximately 2,500 Black Hebrew Israelites presently residing in Israel (started from a group that left the south side of Chicago in the late 1960s and entered Israel with a rhetoric that demanded the country's "fake Jews" leave immediately) still maintains a sense of African identity today, officially calling themselves "African Hebrew Israelites." Moreover, they have jettisoned much of their anti-Semitic rhetoric in an effort to gain full citizenship from the Israeli state, cutting off their ties with, say, Nation of Islam minister Louis Farrakhan as a sign of good faith.

40. Anthroman smilingly divulges, more for himself than their edification, the little he knows about the notion of commodity fetishism, a certain economic anthropomorphism of inanimate goods that seems, somehow, rele-

vant in this context. See Karl Marx, *Capital* (London: J. M. Dent and Sons, 1939).

41. For an evocative ethnographic look at individuals connected to the Branch Davidian movement (a disavowed offshoot of Seventh-Day Adventism), see James D. Faubion, *The Shadows of Waco* (Princeton, NJ: Princeton University Press, 2001). Also, this hyperbolic imagining of an all-out race war (with "Branch Davidians . . . dropping bombs from helicopters right over Harlem") reached a feverish pitch on the eve of Y2K, when the FBI placed the WTU Jews on their "Project Megiddo" list of potential terrorists, which many labeled an updated version of COINTELPRO.

42. Here are some of the titles from our reading list: John Coleman, *Conspirators' Hierarchy: The Story of the Committee of Three Hundred* (Carson City, NJ: America West, 1992), whose author, a former "professional intelligence officer" in Europe, explains a worldwide plot by Satanists to set up a One-World Government and eliminate "all national identity and national pride" so as to destroy the world with corrupted religions, pornography, terrorism, and a global economic policy of starvation and deprivation based on the eighteenth-century writings of Thomas Malthus; Moshe Yohanan Lewis, *History of Edom: The Imposter Jew* (1989, with no publishing information except the fact that Yohanan Lewis holds the copyright), which likens the nation of Israel to an invading army that has used its economic resources to impose foreign interests on the people of America; Arkon Daraul, *A History of Secret Societies* (New York: Citadel Press, 1961), which shows the ubiquity of secret societies around the world; and A. Ralph Epperson, *The New World Order* (Tucson, AZ: Publius Press, 1990), a fast-paced gallop through the Satanist underpinnings of contemporary calls for a new world order. As might be expected within a discourse of conspiracy theory, there was a strong anti-Semitic thrust to much of this literature. We also read through the Bible (including the Apocrypha).

43. This extra-phenotypicality is what it shares with notions of sincerity, but toward very different identificatory ends. I'll unpack this more later on.

44. Epperson's *New World Order* opens with Catholic popes from the nineteenth and early twentieth centuries warning of the "occult forces" behind Communism. As a Seventh-Day Adventist, I actually grew up awaiting the rejuvenation of national "blue laws" (against buying and selling on Sunday), which would be part of a larger plot spearheaded by the pope, the anti-Christ, who would seek to destroy God's Seventh-Day (Saturday) Sabbath keepers. I even brought the guys a copy of one book that argues just such a theory, A. Jan Marcussen, *National Sunday Law* (Thompsonville, IL: Amazing Truth Publications, 1991), which sets the scene for its argument with a discussion of the Iraq/Kuwait conflict in the Middle East. The WTUers are particularly intrigued by the book's numerical verification of the pope's status as anti-Christ, an adding up of the Roman numerals that make up the name *Vivarius Filii Dei* (Vicar of the Son of God) to get 666. Revelation 13:38: "Count the number of the beast; for it is the number of a man; and his number is six hundred threescore and six."

45. For another rendition of the state's magical powers, see Michael Taussig, *The Magic of the State* (New York: Routledge, 1997) or Fernando Coronil, *The Magical State: Nature, Money, and Modernity in Venezuela* (Chicago: University of Chicago Press, 1997).

46. See Ralph Ellison, "A Very Stern Discipline," *Harper's,* March 1967, 76-77.

47. I'm not sure about the significance of the phrase "white blood" here, especially when "blood" might be imagined as a way to talk about commonality and kinship. Possibly, the warlock's renunciation of witchcraft brought him a bit closer to the Black Israelite fold, along with his divulgence of such important secrets.

48. Marilyn Strathern, "Out of Context: The Persuasive Fiction of Anthropology," *Current Anthropology* 28, no. 3 (June 1987): 251-81: "The observer/observed relationship can no longer be assimilated to that between subject and object. The object(ive) is a joint production. Many voices, multiple texts, plural authorship" (264-65).

49. For a discussion of conspiracy theories as a response to "bureaucratic impersonality," see Frederic Jameson, *The Geopolitical Aesthetic* (Bloomington: Indiana University Press, 1993). In his discussion of racial conspiracies among blacks, in which "Jews increasingly become the prime suspects," Charles W. Mills categorizes Jameson's take on conspiracy theories in his *Postmodernism, or the Cultural Logic of Late Capitalism* (Durham, NC: Duke University Press, 1991) as follows: "Frederic Jameson suggests that the conspiracy theory is a kind of half-baked Hegelianism, a degraded attempt at the whole. There is a lot to this, but I would add that it is an attempt to think the whole with the political and psychological virtue of *highlighting human agency*" (*Blackness Visible: Essays on Philosophy and Race* [Ithaca, NY: Cornell University Press, 1998], 89).

CHAPTER FIVE

1. Al Sharpton's National Action Network shared a building with the WTU Black Hebrews in the 1990s. An electrical fire destroyed much of that space in January 2003. One of the WTUers had to be rescued by city firefighters.

2. For a discussion that explicitly links the "marketplace of ideas" to Habermasian notions of the public sphere (in a broader critique about the democratizing limits of free speech in certain national contexts), see Jack Snyder and Karen Ballentine, "Nationalism and the Marketplace of Ideas," *International Security* 21, no. 2 (1996): 5-40.

3. See Jürgen Habermas, *The Structural Transformation of the Public Sphere: An Inquiry into a Category of Bourgeois Society* (Cambridge, MA: MIT Press, 1989) for a foundational articulation of how rational-critical debate/discourse helped to constitute political modernity. Of course, many scholars argue that an irrational xenophobia and exclusionism (far more pronounced than Habermas allows) has always defined this discursive space. For an anthology that highlights some of these critiques (as well as Habermas's own reassessment of his earlier formulation), see Craig Calhoun, ed., *Habermas and*

the Public Sphere (Cambridge, MA: MIT Press, 1992). For an anthropological critique of "rational" modernity's dependence on the concomitant construction of a demonized and irrationalized other, see Stephan Palmié, *Wizards and Scientists: Explorations in Afro-Cuban Modernity and Tradition* (Durham, NC: Duke University Press, 2002).

4. For a discussion of conspiracies "in extremis," see George E. Marcus, *Paranoia within Reason: Casebook on Conspiracy as Explanation* (Chicago: University of Chicago Press, 1998). For a description of the porous boundaries between rationality and irrationality in the context of late capitalist globality, see Jean Comaroff and John L. Comaroff, "Millennial Capitalism: First Thoughts on a Second Coming," *Public Culture* 12, no. 2 (2000): 291–343. For a discussion about the "rational irrational" links between religion and Marxism, spirituality and political action, see Roger N. Lancaster, *Thanks to God and the Revolution: Popular Religion and Class Consciousness in the New Nicaragua* (New York: Columbia University Press, 1988). And for a canonical anthology on the black public sphere, see The Black Public Sphere Collective, ed., *The Black Public Sphere: A Public Culture Book* (Chicago: University of Chicago Press, 1995).

5. Cultural critic Raymond Williams has done some of the most influential work on notions of "the structure of feeling," defining the phrase and redefining his own earlier delineations. See *Culture and Society, 1780–1950* (New York: Columbia University Press, 1983), *Marxism and Literature* (Oxford: Oxford University Press, 1977), and *Resources of Hope: Culture, Democracy, Socialism* (London: Verso, 1989).

6. I am invoking the version of vernacularity found in Grant Farred, *What's My Name: Black Vernacular Intellectuals* (Minneapolis: University of Minnesota Press, 2003). Farred's invocation of "vernacular intellectuals" owes a debt to earlier Gramscian discussions of "organic intellectuals," though the term *vernacularity* attempts to carve out its own theoretical terrain.

7. For an overview of Seventh-Day Adventism's construction of gendered congregants and its socialization of youthful bodies, see Laura Lee Vance, *Seventh-Day Adventism in Crisis: Gender and Sectarian Change in an Emerging Religion* (Urbana: University of Illinois Press, 1999). Other provocatively written books on how Seventh-Day Adventism crafts individualized selves include Stephen Hunt, ed., *Christian Millenarianism: From the Early Church to Waco* (Bloomington: Indiana University Press, 2001); and Walter Ralston Martin, *The Truth about Seventh-Day Adventism* (Grand Rapids, MI: Zondervan Publishing House, 1960).

8. For more on Seventh-Day Adventist religious beliefs and their connections to other marginalized religious groups' cosmologies, see Calvin Edwards, *Seeking After Light: A. F. Ballenger, Adventism, and American Christianity* (Berrien Springs, MI: Andrews University Press, 2000); Gregory Hunt, *Beware This Cult! An Insider Exposes Seventh-Day Adventism and Their False Prophet Ellen G. White* (Belleville, Ontario, Canada: Hunt, 1981); and Anthony A. Hoekema, *The Four Major Cults: Christian Science, Jehovah's Witnesses, Mormonism, Seventh-Day Adventism* (Grand Rapids, MI: Wm. B. Eerdmans, 1963).

9. For a political economy of early hip-hop, see Tricia Rose, *Black Noise:*

Rap Music and Black Culture in Contemporary America (Hanover, NH: University Press of New England, 1994); or Nelson George, *Buppies, B-Boys, Baps, and Bohos: Notes on Post-Soul Black Culture* (Cambridge, MA: Da Capo Press, 2001).

10. An emcee introduces one of Brother Bey's self-edited tapes (discussed later on in this chapter) with an amazing linguistic display that invokes Bush's "Skull and Bones" affiliation at Yale, the conspiratorial Illuminati, and details about merchandise sold on Bey's table. He ends with a couplet that highlights the vending operation's literal geographical location: "On 125, listen close, you gotta follow, we right across from the white man's Apollo." This is a different racialization of the Apollo than what we will read about in chapter 8, "Real Names."

11. All of these figures are famous in their own specific way. For instance, Khallid Muhammad, one of the Nation of Islam's most articulate ministers, started the New Black Panther Party. Ivan Van Sertima wrote a canonical Afrocentrist text, *They Came Before Columbus* (New York: Random House, 1976); Frances Cress Welsing is the author of a highly popular racial conspiracy theory, "The Color Confrontation Theory," which links white supremacy to genetic inferiority, and Ashra Kwesi lectures on Egypt all over the world. My first vending purchase from Bey was a videotape of Ashra Kwesi's "Judaism, the Stolen Religion from Afrika." For a general discussion about the Middle East's importance to African American identities (and especially to forms of Afrocentrism), see Melani McAlister, *Epic Encounters: Culture, Media, and U.S. Interests in the Middle East, 1945–2000* (Berkeley and Los Angeles: University of California Press, 2001).

12. See James Allen, ed., *Without Sanctuary* (Santa Fe, NM: Twin Palms Publishing, 2000) for a discussion of many of these lynching photos.

13. This invocation of "black and white devils" indexes a seminal Rastafarian chant, the Nyabinghi, which is usually glossed as "Death to Black and White Oppressors."

14. I wrote about an earlier Million Youth March in the first chapter of *Harlemworld: Doing Race and Class in Contemporary Black America* (Chicago: University of Chicago Press, 2001), arguing that many African Americans used the incident as a way to distinguish between legitimate and illegitimate community membership.

15. Other versions of York's biography start his life-story in New York City, where he was supposedly born in the 1940s and convicted of a serious crime before subsequently changing his name and starting his first religious group in the 1960s.

16. Anthropologists like Michael Blakey, Alan Goodman, and Lee D. Baker were differently responsible for helping to make ethnographic sense of these eighteenth-century remains—culturally, genetically, and linguistically. At Howard University, physical anthropologists like Blakey and Kittles began DNA-testing the bones in the late 1990s.

17. For interesting how-to books on tracing one's African (American) genealogy, see James D. Walker, *Black Genealogy: How to Begin* (Athens: Univer-

sity of Georgia Center for Continuing Education, 1977); James Rose and Alice Eicholz, *Black Genesis* (Detroit, MI: Gale Research Co., 1978); and Charles Blockson with Ron Fry, *Black Genealogy* (Englewood Cliffs, NJ: Prentice-Hall, 1977).

18. For a cogent and easily digestible discussion of genetics and their relationship to race, see Alexander Alland Jr., *Race in Mind: Race, IQ, and Other Racisms* (New York: Palgrave, 2002).

19. For an ethnographic treatment of race, blood, and belonging in Native America, see Circe Sturm, *Blood Politics: Race, Culture and Identity in the Cherokee Nation of Oklahoma* (Berkeley and Los Angeles: University of California Press, 2002).

20. Women interested in the PatriClan™ test must have a male relative take it for them, a brother or father.

21. For a popular historical overview of the human genome story, see Henry Gee, *Jacob's Ladder: The History of the Human Genome* (New York: W. W. Norton, 2004).

22. For a discussion of how nature, specifically genes and the genome, get "enterprised up," patented, and trademarked into particular forms of racialized and biologized private property, see Donna J. Haraway, *Modest_Witness@ Second_Millennium.FemaleMan©_Meets_OncoMouse™: Feminism and Technoscience* (New York: Routledge, 1997).

23. For an analysis of racial tourism as ancestral pilgrimage in Africa, see Paulla A. Ebron, *Performing Africa* (Princeton, NJ: Princeton University Press, 2002).

24. For a discussion of the stakes at issue with respect to questions of biopolitics, see Michel Foucault, *The History of Sexuality: An Introduction,* vol. 1 (New York: Vintage, 1978). Giorgio Agamben, *Homo Sacer: Sovereign Power and Bare Life* (Stanford, CA: Stanford University Press, 1998) explicitly connects biopolitics to a reconfiguration of Carl Schmitt's analysis of sovereignty.

25. For a recent reconfiguration of diaspora studies within the discipline of anthropology (one that defines *diaspora* "as a globally mobile category of identification"), see Brian Keith Axel, "The Context of Diaspora," *Cultural Anthropology* 19, no. 1 (2004): 26–60. For an earlier (and now rather canonical) rendition of the relationship between diaspora studies and anthropology, see David Scott, "That Event, This Memory: Notes on the Anthropology of African Diasporas in the New World," *Diaspora* 1, no. 3 (1991): 261–83. Among other interventions, Scott challenges previous analytical conflations of slavery with Africa. For a detailed historical ethnographication of Paul Gilroy's often-cited "Black Atlantic," see J. Lorand Matory, "The English Professors of Brazil: On the Diasporic Roots of the Yoruba Nation," *Comparative Studies in Society and History* 41, no. 1 (1999): 72–103.

26. These classes often reproduce the vitriolic rhetoric that sometimes gets the WTU in trouble during their public preaching sessions. In fact, Wilson did send me an article about the city's unsuccessful attempt to ban the WTU from city streets in 1998. The city took them to court and lost. This effort was part of a larger governmental attempt (Project Megiddo) to monitor hate groups

thought capable of taking advantage of whatever mayhem ensued as a function of Y2K predictions (i.e., instigating race riots in the context of large-scale computer shutdowns and consequent power outages).

27. In a future project tentatively entitled "Global Black Judaism," I want to look more pointedly at Black Hebrew cultural and linguistic practices.

28. This identificatory reckoning is of an entirely different scale than the equally invisible "nanopolitics" of race discussed by the likes of Paul Gilroy. And it may not be a coincidence that the so-called godfather of nanotechnology is another Drexler (K. Eric), like the alleged warlock linked to anthropology at Columbia University. Hmmm?

29. WTU Hebrews have always officially rendered belonging (historically) through the father and not the mother. It may have been a peculiar oddity that some new believers imagined identity through matrilineal lines, possibly bastardizing conventional Ashkenazi or Sephardic forms of Jewish self-reckoning.

30. For differently pitched discussions of the antihumanist kernels within many modernist forms of so-called humanism (and within the foundational premises of Western philosophy more generally), see Robert Young, *White Mythologies: Writing History and the West* (New York: Routledge, 1990); Charles W. Mills, *Blackness Visible: Essays on Philosophy and Race* (Ithaca, NY: Cornell University Press, 1998); and Lucius T. Outlaw Jr., *On Race and Philosophy* (New York: Routledge, 1996).

CHAPTER SIX

1. Bill reserves some of his harshest criticisms for this Harlem filmmaker, upset that she is even wasting her time "making silly little movies" instead of joining his family and helping him to sell his books and watermelons to pedestrians. He says that she is "exactly what's wrong with black women today." Diana has interviewed Bill and Gina several times for the film, and he usually sits and answers her questions, even if he dismisses the entire endeavor as a waste of everyone's time—especially the "weakling" men (like me) who are letting her run the show.

2. See John Aguilar, "Insider Research: An Ethnography of a Debate," in *Anthropologists at Home in North America: Methods and Issues in the Study of One's Own Society,* ed. Donald A. Messerschmidt (Cambridge: Cambridge University Press, 1981), 15–26; Lanita Jacobs-Huey, "The Natives Are Gazing and Talking Back: Reviewing the Problematics of Positionality, Voice, and Accountability among Native Anthropologists," *American Anthropologist* 104, no. 3 (2002): 791–804; Khalil Nakhleh, "On Being a Native Anthropologist," in *The Politics of Anthropology,* ed. Gerrit Huizer and Bruce Mannheim (Paris: Mouton, 1979), 343–52; and Judith Okely, *Own or Other Culture* (London: Routledge, 1996).

3. See Marcus Banks and Howard Morphy, eds., *Rethinking Visual Anthropology* (New Haven, CT: Yale University Press, 1997); Paul Hockings, ed., *Principles of Visual Anthropology* (Berlin: Mouton de Gruyter, 1995); Martin Jay, *Downcast Eyes: The Denigration of Vision in Twentieth-Century French*

Thought (Berkeley and Los Angeles: University of California Press, 1996); and Georgia Warnke, "Ocularcentrism and Social Criticism," in *Modernity and the Hegemony of Vision,* ed. David Michael Levin (Berkeley and Los Angeles: University of California Press, 1993), 287–308.

4. Faye Ginsburg, Lila Abu-Lughod, and Brian Larkin, eds., *Media Worlds: Anthropology on New Terrains* (Berkeley and Los Angeles: University of California Press, 2003), 22. I have not yet gotten to help Bradshaw produce that video.

5. See Thomas Headland and Marvin Harris, eds., *Emics and Etics: The Insider/Outsider Debate* (Newbury Park, CA: Sage, 1990).

6. See Annelise Riles, *The Network Inside Out* (Ann Arbor: University of Michigan Press, 2000) for a Stratheriianly pitched examination of how the *emic* has merged with the *etic,* further complicating anthropological attempts to represent contemporary social phenomena in terms that the subjects themselves also use. This provides another interesting way of rethinking the ethnographic filmmaker in the context of ubiquitous mediatization.

7. Georg Simmel, *The Sociology of Georg Simmel* (New York: Free Press, 1950); Nigel Barley, *The Innocent Anthropologist: Notes from a Mud Hut* (London: British Museum Publications, 1983). Hortense Powdermaker, *Stranger and Friend: The Way of an Anthropologist* (New York: W. W. Norton, 1966) provides another important engagement with this methodological issue. Hockings, *Principles of Visual Anthropology,* makes an emic/etic distinction between filmic and written ethnographies, arguing that films are etic and written monographs emic. Anthropologists have often mined the humanities for theoretical frames that might offer useful responses to the reification of scientific experimentality as the only model for anthropological inquiry; see, for example, Paul Benson, ed., *Anthropology and Literature* (Chicago: University of Illinois Press, 1993); James Clifford and George Marcus, eds., *Writing Culture: The Poetics and Politics of Ethnography* (Berkeley and Los Angeles: University of California Press, 1986); Jonathan Friedman, "The Iron Cage of Creativity: An Exploration," in *Locating Cultural Creativity,* ed. John Liep (London: Pluto Press, 2001); Kathleen Stewart, *A Space on the Side of the Road: Cultural Poetics in an "Other" America* (Princeton, NJ: Princeton University Press, 1996); and Paul Stoller, *Jaguar: A Story of Africans in America* (Chicago: University of Chicago Press, 1999).

8. Again, Riles, *Network Inside Out,* provides a more complicated epistemological and methodological version of this topsy-turvy "inside out" motif.

9. See Roger Sanjek, ed., *Fieldnotes: The Making of Anthropology* (Ithaca, NY: Cornell University Press, 1990).

10. Delmos Jones, "Toward a Native Anthropology," *Human Organization* 29, no. 4 (1970): 252.

11. See Eliza McFeely, *Zuni and the American Imagination* (New York: Hill and Wang, 2001); and Benjamin Paul, "Interview Techniques and Field Relations," in *Anthropology Today: An Encyclopedic Inventory,* ed. A. L. Kroeber (Chicago: University of Chicago Press, 1953), 430–51.

12. See Lila Abu-Lughod, "Fieldwork of a Dutiful Daughter," in *Arab Women in the Field: Studying Your Own Society,* ed. Soraya Altorki and

Camillia Fawzi El-Solh (Syracuse, NY: Syracuse University Press, 1988), 139–61; Jacobs-Huey, "Natives Are Gazing and Talking Back"; and Emiko Ohnuki-Tierney, "'Native' Anthropologists," *American Ethnologist* 11, no. 3 (1984): 584–86.

13. See James Clifford, *The Predicament of Culture: Twentieth-Century Ethnography, Literature, and Art* (Cambridge, MA: Harvard University Press, 1988); and Pauline Rosenau, *Postmodernism and the Social Sciences: Insights, Inroads, and Intrusions* (Princeton, NJ: Princeton University Press, 1991).

14. See Micaela di Leonardo, *Exotics at Home: Anthropologies, Others, and American Modernity* (Chicago: University of Chicago Press, 1998); and Edward Said, *Orientalism* (New York: Pantheon, 1978).

15. Nesha Haniff, "Toward a Native Anthropology: Methodological Notes on the Study of Successful Caribbean Women by an Insider," *Anthropology and Humanism Quarterly* 10, no. 4 (1985): 107.

16. Karla Slocum, "Negotiating Identity and Black Feminist Politics in Caribbean Research," in *Black Feminist Anthropology: Theory, Politics, Praxis and Poetics*, ed. Irma McClaurin (New Brunswick, NJ: Rutgers University Press, 2001), 146.

17. Jones, "Toward a Native Anthropology," 255.

18. Jacobs-Huey, "Natives Are Gazing and Talking Back," 800.

19. Kirin Narayan, "How Native Is the 'Native' Anthropologist?" *American Anthropologist* 95, no. 3 (1993): 671–86.

20. See Aguilar, "Insider Research."

21. See Audre Lorde, *Sister Outsider: Essays and Speeches* (Trumansburg, NY: Crossing Press, 1984).

22. See Faye Harrison, ed., *Decolonizing Anthropology: Moving Further Toward an Anthropology for Liberation* (Washington, DC: American Anthropological Association, 1991).

23. Frantz Fanon, *Black Skin, White Masks* (New York: Grove Press, 1967).

24. Narayan, "How Native Is the 'Native' Anthropologist?" 671, 672.

25. See Slocum, "Negotiating Identity," 146. For instance, why do we not think of earlier monographs by the likes of Max Gluckman and Raymond Firth as native anthropological engagements with South Africa and New Zealand respectively? See Aguilar, "Insider Research," 15.

26. See Brackette F. Williams, "Skinfolk, Not Kinfolk: Comparative Reflections on the Identity of Participant-Observation in Two Field Situations," in *Feminist Dilemmas in Fieldwork*, ed. Diane Wolf (Boulder, CO: Westview Press, 1996), 72–95.

27. See Laura Nader, "Up the Anthropologist—Perspectives Gained by Studying Up," in *Reinventing Anthropology*, ed. Dell Hymes (New York: Vintage, 1972), 284–311. This is some of the reason why attempts to theorize and enact the possibility of middle-class betrayal become, at heart, decidedly ethnographic endeavors—and with specific resonance for the professionally trained and labeled native anthropologist. One can read the works of, say, E. Franklin Frazier, *Black Bourgeoisie* (New York: Free Press, 1965); C. L. R. James, *The C. L. R. James Reader*, ed. Anna Grimshaw (Cambridge, MA: Blackwell, 1992); and bell hooks, *Where We Stand: Class Matters* (New York: Routledge, 2000)

as differently pitched attempts at just such middle-class betrayal. Moreover, these same fault lines are the backbone of criticisms organized around authenticity.

28. See Walter Benjamin, "The Storyteller," in *Illuminations* (New York: Harcourt, Brace, and Jovanovich, 1968), 83–110.

29. See Eric Michaels, "How to Look at Us Looking at the Yanomami Looking at Us," in *A Crack in the Mirror: Reflexive Perspectives in Anthropology,* ed. Jay Ruby (Philadelphia: University of Pennsylvania Press, 1982), 133–46.

30. See Dan Marks, "Ethnography and Ethnographic Film: From Flaherty to Asch and After," *American Anthropologist* 97, no. 2 (1995): 339–47; and Fatimah Tobing Rony, *The Third Eye* (Durham, NC: Duke University Press, 1996).

31. See Anna Grimshaw, *The Ethnographic Eye* (Cambridge: Cambridge University Press, 2001).

32. See Brian Winston, "The Documentary Film as Scientific Inscription," in *Theorizing Documentary Film,* ed. Michael Renov (New York: Routledge, 1993), 37–57.

33. See Grimshaw, *Ethnographic Eye;* and Faye Ginsburg, "Culture/Media: A (Mild) Polemic," *Anthropology Today* 10, no. 2 (1994): 5–15.

34. See Rony, *Third Eye;* see also Ilsa Barbash and Lucien Taylor, *Cross-Cultural Filmmaking: A Handbook for Making Documentary and Ethnographic Films and Videos* (Berkeley and Los Angeles: University of California Press, 1997).

35. See Margaret Mead, "Visual Anthropology in a Discipline of Words," in *Principles of Visual Anthropology,* ed. Hockings, 3–10; Ginsburg, "Culture/Media"; and Jay Ruby, *Picturing Culture: Explorations of Film and Anthropology* (Chicago: University of Chicago Press, 2000).

36. Steven Feld, ed., *Cine-Ethnography: Jean Rouch* (Minneapolis: University of Minnesota Press, 2003), 6; see also Paul Stoller, *The Cinematic Griot: The Ethnography of Jean Rouch* (Chicago: University of Chicago Press, 1992); and Manthia Diawara, *Rouch in Reverse* (San Francisco: California Newsreel, 1995).

37. See Ruby, *Picturing Culture.*

38. See Ginsburg, "Culture/Media," and "Institutionalizing the Unruly: Charting Future for Visual Anthropology," *Ethnos* 63, no. 2 (1996): 173–96; Harald Prins and Jay Ruby, "North American Contributions to the History of Visual Anthropology," *Visual Anthropology Review* 13, no. 3 (2001): 3–4.

39. See Ginsburg, Abu-Lughod, and Larkin, *Media Worlds.*

40. See Ginsburg, "Culture/Media."

41. Faye Ginsburg, "Indigenous Media: Faustian Contract or Global Village?" in *Rereading Cultural Anthropology,* ed. George Marcus (Durham, NC: Duke University Press, 1992), 361; David MacDougall, "Complicities of Style," in *Film as Ethnography,* ed. Peter Crawford and David Turnton (Manchester, UK: University of Manchester Press, 1992), 90–98; Jay Ruby, "The Moral Burden of Authorship in Ethnographic Film," *Visual Anthropology Review* 11, no. 2 (1995): 77–82; and Terrance Turner, "Defiant Videos: The Kayapo Appropriation of Video," *Anthropology Today* 8, no. 6 (1992): 5–16. (Moreover,

what is even at stake in calling these offerings "ethnographic" films? Should we police that term more or less stringently? The same question might plague my attempt to label this work an instance of ethnography. What's gained and/or lost by such a designation? What remains of the very category itself?)

42. Ruby, "Moral Burden of Authorship."

43. See Rosalind Morris, *New World in Fragments: Film Ethnography and the Representation of Northwest Coast Cultures* (Boulder, CO: Westview Press, 1994). We assume them to be Road Runners vis-à-vis their own cultures, when they may just be a different version of us, Wile E. Coyotes banging their heads against mountainsides.

44. Diawara, *Rouch in Reverse.*

45. Ginsburg, "Culture/Media."

46. Jeff Himpele, "Arrival Scenes: Complicity and Media Ethnography in the Bolivian Public Sphere," in Ginsburg, Abu-Lughod, and Larkin, *Media Worlds,* 302.

47. See Reuben A. Buford May and Mary Pattillo-McCoy, "Do You See What I See: Examining a Collaborative Ethnography," *Qualitative Inquiry* 6, no. 1 (2000): 65–87.

48. See Ruby, *Picturing Culture.*

49. See Ruth Behar, *The Vulnerable Observer: Anthropology That Breaks Your Heart* (Boston: Beacon, 1996).

50. See Philip Carl Salzman, "On Reflexivity," *American Anthropologist* 104, no. 3 (2002): 805–13. In *Picturing Culture* (151–80), Ruby claims that reflexivity in anthropology provides for greater methodological rigor, making ethnographic research more scientifically sound (even though he thinks that it has been hijacked by postmodernists).

51. See Tina M. Campt, *Other Germans: Black Germans and the Politics of Race, Gender and Memory in the Third Reich* (Ann Arbor: University of Michigan Press, 2004), especially the final chapter.

52. See W. E. B. Du Bois, *The Souls of Black Folk* (1903; reprint, New York: Dover, 1994). For a discussion of "stereoscopy," see Messerschmidt, *Anthropologists at Home.*

53. See Du Bois, *Souls of Black Folk,* 2. Richard Wright, in *The Outsider* (New York: Harper and Row, 1965), does invoke the notion of "double vision" explicitly and specifically. Also see Okely, *Own or Other Culture,* for a different articulation of the "double vision" inherent to native anthropologizing. For an engaging discussion of the "bifurcated" ethnographic self, one that melds productively into an analysis of how we can see/write in a two-pronged way, see Vincent Crapanzano, "On the Writing of Ethnography," *Dialectical Anthropology* 2 (1977): 179–94.

54. Messerschmidt, *Anthropologists at Home.* See also, Jeff P. Himpele, "Arrival Scenes: Complicity and Media Ethnography in the Bolivian Public Sphere," in *Media Worlds,* ed. Ginsburg, Abu-Lughod, and Larkin, 301–16.

55. See Ruby, "Moral Burden of Authorship."

56. Rony, *Third Eye,* 198.

57. See W. J. T. Mitchell, "Showing Seeing: A Critique of Visual Culture," *Journal of Visual Culture* 1, no. 2 (2002): 165–82.

58. Some of these same psychologized attempts at reflexivity can return the discussion to film—for example, Stan Brakhagian moments when the pro-filmic becomes the pre-filmic, a way to talk about the kinds of "seeing" that purportedly come before discourse and culture, see David E. James, "Stan Brakhage: The Filmmaker as Poet," in *Allegories of Cinema,* ed. David E. James (Princeton, NJ: Princeton University Press, 1989), 29–57. In the context of a discussion about "new ethnography," some call for a "dialogic vulnerability" that retains an explicit invocation of the intersubjective bases of all ethnographic encounters; see H. Lloyd Goodall, *Writing the New Ethnography* (New York: AltaMira Press, 2000), 14. For a discussion of Marlon Riggs's film *Black Is, Black Ain't,* which chronicles the filmmaker's slow death from AIDS and challenges our assumptions about the difference between insider and outsider filmmakers, see E. Patrick Johnson, *Appropriating Blackness: Performance and the Politics of Authenticity* (Durham, NC: Duke University Press, 2003), especially chap. 1, "The Pot Is Brewing." Jeanne Livingston's film *Paris Is Burning* has been critiqued by the likes of bell hooks and Judith Butler, among others, in terms of its representational presuppositions—and in ways that hint at some of the same dilemmas highlighted here.

59. See Jay Ruby and Barbara Myerhoff, "Introduction," in *A Crack in the Mirror,* ed. Ruby, 1–35; as well as the film by Barbara Myerhoff, *Number Our Days* (Los Angeles: Direct Cinema, Ltd., 1983), and the identically titled book *Number Our Days* (New York: Dutton, 1979).

60. For a theoretical and historical engagement with minstrelsy, see Eric Lott, *Love and Theft: Blackface Minstrelsy and the American Working Class* (New York: Oxford University Press, 1993); and Michael Rogin, *Black Face, White Noise: Jewish Immigrants in the Hollywood Melting Pot* (Berkeley and Los Angeles: University of California Press, 1996).

61. In the late 1980s, a New Yorker affiliated with one of the ghetto fabulous websites discussed in chapter 2, "Real Harlemites," took advantage of Hollywood's neighborhood neglect by duplicating and selling thousands of illegal VHS tapes of first-run motion pictures. He even claims to have been the first person to bring the illegal videotape sales market to Harlem, New York—and to the tune of tens of thousands of dollars of personal profit every single week.

62. For a discussion of this ubiquitous "mediatization" and what it means for social theory, see Philip Auslander, *Liveness: Performance in a Mediatized Culture* (New York: Routledge, 1999).

63. As another indication of self-conscious visuality in contemporary America, many Harlem churches are videotaping their own services nowadays—either selling them to congregants or archiving sermons for posterity. And, of course, Brother Bey videotapes and sells his own religious debates on the sidewalk.

64. Marcel Mauss, *The Gift: The Form and Reason for Exchange in Archaic Societies* (New York: W. W. Norton, 1990).

65. Ibid., 11–12.

66. David Graeber, *Toward an Anthropological Theory of Value: The False Coin of Our Own Dreams* (New York: Palgrave, 2001), 154.

67. Vincent Crapanzano, "Reflections on Hope as a Category of Social and

Psychological Analysis," *Cultural Anthropology* 18, no. 1 (2003): 19. For a specifically ethnographic engagement with desire's relationship to the mass media, see Anne Allison, *Permitted and Prohibited Desires: Mothers, Comics, and Censorship in Japan* (Berkeley and Los Angeles: University of California Press, 2000).

68. Bea Medicine, *Learning to Be an Anthropologist and Remaining "Native": Selected Writings* (Urbana and Chicago: University of Illinois Press, 2001), 3.

CHAPTER SEVEN

1. The catchy chorus to the cartoon's theme song included one recurring phrase: "Transformers, more than meets the eye."

2. At least one of the two WTU hip-hop priests, Hamanatazachahmath, apparently embraced a version of Africanness contrary to the kind I usually heard voiced in NYC. He allegedly posted the following on a heavy-metal Web site in July 2000: "Where am I from? Africa, bitch. What is my ethnicity? Pure BLACK, mofo. 1 Thessalonians 5:18 'In every thing give thanks: for this is the will of God in Christ Jesus concerning you.' Psalms 50:5 'Gather my saints together unto me; those that have made a covenant with me by sacrifice.' Says the Bible, that black people wrote, and that we shall [defecate?] on your face when you are enslaved in Heaven. Die whitey! And Jesus says: Matthew 10:26 'Fear them not therefore: for there is nothing covered, that shall not be revealed; and hid, that shall not be known.' So let it be proclaimed across the land, WHITES ARE EVIL." It is signed "Priest Hamanatazachahmath ISRAEL@ICWTU.COM."

3. For a discussion of American hip-hop's regional specificities, see Nelson George, *Hip Hop America* (New York: Penguin Books, 1991); Tricia Rose, "Black Texts/Black Contexts" in *Black Popular Culture,* ed. Gina Dent with Michele Wallace (Seattle, WA: Bay Press, 1992), 223–27; Adam Sexton, ed., *Rap on Rap: Straight-Up Talk on Hip-Hop Culture* (New York: Delta Books, 1995); and William Shaw, *West Side: Young Men and Hip Hop in L.A.* (New York: Simon and Schuster, 2000). By "nationalistic" I mean to invoke a certain variety of *black* nationalist discourse linked to groups like Public Enemy, X-Clan and Dead Prez. For a discussion of the postimperial moment, see Michael Hardt and Antonio Negri, *Empire* (Cambridge, MA: Harvard University Press, 2000). One could potentially wire this theory of empire to a discussion of hip-hop's decidedly international and supranational circuits. Moreover for a discussion of hip-hop's interdependent relationship with the political economy of local black communities, see Mark Anthony Neal, *What the Music Said: Black Popular Music and Black Public Culture* (New York: Routledge Press, 1999).

4. "It ain't where ya from, it's where ya at" is a common refrain in hip-hop culture, also offered up in Mos Def's song, "Habitat," from the album *Black on Both Sides* (1999), which I analyze later in this chapter.

5. For a discussion of my previous use of the term, see *Harlemworld: Doing Race and Class in Contemporary Black American* (Chicago: University of Chicago Press, 2001), especially the introduction. Harlemworld was also the name of a hip-hop club from the 1980s at 116th and Lenox. That same space

is now one of the primary stops on a contemporary hip-hop sightseeing tour in Northern Manhattan. This link between cultural tourism and black music is theorized at length in David Grazian, *Blue Chicago: The Search for Authenticity in Urban Blues Clubs* (Chicago: University of Chicago Press, 2003).

6. See Timothy Mitchell, ed., *Global Noise: Rap and Hip-Hop outside the USA* (Middletown, CT: Wesleyan University Press, 2001), especially Ian Condry's piece on Japanese hip-hop.

7. For a sense of this hip-hop pioneer's thoughts on the metaphysical realities of contemporary black life and "Hiphop Kulture," see KRS-One, *Ruminations* (New York: Welcome Rain Publishers, 2003), especially chap. 6, "It Ain't Where Ya From, Its Where Ya At!" In chapter 8, "The Spiritual Meaning of 911," he invokes a "spiritual numerology" that meshes nicely with Bill and Minister Farrakhan's earlier analyses: "September 11th is the 254th day of the year. 2 + 5 + 4 = 11. . . . After September 11th, there are 111 days left to the end of the year. 119 is the country code of Iraq and Iran. 1 + 1 + 9 = 11. The first plane to hit the World Trade Center was flight 11, which had 92 people on board. 9 + 2 = 11." The perceptive reader might add that KRS-One's own discussion of this "master number" actually starts on page 164 of the book: 1 + 4 + 6 = 11.

8. This is reminiscent of the Rastafarian predilection to read everything oppositionally—for example, understand as *over*stand.

9. Many readers interpret Paul Gilroy, *Against Race: Imagining Political Culture Beyond the Color Line* (Cambridge, MA: Harvard University Press, 2000) as including such a dismissal, and he seems to take a particularly hard swipe at rapper Ice Cube.

10. See Neal, *What the Music Said.* Also, Tricia Rose, *Black Noise: Rap Music and Black Culture in Contemporary America* (Hanover, NH: University Press of New England, 1994).

11. There is also the elitist renunciation of hip-hop in public venues by jazz purists like Stanley Crouch and Wynton Marsalis.

12. MA$E actually left hip-hop in 1999 to become a full-time minister. Before returning to hip-hop in 2004 (as a continuation of his religious ministries), he published a book describing his spiritual journey. See Mason Betha, *Revelations: There's a Light after the Lime* (New York: Simon and Schuster, 2001).

13. Émile Durkheim, *The Division of Labor* (New York: Free Press, 1984).

14. For discussion of "collective consciousness" see Émile Durkheim, *Sociology and Philosophy* (New York: Free Press, 1974). Of course, my notion of a social grouping within hip-hop culture (and within contemporary black America more generally) is less predicated on spatial contiguity (Durkheim's node) than on imagined commonalities that outstrip spatial distances.

15. For a discussion of hip-hop as work and the occupationalization of play, see Robin Kelley, *Yo Mama's Disfunktional! Fighting the Culture Wars in Urban America* (Boston: Beacon, 1997), especially 43–77.

16. A similar story of the relationship between the legal, low-wage service sector and the underground economy is told in Sudhir Alladi Venkatesh, *American Project: The Rise and Fall of a Modern Ghetto* (Cambridge, MA: Harvard University Press, 2000).

17. Nelson George, *Buppies, B-Boys, Baps, and Bohos: Notes on Post-Soul Black Culture* (Cambridge, MA: Da Capo Press, 2001), 44.

18. Some renditions of early hip-hop excise graffiti from this originary space, claiming that it was always already clearly distinct from hip-hop culture—and only ever tangentially connected.

19. The "New Jack Swing" stylings of Teddy Riley in the late 1980s can serve as a key moment that helps mark the switch from deejays to producers. The recently released documentary film *Scratch* speaks to the growing autonomy of contemporary deejay culture, complete with its own "university" of turntablism in downtown Manhattan.

20. There is also a growing move to include live musical accompaniment to hip-hop performances, although this usually includes a deejay as one of the band members. Philadelphia's The Roots exemplifies this push.

21. Eric B. and Rakim's first hip-hop hit was "Eric B. for President" in 1986. Back then, a deejay could even playfully run for public office, with an emcee as mere running mate and second fiddle.

22. For a discussion of community "old heads," see Elijah Anderson, *Streetwise: Race, Class, and Change in an Urban Community* (Chicago: University of Chicago Press, 1990). Clearly, people like KRS-One and Chuck D. fit the bill. I take the "four field" notion from anthropology. In hip-hop, as in anthropology, the fields are often not in any consistent conversation, so you have, say, "5pointz" (a celebrated graffitied landscape) in Queens and Scratch DJ Academy (a school for fledgling deejays) in Greenwich Village—discrete spheres with discrete constituencies.

23. Jay-Z's line—"I'm overcharging them for what they did to the Cold Crush"—speaks to hip-hop's current attempts to avenge their genre's exploitation in the 1970s and 1980s.

24. This diversification is reminiscent of the Pentecostal preacher who runs the church where Bill stores his watermelon materials, a preacher who—challenging the divide between sacred and profane—also designs and sells her own clothing to congregants. In a hip-hop context, such commercial gestures serve as one of the potential nodes of illegitimacy, compromising supposed authenticity if it is determined that emcees have sold out to the market for the sake of personal profit. One is supposed to make money, but on one's own terms. I try to explain this more later on in the chapter.

25. For a provocative discussion of how hip-hop culture has supplanted the authority of civil rights discourse, see Todd Boyd, *The New H.N.I.C.: The Death of Civil Rights and the Reign of Hip-Hop* (New York: New York University Press, 2003).

26. For a philosophical discussion that links such sincere soundings to improvisational freedoms, see Fred Moten, *In the Break: The Aesthetics of the Black Radical Tradition* (Minneapolis: University of Minnesota Press, 2003).

27. I take this gesture from Jay-Z, who calls himself "the Frank Sinatra of this rap game," a point of comparison decidedly beyond hip-hop culture.

28. For an examination of the "post-soulic," see Nelson, *Buppies, B-Boys, Baps, and Bohos;* see also Mark Anthony Neal, *Soul Babies: Black Popular Culture and the Post-Soul Aesthetic* (New York: Routledge, 2002).

29. Obviously, this notion of Islam gets rewritten in America immediately after the terrorist attacks of September 11, 2001. I use these attacks to open an argument about naming in the next chapter.

30. For a theoretical discussion of these contact zones, see Mary Louise Pratt, *Imperial Eyes: Travel Writing and Transculturation* (London: Routledge, 1992). See also, James Clifford, *Routes: Travel and Translation in the Late Twentieth Century* (Cambridge, MA: Harvard University Press, 1997), 188–219. "Bed-Stuy" is their Bedford-Stuyvesant neighborhood in Brooklyn.

31. See Frances Cress Welsing, *The Isis Papers: The Keys to the Colors* (Chicago: Third World Press, 1991) for a sense of the Welsingesque. This is also one of the books that I read with the Black Hebrews, from cover to cover, in 1994.

32. Mos Def says he used to speak the king's English, but now embraces a more vernacularized black English.

33. I am thinking here of Houston Baker's helpful distinction between the "mastery of form" and the "deformation of mastery," in *Modernism and the Harlem Renaissance* (Chicago: University of Chicago Press, 1987).

34. Examples of this abound: Nas and Lauryn Hill, De La Soul and Chaka Khan, Melle Mel and Chaka Khan, Method Man and Mary J. Blige, Jay-Z and Beyoncé, Kanye West and Chaka Khan. The list goes on and on and on. (These are only some of *my* favorites.) The late 1980s and 1990s found a few R&B acts (like Bell Biv DeVoe, Bobby Brown, and Montell Jordan) attempting, somewhat successfully, to cross the line between singing and rhyming. Prince also made forays into his own hip-hop style, with far less commercial success. Michael Franti, of the group Spearhead, is a West Coast example of an emcee unafraid to sing (or of such singing compromising his own masculinity). The group Bone Thugs-n-Harmony had a sincere sing-songy style in the 1990s. Just as interesting is the current attempt by artists like Ja Rule and Nelly not only to collaborate with younger R&B divas (Nelly and Destiny's Child's Kelly, Ja Rule and everybody!) but also to split the difference between singing and rhyming with a kind of sing-songy rapping style. Ja Rule, for one, often tries to end many of his lines on an elongated final note ("What would I be without my babaaaa? The thought alone might break meeeee"). One could compellingly read this as a slight return of the singerly repressed. As I finish this manuscript, Kanye West is the most recent example of hip-hop's embrace of both singing and Christianity.

35. In a recent collaboration with Jay-Z, R. Kelly has become more adamant about rhyming as well as singing. This may be a post-sex-scandal R. Kelly (as I write this, the legal case is still pending) who no longer "gives a fuck," a position I talk about later on in this chapter.

36. For a powerful theoretical and ethnographic response to hip-hop's engagement with black women, see Kyra Gaunt, "Translating Double-Dutch to Hip Hop: The Musical Vernacular in Black Girls' Play," in *Language, Rhythm, and Sound: Black Popular Cultures into the Twenty-first Century,* ed. Joseph Adjaye and Adrianne Andrews (Pittsburgh, PA: University of Pittsburgh Press, 1997), 146–63; and Gwendolyn D. Pough, *Check It While I Wreck It: Black Womanhood, Hip-Hop Culture, and the Public Sphere* (Boston: Northeastern University Press, 2004). Also see Imani Perry, *Prophets of the Hood: Politics*

and Poetics in Hip-Hop (Durham, NC: Duke University Press, 2004). For other persuasive discussions about the political significances of hip-hop, see Bakari Kitwana, *The Hip-Hop Generation: Young Blacks and the Crisis in African-American Culture* (New York: Civitas Books, 2002); and Yvonne Bynoe, *Stand and Deliver: Political Activism, Leadership and Hip-Hop Culture* (New York: Soft Skull Press, 2004). For a canonical academic anthology on hip-hop, see Murray Forman and Mark Anthony Neal, eds., *That's the Joint: The Hip-Hop Studies Reader* (New York: Routledge, 2004).

37. This became an even more difficult juggling act when Hammer went "hardcore" but still tried to keep his dancing central. This proved to be the final nail in his coffin. Some people look at Big Daddy Kane's embrace of emphatic dancing in the 1990s as the beginning of the end for him, too.

38. Historian Jeffrey Ogbar's paper at the Caribbean Studies Association Conference in 2002 was quite helpful on this point.

39. Wyclef's use of country music and popular 1980s rock songs is part of the same genre-bending. I'll only talk about Mos Def in the rest of this chapter, but Wyclef's rewriting of a classic Kenny Rogers tune (and having Rogers himself sing that hip-hopped version on a recent album) is part and parcel of the same interventionism. However, Wyclef's invocation of Bob Marley and reggae is a diasporic gesture that does not challenge black American masculinity in quite the same nation-specific way as Mos Def's use of blues and rock music.

40. From the album *Black on Both Sides* (Rawkus Records, 1999).

41. Kid Rock and Eminem are also examples of this same deconstruction from the other side of the racial tracks.

42. For a musicological discussion of rock music's vocal musicianship, see Richard Middleton, "Rock Singing," in *The Cambridge Companion to Singing,* ed. John Potter (Cambridge: Cambridge University Press, 2000), 28–41.

43. Maureen Mahon, "Black Like This: Race, Generation, and Rock in the Post–Civil Rights Era," *American Ethnologist* 27, no. 2 (May 2000): 283–311; and see her book *Right to Rock: The Black Rock Coalition and the Cultural Politics of Race* (Durham, NC: Duke University Press, 2004).

44. For a recent anthology on white appropriations of black culture, see Greg Tate, ed., *Everything but the Burden: What White People Are Taking from Black Culture* (New York: Broadway, 2003).

45. This is from Mos Def's "Rock N Roll," *Black on Both Sides* (Rawkus Records, 1999).

46. On this album, Mos Def still references canonical hip-hop figures like Rakim, retelling some of their most classic hip-hop lines. For a substantive ethnographic and linguistic look at hip-hop, see H. Samy Alim, "Hip-Hop Nation Language," in *Language in the USA,* ed. Edward Finnegan and John Rickford (New York: Cambridge University Press, 2004), 387–409.

47. Mos Def begins the song with a riff on the Red Hot Chili Peppers' opening for "Under the Bridge." He sings, "Sometimes I feel like I don't have a partner / Sometimes I feel like my only friend / is the city I live in, is beautiful Brooklyn" ("Brooklyn," from *Black on Both Sides* [Rawkus Records, 1999]).

48. This is a "notable quotable" from Queen Latifah, copied down from a prefilm slideshow at a Durham, North Carolina, movie theater.

49. See Charles Taylor, *The Ethics of Authenticity* (Cambridge, MA: Harvard University Press, 1992).

CHAPTER EIGHT

1. Of course, this may seem like quite a major turnaround for the producer most notorious for the anticop rhetoric of "Fuck tha Police" (discussed in chapter 4, "Real Jews"). Some might skeptically read the move (especially with so many police and firefighters killed in the attacks) as Dre's attempt to put the final nail in the coffin of mainstream discussions about his NWA-based anticop past.

2. See Geoffrey Hartmann, *Scars of the Spirit: The Struggle against Inauthenticity* (New York: Palgrave, 2002), 27.

3. This takes us back to Vincent Crapanzano's distinction between *hope* and *faith* in "Reflections on Hope as a Category of Social and Psychological Analysis," *Cultural Anthropology* 18, no. 1 (2003): 3–32. For a look at faith among contemporary African American Christian women, see Marla Frederick, *Between Sundays: Black Women and Everyday Struggles of Faith* (Berkeley and Los Angeles: University of California Press, 2003), particularly the contextualization of televangelist Frederick Price's work in the chapter entitled "Name It and Claim It."

4. The fact that this Apollo Theater is vernacularly racialized as both black (in its difference from the World Trade Center) and white (as a kind of Trojan horse within the black community) sheds light on the semiotic malleability of concrete social spaces. Whereas Brother Bey's pitchman called upon the Apollo's latent whiteness to critique commonsense assumptions about its obvious black difference (specifically from places like the World Trade Center), Kevin used that same taken-for-granted black difference to ground his racialist objections to the war, which Brother Bey and his tape's opening emcee would probably endorse.

5. For a discussion of this history, see Louella Jacqueline Long and Vernon Robinson, *How Much Power to the People? A Case Study of the New York State Urban Development Corporation's Involvement with Black Harlem* (New York: Columbia University Urban Center, 1971). Also, see Eric Darton, *Divided We Stand: A Biography of New York's World Trade Center* (New York: Basic Books, 1999).

6. Even before that, Rockefeller found it necessary to call the state's legislators from Martin Luther King Jr.'s funeral in an effort to persuade them to sign his New York State Urban Development Act in the first place, creating the UDC, which Rockefeller labeled a "super agency" for urban redevelopment. See Long and Robinson, *How Much Power to the People?*

7. This text justifies itself, relevantly for us, "as a simple and sincere account," as a transparent autobiography. For the reference to this invocation, and a longer critique of autobiography's claims on the sincere or the authentic, see Hartmann, *Scars of the Spirit.*

8. Indeed, Austin warned against the ultimate analytical usefulness of even making hard and fast distinctions between performatives and constatives.

See John L. Austin, *How to Do Things with Words* (Cambridge, MA: Harvard University Press, 1977) and the reemphasis of this point (toward very different ends), in Eve Kosofsky Sedgwick, *Touching Feeling: Affect, Pedagogy, Performativity* (Durham, NC: Duke University Press, 2003). The constative speech-act is an enabling myth, the Baudrillardian Disneyland that counterfactually fools us into believing Los Angeles itself must be real. See Jean Baudrillard, *Simulacra and Simulation* (Ann Arbor: University of Michigan Press, 1994).

9. See Ann Laura Stoler, *Race and the Education of Desire: Foucault's History of Sexuality and the Colonial Order of Things* (Durham, NC: Duke University Press, 1995), and *Carnal Knowledge and Imperial Power: Race and the Intimate in Colonial Rule* (Berkeley and Los Angeles: University of California Press, 2002).

10. Of course, many Caribbeanist anthropologists would dispute overly simplistic renditions of creolization and cultural hybridity; see Aisha Khan, "Journey to the Center of the Earth: The Caribbean as Master Symbol," *Cultural Anthropology* 16, no. 3 (2001): 271–302. For a related anthropological discussion calling for greater specificity in academic discussions of hybridity, see Joel Robbins, *Becoming Sinners: Christianity and Moral Torment in Papua New Guinea* (Berkeley and Los Angeles: University of California Press, 2004).

11. The film's closing montage contains a mixture of characters (including Nelson Mandela) addressing the camera directly and declaring themselves Malcolm X.

12. See Henry Louis Gates Jr., *The Signifying Monkey: A Theory of Afro-American Literary Criticism* (New York: Oxford University Press, 1988).

13. See Kathleen Stewart, *A Space on the Side of the Road: Cultural Poetics in an "Other" America* (Princeton, NJ: Princeton University Press, 1996). Kathleen Stewart's discussion of local nicknames linking forgotten histories to stories retold, sometimes with different accents and emphases, is specifically relevant here.

14. See Saul Kripke, *Naming and Necessity* (Cambridge, MA: Harvard University Press, 1980) for a discussion of rigid designators and definite descriptions, for a parsing of the distinction between simple and cluster descriptivism—and all in an attempt to pin down the philosophical specificities of naming as referential practice.

15. The Holy Ghost scene was described, with Tyrone's name unchanged, in an earlier version of chapter 3, "Ethnophysicality, or an Ethnography of Some Body," in *Soul: Black Power, Politics, and Pleasure,* ed. Monique Guillory and Richard C. Green (New York: New York University Press, 1997).

16. See Sjaak van der Geest, "Confidentiality and Pseudonyms: A Fieldwork Dilemma from Ghana," *Anthropology Today* 19, no. 1 (2003): 14–18.

17. See James West, *Plainville, U.S.A.* (New York: Columbia University Press, 1945).

18. See Gilbert Herdt, *Guardians of the Flutes: Idioms of Masculinity* (New York: McGraw-Hill, 1981).

19. For Middletown, see Robert Lynd and Helen Lynd, *Middletown: A Study of American Culture* (New York: Harcourt, Brace, and Jovanovich, 1956).

For Eastern City, see Elijah Anderson, *Streetwise: Race, Class, and Change in an Urban Community* (Chicago: University of Chicago Press, 1990).

20. See Carol Stack, *All Our Kin: Strategies for Survival in a Black Community* (New York: Harper and Row, 1975).

21. See Katherine S. Newman, *No Shame in My Game: The Working Poor in the Inner City* (New York: Russell Sage, 1999).

22. See Deborah A. Thomas, *Modern Blackness: Nationalism, Globalization, and the Politics of Culture in Jamaica* (Durham, NC: Duke University Press, 2004).

23. See Linda Green, *Fear as a Way of Life: Mayan Widows in Rural Guatemala* (New York: Columbia University Press, 1999).

24. See Mitchell Duneier, *Sidewalk* (New York: Farrar, Straus, and Giroux, 1999); and Steven Gregory, *Black Corona: Race and the Politics of Place in an Urban Community* (Princeton, NJ: Princeton University Press, 1998).

25. Flyers put up as far away as Brooklyn, New York, would advertise DJ battles, breakdancing competitions, and not-quite-state-of-the-art light shows on Lenox Avenue, aka. Malcolm X Blvd., for parties at Harlem World in the 1980s. For a copy of a Harlem World flyer, see Tricia Rose, *Black Noise: Rap Music and Black Culture in Contemporary America* (Hanover, NH: University Press of New England, 1994).

26. For a discussion of naming in hip-hop culture, specifically among graffiti artists, see Ivor L. Miller, *Aerosol Kingdom: Subway Painters of New York City* (Jackson: University of Mississippi Press, 2002).

27. For a description of the move from MA$E to Reverend Mason Betha, see Mason Betha, *Revelations: There's a Light after the Lime* (New York: Simon and Schuster, 2001). With such Reverend Bethas, Reverend Runs (from Run-DMC), J-Hovas, and Big Baby Jesuses, it becomes clear just how naming marks hip-hop's volatile mixture of the sacred and profane.

28. Some emcees imply that in the 1970s and early 1980s these hip-hop names might also have been gestures at anonymity geared toward avoiding capture by the police whenever they were pirating street lamps for electricity during unlicensed block-parties.

29. See Rose, *Black Noise.*

30. See W. E. B. Du Bois, *The Souls of Black Folk* (1903; reprint, New York: Dover, 1994).

31. See Annelise Riles, *The Network Inside Out* (Ann Arbor: University of Michigan Press, 2000). For a specific discussion of race and social value vis-à-vis the authorial differences between vernacular and academic understandings, see Lindon Barrett, *Blackness and Value: Seeing Double* (Cambridge: Cambridge University Press, 1998).

32. For an implicit discussion of cosmopolitanism's antiquities in the explicit guise of ethnographic fiction, see Amitav Ghosh, *In an Antique Land* (New York: Knopf, 1993). For a theoretical rereading of Ghosh's anthropological intervention, see James Clifford, *Routes: Travel and Translation in the Late Twentieth Century* (Cambridge, MA: Harvard University Press, 1988).

33. The song is "If He Changed My Name" from *Nina at the Village Gate*

(Roulette Jazz, 1961; reissued on Blue Note Records, 1991), written by Robert MacGimsey, EMI Records.

34. This religious group, led by John Africa, also attempted to defend itself in Philadelphia courts without recourse to state-appointed attorneys many years before Colin Ferguson did.

35. These are the Hebrew names of the two members of the WTU's rap group, Sons of the Power. Even WTU is a made-up abbreviation for a differently abbreviated (and named) social group.

36. Revelation 13:38: "Count the number of the beast; for it is the number of a man; and his number is six hundred, threescore and six." Writing these papal accusations, I can't help but think of William Gibson's quite understated line from the novel *Neuromancer* (New York: Ace Books, 1984): "To call up a demon, you must learn its name."

37. For a look at Vasa/Equiano's role in the beginnings of black autobiography, see Angelo Costanzo, *Surprizing Narrative: Olaudah Equiano and the Beginnings of Black Autobiography* (New York: Greenwood Press, 1987).

38. For a fuller description of this naming gesture, see Houston A. Baker, *Turning South Again: Re-Thinking Modernism/Re-Reading Booker T.* (Durham, NC: Duke University Press, 2001).

39. See Lawrence Jackson, *Ralph Ellison: Emergence of Genius* (New York: John Wiley and Sons, 2002).

40. All of this is contrary to the arguments of Elder Shadrock, one of the leading voices within yet another version of Black-Judaic syncretism, the more explicitly Christian-identified Israelite Nation World Wide Ministries. Elder Shadrock's point is that Moses never changed his name—and so neither should anyone else.

41. See Barry Gottehrer, *The Mayor's Man* (Garden City, NY: Doubleday, 1975), 101.

42. Bruno Latour, *We Have Never Been Modern* (Cambridge, MA: Harvard University Press, 1993), describes unmasking as a quintessentially modernist project: "To unmask: that was our sacred task, the task of us as moderns. To reveal the true calculations underlying the false consciousnesses, or the true interests underling the false calculations. Who is not still foaming slightly at the mouth with that particular rabies?" (44).

43. See Louis Dumont, *Homo Hierarchicus: The Caste System and Its Implications* (Chicago: University of Chicago Press, 1980).

44. During one of the earliest rallies of 1994 aimed at challenging Mayor Rudolph Giuliani's removal of street vendors from the sidewalk space along 125th Street (including the space in front of the Adam Clayton Powell Building, renamed Africa Square partially as a function of that very public vending), speakers during that Halloween season spent the entire night calling him not Giuliani, but Ghouliani—a demonization through renaming that still stands out as one of the most memorable (and hilarious) rhetorical interventions on the level of cultural politics that year. For more discussion of this event (and even a picture of Giuliani as ghoul), see John L. Jackson Jr., *Harlemworld: Doing Race and Class in Contemporary Black America* (Chicago: University of Chicago Press, 2001), chap. 1.

45. For instance, see Roland G. Fryer and Steven D. Levitt, "The Causes and Consequences of Distinctively Black Names" (NBER Working Paper W9938, National Bureau of Economic Research, Cambridge, Mass., 2003).

46. For an understanding of authenticity as etymologically rooted in earlier definitions of external authority, see Hartmann, *Scars of the Spirit*.

47. For the earlier discussion of Francis Parker Yockey, see chapter 1.

48. See Mark Fenster, *Conspiracy Theories: Secrecy and Power in American Culture* (Minneapolis: University of Minnesota Press, 1999).

49. For some, "rap" is almost the antithesis of hip-hop. It is the media industry's vacuously streamlined cash-cow. Here, the very term *rap* designates yet another kind of "white man's Apollo." It names a different kind of musical and cultural form.

50. See Hortense Spillers, "Mama's Baby, Papa's Maybe: An American Grammar Book," *Diacritics* 17, no. 2 (1987): 64–81, for an influential discussion of slavery and manipulations of paternity in American history and culture.

51. For a historically situated theory of the new "nigga," see Ronald A. Judy, "On the Question of Nigga Authenticity," *Boundary 2* 21, no. 3 (1994): 211–30.

52. See Vincent L. Wimbush, "Introduction: Reading Darkness, Reading Scriptures," in *African Americans and the Bible: Sacred Texts and Social Textures* (New York: Continuum, 2000).

53. See Ralph Cintron, *Angel's Town: Chero Ways, Gang Life, and Rhetorics of the Everyday* (Boston: Beacon, 1997), 162.

54. See Émile Durkheim and Marcel Mauss, *Primitive Classification* (Chicago: University of Chicago Press, 1963).

55. For a contemporary discussion about the very definition of *democracy* and its potential translation into a specifically Iraqi context, see Noah Feldman, *After Jihad: America and the Struggle for Islamic Democracy* (New York: Farrar, Straus, and Giroux, 2003).

56. For a careful discussion of these business changes and their larger social implications, see Cora Daniels, *Black Power, Inc.: The New Color of Success* (New York: John Wiley and Sons, 2004).

57. See Jayson Blair, *Burning Down My Master's House: My Life at the New York Times* (New York: New Millennium Press, 2004).

58. See Paul Gilroy's referencing of Amiri Baraka's term in *The Black Atlantic: Modernity and Double Consciousness* (Cambridge, MA: Harvard University Press, 1993).

59. The argument comes out of John Ogbu's work, and has one of its most interesting social scientific incarnations in the ethnography of Signithia Fordham, *Blacked Out: Dilemmas of Race, Identity, and Success at Capital High* (Chicago: University of Chicago Press, 1996).

60. Archbishop Don Juan is a famous pimp-turned-pastor profiled in several recent television and film specials on pimps in America, including *American Pimp,* directed by Allen Hughes and Albert Hughes (MGM/UA, 1999).

61. For further explication of these morality plays, see Micaela di Leonardo, *Exotics at Home: Anthropologies, Others, and American Modernity* (Chicago: University of Chicago Press, 1998).

62. For a recent engagement with this famous articulation of organless embodiment, see Slavoj Žižek, *Organs without Bodies: On Deleuze and Consequences* (New York: Routledge, 2003). On the mutual permeability of human bodies, see Ann Weinstone, *Avatar Bodies: A Tantra for Posthumanism* (Minneapolis: University of Minnesota Press, 2004).

63. See Michael Taussig, *The Magic of the State* (New York: Routledge, 1997); see also Fernando Coronil, *The Magical State: Nature, Money, and Modernity in Venezuela* (Chicago: University of Chicago Press, 1997).

64. Taussig, *Magic of the State*, 65, 47, 137.

65. See Donna Haraway, *Modest_Witness@Second_Millennium.Female Man©_Meets_OncoMouse™: Feminism and Technoscience* (New York: Routledge, 1997), 70.

66. The sordid and brutal history of sugar's role in transatlantic exploitation was anthropologically canonized in Sidney Mintz, *Sweetness and Power: The Place of Sugar in Modern History* (New York: Viking, 1985). Nothing is innocent—not sugar and not critiques of sugar's imperial guilt. For a challenge to Mintz's "fetishized" retelling of sugar's global history, see Michael Taussig, "History as Commodity: In Some Recent American (Anthropological) Literature," *Critique of Anthropology* 9, no. 1 (1989): 7–23.

67. See Devin Fergus, "The Founding of Malcolm X University," unpublished paper.

68. See Mark Anthony Neal, *Songs in the Key of Black Life: A Rhythm and Blues Nation* (New York: Routledge, 2003), especially chap. 7, where he cites Paul C. Taylor's "Elvis Effect" to explain "Funky-Ass White Girl" Nyro's connection to Patti LaBelle (nee Patricia Louise Holt) and 1970s funk/soul.

69. See Cornel West, *Democracy Matters: Winning the Fight against Imperialism* (New York: Penguin Press, 2004), 30 and see p. 6 for a discussion of the government's gangsterization after 9/11.

70. For an explanation of black masculinist patriarchy's cocreation of what she calls "Black Superwomen," see Michelle Wallace, *Black Macho and the Myth of the Superwoman* (New York: Verso, 1990). Mos Def assumes the name "Boogie Man" throughout *New Danger*, his 2004 follow-up to *Black on Both Sides*.

71. I am thinking of the object-subject formulations of Jean-Paul Sartre in *Being and Nothingness* (New York: Philosophical Library, 1956), challenged by the Maurice Merleau-Ponty of *The Phenomenology of Perception* (London: Routledge, 1986). See also Fred Moten, *In the Break: The Aesthetics of the Black Radical Tradition* (Minneapolis: University of Minnesota Press, 2003), 137, for a discussion of the Germanic pseudonym (Johannes Koenig) "placed between LeRoi Jones and Amiri Baraka" as "the name of the imaginary native of an imaginary return, the provisional name of the real native whose real return will have always been deferred, the name that marks a highly localized habitation as the site of a transition to an unreachable home." Moten uses this detail to think about naming as an "oscillation between identities" with potentially liberatory consequences.

72. See René Descartes, *Meditations on First Philosophy*, ed. John Cottingham (Cambridge: Cambridge University Press, 1996).

73. For a critique of such problematic invocations of ambivalence and ambiguity, see Rosalind Morris, "All Made Up: Performance Studies and the New Anthropology of Sex and Gender," *Annual Review of Anthropology* 24 (1995): 567–92.

74. As I draft this chapter, black Republican Alan Keyes is all over network television informing Barack Obama (even singing it!) that he is not really black enough to be a "black" congressman, at least not a real one, since his mother is white, his father is a continental African, and he didn't grow up in an urban black ghetto. Of course, in this scenario, Keyes looks like the throwback, and Obama seems to be everyone's next great black political hope.

CHAPTER NINE

1. I am using Walter Benjamin as a writerly model here. For a discussion of Benjamin's version of urban studies, his attempt to "give voice to the 'periphera,' the experiences of those whom modern form of order strive to render silent and invisible," see Graeme Gilloch, *Myth and Metropolis: Walter Benjamin and the City* (Cambridge: Polity Press, 1996), 9. (This same page contains the in-text reference to a "sauntering *flâneur.*")

2. For a discussion of both "deep play" and "thick description," see Clifford Geertz, *The Interpretation of Cultures: Selected Essays* (New York: Basic Books, 1973).

3. For an extended unpacking of this question ("What is inside?"), see Elizabeth Alexander, *The Black Interior* (St. Paul, MN: Graywolf Press, 2004).

4. See Ann Weinstone, *Avatar Bodies: A Tantra for Posthumanism* (Minneapolis: University of Minnesota Press, 2004). Citing Edouard Glissant on the importance of identificatory denseness, David Murray, in *Opacity: Gender, Sexuality, Race, and the "Problem" of Identity in Martinique* (New York: Peter Lang, 2002), argues that opacity can be a form of political resistance. See also Geertz, *Interpretation of Cultures,* for a discussion of ethnography's relationship to its subjects as one that "dissolves their opacity" (14). The argument of this book would see that impulse as the genre's least beneficial by-product.

5. For an interpretation of fundamentalism's discourse, an interpretation that attempts to cut against the idiomatic grain of its unsympathetic and "unborn-again readers," see Susan Friend Harding, *The Book of Jerry Falwell: Fundamentalist Language and Politics* (Princeton, NJ: Princeton University Press, 2000).

6. Geertz, *Interpretation of Cultures,* 103.

7. See Annelise Riles, *The Network Inside Out* (Ann Arbor: University of Michigan Press, 2000). She argues that what we consider "facts are opaque entities; they shield interpretation and close off interest in further questions and answers" (139–40). This is true, but only insofar as the opacities are themselves seen as transparent, looked through as though they were somehow (three dimensionally and fundamentally) the actual thing—and not just our painted images on the sides of glacial rock.

8. See Judith Butler, *The Psychic Life of Power: Theories of Subjection* (Stanford, CA: Stanford University Press, 1997), 14. In an unpublished paper,

"Tainted Love," Justin Izzo likens Butler's "otherwise" to the excesses I would link to sincerity.

9. Saba Mahmood, "Feminist Theory, Embodiment, and the Docile Agent: Some Reflections on the Egyptian Islamic Revival," *Cultural Anthropology* 16, no. 2 (2001): 202–36. Mahmood reads women's roles in Egypt's "mosque movement," especially their understandings of religious practice, as a way to challenge seemingly Eurocentric excesses of Butlerian performativity.

10. See Sam Greenlee, *The Spook Who Sat by the Door* (Detroit, MI: Wayne State University Press, 1989), where an FBI agent—ostensibly tame and invested in "the American Dream"—secretly trains Chicago street gangs to overthrow the government.

11. For a gloss on sincerity as political manifesto, see Hakim Bey, *T.A.Z.: The Temporary Autonomous Zone, Ontological Anarchy, Poetic Terrorism* (New York: Autonomedia, 1985).

12. Henri Lefebvre, *The Urban Revolution* (Minneapolis: University of Minnesota Press, 2003), 188. He describes anthropology as an "uncertain science," making it the perfect disciplinary starting point for an analysis of sincerity's ambiguities. For a pragmatic philosopher's take on the pitfalls and futilities of too-easily-ontologized certainties, see John Dewey, *The Quest for Certainty: A Study of the Relation of Knowledge to Action* (New York: Putnam, 1960).

13. For a discussion of "dialectical criticism," see Steven Caton, *Lawrence of Arabia: A Film's Anthropology* (Berkeley and Los Angeles: University of California Press, 1999).

14. For a historically situated theory of religious doubt (and even its hardening into absolute atheisms), see Jennifer Michael Hecht, *Doubt: A History* (New York: HarperSanFrancisco, 2003).

15. For a discussion of "biological citizenship," see Adriana Petryna, *Life Exposed: Biological Citizens after Chernobyl* (Princeton, NJ: Princeton University Press, 2002). For a definition of "soul citizenship," see Fran Markowitz, Sara Helman, and Dafna Shir-Vertesh, "Soul Citizenship: The Black Hebrews and the State of Israel," *American Anthropologist* 105, no. 2 (2003): 302–12. For an extension of Foucauldian biopolitics into Bataillean rereadings of sovereignty's (political authenticity's?) killerly excesses, see Achille Mbembe, "Necropolitics," *Public Culture* 15, no. 1 (2003): 11–40.

16. MC Threat actually creates what sounds like a hip-hop neologism that is more like *sincerious*—*sincere* and *serious* all rolled into one.

17. For a powerful and moving analytical meditation on the linkages between race and mortality, see Karla FC Holloway, *Passed On: African American Mourning Stories* (Durham, NC: Duke University Press, 2002). See also Sharon P. Holland, *Raising the Dead: Readings of Death and (Black) Subjectivity* (Durham, NC: Duke University Press, 2000).

18. See Henri Lefebvre, *The Urban Revolution* (Minneapolis: University of Minnesota Press, 2003), 157.

19. For a discussion of game theory and the duplicities of all human behavior, see David P. Barash, *The Survival Game: How Game Theory Explains the Biology of Cooperation and Competition* (New York: Times Books, 2003).

For a critique of various stereotypical imaginings of nationhood in Greece, see Michael Herzfeld, *Cultural Intimacy: Social Poetics in the Nation-State* (New York: Routledge, 1997).

20. For a dismissal of "oversincerity" (and an invocation of Lewis Hyde's "Sincerity, with a motive" as explanation for the limitations of irony), see David Foster Wallace, *A Supposedly Funny Thing I'll Never Do Again: Essays and Arguments* (Boston: Little, Brown, 1997), especially "E Unibus Pluram: Television and U.S. Fiction."

Index